Dedication

To Carol and Joe Mottet
T. P. M.

To Betty Newton Peck and Harry Gwinn Peck Sr.
V. P. R.

Contents

8 Teacher Immediacy and the Teacher–Student Relationship 167

9 Teacher and Student Affinity-Seeking in the Classroom 195

Preface

Communication is at the heart of the teaching and learning process. Instructional communication scholars, whose work appears in this handbook, examine how communication links teachers to students and students to teachers. The *Handbook of Instructional Communication: Rhetorical and Relational Perspectives* is a comprehensive distillation of three decades of social scientific research focusing on the role and effects of communication in instructional settings. The handbook was written to address the contemporary challenges facing teachers and trainers in traditional and nontraditional instructional settings. The chapters explain how instructional communication works, why it works, the effects of instructional communication, and how practitioners can use communication most effectively in instructional settings to enhance student learning.

The *Handbook of Instructional Communication* makes research and theory accessible to students who want to learn more about teaching, communication, and learning. It also makes research and theory immediately available to teachers and educational leaders who are responsible for student learning outcomes. The handbook enhances an individual's ability to (1) understand instructional communication research, (2) plan and conduct instructional communication research, (3) practice effective instructional communication, and (4) consult with other teachers and trainers about their use of instructional communication. Individuals who have an interest in becoming primary and secondary teachers, higher education faculty members, community educators, directors of organizational learning, communication consultants, or training and development specialists will find this handbook to be a useful and practical guide.

Rhetorical and Relational Perspectives

The handbook is structured using the rhetorical and relational perspectives that reflect the long-standing traditions in the communication studies discipline. From a rhetorical perspective, instructors intentionally use verbal and nonverbal messages to influence students; the focus is on the message. From the relational perspective, teachers and students mutually create and use verbal and nonverbal messages to manage relationships with each other. Rather than focusing exclusively on message content, teachers and students also acknowledge and address emotions. Although we compare and contrast the rhetorical and relational perspectives, it is neither appropriate nor practical to view these two traditions as polar opposites. These two perspectives simply reflect different emphases of the instructional communication process. The rhetorical approach is more teacher-directed while the relational approach is more collaborative.

The units and chapters of this handbook reflect the social scientific tradition of instructional communication research conducted within the communication studies discipline. Other important research traditions (i.e., critical, social, cultural) were not included for a couple of reasons. First, rather than making the handbook exhaustive of all instructional communication research, we decided to limit the content to ensure depth rather than breadth of content. A focused handbook seemed to complement many of the research programs that have been ongoing for the past three decades. Second, the majority of published research has been conducted using quantitative social scientific research methodologies. Although the social scientific approach to instructional communication research continues, studies using other research traditions (i.e., critical, social, cultural) and methodologies (qualitative, ethnographic) are being published with more regularity. To ensure the proliferation of instructional communication research and theory, this expansion of the research agenda is encouraged.

The Handbook's Organization

The handbook is divided into four units: Foundations; Rhetorical Perspectives; Relational Perspectives; and Theory and Assessment. The first unit, Foundations, includes Chapters 1 and 2. The first chapter introduces readers to the interdisciplinary foundations of instructional communication, the rhetorical and relational perspectives, and the verbal and nonverbal message characteristics that make instructional communication unique from educational psychology and pedagogy. Chapter 2 reviews the history of instructional communication. The second unit, Rhetorical Perspectives, includes Chapters 3–6. Chapter 3 focuses on student communication traits. Chapter 4 reviews teacher credibility and aggressive communication traits. Chapter 5 examines instructional message variables, including content relevance, teacher clarity, and instructional humor. Chapter 6 reviews the seminal and contemporary research focusing on teachers' influence messages.

The third unit, Relational Perspectives, includes Chapters 7–11. Chapter 7 introduces readers to the other side of instructional influence—how student communication behaviors influence teachers and their teaching. Chapter 8 examines teacher immediacy and the teacher–student relationship. Chapter 9 focuses on teacher and student affinity-seeking in the classroom, Chapter 10 on teacher misbehaviors, and Chapter 11 on student resistance. The fourth unit, Theory and Assessment, introduces readers to issues important to researchers and practitioners alike and includes Chapters 12 and 13. In Chapter 12, the authors begin a discussion focusing on instructional communication theory. In Chapter 13, the authors provide the assessment tools that practitioners and instructional leaders need to measure instructional communication effectiveness.

Chapter Organization

Because much of the research that is showcased in this handbook was conducted in a programmatic manner—where one study informs the next—the majority of chapters are organized in a similar manner. This consistent organizational structure allows students, practitioners, and instructional leaders to more easily understand the research and theory discussions, and to extract the communication behaviors and skills that have been shown to enhance instructional outcomes. Chapters 3–11 feature:

- A review of the instructional communication variable and how the variable is conceptualized (defined) and operationalized (measured).
- A discussion as to why the variable remains important to teachers and trainers.
- A study-by-study review of the research. Where appropriate, the program of research is reviewed in a chronological order, revealing how each study made a "unique" and "significant" contribution to the overall program of research.
- A bulleted list of the knowledge claims or conclusions stemming from the program of research.
- A bulleted list of ideas and suggestions for how researchers may advance and continue the program of research.

An Experienced Author Team

The chapter authors are experts in their fields. Many of the authors are award-winning teachers and researchers who have been recognized by their institutions and professional organizations. Many of the authors are listed among the top 100 most prolific researchers in the communication studies discipline, with five being listed among the top 50 most prolific researchers in the discipline. Additionally, the authors have extensive and varied experience working in the teaching and training fields. Many of the authors currently teach or have taught in-service and pre-service public school teachers, graduate teaching assistants, and college and university faculty members about the role and impact of communication in the classroom. Other authors work as corporate trainers and communication consultants. The authors' academic experience coupled with their professional work experience enables them to effectively bridge research and theory with practice. In short, the authors study and investigate communication as an applied science.

Acknowledgments

It is a pleasure to acknowledge the friends and colleagues who improved this book in innumerable ways. First and foremost, the editors would like to thank the chapter authors for their contributions to this handbook. Without their research, this handbook would be incomplete. The editors would also like to thank their team of editors, reviewers, and colleagues who have guided this book project. We thank the Allyn and Bacon team for their commitment to developing authors and book projects. This team of publishing professionals provided continuous and consistent guidance and support of this book project. Their responsiveness is most appreciated. Executive Editor Karon Bowers and Acquisitions Editor Brian Wheel provided guidance and structure for the handbook. Editorial Assistant Heather Hawkins helped manage the numerous details and production deadlines. Marketing Manager Mandee Eckersley promoted and continues to promote our work whenever and wherever possible.

We acknowledge and thank our reviewers, whose comments and reviews enhanced the quality of this handbook. A special thanks to Jerry L. Allen, University of New Haven; Mark Hickson, III, University of Alabama; and Gerard O' Sullivan, Felician College.

Virginia would like to thank Harry Gwinn Peck and Betty Newton Peck for their love and guidance throughout her life.

Tim would like to thank members of his family, including his mom and dad (Carol and Joe), Dan and Barb, Doug and Jane, Julie and Rob, and especially Rick Gonzalez, who provided constant love and support on this book project. Also, Tim would like to thank his friends and colleagues in Communication Studies at West Virginia University and Texas State University–San Marcos. Finally, he thanks his mentors Drs. Steven Beebe, Jim McCroskey, Virginia Richmond, and Marilyn Root, who continue to guide him.

Timothy P. Mottet
Texas State University–San Marcos

Virginia P. Richmond
James C. McCroskey
West Virginia University

About the Authors

Steven A. Beebe (PhD, University of Missouri–Columbia, 1976) is professor and chair of the Department of Communication Studies–San Marcos; he also serves as Associate Dean of the College of Fine Arts and Communication. He teaches a wide variety of communication courses, including interpersonal communication, group communication, public speaking, and communication training and development. Dr. Beebe is author or coauthor of ten widely used communication books, most of which are in multiple editions. His research has appeared in *Communication Education, Communication Quarterly, Communication Research Reports,* and numerous other commnication journals. Dr. Beebe was instrumental in helping to establish new communication studies curricula in Russia through his work with the Russian Communication Association. He's received the Presidential Award for Excellence—Texas State's most prestigious faculty award—in both research and service. The National Speakers Association named him Outstanding Communication Professor in America in 1996. Dr. Beebe can be reached at sb03@txstate.edu.

Joseph L. Chesebro (EdD, West Virginia University, 1999) is an assistant professor in the Department of Communication at the State University of New York (SUNY) at Brockport. He teaches graduate seminars in interpersonal and organizational communication and communication training and development. He teaches undergraduate courses in interpersonal and organizational communication and communication theory. At Brockport, Dr. Chesebro also has conducted instructional communication training for new graduate teaching assistants as well as for faculty members. His research appears in *Communication Education, Communication Quarterly,* and *Communication Research Reports.* He also is coauthor of *Communication for Teachers* with James C. McCroskey. Dr. Chesebro can be reached at jchesebr@brockport.edu.

Cathy A. Fleuriet (PhD, University of Texas at Austin, 1993) serves as Associate Vice -President for Institutional Effectiveness at Texas State University–San Marcos, where she leads initiatives related to organizational communication, strategic planning and assessment, and excellence in teaching and learning. As an associate professor in the Department of Communication Studies, she has taught graduate seminars in instructional communication and communication assessment and previously served as Associate Dean for the College of Fine Arts and Communication. Dr. Fleuriet's research interests include instructional communication, organizational communication, and contemporary rhetoric. Her research appears in *Communication Quarterly, Journal of the Association for Communication Administrators,* and *Southern Communication Journal.* Dr. Fleuriet received the Presidential Award for

Excellence in Teaching, Texas State's highest teaching award, in 1997. She was the College of Fine Arts and Communication's nominee for this award from 1991–1996 and the college nominee for the Presidential Award for Excellence in Research in 1994 and 1995. She has served as chair of the Basic Course Division, as secretary of the Instructional Division for the National Communication Association, and chair of the instructional division for the Southern States Association. Dr. Fleuriet can be reached at cf07@txstate.edu.

Ann Bainbridge Frymier (EdD, West Virginia University, 1992) is an associate professor in the Department of Communication at Miami University, Oxford, Ohio. She teaches graduate courses in research methods and instructional communication and undergraduate courses in persuasion, interpersonal communication, research methods, and a basic course, among others. Dr. Frymier's program of research has examined effective teacher communication behaviors, and she is currently extending it to focus on students' communication and needs in the classroom. Her research appears in *Communication Education, Journal of Applied Communication Research, Communication Quarterly, Communication Research Reports, Communication Reports,* and *Psychological Reports.* She is a coauthor, with Dr. Marjorie Keeshan Nadler, of an upcoming persuasion theory textbook and served as the president of the Eastern Communication Association in 2002. Dr. Frymier can be reached at frymieab@muohio.edu.

Patricia Kearney (EdD, West Virginia University, 1979) is professor of communication studies and recipient of the Distinguished Scholar Award at California State University, Long Beach. Her research and teaching, both theoretical and applied, focus on communication in the instructional process. A regular member of seven journal editorial boards, Kearney has written a variety of textbooks and industrial training packages, and she has published more than 100 research articles, chapters, and commissioned research reports and instructional modules. She is listed among the 100 most published scholars and among the top 20 published women's scholars in her discipline.

Derek R. Lane (PhD, University of Oklahoma, 1996) is an associate professor in the Department of Communication at the University of Kentucky, where he teaches graduate seminars in instructional communication, advanced theory construction, and interpersonal communication. Dr. Lane's research can be classified in the broad area of face-to-face and mediated message reception and processing to affect attitude and behavior change in instructional, organizational, and health contexts. His research is funded by the U.S. Department of Education, the National Institute of Drug Abuse, the National Institute of Mental Health, and the National Science Foundation and appears in *Communication Monographs, Communication Education, Media Psychology, Communication Research Reports, American Journal of Communication,* and the *Journal of Engineering Education.* Dr. Lane is an endowed professor in the UK College of Engineering and is the recipient of several prestigious teaching and research awards. He can be reached at drlane@uky.edu.

Matthew M. Martin (PhD, Kent State University, 1992) is an associate professor and chair in the Department of Communication Studies at West Virginia University. He teaches graduate seminars in persuasion, nonverbal communication, and film criticism. Dr. Martin's current program of research examines the role of personality traits in interpersonal relationships. His research appears in *Communication Education, Communication Quarterly,* and *Communication Research Reports.* He was recently recognized as one of the most prolific scholars in the field of communication studies. Dr. Martin can be reached at mmartin@wvu.edu.

James C. McCroskey (DEd, Pennsylvania State University, 1966) is professor of communication studies at West Virginia University. He teaches courses in instructional communication theory and research, organizational communication, intercultural communication, and communibiology. Dr. McCroskey's areas of research include instructional communication, organizational communication, intercultural communication, health communication, interpersonal communication, communication traits, and communibiology. His research appears in *Communication Education, Communication Monographs, Human Communication Research, Communication Quarterly, Communication Research Reports, Communication Reports, Western States Communication Journal, Southern States Communication Journal, Communication Studies,* and a wide variety of journals in other fields. Dr. McCroskey has received West Virginia University's highest honors in recognition of his teaching and research. In addition to receiving the National Communication Association's Mentor Award and the Kibler Award, the NCA recognizes Dr. McCroskey as the individual who has published more scholarly articles in communication journals than anyone else in the history of the field. Dr. McCroskey can be reached at email@JamesCMcCroskey.com or at www.JamesCMcCroskey.com.

Linda L. McCroskey (PhD, University of Oklahoma, 1998) is an assistant professor in the Department of Communication Studies at Califiornia State University, –Long Beach. She teaches courses in organizational communication, intercultural communication, and communication theory. Dr. McCroskey's current program of research emphasizes the investigation of communication competence and effectiveness in applied contexts. Her research appears in *Communication Education, Journal of Intercultural Communication Research, and Communication Research Reports.* She is coauthor of books and book chapters on instructional and organizational communication. Dr. McCroskey is the current chair of the Instructional and Developmental Division of the International Communication Association. She can be reached at lmccrosk@csulb.edu.

Mary B. McPherson (PhD, Ohio University, 1996) is an assistant professor in the Department of Communication Studies at California State University, Long Beach. Dr. McPherson teaches graduate and undergraduate courses in instructional communication, communication theory and research, and communication training and development. Her most current program of research examines the influence of teacher communication behaviors on students and their learning. Dr. McPherson's research appears in *Communication Quarterly, Journal of Applied Communication Research,* and the *Southern Communication Journal.* She received a Top Paper Award for her research in 2003. Dr. McPherson can be reached at marybmcp@csulb.edu.

Timothy P. Mottet (EdD, West Virginia University, 1998) is an associate professor in the Department of Communication Studies at Texas State University–San Marcos.

He teaches graduate seminars in instructional communication, communication assessment, and communication training and development. Dr. Mottet's current program of research examines the effects of student communication behaviors on teachers and their teaching. Listed among the top 50 most published scholars in the discipline between 1996 and 2001, his research appears in *Communication Education, Communication Quarterly, Communication Research Reports, Journal of Psychology,* and *Psychological Reports.* He is coauthor of *Training and Development: Enhancing Communication and Leadership Skills* with Steven A. Beebe and K. David Roach. At Texas State, Dr. Mottet was a presidential nominee for the Presidential Award for Excellence in Teaching from 2001 to 2003 and a nominee for the Presidential Award for Excellence in Research from 2000 to 2004. Prior to pursuing his doctorate, Dr. Mottet worked as a manager and trainer for Northwest Airlines. Dr. Mottet can be reached at tm15@txstate.edu.

Scott A. Myers (PhD, Kent State University, 1995) is an associate professor in the Department of Communication Studies at West Virginia University. He teaches courses in communication theory, small group communication, and instructional communication. His research interests center primarily on the student-instructor relationship in the college classroom, with his research appearing in *Communication Research Reports, Communication Education, Communication Quarterly,* and *Communication Reports.* Dr. Myers is the former editor of *Communication Teacher* and currently serves as the executive director of Central States Communication Association. He can be reached at smyers@mail.wvu.edu.

Timothy G. Plax (PhD, University of Southern California, 1974) is professor of communication studies at California State Univeristy, Long Beach. He has also served as a member of the faculty at the University of New Mexico and West Virginia University. His organizational experiences include six years as a full-time member of the executive staff at the Rockwell International Corporation and 25 years as an external consultant for numerous Fortune 500 corporations. His programs of research focus on social influence, communication in instruction, and organizational training and development. A member of numerous editorial boards, he has authored a variety of textbooks and industrial training packages. As an academic and a consultant, he has published over 150 manuscripts, including scholarly peer-reviewed articles, book chapters, and commissioned research reports. He is listed among the 25 most published scholars in his discipline. Notable among his distinctions and awards are both the Distinguished Faculty Research and Creative Activity Award and the Associated Students Presidential Award from California State University, Long Beach, and both the Triad of Excellence Award for his work in the Engineering Operation and the Distinguished Research Award from the Aerospace Division of the Rockwell International Corporation.

Virginia Peck Richmond (PhD, University of Nebraska, 1977) is professor of communication studies at West Virginia University. Dr. Richmond teaches courses in nonverbal communication, organizational communication, training and development, and a variety of courses in the WVU off-campus master's degree program in instructional communication. Dr. Richmond has published more than 100 articles on communication in instruction, nonverbal communication, communication apprehension and shyness, interpersonal communication, organizational communication, intercultural communication, and communibiolgy, in addition to numerous books and book chapters. She is listed among the top five most prolific researchers in the discipline. Dr. Richmond has been recognized as an award-winning teacher and researcher by West Virginia University and the Eastern Communication Association. Dr. Richmond can be reached at Virginia.Richmond@mail.wvu.edu.

K. David Roach (EdD, Texas Tech University, 1989) is professor and chair in the Department of Communication Studies at Texas State University. He teaches a range of courses, including organizational communication, communication in instruction and training, nonverbal communication, public speaking, business and professional communication, quantitative research methods, and persuasion. Dr. Roach's research is primarily in the area of instructional communication. His research appears in *Communication Education, Journal of Applied Communication Research, Communication Quarterly, Communication Research Reports, World Communication, The Southern Communication Journal, Texas Speech Communication Journal,* and *The Journal of Graduate Teaching Assistant Development.* He is coauthor of *Training and Development: Enhancing Communication and Leadership Skills* with Steven A. Beebe and Timothy P. Mottet. Dr. Roach was inducted into the Texas Tech University Teaching Academy in 1998. He received the National Communication Association's Scholarship of Teaching and Learning Award in 2000 and was nominated for the Texas Speech Communication Association Teacher of the Year Award in 2002.

Melissa Bekelja Wanzer (EdD, West Virginia University, 1995) is an associate professor in the Department of Communication Studies at Canisius College. She teaches graduate seminars in interpersonal communication, research methods, persuasion, and small group communication. Dr. Wanzer also teaches undergraduate courses in family, gender, social problems, and basic and advanced interpersonal communication. Dr. Wanzer's current instructional research examines differences between student/professor communication problems in the classroom for students with and without disabilities. Also, Dr. Wanzer is currently working with Dr. Ann Bainbridge Frymier on developing a comprehensive typology of appropriate and inappropriate examples of teacher humor. Dr. Wanzer's research appears in *Communication Education, Communication Teacher, Communication Quarterly, Health Communication, Journal of Health Communication,* and *Communication Research Reports.* Dr. Wanzer received teaching and research awards from Syracuse University in 1992 and was the 2004 faculty recipient of the Dr. I. Joan Lorch Women Studies Award at Canisius College. Dr. Wanzer can be reached at wanzerm@canisius.edu.

Unit I

Foundations

1

Foundations of Instructional Communication

Timothy P. Mottet
Texas State University–San Marcos

Steven A. Beebe
Texas State University–San Marcos

Introduction

"Education," suggested B. F. Skinner, "is what survives when what has been learned has been forgotten." Increasingly, there is evidence that students at all levels of education are forgetting what they have learned, assuming that learning occurred in the first place. Studies indicate that only 40 percent of U.S. high school seniors were proficient in reading (Donahue, Voelkl, Campbell, & Mazzeo, 1999) and just 30 percent were proficient in math (Reese, Miller, Mazzeo, & Dossey, 1997). According to a 2002 survey conducted by RoperASW, a scant 12 percent of young Americans could identify Afghanistan on a map, 13 percent could identify Iraq and Iran, and only 14 percent could identify Israel (Toppo, 2002).

Research suggests that student learning is in jeopardy because students are not appropriately engaged in the learning process (Pascarella & Terenzini, 1991). Fewer than 58 percent of a national sample of first-year college students indicated that they asked questions in class or contributed to class discussions (National Survey of Student Engagement, 2000). Only half of the students reported that they had an above-average to good-quality relationship with their teachers (National Survey of Student Engagement, 2000). Forty-five percent of first-year students reported never discussing ideas from classes or readings with a faculty member, engagement behaviors that have been shown to lead to higher levels of personal development and learning (Astin, 1984, 1993; Martin, Mottet, & Myers, 2000; Pascarella & Terenzini, 1991).

Another problem facing American education is the growing shortage of teachers at all levels of education (Archer, 1999; Coffin, 2002; DeFleur, 1993; Evelyn, 2001). According to the American Association of Community Colleges, 30 percent of the almost 100,000 community-college faculty members are likely to retire or otherwise leave their teaching positions in the next three years (Evelyn, 2001). Many attribute these shortages to burgeoning student enrollments and teacher retirements (Archer, 1999; Coffin, 2002; DeFleur, 1993; Evelyn, 2001). Although one-fourth will leave the profession because of retirement (National Education Association, 1997), Archer (1999) reports that between 20 and 30 percent of new primary and secondary teachers quit within their first five years. Another study documents that more than 30 percent of all teachers, and up to 50 percent of teachers in large urban districts, leave their jobs within five years (Gregorian, 2001).

Precisely why are teachers leaving the profession? One researcher suggests two primary reasons, both related to student responsiveness: (1) a teacher's perception of his or her own effectiveness (self-efficacy) and (2) teaching satisfaction (Ingersoll, 2001). Perceived lack of student interest and engagement, which can evolve into disciplinary problems, negatively influence both teacher self-efficacy and satisfaction (Langdon, 1996). In short, the classroom dynamic between teachers and students is a primary factor that contributes to teacher attrition.

For over 30 years, researchers in the field of communication have examined teaching and learning as a communication process with the goal of enhancing teaching effectiveness and student learning. The area of study known as *instructional communication* (McCroskey, Richmond, & McCroskey, 2002), examines teaching and learning using communication theory and research conclusions to explain, predict, and control instructional outcomes. Drawing on the growing body of instructional communication theory and research, the *Handbook of Instructional Communication: Rhetorical and Relational Perspectives* places communication at the heart of the teaching and learning process by describing both *how* and *why* communication works in instructional settings.

This handbook is written to address the contemporary challenges that face educators. An enhanced understanding of how and why communication functions in the learning process can help educators address issues of both self-efficacy and teaching satisfaction. Specifically, this book will help upper-division undergraduate students majoring in communication, graduate students interested in instructional communication, graduate teaching assistants across all disciplines, K–12 in-service teachers pursuing graduate course work, training practitioners, and educational leaders (1) learn about instructional communication research, (2) plan instructional communication research, (3) practice effective instructional communication, and (4) consult with other educators about their use of instructional communication. Individuals who have an interest in becoming primary and secondary teachers, higher education faculty members, community educators, communication consultants, and training and development specialists will benefit from this book.

To accomplish these goals, the book is divided into four units. The first unit (Chapters 1–2) focuses on the foundations of instructional communication. The second (Chapters 3–6) and third units (Chapters 7–11) examine instructional communication from rhetorical and relational perspectives, respectively. The fourth unit (Chapters 12–13) describes how to conduct instructional communication research as well as practice effective instructional communication.

In this chapter we introduce the three foundational disciplines that have influenced instructional communication: educational psychology, pedagogy, and communication. After describing the disciplinary roots of instructional communication, we describe important contributions each discipline has had on instructional communication theory and research. We give special emphasis to the rhetorical and relational nature of communication as foundational principles, which frame instructional communication theory and research.

Instructional communication is the process by which teachers and students stimulate meanings in the minds of each other using verbal and nonverbal messages. Although influenced by McCroskey (1968), this definition is not limited to the traditional primary, secondary, and higher education classroom, but can also be applied to nontraditional instructional settings, such as the training and continuing-education classroom.

In the past, definitions of instructional communication have focused on the one-directional communication process of how teachers influence student learning. Sorensen and Christophel (1992), for example, discuss instructional communication as an "integration of the management of communication messages and the facilitation of learning. . . . [E]ffective instructional communication is a delicate balance of using strategies that control perceptions, that control behavior, and that ultimately maximize students' potential to learn" (p. 35). What this definition ignores is how students' instructional communication influences teachers and their teaching. In this book, instructional communication is recognized and acknowledged as a *transactional process* in which teachers and students mutually influence each other with their verbal and nonverbal messages. Viewing communication as a transactional process not only addresses student learning, compliance, and motivation, but also acknowledges teacher self-efficacy, compliance, and satisfaction. All individuals involved in the learning process, not just teachers, have an impact upon learning.

As illustrated by Figure 1.1, the teaching and learning process, at its core, is also a transactional communication process. In an early conceptualization of

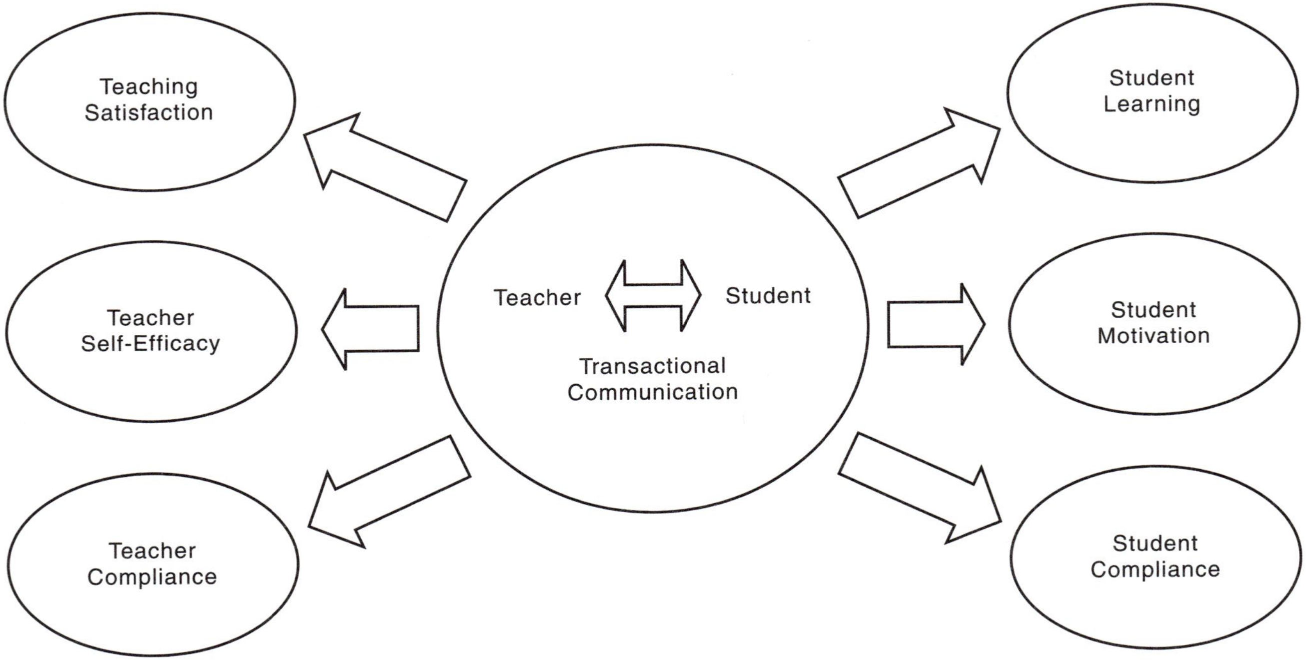

FIGURE 1.1 *Instructional Communication as Mutual Influence.*

instructional communication, Hurt, Scott, and McCroskey (1978) explained the role of communication in the teaching and learning process in the following way:

> Knowledge is valuable in itself, but no matter how much one knows, there is no guarantee he or she can teach that knowledge to others. Communication is the crucial link between a knowledgeable teacher and a learning student. From the vantage point of a professional educator, then, the difference between knowing and teaching is communication in the classroom. (p. 3)

Building upon this classic approach to classroom communication, the underlying paradigm of the *Handbook of Instructional Communication: Rhetorical and Relational Perspectives* continues to put communication at the center of teaching and learning by emphasizing how teachers and students stimulate meanings in the minds of each other using verbal and nonverbal messages. Communication within the classroom inextricably links teachers to students and students to teachers.

To more fully understand contemporary instructional communication theory and research it is important to trace the evolution of the discipline by examining its interdisciplinary roots.

Interdisciplinary Foundations of Instructional Communication

Instructional communication is interdisciplinary. It integrates theory and research from three rich and diverse disciplines: educational psychology, pedagogy, and communication. We will describe these three interrelated, yet distinct, disciplines and examine pertinent theoretical and research issues.

Educational Psychology: An Emphasis on the Learner

Educational psychology investigates the underlying psychological and intellectual processes that explain and predict student learning. Specifically, the focus of educational psychology research is on the individual learner. This discipline explores such questions as: How do students learn? What student personality characteristics or traits are most receptive to various approaches to learning? How do students process and use information? The founding principles of educational psychology address how cognitive, affective, and behavioral processes influence learning outcomes in three domains: cognitive, affective, and behavioral (Bloom 1956).

Cognitive Learning. Cognitive learning focuses on the acquisition of knowledge and the ability to understand and use knowledge. Bloom (1956) identified six distinct, hierarchical levels, which describe the sequence of how students acquire, use, and ultimately evaluate knowledge: knowledge recall, comprehension, application, analysis, synthesis, and evaluation. At the lower levels of cognitive learning, students are asked to recall, explain, and then apply information in a meaningful way. For example, asking students to recall when the Holocaust occurred, their understanding of why it occurred, and how they might use the Holocaust to better understand genocide and other hate crimes that are a part of contemporary life illustrate a student's ability to recall, explain, and apply knowledge. At higher levels of cognitive learning, students are asked to analyze, synthesize, and evaluate information. Asking students to dissect or investigate the events leading up to the Holocaust, explain its effects on the development of Western civilization, and evaluate current social prejudices and sanctions from the standpoint of what was learned by studying the Holocaust illustrate higher levels of cognitive learning.

Anderson and Krathwohl (2001), along with their colleagues, complemented Bloom's (1956) original hierarchy or taxonomy of cognitive learning with a revised taxonomy that includes four types of knowledge: factual, conceptual, procedural, and metacognitive. Factual knowledge focuses on pieces of information that are discrete, isolated, and detailed. Conceptual knowledge includes classifications, principles, theories, and models. Procedural knowledge features processes on how to do something, including skills, techniques, and methods. Metacognitive knowledge includes an individual's awareness of their own knowledge and how they process knowledge.

In summary, Bloom's (1956) original taxonomy and Anderson and Krathwohl's (2001) revised taxonomy of cognitive learning reveal the processes by which information is converted into knowledge and made meaningful. Effective teachers aid students in this conversion process by investing considerable time before they enter the classroom organizing their content, as well as finding ways to illustrate their content through the use of relevant examples. Effective teachers anticipate student confusion and find ways to prevent student misunderstanding.

Affective Learning. Addressing, changing, or reinforcing students' attitudes, beliefs, values, and underlying emotions or feelings as they relate to the knowledge and skills they are acquiring is the domain of affective learning. Krathwohl, Bloom, and Masia (1964) identified five levels of affective responses: receiving, responding, valuing, organizing, and value complex. Lower levels or concrete forms of affective learning include students being willing to minimally receive and respond to classroom information. The mere presence of students attending class while learning about the Holocaust, or students being willing to ask and answer questions regarding this historical event, are examples of lower-level affective learning. Higher levels or more abstract forms of affective learning include students who have modified their attitudes, beliefs, and values in such a way that they perceive their world differently. This change in worldview or paradigmatic shift would be manifested in self-motivated behaviors such as a student who begins to question and challenge a group's propaganda that is hateful.

Affective learning occurs when students take ownership of their learning and is manifested when students enact behaviors that demonstrate that they respect, appreciate, and value the knowledge and skills they are acquiring. Another indication that affective learning has occurred is when students become self-motivated rather than other-motivated. For example, students continue to discuss the Holocaust once the unit is over. On their own, they plan a trip to the Holocaust museum in Washington, DC, because they want to learn more about this historical event. Krathwohl et al., (1964) describe affective learning as a process of internalization where "the phenomenon or value successively and pervasively becomes a part of the individual" (p. 28).

Effective teachers aid students in this internalization process by adapting their instruction to their students' attitudes, beliefs, and values. Master teachers find ways of "turning students on" to the knowledge. These teachers make knowledge approachable and palatable to students by getting to know their students and then using that knowledge to customize the educational experience. A skilled teacher, for example, discovers ways of getting a group of conservative, rural, male students to value and appreciate feminist critique. The first author of this chapter vividly remembers a high school math teacher saying, "My job is to teach you math, not to make you like it." Actually the math teacher's job was to do both, at least according to those interested in affective learning. Whether or not reluctant learners ultimately value and appreciate feminist critique or algebra often depends on the teacher. Most students do not come to the classroom inherently valuing what learning is prescribed. They must be taught how to value knowledge.

Behavioral Learning. Behavioral learning, also referred to as *psychomotor learning,* focuses on physical action and the development of physical skills. Behavioral learning occurs when students are told how to perform the new skill or set of behaviors, observe others who model the desired behaviors, practice the desired behaviors, and receive feedback from an instructor regarding the performed behaviors. According to Bandura (1969), students are more motivated to learn and perform a set of behaviors (affective learning) if they perceive the new skills as being valuable and relevant to their lives, rewarded, obtainable, and performed by models who are similar to themselves.

Behavioral learning has not received as much attention in the research literature as the other two types of learning (Bloom, 1956; Krathwohl et al., 1964). This is unfortunate, especially since much of primary and secondary education focuses on psychomotor development, as do most training and development instructional environments. Lower-level behavioral learning includes reflexive actions or learning how to control behaviors, such as manipulating a mouse when operating a computer. Higher-level behavioral learning includes highly skilled movements or complex behaviors, such as learning how to play a musical instrument.

Effective teachers and trainers aid students and trainees in acquiring new skills by investing considerable time breaking down a behavior into its various component parts called a *skill set.* Developing an outline of the skill steps to be performed, sometimes called a *task analysis,* is an early stage of behavioral curriculum development. After being told how to perform a skill, teachers and trainers should then model the skill set for the students. To clinch ownership of the newfound skill, effective educators provide students or trainees with appropriate opportunities for drill and practice. Skillfully performed behaviors should then be reinforced through teacher feedback while inappropriate performance behaviors are addressed with corrective feedback. Both confirming and corrective feedback should be provided to the student in a timely manner.

Teaching effectiveness is a teacher or a trainer's ability to enhance behavioral learning by properly diagnosing students' behavioral performance. For students to master the behavioral performance, teachers need to identify a behavior or set of behaviors that need to be modified. For example, when teaching students how to speak with verbal fluency, communication instructors can see and hear subtle articulation and pronunciation disfluencies that need correction. They can provide the student with corrective feedback, such as appropriate placement of the tongue and encouragement that will allow the student to modify the speaking behavior.

Educational psychology, especially the seminal work of Bloom and his colleagues, continues to inform teaching and learning by asking teachers to identify the type and level of cognitive, affective, and behavioral learning they are seeking in their students. Once learning outcomes are identified, teachers can then begin the instructional process by selecting appropriate teaching/training methods.

Pedagogy: An Emphasis on the Teacher

Pedagogy is the systematic study of teaching and teaching methods. This academic field of study includes an examination of the history and philosophy of teaching, theories of teaching, curriculum development, and educational assessment. In addition to these topics, scholars who study pedagogy explore the following issues: (1) how teachers can best manage student classroom behavior, (2) how teachers may enhance student motivation, (3) how teachers can engage students through various teaching strategies, and (4) how teachers can most effectively lecture, conduct experiential activities, and facilitate group discussion. Pedagogy is primarily directed at teacher behaviors and self-perceptions of teacher efficacy and teaching satisfaction that contribute to enhanced learning, in contrast to educational psychology, which focuses on students and attributes of student learning.

There is an ongoing debate among teacher educators summarized in the following question: What's more important, instructional content (*what* is taught) or instructional pedagogy (*how* the content is taught)? (Ball, 2000; Darling-Hammond, Chung, & Frelow, 2002; Shulman, 1986; Wilson, Floden, & Ferrini-Mundy, 2002). Shulman (1986) further distilled the issue as a difference between knowing and teaching. In practical terms, the answer to the content versus pedagogy question has important implications for teacher educators. Fueling this discussion is the oft-quoted maxim, "Those who can—do; those who can't, teach." The pejorative implication of this epithet is, teachers are failed practitioners. For example, if you study theater, you become an actor. If you fail as an actor, you "fall back" on teaching as a way to support yourself. This cultural belief implies that everyone is a natural teacher and little, if any, time should be invested in the formal study of teaching and in developing the skill of teaching.

The origins of this demeaning image of a teacher's capacities originated with George Bernard Shaw and are documented in Shulman (1986), and they run quite counter to the words of Aristotle who made these observations about teaching in *Metaphysics* (cited in Wheelwright, 1951):

> We regard master-craftsmen as superior not merely because they have a grasp of theory and know the reasons for acting as they do. Broadly speaking, what distinguishes the man who knows from the ignorant man is an ability to teach, and this is why we hold that art and not experience has the character of genuine knowledge (episteme)—namely, that artists can teach and others (i.e., those who have not acquired an art by study but have merely picked up some skill empirically) cannot. (p. 69)

Here, Aristotle suggests that teaching is a highly developed skill that is mastered only by understanding theory and by putting the theory into practice. Aristotle considered teaching to be the highest form of understanding, meaning that teaching forces an individual to truly understand the content he or she is trying to convey to others (Palmer, 1998).

Despite the opinions of Aristotle, legislators and citizens, who ultimately control American public education, continue to advocate that content knowledge rather than pedagogical method is the preferred way of developing teachers (McCroskey, Richmond, & McCroskey, 2002). In many American colleges and universities, preservice teachers no longer complete a degree in education, but complete a degree in their content area with a companion certification in teaching (Gregorian, 2001). Based on recent educational statistics, it appears that the emphasis on content knowledge over pedagogical method may not be yielding the results that legislators and lay people had hoped for (Wilson, Floden, & Ferrini-Mundy, 2002). Students continue to struggle with the basics. As noted earlier, only 40% of high school seniors are considered proficient in reading (Donahue, Voelkl, Campbell, & Mazzeo, 1999) and only 30% are considered proficient in math (Reese, Miller, Mazzeo, & Dossey, 1997).

The trend in higher education mirrors what is found in the education and training of primary and secondary educators. Each year, college students are taught by faculty who are experts in their respective fields; however, these content experts may often have a difficult time conveying their expertise to students. When students fail to understand, some faculty members become frustrated and blame students for their lack of understanding, rather than blaming themselves for their failure to create understanding with students (Palmer, 1998). Professionals in the field of pedagogy might argue that this lack of student understanding reflects a teacher's lack of pedagogical training rather than a teacher's lack of content understanding. Evidence to support this claim is the fact that most college faculty members receive minimal education and training in pedagogy (Boyer, 1990; Evelyn, 2001; Gaff, 2002; Meacham, 2002; Nelson & Morreale, 2002). Nyquist, Austin, Sprague, and Wulff (2001) found that doctoral students were most concerned about the lack of systematic and comprehensive programs designed to help them teach and the lack of feedback and mentoring about their teaching. Again, it is assumed that everyone can teach. Most college faculty members who hold a terminal degree, such as the PhD, EdD, or MFA, have completed approximately 200 college credit hours in their academic fields of study and approximately three credit hours in pedagogy for those fortunate enough to obtain a teaching assistantship while in graduate school (Boyer, 1990; Weimer, 2002).

The study of pedagogy continues to inform teaching practices on all levels of education. Whether teachers and trainers should invest more time acquiring knowledge in their content area or in pedagogy remains an issue of contention among teachers. Shulman (1986) has done an excellent job of reframing the knowing and doing distinction (those who can—do; those who can't, teach) that has plagued and demoralized many in the teaching profession for decades. Shulman's work reminds the public that teaching is more than a set of innate skills that all people possess. Like Aristotle, Shulman argues that effective teachers are master craftspersons and artisans who have a mindful grasp of both educational theory and pedagogy.

Communication: An Emphasis on the Meaning of Messages

Communication is the process of stimulating meaning in the minds of others using verbal and nonverbal messages (McCroskey, 1968). Communication researchers place an emphasis on how meaning is created through the use of verbal and nonverbal messages. The communication discipline should not be confused with the study of communications (note the "s"), which examines mediated messages. The study of communications, unlike communication, places considerable emphasis on the channel or medium such as television, radio, film, or newspapers that conveys messages to the targeted audience.

Instructional communication researchers view the teaching–learning process as an inherent communication process. Stated another way, teaching and learning could not occur without communication. To better understand the teaching–learning process as communication, it is useful to identify fundamental communication characteristics and models, including both verbal and nonverbal message systems.

One set of models commonly used by communication educators charts the evolution of communication as action, interaction, and transaction (Beebe, Beebe, & Ivy, 2004). These three models depict theoretical assumptions that illuminate how communication is both described and enhanced.

Communication as Action. The action model of communication, shown at the top of Figure 1.2, depicts communication as a linear, one-way process where meaning is stimulated in the minds of others using verbal and nonverbal messages. This model, patterned after the work of Lasswell (1948) and Shannon and Weaver (1949), is applicable to classroom contexts where the instruction is teacher-centered rather than teacher/student-centered. In the instructional context, communication as action would look and sound like a lecture that a teacher presents to a group of students.

Communication as Interaction. The interactive model of communication, shown in the center of Figure 1.2, adds the concept of feedback. This model illustrates communication as a message exchange process where the source-selected meaning

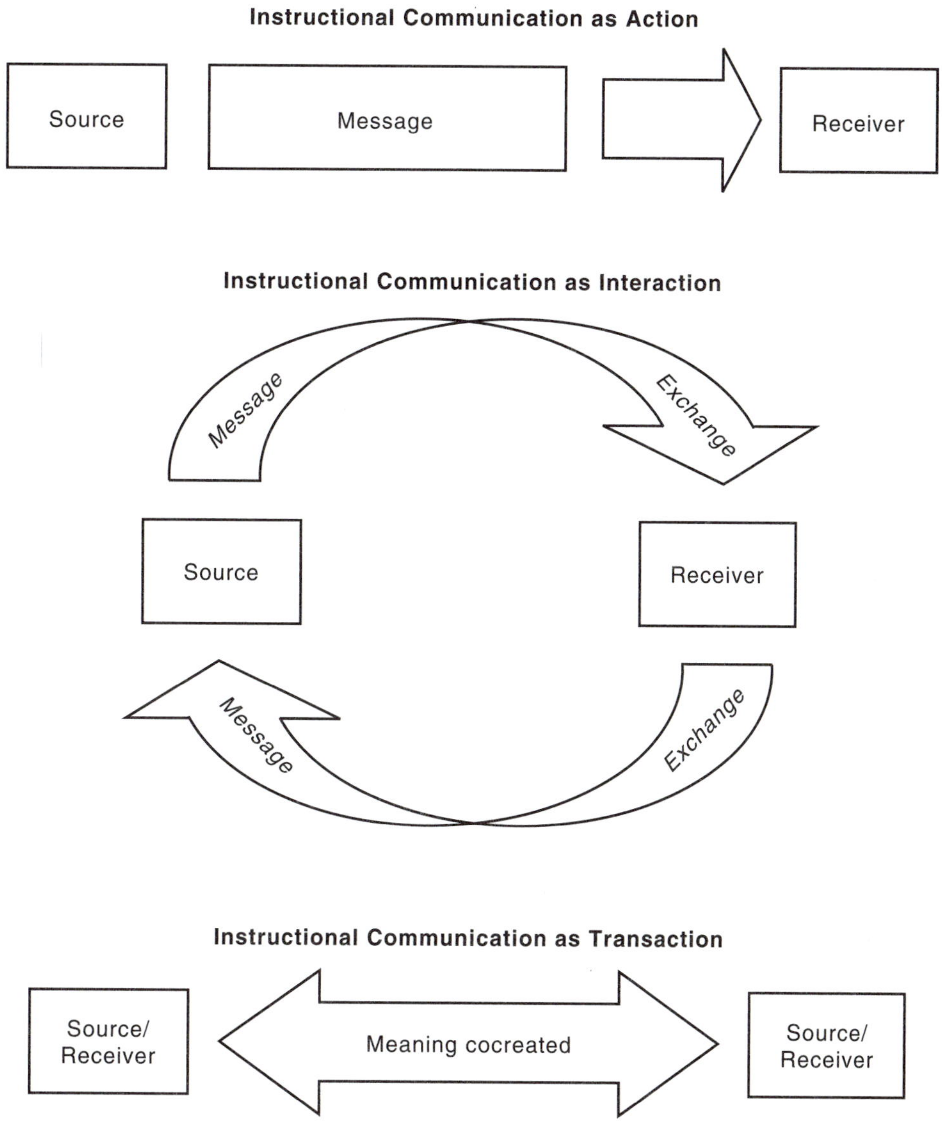

FIGURE 1.2 *Instructional Communication Models.*

is verified, refined, and adapted based on the verbal and nonverbal responses (feedback) that the source obtains from the receiver. Norbert Weiner's research in cybernetics influenced models of human communication by adding a feedback loop (Rogers, 1994). The feedback loop was also reflected in Wilbur Schramm's (1954) model of human communication.

Applied to the classroom, communication as interaction occurs when teachers remain receptive to the verbal and nonverbal feedback they receive from their students and then, after receiving the feedback, adapt their instructional messages accordingly. Teachers who believe in a mastery approach to teaching and learning use feedback to enhance learning outcomes (Bloom, 1976).

Communication as Transaction. The transactional model of communication at the bottom of Figure 1. 2, depicts communication as a process where meaning is cocreated or mutually stimulated by the source *and* the receiver, who send and receive verbal and nonverbal messages simultaneously. Communication as transaction is a nonlinear process (Berlo, 1960). The beginning and ending of communication is virtually indistinguishable. Like the air we breathe, communication is an ever-present element in connecting ourselves with others.

Communication as transaction occurs in the classroom when teachers and students are comfortable enough to engage in conversations. Source and receiver distinctions become less important when both teachers and students are sources and receivers simultaneously. Ideas and meanings are shared and through a mutual expression of ideas and feelings, teachers and students influence each other until shared meaning is created. Transactional communication is evident when teachers respect students' ideas and feelings, and students respect teachers' ideas and feelings. Teachers and students openly debate ideas, clarify meanings, and influence each other until meaning is shared.

Depending on the situation and learning goals, communication in instructional contexts can be enacted as action, interaction, or transaction. From a communication-as-action perspective, the focus is on the message and conveying source-selected meanings to students. Teachers hope that their messages ultimately influence how students understand the content and how students ultimately use the information or change their behaviors as a result of internalizing the course content.

As instructional communication becomes more transactional, it becomes more focused on the other's feelings or *affective responses.* The relationship, rather than the messages, yields the influence. Through the relationship, teachers and students grant each other permission to influence one another. As shown in Figure 1.3,

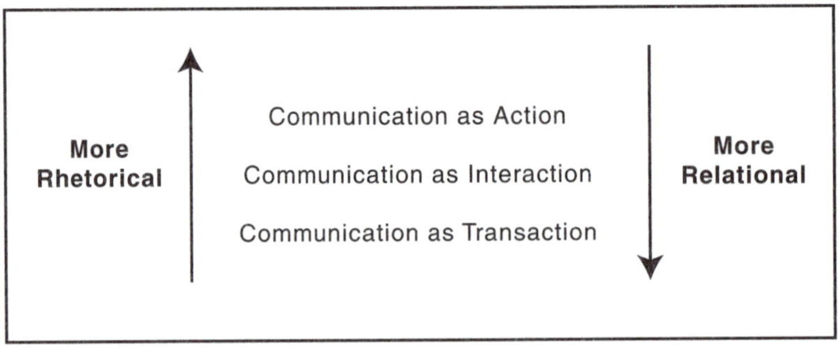

FIGURE 1.3 ***Instructional Communication as a Rhetorical and Relational Process.***

viewed as a continuum, with action on one end and transaction on the other, teachers and students adopt a learning paradigm that is most appropriate for achieving the optimal learning outcome.

In each of the three models, communication messages are expressed both verbally and nonverbally. Virtually all communication between and among humans involves the use of linguistic symbols (verbal communication) and behavior other than written or spoken language (nonverbal communication) that stimulates meaning. Verbal and nonverbal messages have been shown to differ in three ways: content versus relational functions, cognitive versus affective influence, and intentional versus unintentional behavioral control. These fundamental message characteristics aid researchers in studying communication in general and instructional communication in particular to diagnose and prescribe more accurately communication behaviors that may enhance instructional effectiveness.

Content Versus Relational Functions. Watzlawick, Bavelas, and Jackson (1967) theorized that verbal and nonverbal messages function differently in social interactions. Verbal messages function to convey the linguistic information of the message. The content of a message consists of *what* is said. Nonverbal messages function to establish the nature of the relationship; they tend to stimulate meaning about the quality of the interaction that is taking place. The relational dimension of a communication message consists of *how* a message is presented.

Verbal messages typically are content rich and relationally lean. Nonverbal messages are just the opposite; they are infused with cues about power, emotion, and attitudes. Instructional communication researchers, aware of the dynamics of both dimensions of communication, investigate how these dimensions of communication interact to create meaning.

Cognitive Versus Affective Influence. Cognitive learning emphasizes knowledge; affective learning emphasizes feelings. Verbal messages have their primary impact on cognitive responses, whereas nonverbal messages have their primary impact on affective responses (Burgoon, 1994). This difference has important implications for both cognitive and affective learning outcomes. Cognitive learning is more likely to occur when students transform data into information and information into knowledge. Students' abilities to recall, understand, apply, analyze, synthesize, and evaluate knowledge, which are all cognitive processes, are highly influenced by how teachers use verbal messages (Thomson & Tulving, 1970).

Affective learning is more likely to occur when students are receptive to information and respond positively to ideas presented. Students' abilities to receive, respond, value, and internalize new information, which are each affective responses, is highly influenced by how teachers express nonverbal messages, or their degree of nonverbal immediacy (McCroskey & Richmond, 1992). Nonverbal immediacy represents sets of nonverbal communication behaviors that reduce physical and psychological distance between teachers and students (Andersen, 1979; Mehrabian, 1969). Immediacy is a perception of closeness. Nonverbal immediacy behaviors include demonstrating variety in vocal pitch, loudness, and tempo, smiling, leaning toward a person, face-to-face body position, decreasing physical barriers (such as a podium or a desk) between themselves and their students, overall relaxed body movements and positions, spending time with students, and informal but socially appropriate attire.

Intentional Versus Unintentional Behavioral Control. Verbal messages tend to be intentionally crafted and communicated, whereas nonverbal messages are more likely to be unintentionally expressed (Knapp, Wiemann, & Daly, 1978). A certain level of cognition or conscious awareness is required for people to transmit verbal messages (Burgoon, 1994). Therefore, verbal messages tend to be intentional. This level of cognitive engagement is not required, however, for the expression of nonverbal messages. Nonverbal messages are more likely to be expressed outside of the communicator's conscious awareness (Burgoon, 1994). Therefore, nonverbal messages tend to be unintentional.

Because many nonverbal messages are often expressed outside of one's awareness, many teachers fail in their attempts to hide or mask how they feel about their teaching content or their students (Richmond, 1997). Unintentionally expressed nonverbal messages are often referred to as *nonverbal leakage cues* (Ekman & Friesen, 1969). Research suggests that when a person's verbal and nonverbal messages are incongruent, receivers of these messages interpret the nonverbal messages as more believable than the verbal messages (Burgoon, 1994).

A discussion of nonverbal and verbal message systems as well as communication as action, interaction, and transaction provide fundamental assumptions about the nature of human communication. These assumptions have helped instructional communication researchers to better understand the teaching and learning process as a communication process. Applications of these assumptions, along with paradigms gleaned from educational psychology and pedagogy provide fundamental underpinnings of instructional communication research and theory.

Interdisciplinary Contributions to Instructional Communication

Instructional communication integrates the research and theory that the educational psychology, pedagogy, and communication disciplines have generated. As shown in Figure 1.4, instructional communication is the disciplinary intersect of educational psychology, pedagogy, and communication.

To illustrate how educational psychology, pedagogy, and communication contribute to our understanding of instructional communication, we will examine theory and research applications from educational psychology and pedagogy. Specifically, educational psychology has helped instructional communication researchers better understand affective learning from a student's perspective. The study of pedagogy offers a more detailed look at how teacher self-perceptions influence teaching and learning. Drawing upon both of these disciplines, we will

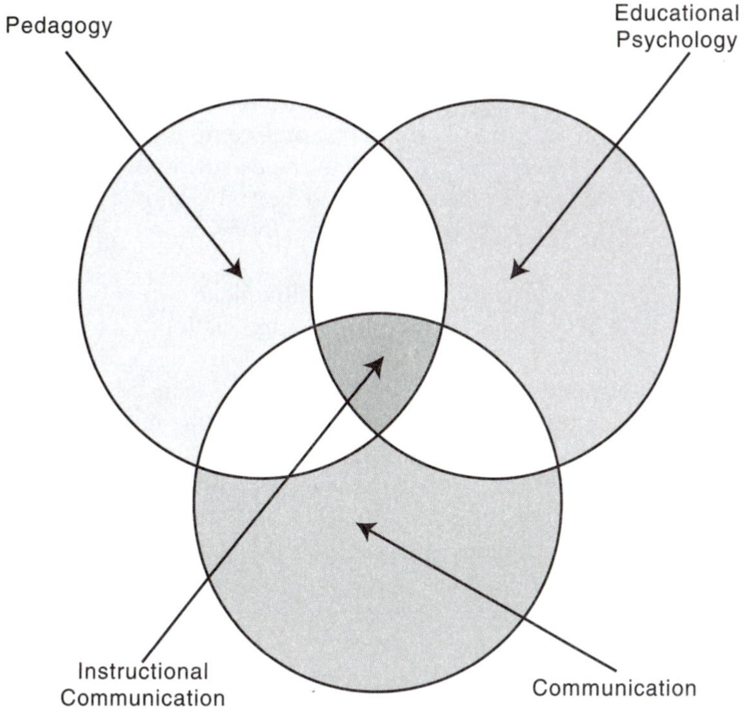

FIGURE 1.4 ***Instructional Communication occurs at the Intersection of Educational Psychology, Pedagogy, and Communication.***

conclude this chapter by examining how communication, from both rhetorical and relational perspectives, links teaching with learning and learning with teaching.

Educational Psychology: Student Affective Learning

Researchers in educational psychology have helped instructional communication researchers explore the relationship between affective learning and cognitive learning. Krathwohl and his colleagues' (1964) conceptualization and taxonomy of affective learning has been particularly informative in helping instructional communication researchers understand how communication functions in the classroom. They define the affective domain of learning as "the objectives that emphasize a feeling or tone, an emotion or degree of acceptance or rejection" (p. 7). Unfortunately, the affective component is often ignored or neglected in teacher education programs. Many of the authors of this book have worked with or are currently working with experienced primary and secondary educators pursuing master's degrees in instructional communication. It is not uncommon to hear them ask, "Why are we now just being introduced to affective learning?"

There are a number of reasons why affective learning has been omitted from traditional teacher education programs. First, many state and national education policies use (and arguably sometimes abuse) standardized testing to document educational effectiveness (McNeil, 2000). School administrators in the United States often focus on cognitive learning outcome comparisons between school districts, states, and countries (Sacks, 2001) to the exclusion of the other domains of learning. Cognitive learning outcomes and how the United States compares to other countries are often fodder for headlines in the nation's leading newspapers (Toppo, 2002).

Second, affective learning, unlike cognitive learning, occurs more slowly. It may take years for students to develop an appreciation for a particular content area (Krathwohl et al., 1964). Such evolutionary learning is difficult to track with the typical assessment measures used in primary, secondary, and higher educational settings. Cognitive and behavioral learning outcomes are more immediate for administrators, teachers, parents, and taxpayers (Krathwohl et al.). Cognitive learning outcomes, therefore, satisfy many educational leaders' needs for immediate feedback data.

Third, many U.S. citizens consider affective learning incompatible with the value Americans place on public versus private information (Krathwohl et al., 1964). Cognitive learning, or students' academic achievement, is considered public information and affective learning, or students' attitudes about what they are learning, is considered private information (Krathwohl et al.). Deans' lists and other academic honors are often published in local newspapers, whereas students' attitudes about what it is they are learning or their respect for learning in general are almost never made public and therefore are never rewarded. In fact, some educators would argue that anti-intellectual attitudes are rewarded more so than intellectual attitudes (Gitlin, 2000; Ravitch, 2004). It also seems appropriate to communicate and showcase anti-intellectual attitudes in the public arena. The first author recalls seeing a bumper sticker proudly proclaiming "My Kid Beat Up Your Honor Student."

Many parents are uncomfortable with teachers telling their children the attitudes they should possess about certain content they are learning in school. The question parents often express is, "Whose values are teachers imparting to our children?" Some parents consider values clarification and affective-based education to be synonymous with brainwashing and consider attitude and value formation to be the responsibility of the family rather than educational institutions (Krathwohl et al., 1964).

Despite the public's obsession with cognitive learning, instructional communication researchers believe affective learning to be a more valid indicator of instructional effectiveness than cognitive learning (Richmond & McCroskey, 1992). This belief is warranted for several reasons. First, affective learning is an educational learning outcome that can be reliably measured and a learning outcome that is meaningful to instructors. The first affective learning measure to be used by instructional communication researchers originated with the work of Andersen (1979) and McCroskey (1966). Their instrument assessed three general areas of affect: (1) affect toward the content/subject matter, (2) affect toward the instructor (teacher evaluation), and (3) affect toward the behaviors taught in the class. It also measured three belief constructs: (1) The probability of taking another course in the subject matter, (2) The probability of taking another course with the instructor, and (3) The probability of using the behaviors taught in the class.

McCroskey (1994) revised the affective learning measure, arguing that the measure was flawed. One flaw was that the instrument contained two sets of items (four items in each set) that evaluated the teacher rather than affective learning. McCroskey argued that (a) assessing students' attitudes about their teacher and (b) assessing students' probability of taking another course with the same teacher, although important, did not fit Krathwohl and his colleagues' (1964) conceptualization and taxonomy of affective learning. According to McCroskey, researchers who include these two sets of teacher evaluation items in their measure have inflated estimates of affective learning.

Another flaw was that the affective learning measure contained two sets of items (four items in each set) that assessed the behaviors taught in the course, even though not all courses included behavioral learning (i.e., history, literature). To remedy this flaw McCroskey (1994) suggested researchers remove the two sets of items that (a) assess students' attitudes about the behaviors taught in the course, and that (b) assess students' probability of using the behaviors taught in the course from the affective learning measure, when a particular course does not include behavioral learning. When a course includes behavioral learning, it is highly recommended that the two sets of behavioral items be included in the affective learning measure because they tap into higher forms of affective learning and enhance the overall validity of the affective learning instrument (Mottet & Richmond, 1998).

The revised Affective Learning Measure (ALM) is reflected in Figure 1.5 and the Affect Toward Instructor (ATI) measure is represented in Figure 1.6. The ALM has been shown to be both valid and reliable (Mottet & Richmond, 1998) and yields learning scores that are immediately interpretable and meaningful, giving teachers and trainers insight into their students' affective learning.

The second reason why instructional communication researchers argue that affective learning is a valid indicator of instructional effectiveness is that teacher communication behaviors, especially their nonverbal behaviors, have been shown to be a stronger predictor of students' affective learning than cognitive learning (McCroskey & Richmond, 1992). This finding is significant, especially since there appears to be numerous validity and reliability problems associated with cognitive learning measurement, which limits the generalizability of current cognitive learning scores (McCroskey & Richmond, 1992). Additionally, affective learning has been shown to predict cognitive learning (Christophel, 1990; Frymier, 1994; Rodriguez, Plax, & Kearney, 1996).

The third reason we favor affective learning over cognitive learning as an indicator of instructional effectiveness is the strong theoretical support that explains and predicts relationships between affective learning and the other two domains of learning (cognitive and psychomotor). Over 2,000 years ago, Aristotle identified pathos (the use of emotions) as one of the primary means to influence others. Contemporary research supports Aristotle's assumptions: Emotions consistently

FIGURE 1.5 ***Affective Learning Measure (ALM).***

Instructions: Using the following scales, evaluate the class you are taking.** Please circle the number for each item that best represents your feelings.

Content/subject matter of the course:

Bad	1	2	3	4	5	6	7	Good
Valuable	1	2	3	4	5	6	7	Worthless*
Unfair	1	2	3	4	5	6	7	Fair
Negative	1	2	3	4	5	6	7	Positive

Your likelihood of actually enrolling in another course of related content if your schedule so permits:

Unlikely	1	2	3	4	5	6	7	Likely
Possible	1	2	3	4	5	6	7	Impossible*
Improbable	1	2	3	4	5	6	7	Probable
Would	1	2	3	4	5	6	7	Would Not*

** The class before this one * Scores reflected for analysis

Note: When behavioral learning is part of a course, then the affective learning measure can be augmented with the following two sets of items. It is important to note, however, that these two sets of items *cannot* be included in a questionnaire instrument when multiple classes are being surveyed using the "prior class" methodology, since researchers will not know whether the "prior class" includes behavioral learning. The "prior class" or "class before this one" method of survey administration is reviewed in Chapter 2.

Behaviors recommended in the course:

Good	1	2	3	4	5	6	7	Bad*
Worthless	1	2	3	4	5	6	7	Valuable
Fair	1	2	3	4	5	6	7	Unfair*
Positive	1	2	3	4	5	6	7	Negative*

In "real life" situations, your likelihood of actually attempting to engage in behaviors recommended in the course:

Likely	1	2	3	4	5	6	7	Unlikely*
Impossible	1	2	3	4	5	6	7	Possible
Probable	1	2	3	4	5	6	7	Improbable*
Would Not	1	2	3	4	5	6	7	Would

* Scores reflected for analysis

influence human behavior (Cacioppo & Gardner, 1999; Metts & Bowers, 1994; Russell & Mehrabian, 1978). After reviewing the literature of communication and psychology, Biggers and Rankis (1983) reported that a large percentage (40 percent or more) of variance in research studies predicting behavior was attributable to people's emotions. In the instructional context, students may use their emotions as information to guide what Hatfield, Cacioppo, and Rapson (1994) referred to as *bivalent* (approach/withdrawal) behavior. Students who self-report high degrees of affective learning are more likely to approach or engage in, their studies while students who self-report low degrees of affective learning are more likely to withdraw from or avoid their studies.

A fourth reason to place greater emphasis on affective learning than currently exists in teacher training is that affective learning principles are compatible

FIGURE 1.6 ***Affect Toward Instructor (ATI) Measure.***

Instructions: Using the following scales, evaluate the teacher in the class you are taking.**
Please circle the number for each item that best represents your feelings.

Course instructor:

Good	1	2	3	4	5	6	7	Bad*
Worthless	1	2	3	4	5	6	7	Valuable
Fair	1	2	3	4	5	6	7	Unfair*
Positive	1	2	3	4	5	6	7	Negative*

The likelihood of my taking another course with the teacher of this course, if I have a choice:

Unlikely	1	2	3	4	5	6	7	Likely
Possible	1	2	3	4	5	6	7	Impossible*
Improbable	1	2	3	4	5	6	7	Probable
Would	1	2	3	4	5	6	7	Would Not*

** The class before this one * Scores reflected for analysis

with contemporary learning theory: Student emotions and learning are related (Goleman, 1997; Mayer, 1986; Mottet & Beebe, 2002; Salovey & Sluyter, 1997). It was once believed that emotions and cognitions were independent of each other; however, research suggests that these two constructs are more closely linked than once thought (Frijda, 1994).

Although some politicians and citizens consider affective learning assessment measures to be inferior to cognitive learning outcomes, many instructional communication scholars believe affective learning outcomes have been underestimated. Affective learning continues to be a strong predictor of cognitive learning (Rodriguez et al., 1996) and allows teachers to reach important cognitive learning outcomes by first focusing on the affective dimension of the teaching and learning process.

Pedagogy: Teacher Self-Perceptions

Educational psychologists focus on students and how they learn. Pedagogical researchers focus on teachers and how they teach. One major impact of the study of pedagogy on instructional communication is the insights that have been discovered about how teacher self-perceptions influence student learning. Two variables that have received considerable attention in the pedagogical research literature and that have influenced instructional communication researchers are teacher self-efficacy and teaching satisfaction.

Teacher self-efficacy is "the extent to which the teacher believes he or she has the capacity to affect student performance" (Berman, McLaughlin, Bass, Pauly, & Zellman, 1977, p. 137). Stated another way, teacher self-efficacy is a "belief or conviction that teachers can influence how well students learn, even those who may be difficult or unmotivated" (Guskey & Passaro, 1994, p. 4). A teacher with high self-efficacy is one who is confident in his or her ability, knowledge, and skill to facilitate student learning.

Ross (1998) found that teacher self-efficacy predicts student outcomes such as achievement and motivation. Teacher self-efficacy has also been shown to predict teacher outcomes such as teachers' adoption of innovation (Fuchs, Fuchs, & Bishop, 1992), professional commitment (Coladarci, 1992), absenteeism (Imants & Van Zoelen, 1995), and dropping out of the teaching profession (Glickman & Tamashiro, 1982).

High self-efficacious teachers have been shown to devote more time to academic instruction (Soodak & Podell, 1993) and have made greater efforts to resolve problems (Chwalisz, Altmaier, & Russell, 1992) than low efficacious teachers. It is also believed that teacher self-efficacy may influence teachers' use of time, choice of classroom management strategies, and questioning techniques (Gibson & Dembo, 1984; Saklofske, Michayluk, & Randhawa, 1988; Woolfolk, Rosoff, & Hoy, 1990).

Teacher job satisfaction is a construct that has been studied in relationship to teacher self-efficacy. Job satisfaction has been defined as "a state of mind determined by the extent to which the individual perceives his/her job-related needs being met" (Evans, 1997, p. 833). Teacher job satisfaction has been shown to be a predictor of teacher retention and school effectiveness (Shann, 1998). According to Fresko, Kfir, and Nasser (1997) and Shin and Reyes (1995), teacher job satisfaction is an antecedent to teacher commitment.

Dinham and Scott (2000) found that teachers were most satisfied by factors that were intrinsic to the role of teaching, such as helping students achieve, modifying students' attitudes and behaviors, and developing positive relationships with students. Pena and Mitchell (2000) found that college educators were most satisfied with their opportunities to educate students and teach courses in their content areas. A flexible work schedule, the opportunity to work independently, and job security were three other highly ranked factors yielding teacher job satisfaction. College faculty members' discontent centered around the quality of students, level of institutional support for research and teaching, teaching load, and compensation.

Pedagogical research suggests that the teacher–student relationship has much to do with enhancing teacher self-efficacy and job satisfaction. According to Shann (1998) and also to Kim and Loadman (1994), the teacher–student relationship was the number one predictor of teacher job satisfaction among primary and secondary educators. Instructional communication researchers are uniquely qualified to examine how the teacher–student relationship influences teachers and their teaching. Chapter 7 summarizes in more detail the instructional communication research that has been conducted in this area, which ultimately builds on the significant contributions of pedagogical researchers.

Instructional Communication: Examining Rhetorical and Relational Processes

The communication discipline has two rich traditions that continue to inform the academy today—rhetorical and relational (Cohen, 1994; Howell, 1954; McCroskey & Richmond, 1996; Shepherd, 1992; Wallace, 1954). Both of these traditions have influenced the study of instructional communication. The remainder of this chapter and the over-arching schema of this book will be framed from both the rhetorical and the relational communication perspectives.

Instructional Communication as a Rhetorical Communication Process

From a rhetorical perspective, teachers use verbal and nonverbal messages with the intention of influencing or persuading students. To persuade is to craft messages that change or reinforce attitudes, beliefs, values, or behaviors. As noted by McCroskey and Richmond (1996), "The function of rhetorical communication is to get others to do what you want or need them to do and/or think the way you want or need them to think—to persuade them" (p. 234).

The rhetorical function of communication, which draws upon the classical tradition of rhetoric with roots in the fifth century BCE, is source- or, in the case of instruction, teacher-centered. During the European Renaissance, rhetoric or the study of rhetoric, was one of the original seven liberal arts (Sproule, 1991). Mastery of rhetoric exemplified the mark of an educated person, or as Roman educator Fabius Quintillian noted, "a good man speaking well." Instructional communication from the rhetorical perspective is more likely to emulate linear forms of communication in which teachers are the source of instructional messages and students are expected to be compliant receivers of instructional messages.

Aristotle's *Rhetoric,* written in 333 BCE, continues to be one of the discipline's most influential works and is considered to be the first textbook in public speaking. To Aristotle, the means of persuasion are primarily ethos (the personal character of the speaker), pathos (the use of emotion), and logos (the logical, rational nature of the message). If teachers are to be successful in their attempts to transfer or convey source-centered meaning to their students, students must first perceive them to be credible or believable. (Ethos, or teacher credibility, will be the primary focus of Chapter 4.) Teachers must also help students learn by using verbal and nonverbal messages that stimulate students' affective or emotional responses. (Various instructional message variables that have been shown to influence students' affective responses will be the primary focus of Chapter 5.) Finally, teachers must present logical, rational messages using appropriate evidence and reasoning.

Another way of examining instructional communication from the rhetorical perspective is by using the classical canons of rhetoric: invention, arrangement, style, memory, and delivery. The five canons of rhetoric were proposed by Roman rhetoricians as a shorthand roster of speaking skills. Each canon is primarily concerned with the communication encoding process (Covino & Jolliffe, 1995). The influence of four of the five canons is evident in contemporary research in instructional communication.

Invention focuses on how teachers create instructional messages for students. In order for a teacher to stimulate source-selected meaning in the minds of students, teachers create and use examples, narratives, and illustrations that are relevant to their students' lives and experiences. Master teachers spend considerable time, out of the classroom, "inventing" as they prepare for their classes. This "behind the scenes" invention process remains invisible to most students and citizens who sometimes criticize teachers for only working partial days. Effective teachers anticipate student confusion and have numerous examples, narratives, and illustrations in their repertoire to help students through their confusion.

Arrangement, which is sometimes referred to as disposition, is the art of organizing the instructional material so that it meets students' needs. If instructional messages are appropriately arranged, they are more likely to stimulate the meaning that teachers intend. Anderson (1995) suggests that for students to learn content, teachers must either create a new schema or an organizational system for students, or show students how the new content fits into their already existing schema.

Style "gives presence" to ideas (Covino & Jolliffe, 1995, p. 23). Good style means phrasing instructional messages so that they are relevant, clear, interesting, and appropriate. Instructional communication researchers have examined such style variables as content relevance (Frymier & Shulman, 1995), message clarity (Chesebro & McCroskey, 1998, 2001), and humor (Wanzer & Frymier, 1999). These instructional message variables have been shown to influence learning outcomes.

Closely related to style is the canon of delivery. Instructional communication researchers have investigated the influence of teacher delivery, operationalized as "teacher immediacy cues" (Andersen, 1979), on student motivation and learning. The study of how teachers speak, move, and express themselves primarily through nonverbal means reflects the initial importance of delivery, as debated by both Greek and Roman rhetoricians.

These classical paradigms continue to inform instructional communication theory and research. From a rhetorical perspective, instructional communication is customized for a particular group of students with the goal of influencing them. The influence occurs by inventing, arranging, and delivering instructional messages that are adapted to how students think and feel about certain topics.

Instructional Communication as a Relational Communication Process

A second perspective examines instructional communication as a relational process is which both teachers and students mutually create and use verbal and nonverbal messages to develop a relationship with each other. A relationship is an ongoing connection made with another person through communication (Beebe, Beebe, & Redmond, 2003). From a relational perspective, rather than focusing exclusively on message content, teachers and students also acknowledge and address emotions. The relational perspective draws upon contemporary models of communication in which meaning is mutually created and shared between individuals. According to McCroskey and Richmond (1996) the relational approach examines communication from a transactional or co-orientational perspective, "[t]hat is, two (or more) people coordinate their communication to reach a shared perspective satisfactory to all. Of paramount concern is the relationship between the two people and the perceived well-being of the 'other'" (p. 234).

It was not until the early part of the twentieth century that communication researchers investigated communication processes using social scientific methods, rather than relying exclusively on rhetorical research methods. Using social science research methods, an increasing number of researchers sought to explain, predict, and control communication phenomena that occurred in a variety of communication contexts, such as public settings, organizations, small groups, instructional settings, and interpersonal relationships. In addition to new social scientific research methodologies, philosophical perspectives about human relationships also had an impact upon how we think about how humans relate to one another.

Philosopher Martin Buber influenced the thinking of relational communication when he suggested that true dialogue is the essence of authentic communication (Buber, 1958). Communication, according to Buber, consists of two contrasting relationship qualities. First, some relationships are more impersonal; Buber (1958) called this an "I–It" relationship. In an "I–It" impersonal relationship, communicators interact with one another by relying upon expected roles. In the context of the classroom, a teacher who views his or her student as simply a vessel to be filled with information selected by the teacher is operating from an "I–It" perspective. A second kind of relationship Buber called "I–Thou." In this relationship there is authentic dialogue that stems from an open, honest, spontaneous, nonjudgmental perspective. Applied to the classroom, an "I–Thou" relationship between teacher and students occurs when teachers and students expect learning to be mutually beneficial. Both teacher and student interact with one another as unique individuals rather than in stereotyped teacher–student roles. We are not suggesting that the goal of all teacher–student relationships is to emulate Buber's "I–Thou" paradigm. Buber's work has, however, influenced communication researchers and theorists sufficiently to consider the possibility of adopting the "I–Thou" relational communication assumption when appropriate.

One hallmark of the relational approach to instructional communication includes an emphasis on both teacher and student feelings and emotions—how teachers and students perceive and affectively respond to each other (Ellis, 2000, 2004). The affective realm influences teachers' motivation to teach and students' motivation to learn. A discussion of the affective domain on both teaching and learning is the focus of Chapters 7–11.

Although instructional communication from the relational perspective focuses on both verbal and nonverbal messages, the bulk of the research examines teachers' and students' nonverbal messages. Nonverbal messages have been shown to stimulate the majority of the emotional or social meaning in messages (Burgoon, Buller, & Woodall, 1996; Mehrabian, 1972). Teachers who are nonverbally expressive or "immediate" in the classroom positively influence students' liking for teachers (Frymier, 1994), students' motivation to learn (Richmond, 1990), and students' perceived learning (McCroskey & Richmond, 1992). Additionally, nonverbally expressive teachers have been shown to be more influential in students' lives than nonverbally unexpressive teachers in that students are more willing to comply with their teachers' requests (Plax & Kearney, 1992) and less willing to resist their teachers (Kearney & Plax, 1992).

Similarly, students who convey positive feelings for their teachers through nonverbal messages have also been shown to influence teachers and their teaching (Mottet & Richmond, 2002). Nonverbally responsive students positively influence teachers' liking for students, their motivation to teach, their self-efficacy, and their overall teaching satisfaction more than nonverbally unresponsive students (Mottet, 2000; Mottet, Beebe, Raffeld, & Medlock, 2004; Mottet, Beebe, Raffeld, & Paulsel, 2004). Also, students have been shown to affect their teachers' compliance tendencies in that nonverbally responsive students are significantly more influential than nonverbally unresponsive students in getting teachers to comply with their instructional requests such as allowing students to turn in late work or raising a student's grade if it falls on the cusp of a higher grade. (Mottet, Beebe, Raffeld, & Paulsel, 2004).

From the relational perspective, instructional communication is more spontaneous and less strategic than the rhetorical perspective. It is believed that many teachers, and students alike, are unaware of the messages, especially nonverbal messages, that are expressed in the classroom and how these implicit messages influence teacher outcomes (i.e., teaching satisfaction, teacher compliance, teacher self-efficacy) and student outcomes (i.e., student learning, student compliance, student motivation).

Drawing upon both rhetorical and relational perspectives, instructional communication theory and research is becoming more accessible to teachers (Chesebro & McCroskey, 2002; McCroskey & Richmond, 2006). There are at least 21 graduate programs that offer advanced degrees or a curricular emphasis in instructional communication (National Communication Association, 2005). Teachers are becoming increasingly aware of how to use communication in the classroom, and this advanced study in instructional communication is enhancing their instructional effectiveness (Richmond, McCroskey, Plax, & Kearney, 1986). Teachers are realizing how student communication messages influence them and their teaching and are becoming more aware of how learning occurs within the context of the teacher–student relationship. Teachers who use rhetorical and relational messages strategically, such as clear and relevant instructional messages, nonverbal immediacy cues (i.e., forward body leans, eye contact, head nods), and affinity-seeking behaviors (i.e., complementing others, making onself interesting to others), are beginning to understand how relational power and instructional influence work in the classroom.

Although we compare and contrast the rhetorical and relational paradigms, it is neither appropriate nor practical to view these two traditions as polar opposites. These two perspectives simply reflect different emphases of the communication process. To borrow Aristotle's opening sentence in the *Rhetoric,* "Rhetoric is the counterpart of dialectic." In other words, rhetorical communication is the counterpart of relational communication. They are two sides of a coin. Both perspectives have the same goal—to facilitate communication. In the context of instructional communication, the goal is to facilitate learning. The rhetorical approach is more teacher-directed while the relational approach is more collaborative.

The communication discipline has given researchers and teachers a new set of tools for examining teaching effectiveness, student learning, and how these two variables are related. Rather than relying exclusively on theories from educational psychology or pedagogy, instructional communication researchers use rhetorical and relational theories and constructs to explain and predict teaching and learning.

Summary

This chapter introduced the study of instructional communication. Instructional communication is the process of teachers and students stimulating meanings in the minds of each other using verbal and nonverbal messages. As an interdisciplinary field of inquiry, instructional communication draws upon the disciplines of educational psychology, pedagogy, and communication. Educational psychology focuses on the learner and the underlying psychological and intellectual processes that explain and predict student learning. Pedagogy focuses on the teacher and the methods that teachers use to instruct. Communication focuses on the meaning of messages and how people use verbal and nonverbal messages to stimulate meanings in the minds of others.

The unique contributions of each discipline make instructional communication a vibrant field of study. Educational psychologists offer multiple perspectives on student learning including cognitive, behavioral, and affective. Although each domain of learning remains important, we argued that students' affective learning, which is often ignored in public debates on education and student learning, is a more valid indicator of instructional effectiveness than student cognitive learning. Researchers in pedagogy have allowed us to see how teacher self-perceptions influence student learning, especially perceptions of teacher self-efficacy and teaching satisfaction. The communication discipline's rich tradition of examining communication from either the rhetorical or the relational perspective has allowed us to understand teaching and learning as *both* a rhetorical and a relational process.

Chapter 2, "Instructional Communication: The Historical Perspective", complements the first chapter by discussing the history of instructional communication. Together, these two chapters form Unit 1, which focuses on the foundations of instructional communication.

References

Andersen, J. F. (1979). Teacher immediacy as a predictor of teaching effectiveness. In D. Nimmo (Ed.), *Communication yearbook 3* (pp. 543–559). New Brunswick, NJ: Transaction Books.

Anderson, J. R. (1995). *Cognitive psychology and its implications.* New York: W. H. Freeman.

Anderson, L. W., & Krathwohl, D. R. (Eds.). (2001). *A taxonomy for learning, teaching, and assessing: A revision of Bloom's taxonomy of educational objectives.* New York: Longman.

Archer, J. (1999, March 17). New teachers abandon field at high rate. *Education Week,* p. 20.

Aristotle (1991). *The art of rhetoric* (H. C. Lawson-Tancred, Trans.). New York: Penguin Books.

Astin, A. W. (1984). Student involvement: A developmental theory for higher education. *Journal of College Student Personnel, 25,* 297–307.

Astin, A. W. (1993). *What matters in college? Four critical years revisited.* San Francisco: Jossey-Bass.

Ball, D. L. (2000). Bridging practices: Intertwining content and pedagogy in teaching and learning to teach. *Journal of Teacher Education, 51,* 241–247.

Bandura, A. (1969). *Principles of behavior modification.* New York: Holt, Rinehart & Winston.

Beebe, S. A., Beebe, S. J. & Ivy, D. K. (2004). *Communication: Principles for a lifetime.* Boston: Allyn & Bacon.

Beebe, S. A., Beebe, S. J. & Redmond, M. A. (2003). *Interpersonal communication: Relating to others.* Boston: Allyn & Bacon.

Berlo, D. K. (1960). *The process of communication.* New York: Holt, Rinehart and Winston.

Berman, P., McLaughlin, M., Bass, G., Pauly, E., & Zellman, G. (1977). *Federal programs supporting educational change, Vol. VII. Factors affecting implementation and continuation* (Rep. No. R-1589/7-HEW). Santa Monica, CA: RAND. (ERIC Document Reproduction Service No. 140–432).

Biggers, T., & Rankis, O. (1983). Dominance–submissiveness as an affective response to situations and as a predictor of approach–avoidance. *Social Behavior and Personality, 11,* 61–69.

Bloom, B. S. (1956). *Taxonomy of educational objectives: Handbook I: Cognitive domain.* New York: McKay.

Bloom, B. S. (1976). *Human characteristics and school learning.* New York: McGraw-Hill.

Boyer, E. L. (1990). *Scholarship reconsidered: Priorities of the professoriate.* The Carnegie Foundation for the Advancement of Teaching. San Francisco: Jossey-Bass.

Bryant, D. C. (1953). Rhetoric: Its function and its scope. *Quarterly Journal of Speech, 39,* 401–424.

Buber, M. (1958). *I and thou.* New York: Scribner.

Burgoon, J. K. (1994). Nonverbal signals. In M. L. Knapp & G. R. Miller (Eds.), *Handbook of interpersonal communication* (pp. 229–285). Thousand Oaks, CA: Sage.

Burgoon, J. K., Buller, D. B., & Woodall, W. G. (1996). *Nonverbal communication: The unspoken dialogue.* New York: McGraw-Hill.

Cacioppo, J. T., & Gardner, W. L. (1999). Emotion. *Annual Review of Psychology, 50,* 191–214.

Chesebro, J. L., & McCroskey, J. C. (1998). The relationship between teacher clarity and immediacy and students' experiences of state receiver apprehension when listening to teachers. *Communication Quarterly, 46,* 446–455.

Chesebro, J. L., & McCroskey, J. C. (2001). The relationship of teacher clarity and immediacy with student state receiver apprehension, affect, and cognitive learning. *Communication Education, 50,* 59–68.

Chesebro, J. L., & McCroskey, J. C. (Eds.). (2002). *Communication for teachers.* Boston: Allyn & Bacon.

Christophel, D. M. (1990). The relationships among teacher immediacy behaviors, student motivation, and learning. *Communication Education, 37,* 323–340.

Chwalisz, K. D., Altmaier, E. M., & Russell, D. W. (1992). Causal attributions, self-efficacy cognitions, and coping with stress. *Journal of Social and Clinical Psychology, 11,* 377–400.

Coffin, C. (2002). *Touching the future: Final report.* Washington, DC: American Council on Education.

Cohen, H. (1994). *Speech communication: The emergence of a discipline, 1914–1945.* Annandale, VA: Speech Communication Association.

Coladarci, T. (1992). Teachers' sense of efficacy and commitment to teaching. *Journal of Experimental Education, 60,* 323–337.

Covino, W. A., & Jolliffe, D. A. (1995). *Rhetoric: Concepts, definitions, boundaries.* Boston: Allyn & Bacon.

Darling-Hammond, L., Chung, R., & Frelow, F. (2002). Variation in teacher preparation: How well do different pathways prepare teachers to teach? *Journal of Teacher Education, 53,* 286–302.

DeFleur, M. L. (1993). *The forthcoming shortage of communications Ph.D.s: Trends that will influence recruiting.* Working Paper Series from the Freedom Forum Media Studies Center. Arlington, VA: The Freedom Forum.

Dinham, S., & Scott, C. (2000). Moving into the third, outer domain of teacher satisfaction. *Journal of Educational Administration, 38,* 379–392.

Donahue, P. L., Voelkl, K. E., Campbell, J. R., & Mazzeo, J. (1999, March). *NAEP 1998 reading report card for the nation and the states.* Retrieved October 1, 2002 from http://nces.ed.gov/nationsreportcard.

Ekman, P., & Friesen, W. V. (1969). Nonverbal leakage and clues to deception. *Psychiatry, 32,* 88–105.

Ellis, K. (2000). Perceived teacher confirmation: The development and validation of an instrument and two studies of the relationship to cognitive and affective learning. *Human Communication Research, 26,* 264–291.

Ellis, K. (2004). The impact of perceived teacher confirmation on receiver apprehension, motivation, and learning. *Communication Education, 53,* 1–20.

Evans, L. (1997). Understanding teacher morale and job satisfaction. *Teaching and Teacher Education, 13,* 831–845.

Evelyn, J. (2001, June 15). The hiring boom at 2-year colleges: Faculty slots—with tenure—are available, but not to those who boast about their dissertations. *Chronicle of Higher Education.*

Fresko, B., Kfir, D., & Nasser, F. (1997). Predicting teacher commitment. *Teaching and Teacher Education, 13,* 429–438.

Frijda, N. H. (1994). Emotions require cognitions, even if simple ones. In P. Ekman & R. J. Davidson (Eds.), *The nature of emotion: Fundamental questions* (pp. 197–202). New York: Oxford University Press.

Frymier, A. B. (1994). The use of affinity-seeking in producing liking and learning in the classroom. *Journal of Applied Communication Research, 22,* 87–105.

Frymier, A. B., & Shulman, G. M. (1995). "What's in it for me?": Increasing content relevance to enhance students' motivation. *Communication Education, 44,* 40–50.

Fuchs, L. S., Fuchs, D., & Bishop, N. (1992). Instructional adaptation for students at risk. *Journal of Educational Research, 86,* 70–84.

Gaff, J. G. (2002). The disconnect between graduate education and faculty realities: A review of recent research. *Liberal Education, 88,* 6–13.

Gibson, S., & Dembo, M. (1984). Teacher efficacy: A construct validation. *Journal of Educational Psychology, 76,* 569–582.

Gitlin, T. (2000, December 8). The renaissance of anti-intellectualism. *The Chronicle of Higher Education,* p. B7.

Glickman, C., & Tamashiro, R. (1982). A comparison of first-year, fifth-year, and former teachers on efficacy, ego development, and problem solving. *Psychology in Schools, 19,* 558–562.

Goleman, D. (1997). *Emotional intelligence.* New York: Bantam Books.

Gregorian, V. (2001, August 17). Teacher education must become colleges' central preoccupation. *The Chronicle of Higher Education* p. B7.

Guskey, T. R., & Passaro, P. D. (1994). Teacher efficacy: A study of construct dimensions. *American Educational Research Journal, 31,* 627–643.

Hatfield, E., Cacioppo, J. T., & Rapson, R. L. (1994). *Emotional contagion.* New York: Cambridge University Press.

Howell, W. S. (1954). English backgrounds of rhetoric. In K. R. Wallace (Ed.), *History of speech education in America* (pp. 1–47). New York: Appleton-Century-Crofts.

Hurt, H. T., Scott, M. D., & McCroskey, J. C. (1978). *Communication in the classroom.* Reading, MA: Addison-Wesley.

Imants, J., & Van Zoelen, A. (1995). Teachers' sickness absence in primary schools, school climate, and teachers' sense of efficacy. *School Organization, 15,* 77–86.

Ingersoll, R. M. (2001). Teacher turnover and teacher shortages: An organizational analysis. *American Educational Research Journal, 38,* 499–534.

Kearney, P., & Plax, T. G. (1992). Student resistance to control. In V. P. Richmond & J. C. McCroskey (Eds.), *Power in the classroom: Communication, control, and concern* (pp. 85–100). Hillsdale, NJ: Lawrence Erlbaum.

Kim, I., & Loadman, W. (1994). *Predicting teacher job satisfaction.* Columbus: Ohio State University. (ERIC Document Reproduction Service No. ED383707).

Knapp, M. L., Wiemann, J. M., & Daly, J. A. (1978). Nonverbal communication: Issues and appraisals. *Human Communication Research, 4,* 271–280.

Krathwohl, D. R., Bloom, B. S., & Masia, B. B. (1964). *Taxonomy of educational objectives: Handbook II: Affective domain.* New York: McKay.

Langdon, C. A. (1996). The third Phi Delta Kappa poll of teachers' attitudes toward the public schools. *Phi Delta Kappan, 78,* 245–246.

Lasswell, H. (1948). The structure and function of communication in society. In L. Bryson (Ed.), *The communication of ideas* (p. 37). New York: Institute for Religious and Social Studies.

Martin, M. M., Mottet, T. P., & Myers, S. A. (2000). Students' motives for communicating with their instructors and affective and cognitive learning. *Psychological Reports, 87,* 830–834.

Mayer, J. D. (1986). How mood influences cognition. In N. E. Sharkey (Ed.), *Advances in cognitive science 1* (pp. 290–314). New York: Halsted Press.

McCroskey, J. C. (1966). *Experimental studies of the effects of ethos and evidence in persuasive communication.* Unpublished doctoral dissertation, Pennsylvania State University.

McCroskey, J. C. (1968). *An introduction to rhetorical communication.* Englewood Cliffs, NJ: Prentice-Hall.

McCroskey, J. C. (1977). Classroom consequences of communication apprehension. *Communication Education, 26,* 27–33.

McCroskey, J. C. (1994). Assessment of affect toward communication and affect toward instruction in communication. In S. Morreale and M. Brooks (Eds.), *1994 SCA summer conference proceedings and prepared remarks* (pp. 55–71). Annandale, VA: Speech Communication Association.

McCroskey, J. C. (1998). *An introduction to communication in the classroom.* Acton, MA: Tapestry Press.

McCroskey, J. C., & Beatty, M. J. (2000). The communibiological perspective: Implications for communication in instruction. *Communication Education, 49,* 1–6.

McCroskey, J. C., & Richmond, V. P. (1992). Increasing teacher influence through immediacy. In V. P. Richmond & J. C. McCroskey (Eds.), *Power in the classroom: Communication, control, and concern* (pp. 101–119). Hillsdale, NJ: Lawrence Erlbaum.

McCroskey, J. C., & Richmond, V. P. (1996). Human communication theory and research: Traditions and models. In M. B. Salwen & D. W. Stacks (Eds.), *An integrated approach to communication theory and research* (pp. 233–242). Mahwah, NJ: Lawrence Erlbaum.

McCroskey, J. C., & Richmond, V. P. (2006). *An introduction to communication in the classroom: The role of communication in teaching and training.* Boston: Allyn & Bacon.

McCroskey, L. L., & McCroskey, J. C. (2002). Willingness to communicate and communication apprehension in the classroom. In J. L. Chesebro & J. C. McCroskey (Eds.), *Communication for teachers* (pp. 19–34). Boston: Allyn & Bacon.

McCroskey, L. L., Richmond, V. P., & McCroskey, J. C. (2002). The scholarship of teaching and learning: Contributions from the discipline of communication. *Communication Education, 51,* 383–391.

McNeil, L. M. (2000). *Contradictions of social reform: Educational costs of standardized testing.* London: Routledge.

Meacham, J. (2002). Our doctoral programs are failing our undergraduate students. *Liberal Education, 88,* 22–27.

Mehrabian, A. (1969). Some referents and measures of nonverbal behavior. *Behavioral Research Methods and Instrumentation, 1,* 213–217.

Mehrabian, A. (1972). *Nonverbal communication.* Chicago: Aldine-Atherton.

Metts, S., & Bowers, J. W. (1994). Emotions in interpersonal communication. In M. L. Knapp & G. R. Miller (Eds.), *Handbook of interpersonal communication* (2nd ed., pp. 508–541). Beverly Hills, CA: Sage.

Mottet, T. P. (2000). Interactive television instructors' perceptions of students' nonverbal responsiveness and their influence on distance teaching. *Communication Education, 49,* 146–164.

Mottet, T. P., & Beebe, S. A. (2002). Relationships between teacher nonverbal immediacy, student emotional response, and perceived student learning. *Communication Research Reports, 19,* 77–88.

Mottet, T. P., Beebe, S. A., Raffeld, P. C., & Medlock, A. L. (2004). The effects of student verbal and nonverbal responsiveness on teacher self-efficacy and job satisfaction. *Communication Education, 53,* 150–163.

Mottet, T. P., Beebe, S. A., Raffeld, P. C., & Paulsel, M. L. (2004). The effects of student verbal and nonverbal responsiveness on teachers' liking of students and willingness to comply with student requests. *Communication Quarterly, 52,* 27–38.

Mottet, T. P., & Richmond, V. P. (1998). New is not necessarily better: A reexamination of affective learning measurement. *Communication Research Reports, 15,* 370–378.

Mottet, T. P., & Richmond, V. P. (2002). Student nonverbal communication and its influence on teachers and teaching. In J. L. Chesebro & J. C. McCroskey (Eds.), *Communication for teachers* (pp. 47–61) Boston: Allyn & Bacon.

National Communication Association. (2005). Retrieved on February 10, 2005, from http://www.natcom.org/ComProg/GPDHTM/graduate_directory.htm.

National Education Association. (1997). *Status of the American Public School Teacher, 1995–1996.* Washington, DC: Author.

National Survey of Student Engagement (2000). *The NSSE 2000 report: National benchmarks of effective educational practice.* Bloomington, IN: Indiana University Center for Postsecondary Research and Planning. Retrieved July 22, 2002, from the NSSE web site: http://www.indiana.edu.

Nelson, P. D., & Morreale, S. P. (2002). Disciplinary leadership in preparing future faculty. *Liberal Education, 88,* 28–33.

Nyquist, J. D., Austin, A. E., Sprague, J., & Wulff, D. H. (2001). *The development of graduate students as teaching scholars: A four-year longitudinal study, final report.* Seattle: University of Washington.

Palmer, P. J. (1998). *The courage to teach: Exploring the inner landscape of a teacher's life.* San Francisco: Jossey-Bass.

Pascarella, E. T., & Terenzini, P. T. (1991). *How college affects students: Findings and insights from twenty years of research.* San Francisco: Jossey-Bass.

Pena, D., & Mitchell, D. (2000). The American faculty poll. *NEA Higher Education Research Center Update, 6,* 1–8. (ERIC Document Reproduction Service No. ED 442527).

Plax, T. G., & Kearney, P. (1992). Teacher power in the classroom: Defining and advancing a program of research. In V. P. Richmond & J. C. McCroskey (Eds.), *Power in the classroom: Communication, control, and concern* (pp. 67–84). Hillsdale, NJ: Lawrence Erlbaum.

Ravitch, D. (2004). *The language police.* New York: Vintage Books.

Reese, C. M., Miller, K. E., Mazzeo, J., & Dossey, J. A. (1997, February). *NAEP 1996 mathematics report card for the nation and the states.* Retrieved on October 1, 2002 from http://nces.ed.gov/nationsreportcard.

Richmond, V. P. (1990). Communication in the classroom: Power and motivation. *Communication Education, 39,* 181–195.

Richmond, V. P. (1997). *Nonverbal communication in the classroom: A text and workbook and study guide.* Acton, MA: Tapestry Press.

Richmond, V. P., & McCroskey, J. C. (Eds.). (1992). *Power in the classroom: Communication, control, and concern.* Hillsdale, NJ: Lawrence Erlbaum.

Richmond, V. P., & McCroskey, J. C. (1998). *Communication: Apprehension, avoidance, and effectiveness.* Boston: Allyn & Bacon.

Richmond, V. P., McCroskey, J. C., Plax, T. G., & Kearney, P. (1986). Teacher nonverbal immediacy training and student affect. *World Communication, 15,* 181–194.

Rodriguez, J. I., Plax, T. G., & Kearney, P. (1996). Clarifying the relationship between teacher nonverbal immediacy and student cognitive learning: Affective learning as the central causal mediator. *Communication Education, 45,* 293–305.

Rogers, E. M. (1994). *A history of communication study: A biographical approach.* New York: Free Press.

Ross, J. A. (1998). Antecedents and consequences of teacher efficacy. In J. Brophy (Ed.), *Advances in research on teaching* (Vol. 7, pp. 49–74). Greenwich, CT: JAI Press.

Russell, J. A., & Mehrabian, A. (1978). Approach–avoidance and affiliation as functions of the emotion-eliciting quality of an environment. *Environment and Behavior, 10,* 355–387.

Sacks, P. (2001). *Standardized minds: The high prices of America's testing culture and what we can do to change it.* Reading, MA: Perseus.

Saklofske, D., Michayluk, J., & Randhawa, B. (1988). Teachers' efficacy and teaching behaviors. *Psychological Reports, 63,* 407–414.

Salovey, P. & Sluyter, D. J. (Eds.). (1997). *Emotional development and emotional intelligence: Educational implications.* New York: Basic Books.

Schramm, W. L. (1954). *The processes and effects of communication.* Urbana, IL: University of Illinois Press.

Shann, M. H. (1998). Professional commitment and satisfaction among teachers in urban middle schools. *The Journal of Educational Research, 92,* 67–73.

Shannon, C. E., & Weaver, W. (1949). *The mathematical theory of communication.* Urbana, IL: University of Illinois Press.

Shepherd, G. J. (1992). Communication as influence: Definitional exclusion. *Communication Studies, 43,* 203–219.

Shin, H. S., & Reyes, P. (1995). Teacher commitment and job satisfaction: A causal analysis. *Journal of School Leadership, 5,* 22–39.

Shulman, L. S. (1986). Those who understand: Knowledge growth in teaching. *Educational Research, 15,* 4–14.

Soodak, L. C., & Podell, D. M. (1993). Teacher efficacy and student problems as factors in special education referral. *Journal of Special Education, 27,* 66–81.

Sorensen, G. A., & Christophel, D. M. (1992). The communication perspective. In V. P. Richmond & J. C. McCroskey (Eds.), *Power in the classroom: Communication, control, and concern* (pp. 35–46). Hillsdale, NJ: Lawrence Erlbaum.

Sproule, M. J. (1991). *Speechmaking: An introduction to rhetorical competence.* Dubuque, IA: Wm. C. Brown.

Thomson, D. M., & Tulving, E. (1970). Associative encoding and retrieval: Weak and strong cues. *Journal of Experimental Psychology, 86,* 255–262.

Toppo, G. (2002, November 21). Students literally all over the map: Survey reveals USA's geography knowledge weak. *USA Today,* p. 10D.

Wallace, K. B. (1954). *History of speech education in America.* New York: Appleton-Century-Crofts.

Wanzer, M. B., & Frymier, A. B. (1999). The relationship between student perceptions of instructor humor and students' reports of learning. *Communication Education, 48,* 48–62.

Watzlawick, P., Bavelas, J. B., & Jackson, D. D. (1967). *Pragmatics of human communication.* New York: W.W. Norton.

Weimer, M. (2002). *Learner-centered teaching: Five key changes to practice.* San Francisco: Jossey-Bass.

Wheelwright, P. (Ed.). (1951). *Aristotle.* New York: Odyssey.

Wilson, S. M., Floden, R. E., & Ferrini-Mundy, J. (2002). Teacher preparation research: An insider's view from the outside. *Journal of Teacher Education, 53,* 190–204.

Woolfolk, A. E., Rosoff, B., & Hoy, W. K. (1990). Teachers' sense of efficacy and their beliefs about managing students. *Teaching and Teacher Education, 6,* 137–148.

2

Instructional Communication: The Historical Perspective

James C. McCroskey
West Virginia University

Linda L. McCroskey
California State University, Long Beach

Introduction

Instructional communication (also referred to as "communication in instruction") is an area of communication scholarship that centers on the role of communication processes in teaching and training contexts in K–12, college, and other organizational environments. It is one of many areas in applied communication research. Other such areas within the communication discipline include political communication, organizational communication, health communication, intercultural communication, mediated communication, and development communication (diffusion of innovations).

Instructional communication is *not* communication education. However, some of the roots of instructional communication include scholarship from the 1930s through the 1960s in speech education and communication education. Speech/communication education centers on the study of teaching the disciplines of speech and/or communication, not on the larger role of communication in teaching and training across disciplines. Other roots of this area of scholarship are general communication theory and research, theory and research from the field of educational psychology, and theory and research in instruction and training. Just as organizational communication scholarship applies to all types of organizations (not just communication departments), so does instructional communication apply to all levels and types of teaching and training, not just that which occurs in communication departments.

While instructional communication and communication education are separate areas of communication scholarship, they are not totally unrelated. Theory and research generated by instructional communication scholars has direct application to the teaching of communication as a content field—just as it has application to teaching or training in any other content field. In addition, many of the founders of the communication research and theory area we now reference as "instructional communication" were also active scholars in the area of speech/communication education. These dual interests of many of the early writers in this area of study produced considerable confusion for many people who were familiar with speech/communication education scholarship but for whom instructional communication was a totally new concept. In the 1980s, the merging of the Instructional Communication Division of the International Communication Association (ICA) with the interest group of the ICA concerned with the development of communication also added to the confusion. The study of communication development is *not* the study of instructional communication. It is the study of children's development of communication skills and the factors which influence that development. The research and theory generated by developmental scholars, of course, is of considerable interest to instructional communication scholars because of its potential for application in instructional contexts.

From the beginning of instructional communication research, scholars have seen their contributions to the fields of education and/or training as providing the "third leg of a three-legged stool," which is believed to provide the foundation for effective teaching and training. The three "legs" are seen as: (1) competence in the subject being taught (provided by subject-matter experts), (2) competence in pedagogy (provided by scholars in education), and (3) competence in instructional communication (McCroskey, Richmond, & McCroskey, 2002). All these competencies are seen as critical aspects of effective teaching and training, with the source of competence for each representing independent but related scholarly disciplines. Thus, instructional communication researchers are not expected to do research in education or any specific content discipline. Rather, they study the role and impact of communication in the instructional process across all disciplines and contexts.

Origins and History of Instructional Communication

Development of the Professional Area

Although isolated individuals within the field of speech have long been concerned with the role of communication in instructional contexts beyond the speech/communication classroom, it was not until the early 1970s that this area of scholarship received any formal recognition. In 1972, primarily due to the efforts of Barbara Lieb Brilhart, a member of the Speech (now "National") Communication Association's staff, and Robert Kibler, a professor at Florida State University, whose education had included both communication and educational psychology, the Instructional Communication Division was approved by ICA. This was the first subdivision associated with the study of instructional communication to be recognized by any association in the field of communication, although several had subdivisions focusing on teaching speech or communication.

In the deliberations of the governing board of ICA (the senior author of this chapter was a member of that board, representing the Interpersonal Division of the association) it was made clear that this new division was to focus attention on the role of communication in all teaching and training contexts, not just the teaching of communication. At that time, the leadership of ICA saw the association as a collection of research scholars, not teachers (although, most of the members were, and still are, college professors and graduate students). There was no desire to have a division devoted to communication instruction. That was seen to be the province of the Speech Communication Association, which was originally founded by teachers of speech, and not within the realm of interest for ICA members who were "scholars." Over the years, however, these distinctions have come to be seen as less important, and people who are instructional communication scholars and those who are communication education scholars share the subgroups concerned with instruction in all of the professional communication associations in the United States, as well as the one sponsored by ICA.

Being accepted as a legitimate subdivision by ICA was very important for the development of the instructional communication area. This served as validation of the legitimacy of instructional communication scholarship in the field. It provided immediate opportunities to present papers reporting instructional communication research at the annual ICA conventions. When ICA launched its first book series in 1977, the *Communication Yearbook,* instructional communication, like the other seven divisions of the association, was authorized to publish the top papers from the most recent convention as well as provide a chapter relating to instructional communication scholarship. For the period of 1972–1986, ICA became the professional home for virtually all instructional communication scholars, and the *Communication Yearbook* published much of the best research in this area.

In 1975, the governing board of the Speech Communication Association approved changing the name of their journal, *Speech Teacher,* to *Communication Education.* This change reflected changes occurring in the field. More articles reporting on instructional communication began to appear in the newly named journal almost immediately, although the mission of the journal did not specifically recognize such work as being appropriate for submission. When Gustav W. Freidrich, one of the founders of instructional communication scholarship, became editor of the journal in 1979, instructional communication scholarship was recognized formally as an area appropriate for inclusion in the journal. From 1979–1986, instructional communication scholars, therefore, had two excellent publication outlets. As might be expected, this fostered substantial growth in both quantity and quality of scholarship in this area. More "instructional" subgroups were approved in regional associations. Instructional communication scholarship became acceptable for presentation at both national and regional professional conventions.

A significant setback confronted instructional communication scholars in 1986. The governing board of ICA decided to no longer publish the top convention papers in the *Communication Yearbook.* While this action was not directed at instructional scholars or any of the other divisions of the association, the impact was very serious for scholarship in many of the divisions. Because few or no articles were published in ICA's journals relating to several of their divisions, including the instructional division, eliminating the *Yearbook* effectively shut down publication opportunities for ICA members with these interests. As a result, many of the U. S. members with strong interests in instructional communication changed their allegiances from ICA to the National Communication Association and/or one of the regional professional associations.

While this period was somewhat traumatic for instructional communication scholars who had a very strong allegiance to ICA, it had the positive outcome of strengthening the instructional communication groups in the national association and several of the regional associations. This was followed by a period when editors were more open to publication of instructional communication research in the regional journals, particularly the two journals sponsored by the Eastern Communication Association (*Communication Quarterly* and *Communication Research Reports*). Over the past decade and a half, the total number of articles reporting instructional communication research has continuously increased. During the same period, the number and breadth of topics in instructional communication scholarship has expanded as well, as has the type and quality of research models employed.

Development of Instructional Communication Scholarship

Most of the original researchers in instructional communication were people who had been primarily interpersonal communication researchers. In fact, much of the early instructional communication research was framed as interpersonal research. For example, work on nonverbal immediacy in instructional communication (which drew from previous work by Mehrabian, 1966, 1971) was seen as a direct extension of the work on nonverbal immediacy in interpersonal communication contexts (Andersen, 1979). Similarly, work on communication apprehension, as a trait in interpersonal interactions, (McCroskey, 1970, 1977b) was extended to potential communication problems in the classroom (McCroskey, 1977a). This was a logical modus operandi given that there were no books on instructional communication, much less any formal graduate instruction available at any graduate school at that time. In fact, the first book on interpersonal communication written from a social science perspective was not published until 1971 (McCroskey, Larson, & Knapp, 1971). Most of the early researchers in instructional communication were unable even to study interpersonal communication in graduate school. Their graduate education was either in general communication theory, rhetorical theory, or a combination of the two. From a social science perspective, little was known about interpersonal communication and virtually nothing was known about instructional communication. The authors cited above acknowledged in their preface that none of them knew enough about interpersonal communication to write a book on it alone; hence they pooled what they knew to produce a joint effort, a book which was only 246 pages in length and included far fewer than half the topics one would expect in such a book today.

The chapters in this book represent many (but of course, not all) of the significant areas of instructional communication scholarship that have developed over the years. Two major approaches have dominated scholarship in this area. The first of these is the "rhetorical" approach, which views teachers' behaviors as causal influences of student learning. This approach is exemplified by the "process–product" perspective taken by many scholars in the field of educational psychology and "message" studies common to communication researchers who study social influence and persuasion. The second is the "relational" approach, which views the shared development of teacher–student relationships as causal influences of student learning. This approach is exemplified by researchers studying relational, interpersonal, intercultural, health, and organizational interactions. While these two approaches are seen by some as being contradictions of each other, in reality they are just different perspectives from which to view instructional communication. As noted in Chapter 1, instruction involves both rhetorical and relational communication, and the study of only one of these would provide an incomplete picture of instructional communication as a whole. For the most part, scholarship in instructional communication has employed quantitative social scientific methods of study. This probably was a function of these methods being well-suited to studying instructional communication from either a rhetorical or a relational perspective. It also is likely that most of the early researchers in the area were quantitative scholars who were experienced in using these methods in studies of interpersonal and general communication theory. However, the success of the early research in finding very socially significant results from their research may have been the strongest force for influencing scholars to continue to employ these methods.

The West Virginia University Influence

Since the establishment of instructional communication as a recognized area of scholarship in the field of communication, West Virginia University faculty and graduate students have maintained a significant role in the advancement of the area. While assuming such a role was not initially a conscious decision made by anyone in WVU's Communication Studies Department, an unusual set of circumstances led to this reality.

In 1972, right at the time instructional communication was being established as a division in ICA, the senior author of this chapter was appointed as chairperson of WVU's speech department (now Communication Studies). He was directed by the administration to "modernize" the department, increase its research productivity, and expand its outreach efforts for service to the state. The emphasis in the undergraduate and graduate programs was immediately changed from speaking skills to interpersonal communication. The new curriculum was modeled on those in place at Michigan State University and Illinois State University, where the new chairperson had taught previously. All but one of the new faculty hires in the next three years were people whose research efforts were in the area of interpersonal communication and who were quantitative social scientists. These faculty included Michael Burgoon, Lawrence R. Wheeless, H. Thomas Hurt, William (Brad) Lashbrook, Michael D. Scott, Thomas J. Young, Thomas Knutson, and Peter A. Andersen—all of whom were leading young interpersonal communication scholars. The hiring of these young scholars permitted modernization of the department and, at the same time, greatly improved the department's productivity in published research. Within only a few years, national analyses of research productivity placed the WVU department in the top ten in the country.

The third directive of the administration was much more of a challenge—expanding the department's outreach efforts to provide service to the citizens of the state. There were no resources provided for such efforts, hence entrepreneurial efforts were required to generate funding. Because of his background in the area of education (BS in secondary education, MA minor in elementary education, and doctoral minor in educational psychology) the chairperson believed there was a need for K–12 teachers to learn about the role of communication in instruction. In the fall of 1972, he met with the dean of the College of Education, the director of off-campus instruction, and the provost of off-campus programs. This group enthusiastically approved his request that the department be permitted to teach an off-campus graduate class on "Communication in the Classroom" directed toward K–12 teachers. Funds were allocated to guarantee coverage of the costs for two classes if the classes did not pay for themselves. Although no one realized it at the time, this was the beginning of WVU's graduate programs in instructional communication.

In the spring of 1973 an agreement was worked out with the college of education to establish a joint doctoral program in instructional communication. That was the first doctoral program in instructional communication, and it continues relatively unchanged today. The program's first doctoral student (and ultimately its first graduate), Judee Heston (now Burgoon) was assigned to work with the chairperson to design the first off-campus graduate course. She and H. Thomas Hurt (a new hire) each team-taught one of the off-campus classes with the chairperson in the summer of 1973. Enrollments were good, meaning the classes paid for themselves. The response to the classes was very positive, with many students asking for more new classes. Authorization was given by the administration to expand the program for the following summer (1974). More classes, with other new members of the faculty, were instituted—all of which were team-taught by the chair and the inexperienced faculty. As more faculty became experienced in the program, they began serving as lead teachers in the team-teaching format with other new faculty and doctoral students. On-campus MA students also were added as team teachers in 1974. Two of those, John A. Daly and Virginia P. Richmond, continued to teach in the program while they were working on doctoral degrees at other institutions. Daly continued to teach in the program for the next 15 years. Richmond returned to WVU as a faculty member in 1978 and has coordinated the program for over 20 years. They played a very important role in the next several years in helping to develop new courses for the program. Many of the graduates of the doctoral program returned to teach in the program in the summer while holding regular year positions at other universities. The team-teaching model for preparing new faculty has continued to be mandated in this program prior to new faculty or advanced doctoral students teaching classes by themselves or as lead instructors.

By 1975, there was a strong push from students in the off-campus classes to be offered a complete program leading to an MA degree. Approval by the administration for offering such a program as an option in the department's MA program was obtained, and the program graduated its first student, Ann Garvin, in the fall of 1976. This was the first MA program in the instructional communication area, as well as the first wholly-offered MA program offered by WVU. Approximately 2,000 K–12 teachers have completed the degree program since that time.

While most of the off-campus MA graduates have continued their careers as K–12 teachers, many of the graduates of the doctoral program have taken positions in colleges and universities and continued their research efforts in instructional communication. Although the program has intentionally been kept small (typically, no more than six students are permitted in the program at one time), it has been semi-mentor based. Doctoral students take classes both in education and communication studies, but their graduate assistantships are in communication studies. Under the guidance of senior faculty members, these students are trained to teach a wide variety of courses in communication. Many of these courses are mass lecture classes with multiple sections. The doctoral students are also taught to design and administer (i.e., mandate graduate teaching assistants, process exams) these courses as well as teach them. In most cases, advanced doctoral students are also trained to teach graduate classes in instructional communication. All of these students are required to conduct instructional communication research for their doctoral dissertation and most do research in other areas of communication as well. As a result, graduates of the doctoral program are prepared as both instructional communication specialists and communication education specialists, but most graduates also develop other individualized specialties in areas such as persuasion, interpersonal, nonverbal, intercultural, health, or organizational communication.

Although no one at WVU set out to develop the field's first full graduate program in instructional communication, the individual elements of that program met the needs of the department so well that, by 1976, the program had been embraced by all of the new faculty. Each part of the program was supportive of the other parts.

As the WVU program grew, an increased emphasis on "programmatic" research evolved. A "programmatic" approach involves a series of research studies, which all focus on a specific subarea of research. The efforts of faculty, doctoral students, doctoral graduates, and MA students began to merge into several such programs of research. Some of the more successful efforts have dealt with communication apprehension (and extension areas, such as shyness, willingness to communicate, communication competence, compulsive communication, writing apprehension, and receiver apprehension), power and influence, nonverbal immediacy, sociocommunicative orientations and styles, clarity, humor, communication motives, teacher misbehaviors, student resistance, and affinity seeking. Many of these areas are addressed in succeeding chapters of this book.

While the area of instructional communication began by borrowing theories and modeling research strategies from other areas inside and outside the field of communication, more and more instructional communication researchers have advanced their own theories and developed unique research procedures. More recently, instructional researchers have extended their research to other subareas of communication to test the generalizability of their findings in the instructional context to other contexts—such as organizational, interpersonal, health, and intercultural communication. This research, as a function of its replication across communication contexts, is beginning to influence general communication theories. This essentially inductive approach is providing strong evidence that many of the findings of instructional researchers indeed can be extended to other contexts, thereby providing a solid research base for broader communication theories related to such concerns as nonverbal immediacy, communication apprehension, use of humor, sociocommunicative orientation and style, and communicator misbehaviors. Instructional communication is now a major contributor to general communication theory.

The Future of Instructional Communication

Predicting the future for an area of scholarship is at least as difficult as predicting the weather—one really cannot see very far into the future. In the past, when the culture of the field of communication was young and fluid, rapid change could be expected. The efforts of a handful of scholars could launch a whole subarea (such as interpersonal communication) in the field. Because the study of instructional communication, particularly the quantitative social scientific study, is now more mature, the place for such scholarship within the field of communication is better defined and more stable. Change now becomes slower and more difficult as the culture becomes stronger. Nevertheless, some change certainly will occur. Our efforts here are our "guesstimates." Some almost certainly will be proven wrong over time. Hopefully, some will be proven correct over time. Since the past has proven positive for the development of instructional communication, our predictions of what the future may portend for it are optimistic.

Continued Growth

Our first prediction is the one in which we have the most confidence: Instructional communication research will grow and expand. There will be more communication scholars specializing in this research. There will be more, and more varied, topics of study. There will be more researchers whose primary areas of study are not instructional communication, but who will do some instructional research along with that in their primary areas. There will be more journals that are open to publishing instructional manuscripts. There will be more graduate programs that include instructional communication as one of their areas of study. More attention to the research in instructional communication will come from academics in other fields, particularly those interested in the scholarship of teaching and learning, and knowledge generated by instructional communication scholars will be integrated into the efforts of many scholars in other disciplines.

Increased Attention to Technologically Mediated Instructional Communication

The founders of the instructional communication area, for the most part, were interpersonal (human) communication scholars, not media scholars. Hence, comparatively little of the instructional communication research to date has been directed toward mediated instruction. Since antiquity, it has been believed that the best instruction involves live, human interaction. The smaller the student–teacher ratio, the better the instruction. However, with every technological advance enhancing mediated communication since the invention of the printing press, have come loud voices proclaiming the end of "teaching as we know it," and its replacement via the new technology. Obviously, that has not happened yet, and we doubt it ever will. The student on one end of the log and the teacher on the other end, will continue to represent the idealized instructional context.

Communication mediated by technology has expanded geometrically over recent decades. Much has been promised, often by academic administrators trying to survive shrinking budgets or media hacks seeking to market more of their new products, but little has been delivered. In most instances two factors have gotten in their way: (1) Technology typically is more expensive both to purchase and to maintain, often very much more expensive than live teachers and school systems can afford—after the grants run out, and (2) while students initially like the stimulating and innovative atmosphere of new technologies in instruction, before long it all becomes "boring" without personal contact with "real" teachers.

Nevertheless, we predict the growth of research directed toward the role in instruction of technologically mediated communication. We hope, but do not predict, that the primary focus of this scholarship will be directed toward determining how each technological advance in mediated communication can be employed to meaningfully enhance student learning—not just to see if a mediated instructional system can be as good or slightly better than a bad lecturer, as has been the case in the past. There are also research studies where components of mediated instruction added to live instruction have been found to improve instruction, particularly instruction devoted to lower-level cognitive learning. In many of these studies, however, while the effect was statistically significant, it was also very small, hence of little social consequence. Improving learning by 2, 3, or 4 percent of the variance probably is not worth the time, effort, and cost of introducing and maintaining these mediated elements.

Based on work in the past, of greatest concern is the tendency of media researchers to focus exclusively on cognitive learning—to the exclusion of both psychomotor and affective learning. Generating positive affect for the subject matter is what highly effective teachers do. Affective learning is what contributes to students completing courses rather dropping out, choosing to take more classes in the subject matter, valuing what they learn, and becoming life-long learners in the subject studied. It is not that mediated instruction is inherently incapable of producing positive affective learning. The unparalleled success of *Sesame Street* and *Mr. Rogers* has demonstrated it is possible and how much talent and resources it takes to make it successful—talent and resources that are not available to the overwhelming proportion of instructors, departments, or even organizations or institutions at any level of teaching or training. We need, and hopefully will get, statistically significant and socially meaningful research that focuses on how the integration of media technologies into existing instructional systems will enhance student learning while remaining affordable and accessible to educational institutions.

Increased Culture-Centered Instructional Communication Research

Much, but not all, of the instructional communication research to date has been monocultural. That is, the overwhelming proportion of instructional communication research has been conducted by U.S. researchers representing the Anglo culture of the United States and has involved participants who were also representing the predominant culture of the United States. Although this should not come as a surprise to anyone familiar with the development of communication scholarship in general in the United States, nor should it devalue the research, it does restrict the generalizability of the current body of research. We do not believe that this pattern will continue at the level it is currently. We predict that there will be an increased concern with cultural issues in instructional communication research.

At least three types of culture-centered research in instructional communication research are needed: (1) international instructors teaching predominantly mainstream U.S. students, (2) mainstream U.S. instructors teaching nonmainstream students (both those from cultures outside the United States and those from microcultures within the United States), and (3) monocultural studies conducted outside the United States in which both instructors and students represent a culture other than the mainstream U.S. culture.

The first type, international instructors teaching U.S. students, has received some attention in the past. Qualitative scholars have pointed to an apparent bias—negative and positive—of domestic U.S. students toward international instructors, suggesting that actions are needed to reduce these apparently ethnocentric attitudes. Recent quantitative studies, however, have demonstrated that ethnocentrism has little impact on U.S. students' attitudes toward international teachers. This research confirmed that there is a strong negative reaction by some domestic students toward some international teachers. However, it also determined that many domestic students rate their international teachers even higher than their domestic teachers. The findings of this research indicated that student ethnocentrism predicted only a very small part of the variance in ratings of foreign teachers. In contrast, measures of instructor communication behaviors, previously identified as effective in instructional communication research with mainstream U.S. instructors and students, were highly predictive of students' ratings of foreign teachers (McCroskey, 2002; 2003). These studies suggest that domestic students respond positively or negatively to their foreign instructors not because of their bias toward them as foreign but because of the foreign instructors' conformance on nonconformance with the students' culturally based expectations with regard to how good teachers are expected to communicate in the classroom. It would appear from this research that the instructors need training in how to adapt to the instructional communication system expected by their students, not the students needing training in reducing their ethnocentrism. Clearly, more research is needed in this area.

The second type, mainstream U.S. instructors teaching international students and those from diverse microcultures in the United States, has also received some attention. Many foreign students have difficulty adapting to mainstream U.S. instructional communication systems. Some training programs have been developed to help international students to adapt. Other training programs have focused on helping U.S. mainstream instructors adapt to diverse students. Little, however, has been done to develop a more complete understanding of diverse cultures' expectations for instructional communication. In general, U.S., some other Western, and most Eastern cultures do not have the same sets of instructional communication expectations. While students in the mainstream U.S. culture learn to expect learning to involve considerable participation on their part and interaction with others, many other Western and most Eastern systems focus on instructors lecturing and students listening. Hopefully, future instructional communication researchers will address these issues.

The third type, instructors and students from other monocultures, has received very little attention from instructional communication scholars. What has been done has come from researchers steeped in the U.S. mainstream culture and the research that has been done in that culture. Results of this research have generally indicated that some of the good instructional communication practices identified in U.S. research (such as nonverbal immediacy) also seem to be effective in some other Western as well as Eastern cultures. While this research is of value and hopefully will continue, what is missing is the examination of instructional communication from a wholly different culture's assumptions. Are most of the elements of instructional communication truly pan-culturally effective? Although we are somewhat doubtful in this regard, only future research will be able to determine whether this is or is not correct. If it is not, are there methods used in one culture, but not in another culture, which can be adapted to the other culture successfully? Or, is effective instructional communication a culturally determined matter? We anticipate that in the future, but maybe not the immediate future, these important issues will receive attention from scholars who have specializations in both intercultural and instructional communication. At present, few scholars in communication embrace both of these areas of specialization.

Improving the Measurement of Cognitive Learning

One of the big problems that instructional communication researchers have confronted, but not overcome to the satisfaction of most scholars in this area, is how to measure cognitive learning. According to scholars in educational psychology, there are several levels of cognitive learning—ranging from learning basic facts and other information to analyzing, interpreting, and using complex constructs. However, there is little agreement on how to measure cognitive learning at any of these levels. Most work in the area of communication education has employed final grades, standardized tests, or teacher-made tests as measures of cognitive learning. All of these have severe validity problems. The problem for instructional communication researchers, who, because of the nature of the area, want to be able to generalize across academic courses and areas of learning, is much more severe. The "interim" method accepted by most instructional communication researchers currently involves asking students to indicate how much they think they learned in a given class, and how much they think they could have learned if they had had an ideal teacher. This method also has problems, as noted by numerous critics of the method. This approach was developed by the senior author of this chapter as an act of desperation and frustration with the other available methods. He chanced to read a report compiled by a federal government agency, which reported using a similar method to determine the quality of instruction in schools. While this method has been validated against a measure of factual learning in a well-controlled experiment (Chesebro & McCroskey, 2000), the primary argument for its use remains "because we don't have anything better." We predict that future researchers will continue to search for better methods of measuring cognitive learning in cross-disciplinary instructional communication research.

Improving Models for Instructional Communication Research

Every area of quantitative research, over time, develops its own models for doing research. In the early days of research in a new area, models were borrowed from other areas in the discipline or from other disciplines. For the most part, instructional communication researchers have borrowed their research models from psychology and education. As yet, we have created few unique models of our own. Most of our statistical models have been drawn from psychology, many of which were earlier employed in agricultural research. However, one design model that has since been employed successfully by many instructional communication researchers, was "dreamed up" by the senior author of this chapter (while waiting 11 hours in a Japanese airport with no reading material and no one who spoke English with whom to talk). This is the "class before this one" or "prior class" model. Up until that time, his research and that of his graduate students used intact classes to collect data related to instructional communication. This was highly limiting because many teachers were not willing to let him do research in their classes (because it would likely disrupt their classes or require special effort on their part). This meant that the generalizability of the results from this research would be severely limited.

He sought to find a way to get data on teacher communication behaviors without the consent of the teachers themselves. He knew that he could get cooperation of many teachers if they did not have to do anything special and the data collected had nothing to do with their own behavior, particularly if all the students had to do was complete questionnaires. Because he had access to classes that were taken by students from all across the university, he determined that he could get the data anonymously for virtually every teacher in the university if he simply had his own and cooperative colleagues' students report on other teachers with whom they took classes. He also determined that this procedure probably would meet full approval of the Human Subjects Research Committee. This research model solved the problem of unwilling teachers and provided the kind of data that would generalize across courses and disciplines.

There are still many problems relating to design and data collection facing instructional communication researchers. We predict that instructional communication researchers will continue mainly to employ borrowed models for their research, but that new models unique to this area of scholarship will be forthcoming and will help to enrich future research.

Applications of the Communibiological Paradigm

In the late 1990s, Beatty and McCroskey determined that the previous work on the etiology of communication apprehension, suggesting that it was a learned trait, probably was not correct. Although this had been suspected two decades earlier (McCroskey, 1977b), as a function of their reading literature from the field of psychobiology, they became convinced that the cause of communication apprehension (and other communication traits) was more likely to be genetically-based brain systems (Beatty & McCroskey, 1997; Beatty, McCroskey, & Valencic, 2001; Beatty, McCroskey, & Heisel, 1998; McCroskey, 1998). This led to their advancing "communibiology" as a new paradigm for communication research. This paradigm posits genetically based brain systems as the primary cause of communication traits. Subsequent research (McCroskey, Heisel, & Richmond, 2001) has confirmed that not only is communication apprehension associated with markers of genetic influence, but also that many other communication traits are as well—including *immediacy,* one of the teacher communication traits that has been the frequent focus of instructional communication researchers.

This new paradigm brings into question the etiology of communication behaviors of instructors. While there has always been a question of whether good teachers are "born" or whether they have learned to be good teachers, virtually everyone in education and in instructional communication has operated on the assumption that the latter option is correct. It may not be. Temperament has been demonstrated to have a strong genetic base. Instructor communication behaviors, which are associated with effective teaching, have also been found to be substantially associated with temperament. Meta analyses of twin research have confirmed that there are genetic bases for many communication traits—for both the orientations people have and the ways they behave (Beatty, Heisel, Hall, Levine, & La France, 2002).

Our final prediction is that instructional communication research will be conducted employing the communibiological paradigm and that it will determine that there is a genetic base for the prediction of effective teaching. Where this will take us from that point certainly is not predictable at this point.

References

Andersen, J. F. (1979). Teacher immediacy as a predictor of teaching effectiveness. In D. Nimmo (Ed.). *Communication yearbook 3* (pp. 543–559). New Brunswick, NJ: Transaction Books.

Beatty, M. J., Heisel, A. D., Hall, A. E., Levine, T. R., & La France, B. H. (2002). What can we learn from the study of twins about genetic and environmental influences on interpersonal affiliation, aggressiveness, and social anxiety?: A meta-analytic study. *Communication Monographs, 69,* 1–18.

Beatty, M. J., & McCroskey, J. C. (1997). It's in our nature: Verbal aggressiveness as temperamental expression. *Communication Quarterly, 45,* 446–460.

Beatty, M. J., McCroskey, J. C., & Heisel, A. D. (1998). Communication apprehension as temperamental expression: A communibiological paradigm. *Communication Monographs, 64,* 187–219.

Beatty, M. J., & McCroskey, J. C., w/Valencic, K. M. (2001). *The biology of communication: A communibiological perspective.* Cresskill, NJ: Hampton Press.

Chesebro, J. L., & McCroskey, J. C. (2000). The relationship between students' reports of learning and their actual recall of lecture material: A validity test. *Communication Education, 49,* 297–301.

McCroskey, J. C. (1970). Measures of communication-bound anxiety. *Speech Monographs, 37,* 269–277.

McCroskey, J. C. (1977a). Classroom consequences of communication apprehension. *Communication Education, 26,* 27–33.

McCroskey, J. C. (1977b). *Quiet children and the classroom teacher.* Urbana, IL: Education Resources Information Center.

McCroskey, J. C. (1998). *Why we communicate the ways we do: The 1997 Carroll C. Arnold Lecture to the National Communication Association.* Boston: Allyn & Bacon.

McCroskey, J. C., Heisel, A. D., & Richmond, V. P. (2001). Eysenck's BIG THREE and communication traits: Three correlational studies. *Communication Monographs, 68,* 360–366.

McCroskey, J. C., Larson, C. E., & Knapp, M. L. (1971). *An introduction to interpersonal communication.* Englewood Cliffs, NJ: Prentice-Hall.

McCroskey, L. L. (2002). Domestic and international college instructors: An examination of perceived differences and their correlates. *Journal of Intercultural Communication Research, 31,* 63–83.

McCroskey, L. L. (2003). Relationships of instructional communication styles of domestic and foreign instructors with instructional outcomes. *Journal of Intercultural Communication Research, 32,* 75–96.

McCroskey, L. L., Richmond, V. P., & McCroskey, J. C. (2002). The scholarship of teaching and learning: Contributions from the discipline of communication in instructional communication. *Communication Education, 51,* 383–391.

Mehrabian, A. (1966). Immediacy: An indicator of attitudes in linguistic communication. *Journal of Personality, 34,* 226–234.

Mehrabian, A. (1971). *Silent messages.* Belmont, CA: Wadsworth.

Unit II

Rhetorical Perspectives

3

Understanding the Audience: Students' Communication Traits

James C. McCroskey
West Virginia University

Virginia P. Richmond
West Virginia University

Introduction

From classical times to the present, rhetorical scholars have cautioned communicators that they need to analyze, understand, and adapt to their audience if they are to succeed in communicating effectively. This general injunction to communicators is particularly apt in the instructional context. Although it is less common in some other cultures, instruction in the U.S. culture typically encourages students to interact with their instructor and fellow students as an integral part of the learning process. Such interaction has many positive outcomes, not the least of which is that student communication serves as feedback to the instructor, which enables the instructor to better understand and adapt to individual student needs. Nevertheless, many students rarely, if ever, voluntarily communicate in the classroom. Of course, huge lecture classes provide little opportunity for students to talk. However, in smaller, more potentially interactive, classes it is not uncommon to find as much as 80 percent of the student-initiated communication produced by less than 20 percent of the students. While many instructors go to considerable effort to encourage student participation, many students never respond to those efforts—even when course syllabi indicate that final grades in the course will be based in part (from as little as 5 percent to over 50 percent) on student participation.

Whether or not students need to communicate in the classroom is open for debate. Nevertheless, in the U.S. instructional culture, their need to do so is taken as a given. In many other cultures, this view is not accepted. A number of years ago, the authors made contact with a leading Scandinavian scholar, Dr. Ake Daun, who is a professor at the University of Stockholm in Sweden. He was interested in our research relating to communication apprehension, and we were interested in expanding our research base to include people in Scandinavian cultures. When he visited our campus, he became intrigued with our graduate program in instructional communication, for which he indicated there was no comparable program anywhere in Europe. After we had discussed at length what we were doing, he made a comment that has stuck in our memory: "In Sweden we believe students learn through their eyes and ears. It appears that here in America you believe that they learn through their mouths."

Professor Daun's comment crystalized the distinction between our different cultures in terms of the perceived need for student communication to enhance learning. Clearly, students in many other cultures are able to learn at a very high level without being forced to communicate in the classroom. Nevertheless, in our culture student communication in the classroom is emphasized by the vast majority of teachers/professors, particularly in small classes. However, many of the students seldom, if ever, communicate in the classroom.

Student Orientations Toward Communicating

While instructors may attribute students' lack of communication in their classes to lack of interest in the class, lack of preparation, low motivation, low intellectual ability, or even to their own ineptness as an instructor, in reality students' communication in the classroom is mostly a function of their trait orientations toward communication. This chapter will examine some of these traits and how they may impact instructional outcomes at all levels of instruction. Traits that we will consider are reticence, shyness, willingness to communicate, self-perceived communication competence, communication apprehension, public speaking anxiety, receiver apprehension, and compulsive communication ("talkaholism"). For readers interested in how these constructs are commonly operationalized, measures for each of these constructs can be obtained at www.JamesCMcCroskey.com.

Reticence

The first research program directed at a broad-based orientation toward communication was led by Phillips (1968, 1997). Over the course of more than 30 years of scholarship, his conceptualization of "reticence" was quite fluid. At the outset Phillips (1968) explained the reticent individual as a "person for whom anxiety about participation in oral communication outweighs his [or her] projection of gain from the situation" (p. 40). Later, Phillips (1997) indicated "Our concern is with behaviors generated from the perception an individual has of his or her own incompetence. It has nothing to do with what someone might feel [anxiety] about it. In short, our emphasis is on detecting incompetent performance and providing a remedy" (p. 130).

As we note above, early in the research on reticence, the presumed cause was "anxiety" (see Communication Apprehension on page 55) and the presumed outcome was reduced or absent communication (see Shyness below). Later in the research program, the presumed cause became a "perception an individual has of her or his own incompetence" (see Self-Perceived Communication Competence on page 55) and the presumed outcome was "incompetent performance." Phillips' many efforts to simplify the so-called "problem" he called "reticence" resulted in considerable confusion in the research community, a confusion that continues to be present in many of the writings about communication orientations to this day. That confusion, however, led to extensive reconceptualization and research by the present authors and others attempting to clarify and explain the many problems that were touched on in his work. These efforts have determined that there are several problems, not one, which are distinct from each other, although somewhat correlated with each other. Similarly, this effort has also led to the identification of multiple causal factors, which are distinct from each other, but also somewhat correlated with each other. Understanding the various communication traits of students depends on understanding the distinct constructs that have been clarified over the last four decades. These distinctions are discussed on the next few pages.

Shyness

The communication behavior of students that is most obvious to instructors, even those with little or no formal training in communication, is the tendency of some students to be quiet and seldom talk in the classroom. The most common "lay" description for this kind of student is "shy." This term also is used in much of the work in psychology that relates to quiet people. It frequently has been used to include both the behavior (talking less) and its presumed cause (anxiety). Leary (1983), a psychologist who has published a considerable body of research in this area, prefers to refer to this combination of cause and effect as "social anxiety" and indicates that there are two components of this construct: "internally experienced discomfort" or communication apprehension and "externally observable behavior," or shyness.

The Leary distinction between cause and effect supports the definition of shyness found in communication research: "the tendency to be timid, reserved, and most specifically, talk less" (McCroskey & Richmond, 1982, p. 460). It is presumed that anxiety might be one of the causes of shyness, however, it is also believed that other factors can produce it as well.

Research has established that students who exhibit shy behaviors generate very negative perceptions in the mind of instructors as well as in the eyes of other students (McCroskey & Daly, 1976). These perceptions and behaviors also lead to reduced learning and dislike of school, among other negative outcomes, for the shy student (McCroskey, 1977a).

Willingness to Communicate (WTC)

Willingness to communicate (WTC) refers to "an individual's predisposition to initiate communication with others" (McCroskey & Richmond, 1987; 1998). It is important to distinguish willingness to communicate from shyness. Willingness to communicate is a predisposition toward behavior; shyness is the actual behavior. Although these are very different things, the two are related. People who are low in willingness to communicate are more likely than others to behave in a shy way—to withdraw and be quiet and not initiate communication. However, this relationship is not perfect. That is, even people who are very low in willingness to communicate are likely to talk sometimes, particularly when someone else initiates communication with them. These same people may even initiate communication in some circumstances, particularly when it is in their best interest, such as when they are applying for a job.

In the instructional environment, the students who are highest in willingness to communicate are those who are most likely to initiate communication by raising their hand or just speaking out (Chan & McCroskey, 1987). However, many of the less willing students will respond to instructors' questions to the class as a whole. Those students who are lowest in willingness to communicate, however, are reluctant to answer instructors' direct questions, even when they know the correct answer. Observations of college classes have indicated that when students do not respond to instructors' direct questions, it is much less likely that the instructor will call on them again during the course. It would appear that this instructor behavior is less a function of the instructors' sensitivity to students not wanting to be called on than it is to the fact that nonresponse on the part of a student disrupts the flow of instruction in the classroom and may be embarrassing to the instructor.

It is important to note that some students are highly anxious about communicating with instructors, and as a result may be less willing to communicate with the instructor than other students. This does not mean, however, that all students who are low in willingness to communicate are anxious or fearful. Many are not. They just don't prefer to initiate communication—for any of a wide variety of reasons.

Self-Perceived Communication Competence (SPCC)

As noted above, one of the assumed causes of reticence is an individual's perception of her- or himself as not communicatively competent. This does not necessarily mean that the individual actually is incompetent, only that the individual has that perception. In short, if I think I am incompetent, I will be reticent—even if am actually quite competent (McCroskey, 1997; McCroskey & McCroskey, 1988).

It is important to distinguish this construct from Phillips's view of competence. Phillips assumed that if people perceive themselves as incompetent communicators, they *are* incompetent communicators. Hence, he employed skills training to help students overcome their reticence. The SPCC conceptualization does not make that assumption, hence skills training is not considered appropriate treatment for all people who see themselves as less competent communicators. Many of the people who perceive themselves as incompetent appear to observers as very competent and can communicate quite effectively if they choose to do so. Nevertheless, if a student perceives her- or himself as a noncompetent communicator, he or she is likely to avoid communication in the classroom when possible.

Communication Apprehension (CA)

The study of communication apprehension (CA) has resulted in one of the largest bodies of research in the field of communication, and research in this area continues (Richmond, Martin, & Cox, 1997). CA is defined as "an individual's level of fear or anxiety associated with either real or anticipated communication with another person or persons" (McCroskey, 1970; 1977b; 1978). Because this area of research has been thoroughly summarized and interpreted elsewhere (Daly, McCroskey, Ayres, Hopf, & Ayres, 1997), we will not duplicate that effort here. Rather, we will direct our attention toward the findings of research related to the instructional context.

Approximately 20 percent of the students in college classrooms report being highly apprehensive about communication. These students tend also to report low levels of willingness to communicate, low levels of self-perceived communication competence, and a strong tendency to be shy. Simply put, these are quiet, anxious individuals who dread forced communication in the classroom and seldom will voluntarily initiate such communication. They go to great lengths to adapt to the classroom environment in ways which reduce their likelihood of having to participate (McCroskey & McVetta, 1978). The impact of these students' CA on their success in the instructional environment is very negative. Some specific examples are outlined below.

Perceived Intelligence. Although communication apprehension and intelligence have been found to be uncorrelated (Bashore, 1971), it has been determined that public school teachers perceive apprehensive students to be less intelligent (McCroskey & Daly, 1976).

Less Learning. Highly apprehensive students have been found to learn less. This has been demonstrated with regard to cognitive learning in both an experimental investigation (Booth-Butterfield, 1988) and through examination of student grades (Hurt & Preiss, 1978; McCroskey, Booth-Butterfield, & Payne, 1989) and American College Test (ACT) scores (McCroskey & Andersen, 1976).

Dislike of School. Highly apprehensive students at the middle-school level have been found to dislike their teachers and school in general more than other students, and to be less liked by their classmates (Hurt & Preiss, 1978.) The same holds true for college students (McCroskey & Sheahan, 1978).

Restricted Social Life. Highly apprehensive students have been found to have fewer dates (although they don't differ from students with low apprehension in terms of the number of dates desired), initiate less communication with students outside of class, know fewer faculty members, and dislike the advising system and college as whole (McCroskey & Sheahan, 1978). They are also less likely to participate in extracurricular activities.

Drop Out Rate. Highly apprehensive college students were found in two longitudinal investigations to be more likely to drop out of college than less apprehensive students (McCroskey, Booth-Butterfield, & Payne, 1989). Many of these students drop out even before the end of the first semester.

In sum, highly communication apprehensive students avoid communication in the instructional environment. This leads to less learning and a less desirable social life, and it may even lead to the termination of the individual's formal education.

Public Speaking Anxiety (PSA)

Stage fright and speech fright are terms commonly employed to reference anxiety and fear associated with public speaking. Another common term for this phenomenon is *public speaking anxiety* (PSA). PSA is one form of communication apprehension. For decades this was the only form of CA that was studied in the field of communication, and its predecessor, the field of speech. This was a function of that field focusing almost all of its attention on public speaking performance. Because of this focus, communication apprehension related to other forms of communication (i.e., interpersonal, small group) went unnoticed. It was not until the mid-1960s that the field of communication directed substantial attention to any kind of communication other than giving speeches. This was when the constructs of reticence and communication apprehension were first developed.

The study of PSA has a long and distinguished history. References to it date back into antiquity. At least until the 1970s, most scholars and lay people believed that being able to give public speeches was a strong indicator of intelligence (of course, it isn't). It was even believed by many scholars that one's personality could be improved as a result of training in public speaking (of course, it can't). Serious scientific study of PSA began in the 1930s. The first 25 years of this effort were synthesized in a classic monograph by Clevenger (1959). This research provided the foundation for the later research on communication apprehension.

PSA is considered by many to be the most serious form of communication apprehension. There is some justification for this view, since several large polls have indicated that the number one fear of Americans is having to give a public speech. Also, estimates of the number of people who experience severe PSA run as high as 80 percent. Others argue that because most people, most of the time, can avoid PSA by avoiding having to give public speeches, it is not as severe a problem as high general communication apprehension, which affects an estimated 20 percent of the population.

Whatever view one takes on the seriousness of this issue, it cannot be denied that PSA is a very serious problem in the general context of education. While people tend to think of public speaking classes in school as the only place where apprehensive people will be confronted with their PSA in a classroom, this is far from the truth. From the earliest levels of education through graduate school final oral exams, public speaking is demanded. It begins with "show and tell" in the lower elementary grades and is followed by oral reading, oral book reports, oral current events reports, oral presentations of science and social science pro-jects. It is not just the public speaking classes in high school and college that demand public speaking; public speaking is also required in many classes in other disciplines, often with instructors with no education in communication and no sensitivity to the problems faced by students with high PSA. Simply put, students cannot avoid PSA in school because the teachers won't allow them to do so. The outcomes are sometimes tragic, ranging from students dropping classes, changing majors, or even changing colleges to feeling totally humiliated in front of their classmates, getting physically sick and/or passing out while trying to give the speech, or even being so traumatized that they will never even attempt to speak in public again. Knowing this information should prevent one from being surprised when another national study surveys people to identify the most negative person in their lives—and once again finds that the answer given most is "a teacher."

Compulsive Communication

Some people talk a lot. Some of these people are students. Often instructors would prefer that the student talk less. But for some of these students talking less is something that is extremely difficult at best and may even be virtually impossible. These are compulsive communicators, sometimes referred to as "talkaholics" (McCroskey & Richmond, 1993; 1995). Talkaholic students, about 5 percent of the student population, are driven to communicate. Not only are they *not* shy but they enjoy talking so much that they have no interest in changing, unfortunately for their classmates and often the teacher. If not addressing the entire class, they are talking to a neighbor. They tend to dominate classroom discussion in small classes, including communication in any group activity. Intellectually, they are normal students—neither especially bright nor especially dull—but they invariably get high grades for participation, which often results in inflated final grades. They are relentless in getting their questions answered—either in class or outside of class—by talking with the teacher or other students.

Very importantly, these are usually *not* the people who get referred to as someone who "talks too much." Everyone knows someone whom they think "talks too much." It is common in U.S. culture to hear the expression. However, it is very important to understand that "talking too much" is *not* a quantitative problem of too much talk, but instead a qualitative problem of offensive behavior. We find talkaholics to be unpleasant, obtrusive, or just plain incompetent. They often express views with which we disagree and give us no room to voice our own opinions. When other students get irritated with a talkaholic (and say she or he "talks too much") it usually is because the other students feel they don't get enough opportunity to speak themselves or because they want the talkaholic to stop talking so the class will be dismissed sooner.

Receiver Apprehension (RA)

The final student communication trait we will consider relates to the apprehension around receiving messages rather than the sending of them. Wheeless (1975) advanced the original conceptualization of receiver apprehension. He defined this construct as "the fear of misinterpreting, inadequately processing and/or not being able to adjust psychologically to messages sent by others" (p. 263). He identified a cognitive pattern that reflects low confidence in processing abilities and low psychological self-approval.

Students with high receiver apprehension have been found to be somewhat less effective listeners, to process less information overall, to commit more errors in processing information, and to be less able to critically evaluate messages, among other receiving and interpreting problems (Wheeless, Preiss, & Gayle, 1997). There appears to be a substantial association between receiver apprehension and cognitive processing problems. At this point it is unclear whether the anxiety is the cause of the processing problems or vice versa. At any rate, receiver apprehension has been established as a stable communication trait, which can seriously interfere with learning in typical learning environments.

Effects of Communication Traits in the Classroom

Primary Effects

In general, research has indicated that high reticence, low willingness to communicate, low self-perceived communication competence, high communication apprehension, high public speaking anxiety, and high receiver apprehension are associated with reduced initiation of communication across communication contexts. In contrast, compulsive communication, high willingness to communicate, high self-perceived communication competence, low communication apprehension, low public speaking anxiety, and low receiver apprehension are associated with increased initiation of communication across communication contexts. These results indicate that such trait orientations are powerful and lead to predictable behaviors. They shape individuals' behaviors, whereby they choose or avoid situations where their trait might be problematic for them. By avoiding threatening situations, they avoid problems associated with their strong traits. Students with high public speaking anxiety seldom suffer from that anxiety simply because they typically remain silent in situations where they would be expected to speak out.

However, these orientations can also be examined from a "situational" perspective. It is more difficult to predict the behavior of people who have weak traits, that is, those who do not score particularly low or high on the measures of these traits. These individuals monitor situations at a much lower level than those with strong traits. Hence, they are more responsive to the varying situations. If they find situations to be comfortable, their avoidance response is not triggered. However, if they see the situation as threatening or challenging, they are likely to respond very much like those with strong trait orientations, and will try to avoid that situation. If they can't, they suffer the consequences as those who have strong traits.

While this general pattern applies to most of the traits we have discussed above, each trait is likely to produce somewhat unique effects. The primary effect of willingness to communicate is for the low willing to communicate to engage in shy behavior, while the high willing to communicate will not. People with a high level of self-perceived communication competence generally will be more likely to initiate communication than people with a low level of self-perceived communication competence. If they feel competent in one kind of communication context (interpersonal communication within a group in class, for example) and not competent in another communication context (giving a public speech in class, for example) they are likely to approach interpersonal communication but avoid public speaking.

The effects of trait communication apprehension (and its subset, public speaking anxiety) have received more attention than some of the other traits we have considered. It has been found that there are both internal effects and external effects of communication apprehension. The only effect that is predicted to be universal across the spectrum of individuals who experience all types of communication apprehension is an internally experienced feeling of discomfort (McCroskey, 1997). Only the individual experiencing this effect may know that it actually is occurring. It is quite possible that no evidence of this occurrence will be observable by anyone else. However, there may be clear external effects that are quite observable. These are *avoidance* (the person fearing the internal discomfort prevents it by not entering a situation where it might be expected to occur—like raising their hand in class), *withdrawal* (the person experiencing the discomfort drops the class or declines to talk when called on), *disruption* (attempting to give a report but having trouble remembering what to say, using many vocalized pauses, or keeping the report very brief), and *over communication* (volunteering to speak in class, registering for a public speaking class, going out for the debate team). Over communication represents a "fight" response, whereas avoidance, withdrawal, and disruption are "flight" responses. The "fight" response is comparatively rare. It is estimated that less than 2% of the high communication apprehensives will engage in this behavior. These people are trying to overcome their apprehension. Unfortunately, the attempt is rarely successful. It is not unusual for these individuals to be seen as "talking too much" by others around them.

Secondary Effects

As we have noted above, research has found a number of negative effects to be likely as a function of a student being "quiet." Particulary in communication apprehension research, it has been found that people reporting themselves to be high communication apprehensives suffer from many negative reactions from others (teachers and classmates) around them. For a long time we have believed this to be primarily a function of their engaging in shy behaviors, and talking less (Richmond & McCroskey, 1998). This assumption has been challenged by some recent research (Cole & McCroskey, 2003).

In a naturalistic study, the researchers measured subordinates' perceptions of their supervisors' levels of both shyness and communication apprehension as well verbal aggressiveness. In a second study, they measured students' perceptions of their roommates' levels of the same three variables. Data were also collected with regard to the subordinates' and roommates' perceptions of their supervisors'/roommates' source credibility (competence, trustworthiness, and goodwill) and their own affect/liking for this other person. The results were not consistent with similar studies that measured self-reports of an individual's shyness and communication apprehension and correlated them with similar outcome variables.

The results of both studies found perceived shyness to be unrelated (no statistically significant correlations) to perceived source credibility or affect/liking for the other person. However, in both studies, highly significant correlations ($r = -.52$ to $-.69$ for supervisors; $r = -.35$ to $-.42$ for roommates) between perceived communication apprehension and the criterion variables. Perceived verbal aggression was also negatively correlated with the criterion variables in both studies ($r = -.57$ to $-.71$ for supervisors; $r = -.21$ to $-.56$ for roommates). In short, while perceptions of communication apprehension were substantially negatively correlated with perceptions of both supervisors and roommates, perceptions of shyness were totally unrelated with those perceptions.

The conclusion from this research is that it probably is not being quiet (in this research, perceived shyness) that results in people having negative reactions to others; it is the attributed reason (in this case, anxiety/fear) for the quietness that produces these negative responses. While the contexts of these studies (organizational communication, interpersonal communication) did not involve the classroom directly, the strength of the observed relationships across two contexts certainly should lead us to expect that the same perceptual process observed in the two contexts is likely to be generalizable to the instructional context. The fact that the results of research in instructional communication suggest that quiet students are perceived by teachers to be less bright, less motivated, less interested, and more anxious adds extra support for this assumption.

Causes of Communication Traits

Throughout the history of philosophy, scholars have argued whether "nature" (genetics) or "nurture" (environment, learning) shapes human behavior. For most of the history of scientific research on communication traits it has been assumed that these traits are learned. Because his doctoral minor was in educational psychology (focusing on learning theories and research methodologies), the first author of this chapter was convinced of the validity of this research paradigm. An essential concept generally accepted by scholars and practitioners employing the learning paradigm has been that "anything that is learned can be unlearned." Based on such learning approaches, a number of methods of changing people's behavior or orientations toward behavior (behavior therapies) have been developed and widely employed.

When it became obvious that some means of reducing individuals' levels of communication apprehension was badly needed, virtually all of the attention was directed toward behavior therapies, particularly *systematic desensitization* (learning to associate an anxiety-producing communication event with a relaxed state of mind) and *cognitive restructuring* (identifying and changing irrational beliefs about self and formulating new positive beliefs). This research consistently produced results that were statistically significant, indicating that these therapies were effective methods of reducing communication apprehension. At the time this research began (late 1960s), the accepted approach to theory building was based on statistical significance. Hence, most researchers were confident of the effectiveness of these treatment approaches. As time passed, communication researchers became more aware of the need for theories to account for socially significant, not just statistically significant, variance. When the treatment research was re-examined, it became very obvious that the results of this research did not account for much variance in the communication apprehension of individuals who received treatment. Although most high apprehensives who received treatment showed some improvement, virtually none changed their level to low apprehension, and most did not even become moderate apprehensives. They just became less high. While employing multiple treatments was found to improve the results somewhat, the impact was still comparatively small.

This reanalysis caused the authors of this chapter to become suspicious not only of the methods of treatment they were employing, but also the basic assumption of the paradigm. They concluded that maybe communication traits cannot really be changed meaningfully by methods based on learning theories. By the mid-1970s they began to wonder if there was some other factor that should be considered—such as genetics. As early as 1975, this view was expressed in a convention paper. It was greeted with laughs and lack of acceptance. Since at that time there was no real evidence with which the authors were familiar to support the view, it was pushed to the background and research on other topics moved to the forefront of their attention.

Much later, with breakthrough twin research in psychobiology, the approaching probability of the decoding of the human genome, and increasing acceptance of such writings as those of Herrnstein and Murray (1994), the unthinkable became more thinkable: Genetics actually play a substantial role in human behavior. While collaborating with Michael Beatty in the development of a new book relating to communication and personality, it became clear that genetic influence in communication trait behavior was no longer speculation but rather a proven fact.

Subsequent work with Professor Beatty and others documented this in a series of articles (Beatty & McCroskey, 1997; Beatty, Heisel, Hall, Levine, & La France, 2002; Beatty, McCroskey, & Heisel, 1998; Heisel, La France, & Beatty, 2003; McCroskey, 1998; McCroskey, Heisel, & Richmond, 2001) and a book on the biology of communication (Beatty & McCroskey, 2001). In an extremely well-written and documented book, Pinker (2002) has provided a superb analysis of the genetic/learning dichotomy and the myths associated with each. To the extent that we may have had any surviving concerns about the role of genetics in communication (and other) traits, or that the learning paradigm might deserve to be the dominating research paradigm for trait communication research, Pinker has answered those concerns. The genetic role is large, and the learning paradigm should be reduced to secondary status (if even that).

Implications

Students enter instructors' classrooms with widely divergent orientations toward communication. Many of these orientations are not well adapted to the typical demands of participation and presentation required in U.S. classrooms. If such high communication demands are made, these students are placed in a distinctly disadvantageous position. Other students enter the classroom with different communication orientations, which are well adapted to the typical demands of U.S. classrooms. These students are placed in a distinctly advantageous position. Most instructors are not even aware of these issues and normally will simply follow the traditional patterns of their teaching culture. Informed instructors must choose whether or not to directly discriminate against 20 percent (1 in 5) of their students, making success in the class virtually unattainable by these students and establishing a high probability of their having to choose between dropping the course or failing it. If instructors believe that students learn primarily through their mouths, they are likely to make the choice to discriminate. However, we concur with Professor Daun—students indeed do learn mostly through their eyes and ears. While communication in the classroom should be encouraged, it should be done without force, or threat of punishment for the students who have traits which prevent them from participating fully.

When making this decision, instructors need to keep in mind that these traits are not likely to be changed by the students, nor can the instructor change them by being nice to the students, or by threatening them with punishment for lack of participation or presentation. The bases for these traits are genetic and not subject to choice on the part of the student.

If instructors make what we believe to be the right choice, there are several prescriptions noted below, which they can use to increase the probability for success of students in their classrooms.

1. *Reduce demands for oral participation.* It is fine to encourage it, but not to require it. One way of doing this is to offer extra credit for those students who participate. Students who find such participation difficult can still get the good grade they earn. The more verbal students can benefit from their communication abilities without harming other students.

2. *Do not require public presentations in the class.* While there are exceptions, such as public speaking classes, certain types of foreign language classes, and some seminar-type classes, there is no major reason why students should need to give presentations in most classes. If individualized reports on the part of students are needed in a class, consider giving students the option of either presenting those reports orally or completing them in writing. Let the students choose the communication system that is most comfortable to them. When students have more control over their potential for success, they are much more likely to succeed.

3. *Avoid randomly calling on students for in-class responses.* For many students such behavior on the part of the instructor results in the student focusing on the anticipated terror of being called on rather than carefully attending to the content in the class. Research has indicated that calling on students may reduce the learning of the apprehensive students by 20 percent or more. If you believe calling on students for class participation is absolutely necessary, try to call on only those students who are making eye contact with you or raising their hand. Those who do not want to participate orally will be looking down or away, which you should take as a clear indication of their not wanting to be called upon.

4. *Allow student-selected seating.* Research has determined that students who want to participate orally in class tend to sit in the front and the middle of the classroom. This is where most teachers direct most of their attention. Students who want to be left alone tend to sit along the sides of the class and in the back. Let them do so and respect their choice. In particular, avoid alphabetical seating. This will guarantee that students who want to participate and ones who don't will be in the seats that make them most uncomfortable.

5. *Try to reward communication in the classroom, and ignore nonparticipation.* If quiet students see that communication is rewarded, they are more likely to talk if they feel they have something to say. If communication in class is punished, the quiet students will be more rigid in their quietness, while the most verbal students (even if they are the ones who are punished) will continue to talk.

6. *Be nonverbally immediate in your classroom communication.* Instructor immediacy is one of the most powerful elements of instructional communication. Frymier's (1993) research has determined that even high communication apprehensives respond better to nonverbally immediate instructors.

7. *Avoid evaluation based on oral communication.* A science class is not a speech class, neither are classes in English, history, engineering, or art. Students should be evaluated on what they learn in the subject matter of the class for which they are enrolled, and not penalized because of their ineptness or reluctance in oral presentations. Of course, if you are teaching public speaking, it is appropriate to evaluate oral presentations. Unless the course is required, few highly apprehensive students will be in the class anyway. If it is required, this is most likely the result of ignorant administrators making bad decisions. Invite them to read this chapter and reconsider the requirement.

References

Bashore, D. N. (1971). *Relationships among speech anxiety, trait anxiety, I.Q., and high school achievement.* MS thesis, Illinois State University, Normal, Illinois.

Beatty, M. J., Heisel, A. D., Hall, A. E., Levine, T. R., & La France, B. H. (2002). What can we learn from the study of twins about genetic and environmental influences on interpersonal affiliation, aggressiveness, and social anxiety?: A meta-analytic study. *Communication Monographs, 69,* 1–18.

Beatty, M. J., & McCroskey, J. C. (1997). It's in our nature: Verbal aggressiveness as temperamental expression. *Communication Quarterly, 45,* 446–460.

Beatty, M. J., & McCroskey, J. C. (2001). *The biology of communication: A communibiological perspective.* Cresskill, NJ: Hampton Press.

Beatty, M. J., McCroskey, J. C., & Heisel, A. D. (1998). Communication apprehension as temperamental expression: A communibiological paradigm, *Communication Monographs, 64,* 197–219.

Booth-Butterfield, S. (1988). Inhibition and student recall on instructional messages. *Communication Education, 37,* 312–324.

Chan, B., & McCroskey, J. C. (1987). The WTC scale as a predictor of classroom participation. *Communication Research Reports, 4,* 47–50.

Clevenger, T. Jr. (1959). A synthesis of experimental research in stage fright. *Quarterly Journal of Speech, 45,* 134–145.

Cole, J. G., & McCroskey, J. C. (2003). The association of perceived communication apprehension, shyness, and verbal aggression with perceptions of source credibility and affect in organizational and interpersonal contexts. *Communication Quarterly, 51,* 101–110.

Daly, J. A., McCroskey, J. C., Ayres, J., Hopf, T., & Ayres, D. M. (1997). *Avoiding communication: Shyness, reticence, and communication apprehension.* Cresskill, NJ: Hampton Press.

Frymier, A. B. (1993). The relationships among communication apprehension, immediacy, and motivation to study. *Communication Reports, 6,* 8–17.

Heisel, A. D., La France, B. H., & Beatty, M. J. (2003). Self-reported extraversion, neuroticism, and psychoticism as predictors of peer rated verbal aggressiveness and affinity seeking competence. *Communication Monographs, 70,* 1–15.

Herrnstein, R. J., & Murray, C. (1994). *The bell curve: Intelligence and class structure in American life.* New York: Free Press.

Hurt, H. T., & Preiss, R. (1978). Silence isn't necessarily golden: Communication apprehension, desired social choice, and academic success among middle-school students, *Human Communication Research, 4,* 315–328.

Leary, M. R. (1983). The conceptual distinctions are important: Another look at communication apprehension and related constructs. *Human Communication Research, 10,* 305–312.

McCroskey, J. C. (1970). Measures of communication-bound anxiety. *Speech Monographs, 37,* 269–277.

McCroskey, J. C. (1977a). Classroom consequences of communication apprehension. *Communication Education, 26,* 27–33.

McCroskey, J. C. (1977b). Oral communication apprehension: A summary of recent theory and research. *Human Communication Research, 4,* 78–96.

McCroskey, J. C. (1978). Validity of the PRCA as an index of oral communication apprehension. *Communication Monographs, 45,* 192–203.

McCroskey, J. C. (1997). Willingness to communicate, communication apprehension, and self-perceived communication competence: Conceptualizations and perspectives. In J. A. Daly, J. C. McCroskey, J. Ayres, T. Hopf, & D. M. Ayres (Eds.), *Avoiding communication: Shyness, reticence, and communication apprehension,* 2nd ed. (pp. 75–108). Cresskill, NJ: Hampton Press.

McCroskey, J. C. (1998). *Why we communicate the ways we do: A communibiological perspective* (National Communication Association, Carroll C. Arnold Distinguished Lecture, 1997). Needham Heights, MA: Allyn & Bacon.

McCroskey, J. C., & Andersen, J. F. (1976). The relationship between communication apprehension and academic achievement among college students. *Human Communication Research, 3,* 73–81.

McCroskey, J. C., Booth-Butterfield, S., & Payne, S. K. (1989). The impact of communication apprehension on college student retention and success. *Communication Quarterly, 37,* 100–107.

McCroskey, J. C., & Daly, J. A. (1976). Teachers' expectations of the communication apprehensive child in elementary school. *Human Communication Research, 3,* 67–72.

McCroskey, J. C., Heisel, A. D., & Richmond, V. P. (2001). Eysenck's BIG THREE and communication traits: Three correlational studies. *Communication Monographs, 68,* 360–366.

McCroskey, J. C., & McCroskey, L. L. (1988). Self-report as an approach to measuring communication competence. *Communication Research Reports, 5,* 108–113.

McCroskey, J. C. & McVetta, R. W. (1978). Classroom seating arrangements: Instructional communication theory versus student preferences. *Communication Education, 27,* 99–111.

McCroskey, J. C., & Richmond, V. P. (1982). Communication apprehension and shyness: Conceptual and operational distinctions. *Central States Speech Journal, 33,* 458–468.

McCroskey, J. C., & Richmond, V. P. (1987). Willingness to communicate. In J. C. McCroskey & J. A. Daly (Eds.), *Personality and interpersonal communication* (pp.129–156). Beverly Hills, CA: Sage.

McCroskey, J. C., & Richmond, V. P. (1993). Identifying compulsive communicators: The talkaholic scale. *Communication Research Reports, 10,* 107–114.

McCroskey, J. C., & Richmond, V. P. (1995). Correlates of compulsive communication: Quantitative and qualitative characterizations. *Communication Quarterly, 43,* 39–52.

McCroskey, J. C., & Richmond, V. P. (1998). Willingness to communicate. In J. C. McCroskey, J. A. Daly, M. M. Martin, & M. J. Beatty (Eds.), *Communication and personality: Trait perspectives* (pp. 119–131). Cresskill, NJ: Hampton Press.

McCroskey, J. C., & Sheahan, M. E. (1978). Communication apprehension, social preference, and social behavior in a college environment. *Communication Quarterly, 26,* 41–45.

Phillips, G. R. (1968). Reticence: Pathology of the normal speaker. *Speech Monographs, 35,* 39–49.

Phillips, G. R. (1997). Reticence: A perspective on social withdrawal. In J. A. Daly, J. C. McCroskey, J. Ayres, T. Hopf, & D. M. Ayres (Eds.) *Avoiding communication: Shyness, reticence, and communication apprehension* (pp. 129–150). Cresskill, NJ: Hampton Press.

Pinker, S. (2002). *The blank slate: The modern denial of human natures.* New York: Viking-Penguin Putnam.

Richmond, V. P., Martin, M. M., & Cox, B. (1997). A bibliography of related practice, theory, and research. In J. A. Daly, J. C. McCroskey, J. Ayres, T. Hopf, & D. M. Ayres (Eds.) *Avoiding communication: Shyness, reticence, and communication apprehension,* 2nd ed. (pp. 401–488) Cresskill, NJ: Hampton Press.

Richmond, V. P., & McCroskey, J. C. (1998). *Communication: Apprehension, avoidance, and effectiveness,* 5th ed. Needham Heights, MA: Allyn & Bacon.

Wheeless, L. R. (1975). An investigation of receiver apprehension and social context dimensions of communication apprehension. *Speech Teacher, 24,* 261–268.

Wheeless, L. R., Preiss, R. W. , & Gayle, B. M. (1997). Receiver apprehension, informational receptivity, and cognitive processing. In J. A. Daly, J. C. McCroskey, J. Ayres, T. Hopf, & D. M. Ayres (Eds.), *Avoiding communication: Shyness, reticence, and communication apprehension,* 2nd ed. (pp. 151–187). Cresskill, NJ: Hampton Press.

4

Understanding the Source: Teacher Credibility and Aggressive Communication Traits

Scott A. Myers
West Virginia University

Matthew M. Martin
West Virginia University

Introduction

According to Aristotle in the *Rhetoric,* a speaker's credibility is based on the receiver's perception of the speaker's intelligence, character, and goodwill (Cooper, 1932). Aristotle argued a speaker's credibility is the most powerful rhetorical strategy a speaker has when persuading an audience. In the last century, researchers have identified the following characteristics as defining credibility: caring, competence, composure, dynamism, emotional stability, expertness, extroversion, sociability, and trustworthiness (Berlo, Lemert, & Mertz, 1969; Falcione, 1974 Hovland, Janis, & Kelley, 1953; McCroskey, 1966). Findings involving the study of credibility include that (a) organized speakers are viewed as more credible (McCroskey & Mehrley, 1969), (b) low credible sources can gain credibility by saying competent things (Wheeless, 1973), (c) speakers that handle questions effectively are considered more credible (Ragsdale & Mikels, 1975), and (d) credible speakers have a greater impact on their audience (Infante, 1980). One area of interest for communication researchers interested in studying source credibility is teacher credibility.

In the classroom, source credibility is viewed as "the attitude of a receiver that references the degree to which a source is seen to be believable" (McCroskey, 1998, p. 80) and is perhaps one of the most important variables affecting the teacher–student relationship (Myers, 2001). Generally, teachers who are viewed as credible exert a tremendous amount of influence on their students. Previous researchers have ascertained that students who perceive their teachers as credible are motivated to perform well academically (Frymier & Thompson, 1992; Martin, Chesebro, & Mottet, 1997), are able to recall course information (Wheeless, 1975), and report gains in affective and cognitive learning (Johnson & Miller, 2002; Russ, Simonds, & Hunt, 2002; Teven & McCroskey, 1997). Furthermore, students enrolled in courses with teachers they consider as credible recommend these teachers to their friends (Nadler & Nadler, 2001), have respect for them (Martinez-Egger & Powers, 2002), evaluate them highly (Teven & McCroskey, 1997), plan to take an additional course from them (Nadler & Nadler, 2001), contribute to in-class discussion (Myers, 2003a), and engage in out-of-class communication with them (Myers, 2003a; Nadler & Nadler, 2001).

Given this influence, it is essential for prospective teachers, educators, and administrators to grasp an understanding of the pervasive role teacher credibility plays in the classroom. To reach this end, the purpose of this chapter is threefold. First, the development of the measurement of the teacher credibility construct will be examined. Second, an overview of the research conducted on teacher credibility will be provided, with a specific focus on the relationships between teacher credibility and the teacher communication traits of aggressive communication. Third, a summary of the knowledge claims about teacher credibility will be provided, and directions for future research will be identified.

Development of the Measurement of Teacher Credibility

Over the years, the development of the measurement of the teacher credibility construct has advanced steadily. The teacher credibility construct was originally believed to consist of five dimensions: competence, extroversion, character, composure, and sociability (McCroskey, Holdridge, & Toomb, 1974). *Competence* refers to the degree to which a teacher is perceived to be knowledgeable about a given subject matter, *extroversion* refers to the degree to which a teacher is perceived to be outgoing, *character* refers to the degree to which a teacher is trusted by students, *composure* refers to the degree of emotional control exhibited by a teacher, and *sociability* refers to the degree to which a teacher is considered to be warm and friendly (McCroskey, 1992). Subsequent research has refined teacher credibility to consist of three dimensions: the competence and character dimensions identified by McCroskey, Holdridge et al. (1974) and the dimension of caring, which is the degree to which a teacher is concerned about students' welfare (Teven & McCroskey, 1997). In this section, three studies that have specifically focused on the development of the measurement of teacher credibility will be reviewed.

Study #1: McCroskey, Holdridge, and Toomb (1974)

The study of teacher credibility began in 1974 when a seminal article written by McCroskey, Holdridge, and Toomb was published in *Speech Teacher.* Acknowledging that (a) the research conducted on source credibility to date had focused solely on the perceived credibility of public figures and (b) the dimensionality of source credibility fluctuates based on the source, McCroskey, Holdridge et al. (1974) were determined to develop a measure of source credibility designed specifically to measure students' perceptions of their teachers. Using 53 items taken from existing credibility instruments (i.e., Berlo et al., 1969; Markham, 1968; McCroskey, 1966; Norman, 1963), McCroskey, Holdridge et al. had three samples comprised of 1,880 undergraduate college students complete the items in reference to one of their instructors. A principal components factor analysis (with the findings of each sample analyzed separately) resulted in the identification of five factors of teacher credibility for the first two samples and four factors of teacher credibility for the third sample. The five factors were labeled character, sociability, composure, extroversion, and competence; the four factors were labeled sociability–character, composure, extroversion, and competence.

Subsequent research conducted by McCroskey, Holdridge et al. (1974) examined the reliability, construct validity, and predictive validity of the items that - comprised the five-factor solution. To assess the reliability of the items, 948 undergraduate students completed a 14-item measure of teacher credibility (see Figure 4.1).

Reliability coefficients ranging from .91 (composure) to .94 (extroversion) were obtained for the five dimensions; test–retest reliability coefficients ranging from .82 (competence) to .86 (sociability) were obtained based on 46 students who completed the measure twice with a two-week interval between the two data collection points. Construct validity was deemed acceptable, given that (a) the items used to construct the measure were grounded in credibility research and (b) the emergence of the five-factor solution was based on constructs identified within the credibility literature.

Predictive validity of the teacher credibility measure was established in two ways. The first way centered on examining students' exposure to the teacher. Students who comprised two of the samples used in the first phase of the study were asked two additional questions. These questions were, "If you had room in your

FIGURE 4.1 ***Teacher Credibility Measure.***

Instructions: The following are a set of attitude scales. You are asked to evaluate your teacher in terms of the adjective on each scale. For example, if you think your teacher is very tall, you might mark the following scale as below:

Tall : X ___ ___ ___ ___ ___ ___ ___ : Short

Of course, if you consider your teacher to be shorter, you would mark your "X" nearer the "short" adjective. The middle space on each scale should be considered "neutral." Mark this space if you feel neither adjective on the scale applies to your teacher or if you feel both apply equally.

My teacher in this course . . .

1. Expert	:___ ___ ___ ___ ___ ___ ___:	Inexpert
2. Unreliable	:___ ___ ___ ___ ___ ___ ___:	Reliable
3. Meek	:___ ___ ___ ___ ___ ___ ___:	Aggressive
4. Verbal	:___ ___ ___ ___ ___ ___ ___:	Quiet
5. Bold	:___ ___ ___ ___ ___ ___ ___:	Timid
6. Silent	:___ ___ ___ ___ ___ ___ ___:	Talkative
7. Unselfish	:___ ___ ___ ___ ___ ___ ___:	Selfish
8. Kind	:___ ___ ___ ___ ___ ___ ___:	Cruel
9. Poised	:___ ___ ___ ___ ___ ___ ___:	Nervous
10. Tense	:___ ___ ___ ___ ___ ___ ___:	Relaxed
11. Anxious	:___ ___ ___ ___ ___ ___ ___:	Calm
12. Unsociable	:___ ___ ___ ___ ___ ___ ___:	Sociable
13. Cheerful	:___ ___ ___ ___ ___ ___ ___:	Gloomy
14. Irritable	:___ ___ ___ ___ ___ ___ ___:	Good-natured

Items 1–2 measure "competence," items 3–6 measure "extroversion," items 7–8 measure "character," items 9–11 measure "composure," and items 12–14 measure "sociability."

From "An Instrument for Measuring the Source Credibility of Basic Speech Communication Instructors," by J. C. McCroskey, W. Holridge, and J. K. Tomb, 1974, *Speech Teacher, 23,* 26–33. Republished with permission by *Communication Education* and Taylor & Francis Ltd. http://www.tandf.co.uk/journals.

schedule for an elective course, how likely would it be that you would sign up for another course with this instructor?" (i.e., voluntary exposure) and "Would you suggest that a friend of yours sign up for a course from this instructor" (i.e., recommended exposure). Multiple correlation analyses revealed 45% to 58% of the variance in both voluntary and recommended exposure was predicted by all five dimensions of teacher credibility, with competence and sociability serving as the best predictors. The second way explored the impact of teacher credibility on student recall of information. One hundred and eighteen (N = 118) students in 10 classes listened to a lecture from their teacher that contained information not available from any other source. Students were then tested on this information. Correlation analysis revealed only one significant finding, which was a positive correlation between teacher competence and student recall.

Based on these collective findings, McCroskey, Holdridge et al. (1974) concluded their 14-item measure of teacher credibility was reliable, had satisfactory construct validity, and had sufficient predictive validity (in terms of student exposure, but not student recall). Furthermore, McCroskey, Holdridge et al., recommended researchers consider teacher credibility to consist of five dimensions (i.e., character, sociability, composure, extroversion, competence) rather than four dimensions (i.e., sociability–character, composure, extroversion, competence), in part because "it is better to have too much information about teacher credibility than too little" (p. 29). Additionally, they established that if researchers treated the sociability and the character dimensions as one combined dimension, it is possible the combined score would be meaningless if the two dimensions were operating independently.

Study #2: McCroskey and Young (1981)

The McCroskey, Holdridge et al. (1974) study served as the impetus for the 1981 study reported by McCroskey and Young in the *Central States Speech Journal.* Arguing that the previous study conducted by McCroskey, Holdridge et al. (1974) identified dimensions of source credibility based on instruments that were never intended to measure source credibility (i.e., Markham, 1968; Norman, 1963), McCroskey and Young (1981) were interested in identifying the dimensions of source credibility that paralleled the theoretical research conducted to date on source credibility. They asked 726 college students to provide adjectives that described a "person [they] would be most likely to believe" and a "person [they] would be least likely to believe" (p. 29). These responses, along with a perusal of adjectives present in the ethos literature and contained on measures of source credibility, resulted in the selection of 30 adjective pairs. McCroskey and Young also added six adjective pairs that measured size (e.g., large/small, big/little) and five adjective pairs that had nothing to do with source credibility.

Using these 41 adjective pairs, 2,057 college students enrolled in communication courses were asked to rate the source credibility of one of six targets: a peer (n = 372), a spouse (n = 352), an organization (n = 344), a media source (n = 331), a political figure (n = 323), or a teacher (n = 335). A principal components factor analysis using varimax rotation revealed an eight-factor solution. These eight factors included the five factors previously identified by McCroskey, Holdridge et al. (1974) (i.e., character, sociability, composure, extroversion, competence) and three new factors: size, time, and weight.

Although these results replicated the findings obtained by McCroskey, Holdridge et al. (1974) and identified three additional factors of source credibility, McCroskey and Young (1981) believed only two dimensions—competence and character—were viable representations of source credibility because of their theoretical grounding. They stated that although individuals use the constructs of sociability, composure, extroversion, size, time, and weight to make impressions on other people, these constructs do not measure source credibility and therefore should not be labeled as such. Consequently, they concluded future researchers should restrict their conceptualization of source credibility to a 12-item, two-factor measure (see Figure 4.2).

FIGURE 4.2 ***Measure of Source Credibility.***

Instructions: Please indicate your impression of your teacher by circling the appropriate number between the pairs of adjectives below. The closer the number is to an adjective, the more certain you are of your evaluation.

Competence								
Intelligent	1	2	3	4	5	6	7	Unintelligent
Untrained	1	2	3	4	5	6	7	Trained
Expert	1	2	3	4	5	6	7	Inexpert
Uninformed	1	2	3	4	5	6	7	Informed
Competent	1	2	3	4	5	6	7	Incompetent
Stupid	1	2	3	4	5	6	7	Bright
Character								
Sinful	1	2	3	4	5	6	7	Virtuous
Dishonest	1	2	3	4	5	6	7	Honest
Unselfish	1	2	3	4	5	6	7	Selfish
Sympathetic	1	2	3	4	5	6	7	Unsympathetic
High character	1	2	3	4	5	6	7	Low character
Untrustworthy	1	2	3	4	5	6	7	Trustworthy

From "Ethos and Credibility: The Construct and Its Measurement after Three Decades," by J. C. McCroskey and T. J. Young, 1981, *Central States Speech Journal*, 32, 24–34. Republished with permission by the Central States Communication Association.

It should be noted the purpose of this study was not to develop a measure of teacher credibility. Yet, this measure has been used by many instructional communication researchers (Frymier & Thompson, 1992; Johnson & Miller, 2002; Patton, 1999; Schrodt, 2003a) and until 1997, was only one of two scales available to measure teacher credibility.

Study #3: Teven and McCroskey (1997)

The third study, which was conducted by Teven and McCroskey (1997), was based on an idea generated by McCroskey (1992). In a reexamination of Aristotle's conceptualization of ethos (i.e., competence, trustworthiness, goodwill), McCroskey posited that goodwill (hereafter referred to as caring) was a dimension of teacher credibility to which students respond. He proposed that the overarching caring dimension was comprised of three teacher behaviors: empathy, understanding, and responsiveness. *Empathy* refers to a teacher's ability to identify with students' feelings. When teachers are empathic, students are more likely to engage in out-of-class communication with them (Nadler & Nadler, 2001). *Understanding* centers on how well teachers identify the ideas and needs of their students. When students feel understood by their teachers, they report affect for their teachers, are motivated to study, and are satisfied with their classroom experience (Myers & Bryant, 2002). *Responsiveness* concerns whether teachers are attentive and listen to their students. When teachers are perceived as responsive, they are also considered to be nonverbally immediate (Thomas, Richmond, & McCroskey, 1994) and verbally receptive (Robinson, 1993).

To examine whether caring was a viable dimension of teacher credibility, 235 students completed the 12-item Source Credibility Scale (McCroskey & Young, 1981) and 10 items developed by the researchers based on McCroskey's (1992) conceptualization of caring. These 10 items were "cares about me/doesn't care about me," "has my interests at heart/doesn't have my interests at heart," "self-centered/not self-centered," "unconcerned with me/concerned with me," "insensitive/sensitive," "empathetic/apathetic," "not understanding/understanding," "unresponsive/responsive," "understands how I feel/doesn't understand how I feel," and "doesn't understand how I think/understands how I think" (p. 4).

An iterated principal factor analysis resulted in a three-factor structure: The competence and the character factors identified by McCroskey and Young (1981) as well as a caring factor, with all 10 items loading on this factor. Because of the low-factor loading associated with the "empathetic/apathetic" item, however, the item was discarded, resulting in a nine-item measure of teacher caring. A reliability coefficient of .95 was obtained for this nine-item factor.

Concurrent and predictive validity of the nine-item caring dimension was established by having students complete the Perceived Caring Scale (Koehn & Crowell, 1996), a measure of teacher evaluation and affective learning (McCroskey, 1994), and a measure of cognitive learning (Richmond, McCroskey, Kearney, & Plax, 1987). A correlation of .86 was obtained between the nine-item measure of teacher caring and the Perceived Caring Scale, thus establishing concurrent validity. Predictive validity was established through multiple regression analysis and the computation of partial correlations. Multiple regression analyses revealed 29% to 68% of the variance in teacher evaluation, student affective learning, and student cognitive learning was predicted by all three dimensions of teacher credibility. Furthermore, partial correlations computed between teacher caring and teacher evaluation, student affective learning, and student cognitive learning ranged from .09 to .20, suggesting that teacher caring accounts for some of the variance in student attitudes toward their classroom experience.

Subsequently, this measure was refined by McCroskey and Teven (1999) and is now an 18-item, three-dimension measure. Six items measure competence, six items measure character, and six items measure caring (see Figure 4.3). McCroskey and Teven reported reliability coefficients of .85 for the competence dimension, .92 for the character dimension, and .92 for the caring dimension. Similar reliability coefficients have been obtained for these three dimensions in instructional communication research (Baringer & McCroskey, 2000; Martin, Chesebro et al., 1997; Martinez-Egger & Powers, 2002; Myers, 2001; Thweatt, 1999; Thweatt & McCroskey, 1998; Wrench & Richmond, 2000).

FIGURE 4.3 *Measure of Ethos/Credibility (MEC).*

Instructions: Please indicate your impression of your teacher by circling the appropriate number between the pairs of adjectives below. The closer the number is to an adjective, the more certain you are of your evaluation.

Competence								
Intelligent	1	2	3	4	5	6	7	Unintelligent
Untrained	1	2	3	4	5	6	7	Trained
Inexpert	1	2	3	4	5	6	7	Expert
Informed	1	2	3	4	5	6	7	Uninformed
Incompetent	1	2	3	4	5	6	7	Competent
Bright	1	2	3	4	5	6	7	Stupid
Character								
Honest	1	2	3	4	5	6	7	Dishonest
Untrustworthy	1	2	3	4	5	6	7	Trustworthy
Honorable	1	2	3	4	5	6	7	Dishonorable
Moral	1	2	3	4	5	6	7	Immoral
Unethical	1	2	3	4	5	6	7	Ethical
Phony	1	2	3	4	5	6	7	Genuine
Caring								
Cares about me	1	2	3	4	5	6	7	Doesn't care about me
Has my interests at heart	1	2	3	4	5	6	7	Doesn't have my interests at heart
Self-centered	1	2	3	4	5	6	7	Not self-centered
Concerned with me	1	2	3	4	5	6	7	Unconcerned with me
Insensitive	1	2	3	4	5	6	7	Sensitive
Understanding	1	2	3	4	5	6	7	Not understanding

From "Goodwill: A Reexamination of the Construct and Its Measurement," by J. C. McCroskey and J. J. Teven, 1999, *Communication Monographs, 66,* 90–103. Republished with permission by *Communication Education* and Taylor & Francis Ltd. http://www.tandf.co.uk/journals.

Teacher Credibility and Teacher Aggressive Communication Traits

The research conducted to date on teacher credibility has generally concluded that perceived teacher credibility is associated with teacher effectiveness. Several researchers have noted the positive relationship that exists between teacher credibility and teacher communication behaviors. When teachers demonstrate competence, character, and/or caring, they are considered to be verbally and nonverbally immediate (Johnson & Miller, 2002; Teven, 2001; Thweatt, 1999), to use affinity-seeking strategies (Frymier & Thompson, 1992; Thweatt, 1999), and to use humor (Wrench & Richmond, 2000). Conversely, when teachers demonstrate competence, character, and/or caring, they are less likely to engage in behaviors that interfere with student learning (Thweatt, 1999; Thweatt & McCroskey, 1998). (These studies are examined in greater detail in Unit 3.)

Infante, Rancer, and Womack (2003) argued that a communication trait differs from a personality trait in that a communication trait, focuses on symbolic behavior. "A communication trait is an abstraction constructed to account for enduring consistencies and differences in message-sending and message-receiving behaviors among individuals" (Infante et al., 2003, p. 77). Infante et al. (2003) presented four categories of communication traits: *apprehension traits* (e.g., communication apprehension, receiver apprehension), *presentation traits* (e.g., communicator style, disclosiveness), *adaptation traits* (e.g., communication competence, interaction involvement), and *aggression traits* (e.g., argumentativeness, assertiveness, verbal aggressiveness). Of these four categories, the most attention involving teacher credibility has been paid to the aggression traits. In the following section, we define these aggression traits and review several studies that have explored the relationship between teacher credibility and teacher aggressive communication traits.

Aggressive Communication

A teacher trait that has ramifications on students' perceptions of teacher credibility is aggressive communication (Myers, 2002). Conceptualized by Infante (1987), aggressive communication consists of four traits through which a sender attempts to influence a receiver: assertiveness, argumentativeness, hostility, and verbal aggressiveness. *Assertiveness* is defined as the tendency to be interpersonally dominant, ascendant, and forceful (Infante, 1995) and encapsulates the characteristics associated with extroversion (Infante, 1987). *Argumentativeness* is defined as the predisposition to defend one's position on controversial issues while simultaneously attempting to refute another person's position (Infante & Rancer, 1982). *Hostility* is defined as the use of communication that is threatening and frustrating (Infante, 1987) and contains elements of negativity, suspicion, resentment, and irritability (Infante, 1995). *Verbal aggressiveness* is defined as a message behavior that attacks a person's self-concept in order to deliver psychological pain (Infante & Wigley, 1986). In the communication discipline, the study of aggressive communication has focused primarily on the examination of argumentativeness and verbal aggressiveness.

Three tenets guide a teacher's argumentativeness and verbal aggressiveness traits, which then affect how students perceive a teacher's credibility. First, argumentativeness is considered to be a constructive trait, whereas verbal aggressiveness is considered to be a destructive trait (Infante & Rancer, 1996). Argumentative teachers generally facilitate communication satisfaction and/or increase relational understanding, empathy, and intimacy between themselves and students; verbally aggressive teachers generally decrease relational satisfaction by making students feel less favorable toward the teacher and reducing the quality of the teacher–student relationship. Second, both argumentativeness and verbal aggressiveness can be viewed as an attack, even though the locus of the attack is different. This attack can then lead to an increase in students' levels of arousal and stress (Infante, 1987). Third, whether an aggressive act is judged as being either constructive or destructive depends on who is making the judgment (Infante, 1987). Within the instructional communication discipline, the study of aggressive communication has focused primarily on the study of students' perceptions of their teachers' argumentativeness and verbal aggressiveness (Myers, 2003c).

Classroom Studies

To date, six studies have explored the link between teacher credibility and teacher aggressive communication. In an unpublished study examining the relationship between teacher credibility and teacher aggressive communication, Martin, Weber, and Burant (1997) conducted an experiment in which 167 undergraduate students listened to a seven-minute, audiotaped lecture on kinesics. They posed a research question that asked whether a teacher's use of verbally aggressive messages and slang influence students' perceptions of both the teacher and the lecture. Four different conditions of the lecture were presented, in which the levels of the teacher's use of verbal aggressiveness (i.e., seven verbally aggressive messages) and slang (i.e., 10 expressions) varied. In the first condition, students listened to a lecture that contained verbally aggressive messages, but no slang. In the second condition, students listened to a lecture that contained a combination of verbally aggressive messages and slang. In the third condition, students listened to a lecture that contained slang, but no verbally aggressive messages. In the fourth condition, students listened to a lecture devoid of any verbally aggressive messages and slang. After students listened to one of the four conditions, they completed the Source Credibility Scale (McCroskey, Hamilton, & Weiner, 1974), an adapted version of the Conversational Appropriateness Scale (Canary & Spitzberg, 1987), the Generalized Immediacy Scale (Andersen, 1979), and the Affective Learning Scale (Kearney, Plax, & Wendt-Wasco, 1985). Students were also asked whether the university should hire the teacher.

Martin, Weber et al. (1997) obtained three findings. First, they found that the teacher who used verbally aggressive messages (condition one) was rated lower in perceived competence, character, affect, immediacy, and conversational appropriateness than the teacher who used either slang (condition three) or did not use either verbally aggressive messages or slang (condition four). Second, they found that the teacher who used verbally aggressive messages (condition one) and the teacher who used verbally aggressive messages and slang simultaneously (condition two) were not rated significantly different in perceived competence, character, affect, immediacy, or conversational appropriateness. There was a significant difference, however, in that the teacher who used verbally aggressive messages and slang simultaneously (condition two) was rated lower in perceived character, affect, and conversational appropriateness than the teacher who used only slang (condition three). Third, they found that the teacher who used verbally aggressive messages (condition one) was less likely to receive a recommendation from students to be hired by the university than the teacher in the other three conditions. Based on these results, Martin,

Weber et al. (1997) concluded that teachers should use slang cautiously and should not use verbally aggressive messages at all if they want students to perceive them as being competent and as possessing character.

In another unpublished study, Martin and Valencic (2001) conducted a similar experiment in which they were interested in examining whether teacher sex and student sex mediated the relationship between perceived teacher caring and teacher verbal aggressiveness. While they acknowledged previous research had demonstrated negative outcomes associated with teacher verbal aggressiveness, they wondered if it mattered to a student if a teacher who was verbally aggressive had shown in the past a sincere interest (i.e., caring) in the student. Participants were 492 undergraduate students who received one of four scenarios in which they were to imagine meeting with a teacher to discuss an exam score. In the scenario, the teacher uttered a series of verbally aggressive messages. The four scenarios included a male teacher who was described as caring (scenario one), a male teacher who was described as not caring (scenario two), a female teacher who was described as caring (scenario three), and a female teacher who was described as not caring (scenario four). The verbally aggressive messages in all four scenarios were identical.

Prior to reading the scenario, students were informed this was the second course they had voluntarily chosen to take with the teacher and provided with the same description of the teachers' competence and character. Following the reading of the scenario, participants completed a series of items relating to teacher credibility (Koehn & Crowell, 1996; McCroskey et al., 1974; Teven & McCroskey, 1997), items taken from the Conversational Appropriateness scale (Canary & Spitzberg, 1987) and the Affective Learning scale (Kearney, Plax, & Wendt-Wasco, 1985), and items measuring motivation designed specifically for their study.

Two findings were obtained by Martin and Valencic (2001). First, the results of two multivariate analyses of variance revealed significant main effects for student sex and for perceived caring. Specifically, male students rated the teacher, regardless of the teacher's sex, higher in competence, character, and caring than female students. Additionally, male students rated the teacher, regardless of the teacher's sex, higher in affect and conversational appropriateness than female students. In terms of caring, participants who read the scenarios containing a caring teacher rated these teachers as higher in caring than participants who read the scenarios containing a not caring teacher. Second, although participants were *informed* that the teacher was high in competence and character across all four scenarios, participants still *rated* the teacher relatively low in competence and character. This second finding prompted Martin and Valencic to conclude that regardless of the information given to students about a teacher, teacher use of verbally aggressive messages negatively influences students' perceptions of the teacher's credibility.

Myers (2001) investigated the relationship between the dimensions of perceived teacher credibility (i.e., competence, character, caring) and perceived teacher verbal aggressiveness. Participants were 273 undergraduate students who completed the Measure of Source Credibility (McCroskey & Teven, 1999), a modified version of the Verbal Aggressiveness Scale (Infante & Wigley, 1986; see Figure 4.4),

FIGURE 4.4 ***Modified Version of Verbal Aggressiveness Scale.***

Instructions: Record your impressions of the way the teacher you just identified communicates while teaching. Indicate how often each statement is true for your teacher. Use the following scale:

1 = Almost never true
2 = Rarely true
3 = Occasionally true
4 = Often true
5 = Almost always true

1. My teacher is extremely careful to avoid attacking students' intelligence when he/she attacks their ideas.*
2. When students are acting stubborn, my teacher uses insults to soften their stubbornness.
3. My teacher tries hard to avoid having students feel bad about themselves when he/she tries to influence them.*
4. When students refuse to do a task my teacher knows is important, my teacher tells them they are unreasonable.
5. When students do things my teacher regards as stupid, my teacher tries to be extremely gentle with them.*
6. If students my teacher are trying to influence really deserve it, my teacher attacks their character.
7. When students will not budge on a matter of importance, my teacher loses his/her temper and says rather strong things to them.
8. When students criticize my teacher's shortcomings, my teacher takes it in good humor and does not try to get back at them.*
9. My teacher likes poking fun at students who do things that are stupid in order to stimulate their intelligence.
10. When nothing seems to work in trying to influence students, my teacher yells and screams in order to get some movement from them.

Note. The original scale is a 20-item, self-report measure. This version of the original scale has been modified to a 10-item, other-report measure in that students reference their teacher. Items marked with an asterisk should be reverse-coded before scoring. The higher the summed score, the higher the perceived verbal aggressiveness of the teacher.

Modified from "Verbal Aggressiveness: An Interpersonal Model and Measure," by D. A. Infante and C. J. Wigley, III, 1986, *Communication Monographs, 53,* 61–68. Modified with permission of *Communication Education* and Taylor & Francis Ltd. http://www.tandf.co.uk/journals.

and the Recall of Verbal Aggression Instrument (Infante, Sabourin, Rudd, & Shannon, 1990; see Figure 4.5).

The results indicated a negative relationship between each dimension of teacher credibility (i.e., competence, character, caring) and perceived teacher verbal aggressiveness, although the negative correlations between both perceived teacher character and caring and teacher verbal aggressiveness were higher than the negative correlation obtained between perceived teacher competence and teacher verbal aggressiveness. Additionally, with the exception of a nonsignificant relationship

FIGURE 4.5 ***Recall of Verbal Aggression Instrument.***

Instructions: Record your impressions of the way the teacher you just identified communicates while teaching. Indicate how often each statement is true for your teacher. Use the following scale:

1 = Almost never true
2 = Rarely true
3 = Occasionally true
4 = Often true
5 = Almost always true

1. My teacher says unfavorable things about the character of the students enrolled in the class. (character attack)
2. My teacher makes negative comments about the competence level of students enrolled in the class. (competence attack)
3. My teacher attacks the personal background of students enrolled in the class. (background attack)
4. My teacher expresses dissatisfaction with the physical appearance of students enrolled in the class. (physical appearance attack)
5. My teacher says he/she hopes something bad will happen to students enrolled in the class. (malediction)
6. My teacher teases students enrolled in the class. (teasing)
7. My teacher ridicules the shortcomings of students enrolled in the class. (ridicule)
8. My teacher threatens to punish students enrolled in the class. (threats)
9. My teacher swears at and uses obscene language with students enrolled in the class. (swearing)
10. My teacher uses facial expressions, gestures, and/or eye behaviors that attack the self-concepts of students enrolled in the class. (nonverbal emblems)

From "Verbal Aggression in Violent and Nonviolent Marital Disputes," by D. A. Infante, T. C. Sabourin, J. E. Rudd, and E. A. Shannon, 1990, *Communication Quarterly, 38,* 361–371. Republished with permission of the Eastern Communication Association.

between perceived teacher competence and teasing, perceived teacher competence, character, and caring were negatively correlated with perceived teacher use of 10 types of verbally aggressive messages (i.e., character, competence, background, and physical appearance attacks; malediction; threats; ridicule; swearing; nonverbal emblems). These findings prompted Myers to conclude that perceived teacher character and teacher caring may be more negatively impacted by teacher verbal aggressiveness than perceived teacher competence, in part because college students expect their teachers to be competent. Students who perceive their teachers as possessing less character and demonstrating less caring may attribute these perceptions to a flaw in the teacher's personality, not to a flaw in teacher's ability to play the teacher role.

Teven (2001) explored the relationship between several perceived teacher interpersonal communication behaviors, one of which was verbal aggressiveness, and perceived teacher caring. He hypothesized a negative relationship would exist between perceived teacher verbal aggressiveness and perceived teacher caring.

FIGURE 4.6 ***Modified Version of the Argumentativeness Scale.***

Instructions: Record your impressions of the way the teacher you just identified communicates while teaching. Indicate how often you perceive the statement to be true for your teacher. Use the following scale:

1 = Almost never true
2 = Rarely true
3 = Occasionally true
4 = Often true
5 = Almost always true

1. My teacher enjoys avoiding arguments with students.*
2. My teacher is energetic and enthusiastic when he or she argues.
3. My teacher enjoys a good argument over a controversial issue with students.
4. My teacher enjoys defending his/her point of view on an issue.
5. My teacher is happy when she/he keeps an argument with students from happening.*
6. My teacher prefers talking with students who rarely disagree with her/him.*
7. My teacher considers an argument with students to be an exciting intellectual challenge.
8. My teacher is unable to think of effective points during an argument with students.*
9. My teacher has the ability to do well in an argument with students.
10. My teacher tries to avoid getting into arguments with students.*

Note. The original scale is a 20-item, self-report measure. This version of the original scale has been modified to a 10-item, other-report measure in that students reference their teacher. Items marked with an asterisk should be reverse-coded before scoring. The higher the summed score, the higher the perceived argumentativeness of the teacher.

From "A Conceptualization and Measure of Argumentativeness," by D. A. Infante and A. S. Rancer, 1982, *The Journal of Personality Assessment, 46,* 72–80. Reprinted with permission of *The Journal of Personality Assessment.*

Participants were 249 undergraduate students who completed the Perceived Caring Scale (Teven & McCroskey, 1997) and a modified version of the Verbal Aggressiveness scale. The hypothesis was supported. According to Teven, the results offered in his study provide instructors with another way in which they can determine whether their students perceive them as caring.

Schrodt (2003a) proposed perceived teacher argumentativeness and verbal aggressiveness would affect students' perceptions of feeling understood as well as students' ratings of their teachers' credibility and overall teaching effectiveness. Participants were 228 undergraduate students who completed the Feelings of Understanding/Misunderstanding Scale (Cahn & Shulman, 1984), the Teacher Credibility Scale (McCroskey & Young, 1981), a departmental instructor evaluation form, and modified versions of the Argumentativeness (Infante & Rancer, 1982; Myers & Rocca, 2000; see Figure 4.6) and Verbal Aggressiveness (Infante & Wigley, 1986; Myers & Rocca, 2000; see Figure 4.4) scales. Schrodt obtained two findings. First, he found perceived teacher argumentativeness was positively correlated with perceived teacher competence, but not with teacher character; and perceived teacher verbal aggressiveness was negatively correlated with both perceived

FIGURE 4.7 ***Socio-Communicative Style.***

Instructions: Please indicate how well each of the following personality characteristics describes your teacher.

Always True	Mostly True	Often True	Sometimes True	Seldom True	Rarely True	Never True
7	6	5	4	3	2	1

— 1. Gentle
— 2. Tender
— 3. Acts as a leader
— 4. Responsive to others
— 5. Dominant
— 6. Aggressive
— 7. Warm
— 8. Sympathetic
— 9. Willing to take a stand
— 10. Defends own beliefs
— 11. Forceful
— 12. Compassionate
— 13. Sincere
— 14. Assertive
— 15. Helpful
— 16. Strong Personality
— 17. Competitive
— 18. Sensitive to the needs of others
— 19. Eager to soothe hurt feelings
— 20. Independent

Items 3, 5, 6, 9, 10, 11, 14, 16, 17, and 20 are added for an assertiveness score.
Items 1, 2, 4, 7, 8, 12, 13, 15, 18, and 19 are added for a responsiveness score.

From "Reliability and Separation of Factors on the Assertiveness-Responsiveness Measure," by V. P. Richmond and J. C. McCroskey, 1990, *Psychological Reports, 67*, 449–450. Reprinted with permission from *Psychological Reports.*

teacher competence and character. Second, when examining the extent to which perceived teacher argumentativeness and verbal aggressiveness and student understanding were correlated with perceived teacher credibility and teacher evaluation, he found perceived understanding was most closely related to perceived teacher credibility and teacher evaluation, and to a lesser extent, teacher argumentativeness and verbal aggressiveness. As such, Schrodt concluded teachers' "deployment of argumentative behaviors and simultaneous avoidance of verbally aggressive behaviors enhances students' perceptions of [their] credibility and evaluations" (p. 118).

Although the aforementioned studies focus on teachers' argumentativeness and verbal aggressiveness, another aggressive communication trait that has received considerable attention in the instructional communication discipline is assertiveness. Martin, Chesebro et al. (1997) investigated whether students' perceptions of teachers' sociocommunicative style (i.e., levels of assertiveness and responsiveness) were related to students' perceptions of their teachers' credibility. Participants were 260 undergraduate students who completed the Assertiveness-Responsiveness measure (Richmond & McCroskey, 1990; see Figure 4.7) and six, seven-point semantic differential items for each of the three credibility dimensions of competence, character, and caring (Koehn & Crowell, 1996; McCroskey, Hamilton et al., 1974; Teven & McCroskey, 1997).

Martin, Chesebro et al., found that teachers who were viewed as assertive and responsive were rated the highest across all three dimensions of credibility. Additionally, teachers who were considered assertive but not responsive were viewed as more competent and caring, but having lower character, than teachers who were considered low in both assertiveness and responsiveness. They concluded that when teachers are both assertive and responsive, they will be perceived by students as being competent, possessing character, and expressing caring, more so than teachers who are neither assertive nor responsive.

Knowledge Claims

Based on the research conducted on teacher credibility and aggressive communication traits, several claims can be made. These claims are:

1. Source credibility rests in the minds of students. Although teachers may strategically engage in communication behaviors to promote their competence, character, and caring, unless students perceive and respond to these behaviors accordingly, teachers will not be considered to be credible. Moreover, there is always a chance students will misinterpret the meaning or intent behind a teacher's communication behaviors. When this happens, a teacher's credibility can be enhanced or destroyed. The bottom line, according to Hurt, Scott, and McCroskey (1977), is that "teacher credibility is a perception on the part of the student, and does not necessarily correspond to reality" (p. 119). As such, students' *perceptions* of a teacher's credibility may have more far-reaching implications than a teacher's *actual* credibility.

2. To be perceived as believable, an instructor must be perceived as possessing competence, having character, and being capable of caring. It is possible for an instructor to be higher in one dimension than the other two dimensions, but students perceive their teachers as most credible when they are perceived as exhibiting all three dimensions (McCroskey, 1998).

3. Although teacher competence is essential for students to learn (Hurt et al., 1977), teacher character and caring are just as important. Because the teacher-student relationship is both content- and relationally-driven (Frymier & Houser, 2000), students are motivated to communicate with their teachers for a host of reasons other than needing to acquire knowledge and content-related material. These reasons include a desire to get to know teachers on a personal level, to demonstrate knowledge of the course material, and a desire to make a favorable impression on the teacher (Martin, Myers, & Mottet, 2002). When teachers are perceived to be competent, to have character, and to be caring, it is possible teacher–student communication can be enhanced, both in terms of quality and quantity.

4. In terms of teacher aggressive communication, teacher verbal aggressiveness may have more of a detrimental effect on teacher credibility than teacher argumentativeness. Verbally aggressive teachers are perceived to engage in verbal aggression as a way to attack students' competence, to psychologically distance themselves from students, to criticize students' classroom behaviors, and to discourage student participation in class (Myers, 2003b). Moreover, when teachers are verbally aggressive, students view the classroom climate as defensive (Myers & Rocca, 2001) and are less satisfied with their educational experience (Myers & Knox, 2000). Conversely, argumentative teachers may engage in argumentativeness as a way to increase students' participation, to enhance students' learning, or to keep students' attention (Myers, 1998). As such, aggressive teachers would be well-advised to decrease their use of verbally aggressive behaviors and increase their use of argumentative behaviors in the classroom. Teachers may play more of a role in how students perceive their credibility than was previously believed.

5. Students view teachers who are higher in assertiveness more favorably than teachers who are lower in assertiveness (Martin, Chesebro et al., 1997). When teachers are both assertive and responsive, they are viewed as competent, trustworthy, and caring. Results involving assertiveness in the instructional context (Thomas et al., 1994; Wooten & McCroskey, 1996), the mass communication context (Neupauer, 1996), and the organizational context (Martin & Anderson, 1996; Martin, Anderson, & Sirimangkala, 1999) support the importance of teachers possessing the ability to be assertive. Teachers need to understand that students expect them to be assertive, but not verbally aggressive, when communicating both in and out of the classroom.

Directions for Future Research

Although a great deal of research has been conducted on teacher credibility, there are several avenues of research worthy of further investigation. These avenues include addressing the following five questions:

1. To what degree do teacher demographics (i.e., sex, race, ethnicity, culture, sexual orientation) affect students' perceptions of teacher credibility? Although several studies have examined the influence of teacher sex (Martin & Valencic, 2001; Nadler & Nadler, 2001), teacher race (Patton, 1999), and teacher sexual orientation (Russ et al., 2002) on students' perceptions of teacher credibility, the research conducted in this area is relatively sparse. Because it can be argued that students interact differently with their teachers based on teacher demographics (Bennett, 1982), additional research in this area should be conducted in order to gain a more comprehensive picture of the role teacher demographics plays in students' perceptions of teacher credibility.

2. What role does teacher credibility play, and how is teacher credibility associated with student outcomes, in the K–12 classroom? Currently, not much is known about the role teacher credibility plays in the K–12 classroom. McCroskey (1992) posited the importance of the dimensions of teacher credibility changes as students progress through the educational system. For example, teacher competence usually becomes incrementally important as students move from lower grade levels to high school (Hurt et al., 1977). Yet, little empirical evidence exists that documents these notions. By examining the role teacher credibility plays in the elementary and secondary education classrooms, the study of teacher credibility can be expanded to include students across all educational settings.

3. How does teacher credibility change over time? The bulk of the research conducted on teacher credibility has examined students' perceptions of their teachers' credibility toward the *end* of the semester. Although this methodology makes sense, it is possible students' perceptions of their teachers' credibility change during the semester. In a longitudinal study of teacher credibility, McGlone and Anderson (1973) found perceived instructor competence becomes less of an issue over the course of a semester. They discovered that during the first week of a semester, perceived instructor expertness (i.e., competence) was the primary factor upon which students based their perceptions of teacher credibility. By the third week of the semester, students considered a mix of perceived expertness and trustworthiness (i.e., character) as the primary determinant of teacher credibility; by the fifth week of the semester, students considered trustworthiness as the primary determinant of teacher credibility; and by the final week of the semester, students considered teacher personality (i.e., a mix of character and caring characteristics) as the primary determinant of teacher credibility. Thus, student attention to particular dimensions of teacher credibility may simultaneously increase and decrease as the semester progresses, and should be explored. The reasons behind why students shift their attention from one dimension of teacher credibility to another dimension of teacher credibility should also be explored.

4. Could students' own aggressive communication traits influence how credible they view their teachers to be? Students who are highly aggressive might view a teacher as less credible than students who are not as aggressive. Most recently, Schrodt (2003b) found that students who report moderate to high levels of trait verbal aggressiveness rate their teachers as being more verbally aggressive than students who report low levels of trait verbal aggressiveness. Although research has aptly demonstrated the relationship that exists between students' perceptions of teacher aggressive communication behaviors and teacher credibility, future research will need to explore what role students' aggressive communication traits play, if any, in their evaluations of their teachers' credibility. Of further interest, possibly certain cultures would view teacher aggressive communication behaviors differently, and thus, students of those cultures may differ in their perceptions of teacher credibility.

5. What teacher verbal and nonverbal communication behaviors do students expect, and how can these behaviors enhance (or destroy) students' perceptions of teacher competence, teacher character, and teacher caring? Generally, college students expect their teachers to engage in verbal and nonverbal communication behaviors appropriate for the classroom setting. These behaviors include being approachable, friendly, and affirming (Chen, 2000); at the same time, college students do not expect their teachers to be offensive, indolent, or incompetent

(Kearney, Plax, Hays, & Ivey, 1991). When teachers engage in intense and aggressive displays of anger, these displays are considered by students to be socially inappropriate (McPherson, Kearney, & Plax, 2003). Thus, a further exploration of teacher anger, as well as other verbal communication behaviors, such as humor orientation, affinity seeking, and conversational sensitivity, may be warranted. By exploring this direction, it may be possible to determine whether (and how) teachers' use of these behaviors affect how students view their competence, character, and caring.

References

Andersen, J. F. (1979). Teacher immediacy as a predictor of teaching effectiveness. In D. Nimmo (Ed.), *Communication yearbook 3* (pp. 543–559). New Brunswick, NJ: Transaction.

Baringer, D. K., & McCroskey, J. C. (2000). Immediacy in the classroom: Student immediacy. *Communication Education, 49,* 178–186.

Berlo, D. K., Lemert, J. B., & Mertz, R. (1969). Dimensions for evaluating the acceptance of message sources. *Public Opinion Quarterly, 33,* 563–576.

Bennett, S. K. (1982). Student perceptions of and expectations for male and female instructors: Evidence relating to the question of gender bias in teaching evaluation. *Journal of Educational Psychology, 74,* 170–179.

Cahn, D. D., & Shulman, G. M. (1984). The perceived understanding instrument. *Communication Research Reports, 1,* 122–125.

Canary, D. J., & Spitzberg, B. H. (1987). Appropriateness and effectiveness perceptions of conflict strategies. *Human Communication Research, 14,* 93–188.

Chen, Z. (2000). The impact of teacher–student relationships on college students' learning: Exploring organizational culture in the classroom. *Qualitative Research Reports in Communication, 1,* 76–83.

Cooper, L. (1932). *The rhetoric of Aristotle.* New York: Appleton-Century-Crofts.

Falcione, R. L. (1974). The factor structure of source credibility scales for immediate superiors in the organizational context. *Central States Speech Journal, 25,* 63–66.

Frymier, A. B., & Thompson, C. A. (1992). Perceived teacher affinity-seeking in relation to perceived teacher credibility. *Communication Education, 41,* 388–399.

Frymier, A. B., & Houser, M. L. (2000). The teacher-student relationship as an interpersonal relationship. *Communication Education, 49,* 207–219.

Hovland, C. I., Janis, I. L., & Kelley, H. H. (1953). *Communication and persuasion.* New Haven, CT: Yale University Press.

Hurt, H. T., Scott, M. D., & McCroskey, J. C. (1977). *Communication in the classroom.* Reading, MA: Addison-Wesley.

Infante, D. A. (1980). The construct validity of semantic differential scales for the measurement of source credibility. *Communication Quarterly, 28,* 19–26.

Infante, D. A. (1987). Aggressiveness. In J. C. McCroskey & J. A. Daly (Eds.), *Personality and interpersonal communication* (pp. 157–192). Newbury Park, CA: Sage.

Infante, D. A. (1995). Teaching students to understand and control verbal aggression. *Communication Education, 44,* 51–63.

Infante, D. A., & Rancer, A. S. (1982). A conceptualization and measure of argumentativeness. *Journal of Personality Assessment, 46,* 72–80.

Infante, D. A., & Rancer, A. S. (1996). Argumentativeness and verbal aggressiveness: A review of recent theory and research. In B. R. Burleson (Ed.), *Communication yearbook 19* (pp. 319–351). Thousand Oaks, CA: Sage.

Infante, D. A., Rancer, A. S., & Womack, D. F. (2003). *Building communication theory* (4th ed.). Prospect Heights, IL: Waveland.

Infante, D. A., Sabourin, T. C., Rudd, J. E., & Shannon, E. A. (1990). Verbal aggression in violent and nonviolent marital disputes. *Communication Quarterly, 38,* 361–371.

Infante, D. A., & Wigley, C. J., III. (1986). Verbal aggressiveness: An interpersonal model and measure. *Communication Monographs, 53,* 61–68.

Johnson, S. D., & Miller, A. N. (2002). A cross-cultural study of immediacy, credibility, and learning in the U. S. and Kenya. *Communication Education, 51,* 280–292.

Kearney, P., Plax, T. G., Hays, E. R., & Ivey, M. J. (1991). College teacher misbehaviors: What students don't like about what teachers say and do. *Communication Quarterly, 39,* 309–324.

Kearney, P., Plax, T. G., & Wendt-Wasco, N. J. (1985). Teacher immediacy for affective learning in divergent college courses. *Communication Quarterly, 33,* 61–74.

Koehn, S. C., & Crowell, T. (1996, November). *The development of a perceived caring scale for educators and students.* Paper presented at the annual meeting of the Speech Communication Association, San Diego, CA.

Markham, D. (1968). The dimensions of source credibility of television newscasters. *Journal of Communication, 18,* 57–64.

Martin, M. M., & Anderson, C. M. (1996). Argumentativeness and verbal aggressiveness. *Journal of Social Behavior and Personality, 11,* 547–554.

Martin, M. M., Anderson, C. M., & Sirimangkala, P. (1999). The relationship between use of organizational conflict strategies with socio-communicative style and aggressive communication traits. *Communication Research Reports, 16,* 370–376.

Martin, M. M., Chesebro, J. L., & Mottet, T. P. (1997). Students' perceptions of instructors' socio-communicative style and the influence on instructor credibility and situational motivation. *Communication Research Reports, 14,* 431–440.

Martin, M. M., Myers, S. A., & Mottet, T. P. (2002). Students' motives for communicating with their instructors. In J. L. Chesebro & J. C. McCroskey (Eds.), *Communication for teachers* (pp. 35–46). Boston: Allyn & Bacon.

Martin, M. M., & Valencic, K. M. (2001, November). *The effect of an instructor's caring and instructor's and student's sex when an instructor is verbally aggressive with a student.* Paper presented at the annual meeting of the National Communication Association, Atlanta, GA.

Martin, M. M., Weber, K., & Burant, P. A. (1997, April). *Students' perceptions of a teacher's use of slang and verbal aggressiveness in a lecture: An experiment.* Paper presented at the annual meeting of the Eastern Communication Association, Baltimore, MD.

Martinez-Egger, A. D., & Powers, W. G. (2002, November). *Student respect for a teacher: Measurement and relationships to teacher credibility and classroom behavior perceptions.* Paper presented at the annual meeting of the National Communication Association, New Orleans, LA.

McCroskey, J. C. (1966). Scales for the measurement of ethos. *Speech Monographs, 33,* 65–72.

McCroskey, J. C. (1992). *An introduction to communication in the classroom.* Edina, MN: Burgess.

McCroskey, J. C. (1994). Assessment of affect toward communication and affect toward instruction in communication. In S. Morreale & M. Brooks (Eds.), *Assessing college student competency in speech communication* (pp. 56–71). Annandale, VA: Speech Communication Association.

McCroskey, J. C. (1998). *An introduction to communication in the classroom* (2nd ed.). Acton, MA: Tapestry.

McCroskey, J. C., Hamilton, P. R., & Weiner, A. M. (1974). The effects of interaction behavior on source credibility, homophily, and interpersonal attraction. *Human Communication Research, 1,* 42–52.

McCroskey, J. C., Holdridge, W., & Toomb, J. K. (1974). An instrument for measuring the source credibility of basic speech communication instructors. *Speech Teacher, 23,* 26–33.

McCroskey, J. C., & Mehrley, R. S. (1969). The effects of disorganization and nonfluency on attitude change and source credibility. *Speech Monographs, 36,* 13–21.

McCroskey, J. C., & Teven, J. J. (1999). Goodwill: A reexamination of the construct and its measurement. *Communication Monographs, 66,* 90–103.

McCroskey, J. C., & Young, T. J. (1981). Ethos and credibility: The construct and its measurement after three decades. *Central States Speech Journal, 32,* 24–34.

McGlone, E. L., & Anderson, L. J. (1973). The dimensions of teacher credibility. *Speech Teacher, 22,* 196–200.

McPherson, M. B., Kearney, P., & Plax, T. G. (2003). The dark side of instruction: Teacher anger as classroom norm violations. *Journal of Applied Communication Research, 31,* 76–90.

Myers, S. A. (1998). Instructor socio-communicative style, argumentativeness, and verbal aggressiveness in the college classroom. *Communication Research Reports, 15,* 141–150.

Myers, S. A. (2001). Perceived instructor credibility and verbal aggressiveness in the college classroom. *Communication Research Reports, 18,* 354–364.

Myers, S. A. (2002). Perceived aggressive instructor communication and student state motivation, learning, and satisfaction. *Communication Reports, 15,* 113–121.

Myers, S. A. (2003a, November). *The influence of perceived instructor credibility on college student in-class and out-of-class communication.* Paper presented at the annual meeting of the National Communication Association, Miami, FL.

Myers, S. A. (2003b, April). *A typological analysis of perceived instructor verbal aggressiveness in the college classroom.* Paper presented at the annual meeting of the Central States Communication Association, Omaha, NE.

Myers, S. A. (2003c, April). *Argumentativeness and aggressiveness research in instructional communication contexts.* Paper presented at the annual meeting of the Eastern Communication Association, Washington, DC.

Myers, S. A., & Bryant, L. E. (2002). Perceived understanding, interaction involvement, and college student outcomes. *Communication Research Reports, 19,* 146–155.

Myers, S. A., & Knox, R. L. (2000). Perceived instructor argumentativeness and verbal aggressiveness and student outcomes. *Communication Research Reports, 17,* 299–309.

Myers, S. A., & Rocca, K. A. (2000). The relationship between perceived instructor communicator style, argumentativeness, and verbal aggressiveness. *Communication Research Reports, 17,* 1–12.

Myers, S. A., & Rocca, K. A. (2001). Perceived instructor argumentativeness and verbal aggressiveness in the college classroom: Effects on student perceptions of climate, apprehension, and state motivation. *Western Journal of Communication, 65,* 113–127.

Nadler, M. K., & Nadler, L. B. (2001). The roles of sex, empathy, and credibility in out-of-class communication between faculty and students. *Women's Studies in Communication, 24,* 239–261.

Neupauer, N. C. (1996). Individual differences in on-air television and radio personalities. *Communication Research Reports, 13,* 77–85.

Norman, W. T. (1963). Toward an adequate taxonomy of personality attributes: Replicated factor structure in peer nomination personality ratings. *Journal of Abnormal and Social Psychology, 66,* 574–583.

Patton, T. O. (1999). Ethnicity and gender: An examination of its impact on instructor credibility in the university classroom. *The Howard Journal of Communications, 10,* 123–144.

Ragsdale, J. D., & Mikels, A. L. (1975). Effects of question periods on a speaker's credibility with a television audience. *Southern Speech Communication Journal, 40,* 302–312.

Richmond, V. P., & McCroskey, J. C. (1990). Reliability and separation of factors on the assertiveness-responsiveness measure. *Psychological Reports, 67,* 449–450.

Richmond, V. P., McCroskey, J. C., Kearney, P., & Plax, T. G. (1987). Power in the classroom VII: Linking behavior alteration techniques to cognitive learning. *Communication Education, 36,* 1–12.

Robinson, R. Y. (1993). The usefulness of the verbal receptivity construct in instructional communication research. *Communication Quarterly, 41,* 292–298.

Russ, T. L., Simonds, C. J., & Hunt, S. K. (2002). Coming out in the classroom . . . An occupational hazard: The influence of sexual orientation on teacher credibility and perceived student learning. *Communication Education, 51,* 311–324.

Schrodt, P. (2003a). Students' appraisals of instructors as a function of students' perceptions of instructors' aggressive communication. *Communication Education, 52,* 106–121.

Schrodt, P. (2003b). Student perceptions of instructor verbal aggressiveness: The influence of student verbal aggressiveness and self-esteem. *Communication Research Reports, 20,* 240–250.

Teven, J. J. (2001). The relationships among teacher characteristics and perceived caring. *Communication Education, 50,* 159–169.

Teven, J. J., & McCroskey, J. C. (1997). The relationship of perceived teacher caring with student learning and teacher evaluation. *Communication Education, 46,* 1–9.

Thomas, C. E., Richmond, V. P., & McCroskey, J. C. (1994). The association between immediacy and socio-communicative style. *Communication Research Reports, 11,* 107–114.

Thweatt, K. S. (1999, November). *The impact of teacher immediacy, teacher affinity-seeking, and teacher misbehaviors on student-perceived teacher credibility.* Paper presented at the annual meeting of the National Communication Association, Chicago, IL.

Thweatt, K. S., & McCroskey, J. C. (1998). The impact of teacher immediacy and misbehaviors on teacher credibility. *Communication Education, 47,* 348–358.

Wheeless, L. R. (1973). Effects of explicit credibility statements by more credible and less credible sources. *Southern Speech Communication Journal, 39,* 33–39.

Wheeless, L. R. (1975). Relationship of four elements to immediate recall and student-teacher interaction. *Western Speech Communication, 39,* 131–140.

Wooten, A. G., & McCroskey, J. C. (1996). Student trust of teacher as a function of socio-communicative style of teacher and socio-communicative orientation of student. *Communication Research Reports, 13,* 94–100.

Wrench, J. S., & Richmond, V. P. (2000, November). *The relationships between teacher humor assessment and motivation, credibility, verbal aggression, affective learning, perceived learning, and learning loss.* Paper presented at the annual meeting of the National Communication Association, Seattle, WA.

5

Instructional Message Variables

Joseph L. Chesebro
SUNY Brockport

Melissa Bekelja Wanzer
Canisius College

Introduction

Every day classroom teachers are responsible for reaching and engaging students. This process of "engaging students" typically involves overcoming a number of potential barriers, including students' lack of attention, enthusiasm, or interest in the material being taught. Even if these problems are minimal in one's classroom, an additional challenge is effectively explaining course material. Fortunately, instructional communication research has identified a number of techniques teachers can adopt to overcome these challenges.

In this chapter we focus on the messages teachers use and the ways teachers can use them effectively in the classroom to enhance learning outcomes. As Mottet and Beebe suggest in Chapter 1, effective teaching typically involves the use of a variety of rhetorical strategies. Highly effective teachers will utilize a variety of verbal messages to gain students' attention, make material more interesting, and help students transfer information from their short-term to long-term memories. Not surprisingly, some rhetorical strategies have proved to be more effective than others in facilitating the learning process. More specifically, the research shows that teachers can be more effective in the classroom when they use messages that are clear, relevant, and humorous. This chapter will highlight research on these types of instructional messages, discuss a number of knowledge claims yielded from the research, and provide ideas for future research in these areas.

In the first part of this chapter we examine the construct of relevance, which involves the extent to which course material is linked to students' interests, needs, or future goals. In addition to making course material relevant, teachers should also use clear messages to increase student learning. Research on teacher clarity, recognized as a cluster of behaviors that enhances the fidelity of classroom messages, will be examined more thoroughly in this chapter as well. Effective teaching also involves making the messages interesting or memorable. One way that teachers can improve the classroom environment and facilitate learning is by using humorous messages that are classroom-appropriate.

Content Relevance

The act of gaining and keeping students' attention involves both delivering a message with appropriately engaging nonverbal behaviors (e.g., immediacy) and encoding the message itself in a way that will connect with students. This section focuses on the content of the message itself by examining the message variable of *content relevance.* Content relevance refers to student perception of whether instructional course content satisfies personal needs, personal goals, and/or career goals (Keller, 1983). Although content relevance has not been researched extensively, the research that does exist supports the importance of making content relevant to students' interests, needs, and goals.

Overview of Content Relevance

The significance of content relevance in the classroom first was identified in Keller's work in the area of instructional design (Keller, 1983, 1987). Keller designed a model, Attention, Relevance, Confidence, and Satisfaction (ARCS), with the goal of providing an instructional system for enhancing student motivation to learn (Keller, 1987).

The development of this model was grounded in expectancy–value theory, a theory designed to explain human motivation. According to expectancy–value theory, people will be motivated to do something (1) if they expect to succeed at it (expectancy) and (2) if it is linked to the satisfaction of personal needs (value).

Keller modified the original expectancy–value model and expanded it into four categories (Keller, 1983). The "expectancy" category remained unchanged, but the "value" category was divided into two categories, "interest" and "relevance." Keller argued that something of interest tapped into an individual's curiosity, whereas something relevant was linked to a person's goals. For example, some students might value a topic like systems theory out of curiosity (interest) while others might value systems theory because it relates to their goals for communicating more effectively within a system, such as a family or an organization (relevance). Finally, Keller (1987) added a fourth category, "satisfaction of outcomes," in recognition that the outcome of a behavior can influence whether an individual will want to repeat the behavior. With these four categories in place and renamed, the ARCS model was complete (Keller, 1987).

Keller (1987) then set out to identify specific instructional strategies that fit into each of the four categories. A number of sources, including research findings, information on successful instructional practices, interviews with teachers, and practical teaching guides, were consulted in order to develop a list of strategies. Four research assistants then classified the strategies into one of the four categories of the ARCS model. The specific strategies placed into the relevance category are listed in Table 5.1.

TABLE 5.1 ***Strategies to Make Content More Relevant.***

Strategy Types	*Specific Examples of Each Type of Strategy*
Future usefulness of the material	-Explain how material relates to the learners' future activities. -Ask learners to relate the material to their own future goals.
Present worth of the material	-State ways in which students currently can benefit from learning the content.
Match students' needs to the material	-Provide opportunities for successful achievement. -Provide opportunities for students to exercise responsibility and influence.
Relate material to students' experience	-Explain how material builds on existing skills. -Use analogies familiar to the learner. -Identify the learners' interests and relate them to the material.
Modeling	-Bring alumni from the course in as guest lecturers. -Model enthusiasm for the subject.
Choice	-Provide alternative methods for accomplishing a goal. -Provide personal choices for organizing work.

Adapted from "Strategies for Stimulating the Motivation to Learn," by J. M. Keller, 1987, *Performance and Instruction, 26,* p. 4.

The Study of Relevance in Instructional Communication Research

Keller's model has been applied successfully to instructional design in a number of contexts, including regular classroom instruction, self-paced written instruction, and computer-based instruction (Keller, 1999; Means, Jonassen, & Dwyer, 1997; Small & Gluck, 1994). In a study on motivational strategies used by teachers, relevance was the only strategy related to student's on-task behavior (Newby, 1991). Although relevance was not a focus of this study, its emergence provided initial support for Keller's identification of relevance as an important instructional variable. Following from this early support, the relevance dimension of the model was investigated in an instructional communication context in a series of studies by Frymier and colleagues (Frymier & Shulman, 1995; Frymier & Houser, 1998; Frymier, Shulman, & Houser, 1996).

Frymier and Shulman (1995) developed a 12-item scale to measure students' reports of their teachers' use of relevance strategies in the classroom. Scale items include both high-inference and low-inference items. High-inference items ask respondents for more global or generic perceptions, while low-inference items ask respondents to report on more specific behaviors that require a less subjective interpretation by respondents. Because respondents can focus on specific behaviors, less is left to infer subjectively. For example, "Provides explanations that make the content relevant to me." is a high-inference item, whereas "Gives assignments that involve the application of the content to my career interests." (p. 46), is a low-inference item. The entire scale is provided in Figure 5.1.

FIGURE 5.1 *Content Relevance Scale.*

Directions: Read each statement and use the following scale to indicate how frequently your teacher performs each of the behaviors. There are no right or wrong answers.

Never = 0 Rarely = 1 Occasionally = 2 Often = 3 Very Often = 4

1. ___ Uses examples to make the content relevant to me.
2. ___ Provides explanations that make the content relevant to me.
3. ___ Uses exercises or explanations that demonstrate the importance of the content.
4. ___ Explicitly states how the material relates to my career goals or my life in general.
5. ___ Links content to other areas of content.
6. ___ Asks me to apply content to my own interests.
7. ___ Gives assignments that involve the application of the content to my career interests.
8. ___ Helps me to understand the importance of the content.
9. ___ Uses own experiences to introduce or demonstrate a concept.
10. ___ Uses student experiences to demonstrate or introduce a concept.
11. ___ Uses discussion to help me understand the relevance of a topic.
12. ___ Uses current events to apply a topic.

From " 'What's In It for Me?': Increasing Content Relevance to Enhance Students' Motivation," by A. B. Frymier and G. M. Shulman, 1995, *Communication Education*, *44*, 40–50. Republished with permission by *Communication Education* and Taylor & Francis Ltd. http://www.tandf.co.uk/journals.

The study examined the frequency with which instructors used relevance strategies, the relationships between students' reports of their teachers' relevance behaviors and their own state motivation to learn, and the relative impact of both immediacy and relevance on students' state motivation to learn. Nonverbal immediacy is a perception of physical and/or psychological closeness that is generated by a cluster of nonverbal behaviors, including eye contact, vocal variety, a relaxed body posture, gesturing, and smiling. Immediacy is the study and focus of Chapter 8.

The results of this study indicated a moderately strong correlation between relevance and state motivation. Greater use of relevance strategies was related to increased state motivation to learn. Unlike trait motivation, which refers to a person's motivation to learn in school in general, state motivation refers to motivation to learn in a particular course. While trait motivation is expected to vary little from course to course, state motivation is expected to vary more considerably. An additional aspect of the relevance–motivation finding is worth noting. Relevance explained unique variance in state motivation beyond the effects of verbal and nonverbal immediacy. In other words, the effects due to immediacy were removed from the "equation," and relevance alone still explained variation in motivation scores, independent of any overlap (shared variance) with verbal or nonverbal immediacy. This finding was important because it demonstrated that relevance alone, besides immediacy, played an important role in improving students' motivation to learn. In a similar study, Frymier, Shulman, and Houser (1996) reported that content relevance again was associated with increased motivation to learn, as well as a number of other important instructional outcomes, including students' affect towards the course material and the instructor, students' reports of empowerment, and use of effective learning behaviors.

Frymier and Houser (1998) used an experimental design to investigate the effects of both relevance and immediacy on student motivation and learning. Immediacy was studied because it is thought to be necessary to gain students' attention, thus enabling message factors, such as relevance and clarity, to have an effect. Although immediacy had an effect on motivation and learning, relevance did not. The authors explained the lack of effects for relevance by suggesting that their manipulation of relevance probably was not strong enough. In the experiment, examples were manipulated so that relevant examples would refer to things that were familiar to students and to local events. However, the topic itself (discussing comparisons in speeches) was relevant to the student participants, who themselves were in the process of preparing speeches. A topic less relevant to a public speaking course would have enabled the manipulation to actually change the relevance of each condition. Frymier (2002) reports a similar manipulation problem with an additional relevance study by Behrens (1999). However, even with this problematic manipulation, two measures of relevance were correlated with motivation to study and affective learning ($r = 0.41$ and $r = 0.52$).

An additional type of support for relevance comes from studies that aim to identify effective teaching behaviors, such as those that help motivate students. In studies of this nature, the relevance of content frequently emerges as an important and effective aspect of a teacher's message. In their program of studies on student motivation, Millette & Gorham (2002) report that, from a student perspective, the "perceived relevance of and interest in the subject area" was the most important factor influencing motivation to learn in a given class (p. 144). Similar results are observed by Cruickshank & Kennedy (1986) and Newby (1991).

Knowledge Claims

Collectively, this body of work on content relevance allows for a number of knowledge claims about making content more relevant for students:

1. Making content relevant to students is supported by a collection of studies, which have used a variety of methods, including survey instruments, observation, and open-ended questionnaires.
2. The use of relevance is related to students' reports of increased affect for instructors and subject material, motivation to learn, and a sense of having greater empowerment in the classroom.
3. The only studies that fail to offer support for the relevance of content are suspect because of problems manipulating relevance.

Directions for Future Research

Based on these claims, future areas worthy of research on relevance may focus on some of the following questions:

1. How can relevance be manipulated so that its role in the classroom can be better understood?
2. What are the most effective ways to make content relevant to students?
3. What student characteristics play an important role in the judgment, necessity, and effectiveness of relevance (for example: class rank, major area of study, traditional/nontraditional status)?
4. What learner strategies can students themselves enact that might help them better appreciate the relevance of course content?
5. When teaching in computer-mediated or distance-learning settings, what unique things do teachers have to do to make their content more relevant to students?

In addition to content relevance, teacher clarity has been identified as an important instructional message variable. It has attracted the attention of a number of researchers who have taken different approaches to studying clear messages. These approaches are reviewed next.

Teacher Clarity

Overview of Teacher Clarity

Upon reviewing a considerable number of studies examining teacher behaviors, Roshenshine and Furst (1971) argued that teacher clarity was the most important teacher behavior worth consideration for research and teacher training. (Incidentally, teacher enthusiasm, which is similar to teacher immediacy, was also among the most important variables they identified). Although studies related to clarity had been conducted before their article was published, Rosenshine and Furst generally are credited for bringing clarity to the attention of researchers and practitioners.

As other reviews of the clarity construct have noted (see, for example, Civikly, 1992; Daly & Vangelisti, 2003), there are a variety of definitions for teacher clarity. Cruickshank and Kennedy (1986) defined clarity as "a cluster of teacher behaviors that result in learners gaining knowledge or understanding of a topic, if they possess adequate interest, aptitude, opportunity, and time" (p. 43). Powell and Harville (1990) provided perhaps the most parsimonious definition, stating that clarity is "concerned with the fidelity of instructional messages" (p. 372). These definitions complement each other well. The first leaves a broad interpretation of the considerable number of behaviors, some of which may not be concerned with clarity that can result in learners gaining knowledge of a topic. The second definition leaves room for greater elaboration about what is involved in clear teaching. However, by combining them, one can better understand clarity as *a cluster of teacher behaviors that contributes to the fidelity of instructional messages.* Clarity thereby enables students to better understand a topic, if they have adequate opportunity and motivation.

Research on clarity has followed an interesting trajectory, in the sense that a variety of programs have studied different aspects of teacher behaviors related to clear teaching. A number of impressive reviews of research and clear teaching behaviors are available (Chesebro & McCroskey, 1998b; Civikly, 1992; Cruickshank & Kennedy, 1986; Daly & Vangelisti, 2003). In conducting this review, we will focus on some of the major research programs and single studies that have been conducted since the appearance of the Rosenshine and Furst (1971) article.

The Ohio State Studies

The Ohio State studies on teacher clarity were conducted between 1975 and 1985. These seminal studies began with an attempt to discover the specific teaching behaviors that students perceived as enhancing the clarity of a lesson. The researchers began by surveying over 1,000 junior-high students to (1) recall his or her clearest teacher, and (2) list five things the teacher did when teaching clearly (Cruickshank, Myers, & Moenjak, 1975, cited in Cruickshank & Kennedy, 1986). After filtering out responses that were irrelevant or otherwise not useful, the researchers were left with a list of 110 distinct behaviors, which they then categorized into one of 12 categories, including "teaching things in a step-by-step manner, repeating and stressing directions and difficult points," and "communicating so students understand."

Bush, Kennedy, and Cruickshank (1977) then created instruments with the 110 low-inference behaviors to test the extent to which they could be used to discriminate between clear and unclear teachers. Those behaviors that most distinguished clear from unclear teachers tended to fall within two factors: (1) explaining and (2) providing for student understanding. A similar study by Kennedy et al., (1978) refined the list of behaviors even further and obtained consistent results from students in Australia, Tennessee, and Ohio. Hines (1981, cited in Cruickshank & Kennedy, 1986) then replicated these findings with college-age students, thus addressing one of the primary concerns raised by those who conducted the earlier studies—that the findings would be different for students in different age groups. At this point, the key clear teaching behaviors had been consistent in different geographic locations and at different age groups, which enabled the findings to be generalized with confidence from one population to the next.

However, the relationship between clear teaching, as operationalized in this research program, and desired student outcomes, such as learning, had not been established. This absence of experimental support provided the rationale for Hines et al. (1985) to study the relationship between three measures of a teacher's clarity (ratings from trained observers, student ratings, and teacher self-ratings) and student achievement and satisfaction. The results revealed moderately strong to strong correlations (.34 – .72) between clarity behaviors and both the student achievement and satisfaction outcomes. Furthermore, these findings were observed across all inference levels and all forms of rating (students, observers, and teacher self-ratings). The ratings of the observers had the strongest relation to student achievement and students' ratings of clarity had the strongest relation to students' satisfaction with the quality of instruction. Given the triangulation of measures of clarity, the different inference levels, and the small number of subjects in this study ($N = 32$), which would lessen the likelihood of significant findings, the obtained results provide considerable evidence of the importance of clear teaching, as operationalized by earlier studies in this research program. As a result, the three intermediate-inference dimensions and 12 low-inference behaviors listed in Table 5.2 help comprise one of the strongest and most credible models of clear teaching.

Research on Lecture Cues and Notetaking

Research in this section features attempts to enhance the clarity of lectures using two related strategies. Research on notetaking (or the lack of quantity or quality of) led researchers in this area to recognize the important role that lecture cues can provide in improving the notes students take of lectures (Kiewra, 2002; Titsworth, 2004). Lecture cues help signal important ideas for students, thereby helping ensure that students record the material in their notes. Cues may be provided by writing ideas on a chalkboard, overhead transparencies, orally, and more recently,

TABLE 5.2 ***The Model of Clarity Generated by the Ohio State Studies.***

Category	*Specific Behaviors*
Teacher stresses important aspects of content	-teaching in a step-by-step manner -teaching the lesson at a pace appropriate for understanding -presenting material in a logical manner -providing sufficient time for practice -informing students of the lesson objectives so that they knew what they would be expected to learn at the lesson completion
Teacher explains content by the use of examples	-use of relevant examples -explaining content so that students could understand -providing students with sufficient examples of how to do the work
Teacher assesses and responds to perceived deficiencies in understanding	-explaining content and then stopping so that students could think about it -repeating things when students did not understand -asking questions to find out if students understood -answering students' questions

From "Teacher Clarity and Its Relationship to Student Achievement and Satisfaction," by C. Hines, D. Cruickshank, and J. Kennedy, 1985, *American Educational Research Journal, 22,* 87–99.

PowerPoint. The benefits of using lecture cues are important because improvements in notetaking have been linked to greater recall of lecture material (Aiken, Thomas, & Shennum, 1975; Kiewra, 1985; Kiewra & Benton, 1988). The importance of taking notes effectively led researchers to focus not only on lecture cues, but also on the benefits of providing skeletal outlines to better guide student notetaking (Kiewra, 2002). The benefits of using skeletal outlines and different types of notetaking structures are reviewed extensively by Kiewra (2002).

To maintain a focus on aspects of classroom messages more specifically, the present review will focus on three recent experimental studies involving the use of lecture cues. While educational researchers predominantly have conducted this line of research, Titsworth (2001a; 2001b; 2004) recently integrated this body of work with instructional communication concepts such as immediacy. In each study he used scripted, videotaped lectures to manipulate immediacy and organizational lecture cues to examine their effect on cognitive (Titsworth, 2001a) and affective (Titsworth, 2001b) learning, both immediately after the lecture and again approximately one week after the lecture. In the third study, he examined students' notetaking as an outcome of teacher immediacy and the use of organizational lecture cues. Lecture cues in each study were manipulated by varying whether content was previewed and reviewed, and whether the instructor identified key material.

In the study involving cognitive learning (Titsworth, 2001a), organizational cues accounted for 11% of the variance in students' learning on a detail test (written responses), but the effect on a concept test (multiple-choice items) was not statistically significant. There were no statistically significant effects for immediacy. Notetaking, regardless of organizational cues, contributed to higher scores on the achievement tests (accounting for 7% of the variance in scores on the concept test and 25% of the variance in scores on the detail test). In the second study (Titsworth, 2001b), organizational cues did not significantly influence affective learning scores. This final result is somewhat anomalous with other results regarding the relationship between clarity-like variables and affect. Titsworth posited that other aspects of clarity might be more influential of student affect than organizational cues exclusively. This possibility, along with the diversity of approaches to research relevant to clarity, suggests the need to examine a larger cluster of clarity behaviors, which is the focus of the most recent clarity research program.

In the third study, Titsworth (2004) examined the effects of teacher immediacy and the use of organizational lecture cues on students' notetaking. Two aspects of students' notes were examined: organizational points and details. Organizational points are structural elements within notes, such as clear discrimination between main points (for example, some notes may have a clear structure of main points while others may be structured in a way that makes main points difficult to recognize). Details are specific explanations or definitions provided by the instructor. The results of this study indicated that student notetaking effectiveness was positively related to scores on three types of achievement tests that students took after viewing a lecture (on average, the two types of notetaking effectiveness accounted for 28 percent of the variance in test scores). Organizational cues and immediacy accounted for a small yet significant amount of variance in the details recorded on students' notes. Interestingly, the amount of details recalled was higher in the low immediacy condition. Organizational cues accounted for considerably more variance (36 percent) in organizational points in students' notes, though there was no effect for immediacy on organizational points. In addition to demonstrating the benefits of organizational cues, this study introduced the outcome of students' notes to the instructional communication literature and demonstrated why it might be worthy to study notes as an important outcome in future research.

The Chesebro and McCroskey Studies

The Chesebro and McCroskey program of research initially began with a focus of reducing state receiver apprehension in the classroom. Receiver apprehension occurs when listeners experience anxiety over a "fear of misinterpreting, inadequately processing, and/or not being able to adjust psychologically to messages sent by others" (Wheeless, 1975, p. 263). It was presumed that clear teaching would be a major key to alleviating receiver apprehension for students. The initial program of research was expanded to include a more complete model of clarity that addressed shortcomings in earlier research.

In the first study, students were presented with one of eight scenarios in which the importance of content to students and the teacher's level of clarity and immediacy were manipulated (Chesebro & McCroskey, 1998b). Students were then asked to complete a measure of state receiver apprehension in terms of how they would feel after listening to the lecture described by the scenario. Main effects were observed for all three variables. Those with more clear and immediate teachers reported significantly lower receiver apprehension scores than those with less clear and immediate teachers. This study provided initial support for the positive effects of clarity on the reduction of receiver apprehension. However, with the use of scenarios, this study fell short of representing an actual classroom situation.

Therefore, a second study using a survey research design was conducted (Chesebro & McCroskey, 2001). This study used the established method, which asks students to report on the last class they had attended before the one in which they are taking the survey (Richmond, McCroskey, Kearney, & Plax, 1987). Students reported on the following for one particular class and teacher: state receiver apprehension, motivation, affect for the course and the teacher, their perceptions of how much they had learned, their teacher's nonverbal immediacy, and their teacher's clarity. Clarity in this study was measured using a recently developed short inventory of teacher clarity (TCSI) (Chesebro & McCroskey, 1998a). The complete measure is provided in Figure 5.2.

Clarity was positively related to increased student state motivation to learn, positive affect, and perceived cognitive learning, and was negatively related to receiver apprehension. Although only a perception of cognitive learning was measured in this study (suggesting it may fall short of actual learning), Chesebro and McCroskey (2000) found a strong correlation between students' perceptions of how much they learned and the actual amount they did learn. These findings add credibility to the use of the perceived learning measure. Still, this study measured the relationships between these variables, but did not establish a cause-and-effect relationship.

FIGURE 5.2 ***Teacher Clarity Short Inventory.***

Please indicate your level of agreement with the following items as they refer to your feelings towards this course. Please respond to the following sentences on a 1 to 7 scale, with 1 representing Completely Disagree and 7 representing Completely Agree.

Completely Disagree 1 2 3 4 5 6 7 Completely Agree

___ 1. My teacher clearly defines major concepts.
___ 2. My teacher's answers to student questions are unclear.
___ 3. In general, I understand the teacher.
___ 4. Projects assigned for the class have unclear guidelines.
___ 5. My teacher's objectives for the course are clear.
___ 6. My teacher is straightforward in his lecture.
___ 7. My teacher is not clear when defining guidelines for out of class assignments.
___ 8. My teacher uses clear and relevant examples.
___ 9. In general, I would say that my teacher's classroom communication is unclear.
___ 10. My teacher is explicit in his instruction.

From "The Development of the Teacher Clarity Short Inventory (TCSI) to Measure Clear Teaching in the Classroom," by J. L. Chesebro and J. C. McCroskey, 1998, *Communication Research Reports, 15,* 262–266. Republished with permission of the Eastern Communication Association.

To establish a cause-and-effect relationship between a cluster of clarity behaviors and learning, Chesebro (2003) studied clarity and immediacy using an experimental design. Students viewed 15-minute videotaped lectures in which a teacher varied both clarity and immediacy behaviors, thereby creating a 2 (high/low clarity) X 2 (high/low immediacy) design. Participants were encouraged to take notes as they normally would in class. At the end of the presentation, students were given a few minutes to review their notes. They then completed a short exam based on the lecture, as well as measures of their state receiver apprehension and affect for the material and for the instructor. Main effects for clarity were observed on recall, affect, and receiver apprehension. Students of the clear teacher learned more, experienced less apprehension, and had more positive affect for both the material and the instructor. It is worth noting that clarity predicted a considerable amount of the variance in learning scores (52%), which is similar to the effect for clarity on achievement observed by Hines, Cruickshank, and Kennedy (1985). Immediacy did not have a significant effect on cognitive learning, though it did have effects on affect for the instructor (12% of the variance) and course material (2% of the variance).

Results on effects of clarity behaviors (Chesebro, 2003), provide considerable support for the importance of clear teaching. Now, it is more difficult to question the results generated by using research designs that used scenarios and surveys, because they have been confirmed experimentally. Additionally, it is more difficult to question the experimental results when they have been confirmed using survey research on actual classroom settings. This study also is important because it was the first in the series to operationalize clarity by having an instructor demonstrate clear teaching behaviors that comprise an actual model of clear teaching. To do this, the researchers needed to reexamine much of the research conducted as part of the first two major research programs on clarity, as well as research that may have not been addressed within those programs.

Knowledge Claims

Even with the shortcomings of clarity research and the multiple aspects of clarity that remain to be investigated, existing research has generated a number of credible results.

1. Clear teaching increases student achievement. This has been demonstrated experimentally as well as with students' reports of how much they think they have learned.
2. Clear teaching increases student affect for both instructors and course material. Given the importance of affective learning (McCroskey, 2002), this stands as an important outcome that consistently has been observed in clarity research.
3. Clear teaching reduces student state receiver apprehension in the classroom.
4. The effects of clarity are supported across a variety of populations and have been supported using a variety of research methodologies, including experiments, surveys, scenarios, observations, and the use of both live teachers and more controlled video- and audio-taped presentations.

5. The research on clarity supports Rosenshine and Furst's (1971) assertion that clarity is one of the most important teacher behaviors in the classroom.

Directions for Future Research

A number of future research directions are worth noting:

1. What behaviors might be added to the model of clear teaching? Specific methods of effective explanation would add depth to the model (this skill is reviewed in detail by Rowan, 2003). The effective use of metaphors and analogies also is likely to play a role in enhancing the clarity of a message, as is the use of a variety of teaching methods. Daly and Vangelisti (2003) also review the role that narratives, questions, and learning aids can play in facilitating understanding of classroom messages. The role of repetition of messages also may affect clarity (Booth-Butterfield, 1999). Future research could explore how these message factors relate to clarity.

2. How might clarity be examined as a relational variable? Eisenberg (1984), Kendrick and Darling (1990), and Simonds (1997) conceptualized clarity as a relational variable, by which both students and teachers participate in reaching clarity and understanding. Teachers participate by using clear teaching behaviors, but students also participate by using a number of clarifying tactics. This relational approach has yet to be integrated with the more rhetorical approach taken by the majority of clarity researchers. Still, given the increased focus on mutual influence in the classroom (Mottet & Richmond, 2002; see also Mottet, Beebe, & Fleuriet in Chapter 7), this remains a worthy research question, which deserves attention in future research.

3. How might effectively clear teaching be different in different types of classrooms (entry-level courses vs. more advanced courses vs. graduate courses)? Successful teaching might involve differing levels of clarity at these different levels. For example, in advanced or graduate courses, assignments may want to have some openness (not be precisely defined) to permit students to take a variety of approaches. Additionally, communicating with students from different cultures might necessitate an additional series of clear teaching behaviors.

4. Finally, does clear teaching in distance-learning or computer-mediated environments require additional unique clear teaching behaviors?

Instructional Humor

While student views on technology in the classroom, academic curriculum, clothing, and music may change over the years, their attitudes toward teachers' use of humor in the classroom have remained favorably consistent. For example, as early as 1940, Bousfield had students list the traits they considered the most important in a college professor. Students identified humor as a valuable personal quality that preceded other traits such as voice, poise, appearance, accomplishment in research, and reputation as a scholar. Some 60 years later, Check (2001) conducted a very similar study—once again asking students to identify a variety of traits considered essential for effective college teaching. Not surprisingly, "employment of humor" was third on this list of "must haves" for effective instructors. Graduate students also view humor as an important instructor characteristic. When Fortson and Brown (1998) asked 115 graduate students to describe their "best" instructor in one sentence, they noted that a sense of humor (among other traits) was often part of their descriptions. These studies and others illustrate the unequivocal value students place on their instructors' use of humor in the classroom.

In this final section of the chapter examining instructional message variables, we provide a detailed overview of classic and contemporary research on humor in the classroom. In the first section, we present an overview and rationale for studying humor in the classroom. In the second section, a detailed review of research that has attempted to operationalize humor is offered. In the third section, research exploring the appropriateness of teachers' humor is discussed. In the fourth section, we highlight research on the effectiveness of instructional humor. In the fifth section, we examine the relationship between individual differences and instructors' use of humor. In the final sections, we offer a number of knowledge claims based on extant humor research and advance directions for future research in this area.

Overview of Instructional Humor

Scholars who study humor seem to pose the same underlying question—how is humor beneficial for either the person enacting the humorous messages or the recipient of the humorous messages? For example, in the medical field, where the use of humor may often seem inappropriate, health-care workers regularly use humor as a means of "organizing and influencing social transactions" (DuPre, 1998, p. 183). Nurses use humor to cope with a wide range of work-related situations ranging from a patient's death to dealing with difficult coworkers (Wanzer, Booth-Butterfield, & Booth-Butterfield, 1997). Physicians use humor at work to manage difficult work-related situations (Robinson, 1991) and may even benefit financially when they use a bit of levity and laughter with their patients (Levinson, Roter, Mullooly, Dull, & Frankel, 1997). In a study that explored the factors related to malpractice suits for physicians, Levinson and her colleagues (1997) found that primary-care physicians who used humor with their patients experienced less malpractice claims.

In the corporate sector, humor is beneficial for managers and employees. Interestingly, researchers found that those managers who incorporated humor into their leadership styles had more productive work units (Avolio, Howell, & Sosik, 1996). Additionally, humor-oriented managers are often perceived as more effective and well liked by their employees (Rizzo, Wanzer, & Booth-Butterfield, 1999). Not surprisingly, employees report greater job satisfaction when they perceive their managers as humor oriented (Rizzo et al., 1999). Regardless of the context, humorous messages seem to have a variety of benefits for both the source and the receiver.

Instructional scholars have had a longstanding interest in the benefits of humor in the classroom (see, for example, Aylor & Opplinger, 2003; Bryant Cominsky, & Zillman, 1979; Bryant, Cominsky, Crane, & Zillman, 1980; Bryant & Zillman, 1989; Conkell, Imwold, Ratliffe, 1999; Davies & Apter, 1980; Downs, Javidi, & Nussbaum, 1988; Frymier & Wanzer, 1999a, 1999b; Frymier & Weser, 2001; Gorham & Christophel, 1990; Kaplan & Pascoe, 1977; Sadowski & Gulgoz, 1994; Wanzer, 2002; Wanzer & Frymier, 1999a; 1999b; White, 2001). Why does this message variable receive so much attention from researchers? First and foremost, all types of teachers tend to use humor quite often when interacting with their students (Bryant et al., 1979; Downs et al., 1988). Additionally, use of humor in the classroom has been linked to improved perceptions of the teacher (Scott, 1976), enhanced quality of the student–teacher relationship (Welker, 1977), and higher teaching evaluations (Bryant et al., 1980). When attempting to identify the behaviors of award-winning teachers, researchers noted that they used moderate amounts of humor throughout their lectures (Downs, Javidi, & Nussbaum, 1988). And, most importantly, instructors' use of humor has been linked to student learning outcomes (Gorham & Christophel, 1990; Wanzer & Frymier, 1999a). It is for these reasons and others that instructional scholars have studied this topic extensively.

Operationalization of Instructional Humor

To understand this message variable we must first examine how researchers have operationalized teachers' humor in the classroom. More specifically, what constitutes a humorous message? Researchers have concluded that teachers use a wide range of humorous behaviors in their classrooms (Bryant et al., 1979; Downs et al., 1988; Gorham & Christophel, 1990; Neuliep, 1991) and that some of these behaviors are viewed as more appropriate than others (Frymier & Wanzer, 1999b). There are a number of studies that have attempted to illuminate and, at the same time, classify the types of humorous messages instructors use in the classroom.

Early research by Bryant, Cominsky, and Zillman (1979) sought to develop a comprehensive list of the different types of humor college teachers use. Students were asked to first audiotape then analyze their instructors' messages to decipher the typical types of humor teachers used throughout their lectures. Based on this data, college teachers used humorous messages 3.34 times during a 50-minute class period. Additionally, male instructors used humor in the classroom more often than female instructors. The researchers used deductive methods to identify the following six types of teacher humor: jokes, riddles, puns, funny stories, funny comments, and other/miscellaneous. They also further clarified the type of humor instructors used by coding it as sexual or nonsexual, hostile or nonhostile, related or unrelated to course material, and determined whether it disparaged the student, teacher, or a third person or group. The main way instructors communicated humor in the classroom was through the use of funny stories, with 39% of their sample indicating that they used this behavior.

Subsequent research by Downs et al., (1988) and Javidi and Long (1989) used a category system developed by Nussbaum, Comadena, and Holladay (1985), which involved different types of "play offs" that instructors typically used in the classroom. For example, instructors often directed play offs toward their students, others who are not in the class, course material, and even themselves. These play offs were further qualified based on how they were related or unrelated to the course material (Neuliep, 1991).

While research by Bryant (1979) and Nussbaum et al. (1985) utilized *deductive* methods to develop a typology of typical instructor humor, Gorham and Christophel (1990) adopted *inductive* methods in their research. A deductive typology is one where the items are generated from the theory and existing research. An inductive typology is one where the items are generated from students or the sample under investigation. In their study, students were asked to keep a log of the actual humor behaviors their instructors exhibited over five consecutive class meetings. Specifically, students were instructed to record "things this teacher did or said today which shows he/she has a sense of humor" (Gorham & Christophel, 1990, p. 51). In order to develop their classification system of teacher humor, the researchers used grounded theory constant comparison procedures. Once the data were transcribed and unitized, they were placed into categories and cross-coded. This process resulted in the identification of 13 different categories of humorous behavior (See Figure 5.3).

The majority of the humorous behaviors (categories 1–6) were purposeful humor attempts directed at individual students, the class as a whole, the university or department, national or world events, the subject matter, and the teacher. The researchers noted that students were aware of the teachers' humor attempts

FIGURE 5.3 ***Humor Categories.***

1. Brief tendentious comment directed at an individual student
2. Brief tendentious comment directed at the class as a whole
3. Brief tendentious comment directed at the university, department, or state
4. Brief tendentious comment directed at national or world events or personalities or at popular culture
5. Brief tendentious comment directed at the topic, subject, or class procedures
6. Brief tendentious (self-deprecating) comment directed at self
7. Personal anecdote or story related to the subject/topic
8. Personal anecdote or story not related to the subject/topic
9. General anecdote or story related to the subject/topic
10. General anecdote or story not related to the subject/topic
11. Joke
12. Physical or vocal comedy ("shtick")
13. Other

From "The Relationship of Teachers' Use of Humor in the Classroom to Immediacy and Student Learning," by J. Gorham and D. Christophel, 1990, *Communication Education, 39*, 46–62.

and that the type and amount of humor used by the instructor affected student learning outcomes differently. More specifically, the use of self-deprecating humor and tendentious comments in general were significantly and negatively correlated with student learning.

This study provided several important contributions to the instructional research on humorous messages. First, it clarified and expanded the different types of humor that instructors used in the classroom through the use of inductive methods. Additionally, this research illustrated the importance of the type and amount of humor that the instructor used in the classroom. We now know that not all types of humor are equally effective in influencing student learning outcomes and that instructors can maximize learning outcomes by strategically using certain types of humor (e.g., personal anecdotes not related to the subject, general anecdotes related to the subject) and avoiding others (e.g., tendentious comments directed at students, self-disparaging comments).

The research discussed in the previous sections has illustrated the types of humor that *college* professors use in the classroom. Neuliep (1991) explored the humorous behaviors that *high school* teachers use, the perceived appropriateness of different humorous behaviors, and the reasons high school teachers give for using humor in their classrooms. Interestingly, he found that high school teachers typically use the same types of humorous messages as college professors but to a lesser extent. Using Gorham and Christophel's (1990) humor categories, teachers were also asked to indicate the appropriateness of the 13 humorous behaviors. High school teachers viewed almost all of the humor behaviors as at least slightly appropriate for the classroom. Some of the reasons high school teachers gave for using humor in the classroom were to put students at ease, as an attention-getting device, to show that the teacher is human, and to keep the class informal. Neuliep's (1991) research confirmed the existence of Gorham and Christophel's (1990) humor categories and provided some preliminary information on the types of humorous messages that high school instructors view as appropriate in the classroom.

Appropriateness of Instructional Humor

Although this research helps us understand the many different types of humor instructors use in the classroom, it does not provide a great deal of insight into the extent to which students find certain types of humor appropriate in the classroom. Preliminary research by Wanzer and Frymier (1999b) identified examples of appropriate and inappropriate types of humor that teachers use in the classroom. Unlike previous research, which just asked students to identify examples of teacher-generated humor (Gorham & Christophel, 1990), Wanzer and Frymier also asked students to distinguish between appropriate and inappropriate types of teacher humor. From the student-generated examples, they identified eight categories of appropriate teacher humor and ten categories of inappropriate humor (See Figure 5.4).

Not surprisingly, categories of appropriate humor were similar to those identified by other researchers. For example, students perceived humor related to course material, humor that was unrelated to course material, nonverbal behaviors,

FIGURE 5.4 ***Categories of Appropriate and Inappropriate Humor.***

Appropriate Teacher Humor
1. Related Humor
2. Unrelated Humor
3. Impersonation
4. Nonverbal Behaviors
5. Disparaging Humor
6. Humorous Props
7. Sarcasm
8. Unintentional Humor

Inappropriate Teacher Humor
1. Making Fun of Student
2. Humor Based on Stereotypes
3. Failed Humor
4. Sexual Humor
5. Irrelevant Humor
6. Sarcasm
7. Swearing
8. Joking about Serious Issues
9. Personal Humor
10. Sick Humor

From *"Being Funny in the Classroom: Appropriate and Inappropriate Humor Behaviors,"* by M. B. Wanzer and A. B. Frymier, 1999, paper presented at the Eastern Communication Association convention in Charleston, West Virginia.

disparaging humor, humorous props, sarcasm, and unintentional humor as appropriate behaviors to use in the classroom. What was perplexing about Wanzer and Frymier's findings were that some of the inappropriate teacher behaviors that students identified also emerged as appropriate. Teachers' use of sarcasm and irrelevant humor were identified as both appropriate and inappropriate types of humor in the classroom. The researchers comment on this finding, noting that, "the differences in perceptions of teacher humor may stem from the type of teacher who is using the humor as opposed to the type of humor being used" (Wanzer, 2002, p. 121). Some instructors may be more effective in delivering humorous messages and therefore are afforded more flexibility in the types of humor they can employ in the classroom. In addition to the type of teacher who is using the humor, what determines the appropriateness or inappropriateness of humor is the larger cultural context, which includes our changing values, beliefs, and attitudes.

Students also identified additional types of humorous messages as inappropriate for teachers to use in the classroom: making fun of students, humor based on stereotypes, failed humor, sexual humor, swearing, joking about serious issues, and personal humor. The most frequently cited type of inappropriate humor was "making fun of students." Other researchers (Gorham & Christophel, 1990; White, 2001) point out the potential problems with teacher humor that targets students. Using the findings from the Wanzer and Frymier (1999b) research and other studies with similar conclusions, we strongly encourage teachers to refrain from using humor that targets students in order to create more positive and productive learning environments.

Based on the research discussed to date, teachers seem to use a variety of humorous messages in the classroom that may include, among others, humorous stories, jokes or anecdotes that may or may not be related to course material, comments directed at students, themselves, or a third party, and even nonverbal types of humor such as a vocalic cue that suggests sarcasm or irony. Now that we understand the types of humor that teachers use in the classroom, the next and most obvious question is whether an instructor's use of humor is related to student learning. Unfortunately, the answer to this question is not a straightforward one.

Effectiveness of Instructional Humor

Humor has been shown to be effective in the classroom. For example, teachers' use of humor can help to reduce tension and to improve the relationship between teachers and students (Bryant & Zillman, 1989). Others (Highet, 1963; Baughman, 1979) note that teachers' use of humor in the classroom can increase student interest in course material and help maintain students' attention during classes. Teachers who use humor effectively in the classroom can improve the classroom environment and make learning a more pleasant and even "happy" experience (Davies & Apter, 1980). However, most instructional scholars would agree that the most important outcome of an instructor's use of humor in the classroom is student learning. Fortunately, there is a great deal of research that has illustrated a positive and significant relationship between teacher humor and student learning (see, for example, Chapman & Crompton, 1978; Davies & Apter, 1980; Gorham & Christophel, 1990; Vance, 1987; Wanzer & Frymier, 1999a; Ziv, 1988).

Early research, which tested the humor–learning relationship (e.g., Chapman & Crompton, 1978; Davies & Apter, 1980), compared children's ability to comprehend material in two different conditions. Child participants were exposed to either humorous or nonhumorous information and then later tested for differences in recall of that same information. In both the Chapman & Crompton (1978) and Davies and Apter (1980) studies, children exposed to the humorous information were able to retain more information than those who received the nonhumorous information.

Research by Vance (1987) provided support for the relationship between unrelated humor and retention. This study used three humorous conditions and one control to test the impact of unrelated humor. In order to simulate states of low interest and low arousal, children participants listened to an audiotaped reading of a familiar story. Next, the participants were either: (1) exposed to a humorous experience that was immediately followed by a serious presentation of novel information (*contiguous/immediate condition*), (2) exposed to an identical humorous experience followed one week later by exposure to novel information (*contiguous/postponed condition*), or (3) presented with novel information with humor incorporated within the educational message (*integrated condition*). As the researchers suspected, child participants in the immediate and postponed contiguous conditions scored the highest in recall of novel information. Thus, the researchers concluded that attaching humor to information can improve recall. Bryant and Zillman (1989) concur and note that when children's attention and motivation to learn is low, attaching humor to course material, even if it is unrelated humor, can help them retain information later.

Ziv's (1988) work rectified many of the earlier weaknesses in empirical research, which had tested the relationship between humor and learning. Unlike earlier research, Ziv's (1988) study was conducted in a real college setting rather than an artificial one. Additionally, he examined an instructor's use of humor over an entire semester rather than just adopting a one-shot approach. In his study, Ziv (1988) divided female students enrolled in an introductory psychology course into one of two groups. In one group, the teacher incorporated humorous messages throughout the semester, while in the second group, the teacher refrained from using any humor in her or his teaching. Not surprisingly, student test scores were higher for those exposed to the humorous messages throughout the semester. This study provided support for the notion that the impact of humorous messages on learning may be more powerful when used throughout the semester rather than just a one-shot application.

Another way of explaining the relationship between teachers' use of humor and student learning is that humor is a type of immediacy behavior. Immediacy "refers to the degree of perceived physical or psychological distance between people in a relationship" (Richmond, 1992, p. 196). Immediate teachers utilize verbal and nonverbal behaviors in an attempt to reduce physical and psychological distance between themselves and their students. Unlike the humor research that yields mixed results in terms of learning outcomes, the immediacy research has provided almost unequivocal support for the relationship between teacher immediacy and student learning (see, for example, Richmond, 2002). As Gorham and Christophel (1990) state "while a particular bit of humor may not enhance retention and may not even be perceived as funny to a particular subject—an ongoing teacher–student relationship in which humor has contributed to immediacy might affect arousal, retention, and learning" (p. 48). Gorham and Christophel (1990) found that highly immediate instructors used 63% more humor than low and moderate immediate teachers. Additionally, teachers who were high in immediacy were seven times more likely to use physical humor/vocal humor than low immediacy teachers. The researchers suggest that the humor–learning relationship is best understood when teacher humor is studied in combination with teacher immediacy.

More recently, instructional scholars have examined how individual differences affect the relationship between humor and learning. Do certain types of teachers use humor more often in the classroom? What types of teachers are the most skilled at using humor in the classroom?

Instructional Humor and Individual Differences

Humor orientation (HO) is a communication-based personality trait that can be assessed by the Humor Orientation Scale (HOS) (Booth-Butterfield & Booth-Butterfield, 1991). Individuals scoring high on the HOS use humor frequently, perceive themselves as effective in communicating humorous messages, and are typically perceived as funnier than individuals who score low on the HOS (Booth-Butterfield & Booth-Butterfield, 1991; Wanzer, Booth-Butterfield, & Booth-Butterfield, 1995). Wanzer and Frymier (1999a) found that instructors who were perceived by their students as high in humor orientation were also perceived as more immediate than instructors who were low in humor orientation. Additionally, when examining differences in student learning based on student and teachers' humor orientation scores, learning scores were the highest when a high humor-oriented student was paired with a high humor-oriented instructor. Alternatively, learning scores were lowest when a high humor-oriented student was paired with a low humor-oriented instructor. Both high and low humor-oriented students learned the most from instructors they perceived as high in humor orientation.

Frymier and Weser (2001) also examined student traits as they related to expectations of teachers' behaviors. Specifically, the researchers assessed students' communication apprehension, grade and learning orientation, and humor orientation in relationship to their expectations for teachers' use of verbal and nonverbal immediacy behaviors, clarity behaviors, and humor behaviors. Students who were high in grade and learning orientation reported the highest expectations for instructor immediacy, clarity, and humor behaviors. Students who were the most focused on achieving high grades also placed high expectations on their instructors' use of humor in the classroom. The researchers speculated that grade-oriented students may place more emphasis on teachers to relieve the "tedium" associated with learning. Grade-oriented students may also care more about the teacher's use of humor because they know that they can retain information with greater ease when the instructor makes the material interesting and memorable (Frymier & Weser, 2001).

Interestingly, students who were more humor-oriented also expected their instructors to use more verbal and nonverbal immediacy behaviors in the classroom (Frymier & Weser, 2001). Similar to teachers, students who use more humorous behaviors probably enact more verbal and nonverbal immediacy behaviors (Gorham & Christophel, 1990; Wanzer & Frymier, 1999a, 1999b). Finally, while humor-oriented students did expect their instructors to use humorous behaviors, the correlation between student HO and expectations of teachers' behaviors was quite low. The researchers suspect that because instructors are not generally known for using a great deal of humor in the classroom, humor-oriented students may not expect teachers to use humor that often (Frymier & Weser, 2001).

In addition to learning more from instructors perceived as high in humor orientation, students are also more likely to visit them outside of class both formally and informally (Aylor & Oppliger, 2003). Aylor and Opplinger (2003) explored teacher humor orientation and sociocommunicative style as predictors of student outside-of-class communication (OCC). They speculated that students would be more likely to visit instructors perceived as humor-oriented and report greater satisfaction with these interactions. Both of their hypotheses were supported with student perceptions of humor orientation being positively and significantly correlated with frequency of OCC and satisfaction with communication. When comparing sociocommunicative style with humor orientation as predictors of OCC, humor orientation was a stronger prediction of the frequency of OCC, but responsiveness was a superior predictor of satisfaction with OCC. Based on their findings, the researchers encourage instructors to use more humorous communication in class to increase OCC with their students. Notably, OCC has been positively linked to student retention (Milem & Berger, 1997) and academic performance (Pascarella, 1980).

The Gorham and Christophel (1990) and Wanzer and Frymier (1999a, 1999b) studies shed light on the kinds of teachers who are more likely to use humor in the classroom. Thus, we now know that those teachers who are immediate and higher in humor orientation will be more likely to use humor effectively in the classroom. Use of humor in the classroom is also related to experience (Javidi & Long, 1989), with experienced teachers using more humor in the classroom than less experienced teachers. Humor use is also related to the instructor's sex. Male instructors are more likely to use humor in the classroom than female instructors (Byant et al., 1979). Gorham and Christophel (1990) examined gender differences in the types of humor that teachers used and found that the relationship between teachers' use of certain types of humor and student learning only existed for male instructors.

Knowledge Claims

The last 30 years of research on humor has provided us with a great deal of information on how to use humor productively in the classroom. Additionally, we know a great deal about the ways that instructors use humor and the types of instructors that are most likely to use humor effectively. Based on the extensive research on humor we can conclude the following:

1. Research indicates that all types of teachers (primary, secondary, and college) use humorous messages as part of their instructional techniques (Bryant et al., 1979; 1980).

2. Humorous messages serve a variety of purposes in the classroom. For example, humor can be used to gain and keep students' attention, generate interest in course material, put students at ease, and facilitate healthy relationships between teachers and students (Linfield, 1977; Welker, 1977).

3. Effective teachers consider the amount of humor they use in the classroom. Award-winning teachers typically use moderate amounts of humor when teaching (Downs, Javidi, & Nussbaum, 1988). Research indicates that teachers should use moderate, not excessive amounts of humor in the classroom and that too much of a good thing can be perceived as a bad thing. As Gorham and Christophel (1990) note, students may like more humor in the classroom but put little stock in what the teacher says.

4. Teachers should be encouraged to use humor in the classroom to increase learning. However, teachers must also take into account the type of humorous messages that they use and realize that there are certain kinds of humor that are more effective than others in facilitating learning in the classroom. For example,

Gorham and Christophel (1990) found that self-disparaging humor and tendentious humor that targeted specific students were not related to learning, while personal anecdotes that were not related to the subject/topic and general anecdotes that were related to the topic/subject *did* increase learning in the classroom.

5. Some types of humorous messages may be perceived by students as inappropriate in the classroom and should probably be avoided. For example, teachers should probably avoid humorous messages that target specific students (as indicted by Gorham & Christophel, 1990; Wanzer & Frymier, 1999b), are sexual in nature, or involve profanity. Teachers should also note that students could misinterpret humor that is based on stereotypes or is sarcastic in nature; thus, these types of humor should probably be avoided or used sparingly (Wanzer & Frymier, 1999b).

6. Teachers should make attempts to use humorous messages throughout their lectures in an attempt to encourage outside-of-class communication with students. Based on research by Aylor and Opplinger (2003), teachers should attempt to adopt a humorous communication style in order to facilitate outside-of-class communication. Students will visit instructors more frequently when they use humor in the classroom. Additionally, when students engage in OCC, teachers should be sure to adopt a highly responsive demeanor (e.g., remain attentive, encouraging, caring, show empathy, etc).

7. Instructors who do not feel comfortable telling funny jokes, stories, or anecdotes can instead use humorous props or visual aids. Sadowski and Gulgoz (1994) found that content-relevant cartoons served as a valuable instructional tool. Students that received cartoon examples performed better on tests than students who did not receive cartoon examples. Thus, instructors could utilize humorous props such as cartoons, pictures, costumes, and objects in an effort to generate humor in the classroom and increase student learning.

8. Instructors who feel that they are unable to tell funny jokes, stories, or anecdotes in the classroom should strive to be immediate in the classroom (Wanzer, 2002). As mentioned previously, being immediate and using humor often involve the same behaviors (e.g., laughing, smiling, use of gestures, and dramatic voice, etc).

Directions for Future Research

It appears that humor is effective in facilitating learning in the classroom and, in some cases, can even motivate students to enact behaviors recommended by teachers (see, for example, Conkell et al., 1999). Listed below are some ideas for future research in this area:

1. What types of humor are most effective in facilitating learning in the classroom? This question could be explored by creating scenarios where instructors enacted different types of humorous messages (e.g., related/unrelated humor, self-deprecating humor, nonverbal humor, humor directed at specific students, etc.) and then compare learning outcomes based on humor type.

2. What types of humor detract from the learning experience? Preliminary work conducted by Wanzer and Frymier (1999b) should be replicated and extended in order to find a more comprehensive list of humorous messages that are inappropriate in the classroom. Individuals who are interested in learning more about humor in the classroom should further explore the concept of "appropriateness." What types of messages do students perceive as inappropriate or offensive in the classroom setting? Also, are there cultural differences in student perceptions of appropriate and inappropriate teacher humor?

Summary

We began this chapter by mentioning the various barriers teachers face daily. With the three message variables in this chapter, we have outlined the main ways teachers can craft classroom messages to overcome these barriers. We did this first by discussing content relevance. We then examined teacher clarity. Finally we reviewed instructional humor. Still, one issue remains for consideration. It involves the variety in student perceptions and schemata. Students bring to the classroom a variety of backgrounds, interests, experiences, personalities, and levels of knowledge about the course content. Therefore, what is relevant, clear, and funny to one student may be irrelevant, unclear, and not-so-funny to the next. Most teachers probably can recall getting contradictory comments on evaluations such as, "takes too long to cover content" and "goes too fast" from students in the same class. This leads us in the direction of an often-mentioned variable that has yet to be formally conceptualized and researched in the instructional communication literature—*instructional variety.* Many teaching handbooks will suggest variety in teaching, but specific research on variety as a variable is lacking. When considering important classroom message variables, the variety of the messages we use may itself be a promising message variable worthy of future research. We suspect that the *most effective* instructors exhibit variety in addition to successfully using the message variables discussed in this chapter, but this likelihood remains to be investigated systematically.

References

Aiken, E. G., Thomas, G. S., & Shennum, W. A. (1975). Memory for a lecture: Effects of notes, lecture rate and informational density. *Journal of Educational Psychology, 67,* 439–444.

Avolio, B. J., Howell, J. M., & Sosik, J. J. (1996). *A funny thing happened on the way to the bottom-line.* Paper presented at the annual meeting of the Society of Industrial and Organizational Psychology, San Diego, CA.

Aylor, B. & Opplinger, P. (2003). Out-of-class communication and student perceptions of instructor humor orientation and socio-communicative style. *Communication Education, 52,* 122–134.

Baughman, M. D. (1979). Teaching with humor: A performing art. *Contemporary Education, 51,* 26–30.

Behrens, F. H. (1999). *Do relevance strategies affect a student's motivation to learn?* Unpublished master's thesis, Miami University, Oxford, OH.

Booth-Butterfield, S. (1999). Personal conversation.

Booth-Butterfield, M., & Booth-Butterfield, S. (1991). Individual differences in the communication of humorous messages. *Southern Communication Journal, 56,* 32–40.

Bousfield, W. A. (1940). Students' ratings of qualities considered desirable in college professors. *School & Society, 51,* 253–256.

Bryant, J., Cominsky, P., Crane, J. S., & Zillman, D. (1980). Relationship between college teachers' use of humor in the classroom and students' evaluations of their teachers. *Journal of Educational Psychology, 72,* 511–519.

Bryant, J., Cominsky, P., Zillman, D. (1979). Teachers' humor in the college classroom. *Communication Education, 28,* 110–118.

Bryant, J., & Zillman, D. (1989). Using humor to promote learning in the classroom. *Journal of Children in Contemporary Society, 20,* 49–78.

Bush, A., Kennedy, J., & Cruickshank, D. (1977). An empirical investigation of teacher clarity. *Journal of Teacher Education, 28,* 53–58.

Chapman, A. J., & Crompton, P. (1978). Humorous presentations of materials and presentation of humorous materials: A review of the humor and memory literature two experimental studies. In M. M. Gruneberg, P. E. Morris, & R. N. Sykes, (Eds.), *Practical Aspects of Memory.* London: Academic Press.

Check, J. F. (2001). Positive traits of the effective teacher—negative traits of the ineffective one. *Education, 106,* 326–334.

Chesebro, J. L. (2002). Teaching clearly. In J. L. Chesebro & J. C. McCroskey (Eds.), *Communication for teachers* (pp. 93–103). Boston: Allyn & Bacon.

Chesebro, J. L. (2003). Effects of teacher clarity and nonverbal immediacy on student learning, receiver apprehension, and affect. *Communication Education, 52,* 135–147.

Chesebro, J. L., & McCroskey, J. C. (1998a). The development of the teacher clarity short inventory (TCSI) to measure clear teaching in the classroom. *Communication Research Reports, 15,* 262–266.

Chesebro, J. L., & McCroskey, J. C. (1998b). The relationship between teacher clarity and immediacy and students' experiences of state receiver apprehension when listening to teachers. *Communication Quarterly, 46,* 446–455.

Chesebro, J. L., & McCroskey, J. C. (2000). The relationship between students' reports of learning and their actual recall of lecture material. *Communication Education, 49,* 297–301.

Chesebro, J. L., & McCroskey, J.C. (2001). The relationship of teacher clarity and immediacy with student state receiver apprehension, affect, and cognitive learning. *Communication Education, 50,* 59–68.

Civikly, J. M. (1992). Clarity: Teachers and students making sense of instruction. *Communication Education, 41,* 138–152.

Conkell, C. S., Imwold, C., Ratliffe, T. (1999). The effects of humor on communicating fitness concepts to high school students. *Physical Educator, 56,* 8–18.

Cruickshank, D. R., & Kennedy, J. J. (1986). Teacher clarity. *Teaching & Teacher Education, 2,* 43–67.

Cruickshank, D. R., Myers, B., & Moenjak, T. (1975). *Statements of clear teacher behaviors provided by 1009 students in grades 6–9.* Unpublished manuscript, Ohio State University, Columbus.

Daly, J. A., & Vangelisti, A. L. (2003). Skillfully instructing learners: How communicators effectively convey messages. In J. O. Green & B. R. Burelson (Eds.), *Handbook of communication and social interaction skills* (pp. 871–908). Mahwah, NJ: Lawrence Erlbaum.

Davies, A. P. & Apter, M. J. (1980). Humour and its effect on learning in children. In P. E. McGhee & A. J. Chapman (Eds.), *Childrens' Humour.* (pp. 237–235). New York: Wiley.

Downs, V. C., Javidi, M., & Nussbaum, J. F. (1988). An analysis of teachers' verbal communication within the college classroom: Use of humor, self-disclosure, and narratives. *Communication Education, 37,* 127–141.

DuPre, A. (1998). *Humor and the healing arts.* Mahwah, NJ: Lawrence Erlbaum.

Eisenberg, E. M. (1984). Ambiguity as strategy in organizational communication. *Communication Monographs, 51,* 227–242.

Fortson, S. B. & Brown, W. E. (1998). Best and worst university instructors: The opinions of graduate students. *College Student Journal, 32,* 572–576.

Frymier, A. B. (2002). Making content relevant to students. In J. L. Chesebro & J. C. McCroskey (Eds.), *Communication for teachers* (pp. 83–92). Boston: Allyn & Bacon.

Frymier, A. B., & Houser, M. L. (1998). Does making content relevant make a difference in learning? *Communication Research Reports, 15*, 121–129.

Frymier, A. B., & Shulman, G. M. (1995). "What's in it for me?": Increasing content relevance to enhance students' motivation. *Communication Education, 44*, 40–50.

Frymier, A. B., Shulman, G. M., & Houser, M. (1996). The development of a learner empowerment measure. *Communication Education, 45*, 181–199.

Frymier, A. B., & Wanzer, M. B. (1999a, November). *Student perceptions of teacher humor use in relationship to learning and motivation: Examining appropriate and inappropriate teacher humor.* Paper presented at the annual convention of the National Communication Association, Chicago, IL.

Frymier, A. B., & Wanzer, M. B. (1999b, April). *Being funny in the classroom: Appropriate and inappropriate humor behaviors.* Paper presented at the annual convention of the Eastern Communication Association, Charleston, WV.

Frymier, A. B., & Weser, B. (2001). The role of student predispositions on student expectations for instructor communication behavior. *Communication Education, 50*, 314–326.

Gorham, J., & Christophel, D. (1990). The relationship of teachers' use of humor in the classroom to immediacy and student learning. *Communication Education, 39*, 46–62.

Highet, G. (1963). *The art of teaching.* New York: Knopf.

Hines, C. (1981). *A further investigation of teacher clarity. The observation of teacher clarity and the relationship between clarity and student achievement and satisfaction.* Unpublished doctoral dissertation, Ohio State University, Columbus.

Hines, C., Cruickshank, D., & Kennedy, J. (1985). Teacher clarity and its relationship to student achievement and satisfaction. *American Educational Research Journal, 22*, 87–99.

Javidi, M. N., & Long, L. W. (1989). Teachers' use of humor, self-disclosure, and narrative activity as a function of experience. *Communication Research Reports, 6*, 47–52.

Kaplan, R. M., & Pascoe, G. C. (1977). Humorous lectures and humorous examples: Some effects upon comprehension and retention. *Journal of Educational Psychology, 69*, 61–65.

Keller, J. M. (1983). Motivational design of instruction. In C. M. Reigeluth (Ed.), *Instructional design theories: An overview of their current status* (pp. 383–434). Hillsdale, NJ: Lawrence Erlbaum.

Keller, J. M. (1987). Strategies for stimulating the motivation to learn. *Performance and Instruction, 26*, 1–7.

Keller, J. M. (1999). Using the arcs motivational process in computer-based instruction and distance education. *New Directions for Teaching and Learning, 78*, 39–47.

Kendrick, W. L., & Darling, A. L. (1990). Problems of understanding in classrooms: Students' use of clarifying tactics. *Communication Education, 39*, 15–29.

Kennedy, J., Cruickshank, D., Bush, A., & Myers, B. (1978). Additional investigations into the nature of teacher clarity. *Journal of Educational Research, 72*, 3–10.

Kiewra, K. A. (1985). Providing the instructor's notes: An effective addition to student notetaking. *Educational Psychologist, 20*, 33–39.

Kiewra, K. A. (2002). How classroom teachers can help students learn and teach them how to learn. *Theory into Practice, 41*, 71–80.

Kiewra, K. A., & Benton, S. L. (1988). The relationship between information-processing ability and note taking. *Contemporary Educational Psychology, 13*, 33–44.

Land, M. (1979). Low-inference variables and teacher clarity: Effects on student concept learning. *Journal of Educational Psychology, 71*, 795–799.

Land, M., & Smith, L. (1979). The effect of low inference teacher clarity inhibitors on student achievement. *Journal of Teacher Education, 31*, 55–57.

Levinson, W., Roter, D. L., Mullooly, J. P., Dull, V. T., & Frankel, R. M. (1997). The relationship with malpractice claims among primary care physicians and surgeons. *The Journal of the American Medical Association, 227*, 553–559.

Linfield, E. G. (1977). The function of humor in the classroom. In A. J. Chapman & H. C. Foot (Eds.), *It's a funny thing, humor.* Oxford, England: Pergamon Press.

McCroskey, J. C. (2002). Learning goals and objectives. In J. L. Chesebro & J. C. McCroskey (Eds.), *Communication for teachers* (pp. 3–7). Boston: Allyn & Bacon.

Means, T. B., Jonassen, D. H., & Dwyer, F. M. (1997). Enhancing relevance: Embedded arcs strategies versus purpose. *Educational technology research and development, 45,* 5–18.

Milem, J. F., & Berger, J. B. (1997). A modified model of college student persistence: Exploring the relationship between Astin's theory of involvement and Tinto's theory of student departure. *Journal of College Student Development, 38,* 387–400.

Millette, D. M., & Gorham, J. (2002). Teacher behavior and student motivation. In J. L. Chesebro & J. C. McCroskey (Eds.), *Communication for teachers* (pp. 141–154). Boston: Allyn & Bacon.

Mottet, T. P., & Richmond, V. P. (2002). Student nonverbal communication and its influence on teachers and teaching. In J. L. Chesebro & J. C. McCroskey (Eds.), *Communication for teachers* (pp. 47–64). Boston: Allyn & Bacon.

Neuliep, J. W. (1991). An examination of the content of high school teachers' humor in the classroom and the development of an inductively derived taxonomy of classroom humor. *Communication Education, 40,* 343–355.

Newby, T. J. (1991). Classroom motivation: Strategies of first-year teachers. *Journal of Educational Psychology, 83,* 195–200.

Nussbaum, J. F., Comadena, M. E., & Holladay, S. J. (1985). *Verbal communication within the college classroom.* Paper presented at the meeting of the International Communication Association, Chicago, IL.

Pascarella, E. T. (1980). *How college affects students: Findings and insights from twenty years of research.* San Francisco: Jossey-Bass.

Powell, R. G., & Harville, B. (1990). The effects of teacher immediacy and clarity on instructional outcomes: An intercultural assessment. *Communication Education, 39,* 369–379.

Richmond, V. P. (1992). *Nonverbal communication in the classroom.* Edina, MN: Burgess International Group.

Richmond, V. P. (2002). Teacher nonverbal immediacy. In J. L. Chesebro & J. C. McCroskey (Eds.), *Communication for teachers* (pp. 65–82). Boston: Allyn & Bacon.

Richmond, V. P., McCroskey, J. C., Kearney, P., & Plax, T. G. (1987). Power in the classroom VII: Linking behavior alteration techniques to cognitive learning. *Communication Education, 36,* 1–12.

Rizzo, B., Wanzer, M. B., & Booth-Butterfield, M. (1999). Individual differences in managers' use of humor: Subordinate perceptions of managers' humor orientation, effectiveness, and humor behaviors. *Communication Research Reports, 16,* 370–376.

Robinson, V. M. (1991). *Humor and the health professions: The therapeutic use of humor in the health care.* Thorofare, NJ: Slack.

Rosenshine, B. V., & Furst, N. (1971). Research on teacher performance criteria. In B. O. Smith (Ed.), *Research in teacher education* (pp. 37–72). Englewood Cliffs, NJ: Prentice-Hall.

Rowan, K. E. (2003). Informing and explaining skills: Theory and research on informative communication. In J. Green & B. Burleson (Eds.) *Handbook of communication and social interaction skills* (pp. 403–438). Mahwah, NJ: Lawrence Erlbaum.

Sadowski, C. J., & Gulgoz, S. (1994). An evaluation of the use of content-relevant cartoons as a teaching device. *Journal of Instructional Psychology, 21,* 368–370.

Scott, T. M. (1976). Humor in teaching. *Journal of Physical Education and Recreation, 7,* 18.

Simonds, C. J. (1997). Classroom understanding: An expanded notion of teacher clarity. *Communication Research Reports, 14,* 279–290.

Small, R. V., & Gluck, M. (1994). The relationship of motivational conditions to effective instructional attributes: A magnitude scaling approach. *Educational Technology, 34,* 33–40.

Smith, L. (1985). Teacher clarifying behaviors: Effect on student achievement and perceptions. *Journal of Experimental Education, 53,* 162–169.

Smith, L., & Cotten, M. (1980). Effect of lesson vagueness and discontinuity on student achievement and attitudes. *Journal of Educational Psychology, 72,* 670–675.

Smith, L., & Land, M. (1981). Low-inference verbal behaviors related to teacher clarity. *Journal of Classroom Interaction, 17,* 37–42.

Titsworth, B. (2001a). The effects of teacher immediacy, use of organizational lecture cues, and students' notetaking on cognitive learning. *Communication Education, 50,* 283–298.

Titsworth, B. (2001b). Immediate and delayed effects of interest cues and engagement cues on students' affective learning. *Communication Studies, 52,* 169–179.

Titsworth, B. (2004). Students' notetaking: The effects of teacher immediacy and clarity. *Communication Education, 53,* 305–320.

Vance, C. M. (1987). A comparative study on the use of humor in the design of instruction. *Instructional Science, 16,* 79–100.

Wanzer, M. B. (2002). Use of humor in the classroom: The good, the bad, and the not-so-funny things that teachers say and do. In J. L. Chesebro & J. C. McCroskey (Eds.), *Communication for teachers* (pp. 116–125). Boston: Allyn & Bacon.

Wanzer, M. B., Booth-Butterfield, M., & Booth-Butterfield, S. (1995). The funny people: A source orientation to the communication of humor. *Communication Quarterly, 44,* 42–52.

Wanzer, M. B., Booth-Butterfield, M., & Booth-Butterfield, S. (1997). *If we didn't use humor we'd cry: Predispositional and situational influences on humorous coping communication in health care settings.* Paper presented at the National Communication Association conference, Chicago, IL.

Wanzer, M. B., & Frymier, A. B. (1999a). The relationship between student perceptions of instructor humor and students' reports of learning. *Communication Education, 48,* 48–62.

Wanzer, M. B., & Frymier, A. B. (1999b). *Being funny in the classroom: Appropriate and inappropriate humor behaviors.* Paper presented at the Eastern Communication Association convention in Charleston, WV.

Welker, W. A. (1977). Humor in education: A foundation for wholesome living. *College Student Journal, 11,* 252–254.

Wheeless, L. R. (1975). An investigation of receiver apprehension and social context dimensions of communication apprehension. *The Speech Teacher, 24,* 261–268.

White, G. W. (2001). Teachers' report of how they used humor with students perceived use of such humor. *Education, 122,* 337–347.

Ziv, A. (1988). Teaching and learning with humor: Experiment and replication. *Journal of Experimental Education, 57,* 5–15.

6

Teachers' Influence Messages

K. David Roach
Texas Tech University

Virginia P. Richmond
West Virginia University

Timothy P. Mottet
Texas State University–San Marcos

Introduction

It is a teacher's job to influence. Teachers demonstrate, share, and facilitate. Teachers motivate and try to inspire students to learn. Teachers persuade and inform. In an instructional setting, a relationship is formed and maintained between a teacher and a student in order to stimulate and facilitate student learning. This relationship is built and sustained by communication. Without communication and a relationship, a teacher cannot influence students. It is important to keep in mind that teacher influence should be a means to student learning and development. This unit of the book has examined instructional communication from the rhetorical perspective. Specifically, Chapter 3 provided an examination of audience. Chapter 4 examined the source. And Chapter 5 examined the message. This chapter continues focusing on the rhetorical perspective by focusing on how teachers use information from audience, source, and message to influence students.

In 1983, a program of research was launched by McCroskey and Richmond to explore influence as it operates in instructional settings. Over the next several years, this program of research provided rich insight into the role, operation, and impact of influence in the classroom. In 1992, Richmond and McCroskey's book, *Power in the Classroom,* provided an excellent survey of research examining power and compliance gaining in instructional settings. The topics covered in this 1992 book included not only influence in the classroom, but also how teacher influence messages were impacted by other communication variables such as affinity, motivation, immediacy, and communicator style.

Instructional communication research examining teacher power and influence messages remains salient in the twenty-first century, especially as pedagogical models of instruction continue to shift from teacher-centered to student-centered, which ultimately give students more power (Weimer, 2002). Research continues to shed light on student incivility (Boice, 1996, 2000) and teacher misbehaviors (Kelsey, Kearney, Plax, Allen, & Ritter, 2004), which influence how power is enacted and negotiated in the classroom. For example, Chory-Assad and Paulsel (2004) found that instructors' antisocial influence messages (i.e., messages that punish) were negatively correlated with student perceptions of classroom justice. Classroom justice refers to "perceptions of fairness regarding outcomes or processes that occur in the instructional context" (p. 101). Chory-Assad and Paulsel's research found that students act out in an aggressive manner to teachers who use antisocial influence messages to restore what they perceive to be the lack of justice or classroom equity. This research suggests that instructors may be partially responsible for the incivility they experience in the classroom.

This chapter examines teachers' influence messages by first defining power as a relational phenomenon. Second, it reviews the seminal research on teachers' use and effects of influence messages. Third, it examines current research or how the seminal programs of research have been extended. Fourth, it discusses issues related to how researchers measure teachers' influence messages. The chapter concludes with a review of the knowledge claims and directions for future research.

Power as a Relational Phenomenon

Before exploring the research literature, it is important first to define what we mean by power as a relational phenomenon. From a communication perspective, power is a product that emerges from a relationship. Interpersonal or relational power is "an individual's potential to have an effect on another person's or group of persons' behavior. . . . It is the capacity to influence another person to do something" (Richmond, McCroskey, Davis, & Koontz, 1980, p. 38). According to Hartnett (1971):

> One of the most common misconceptions of power has treated power as if it were only an attribute of a person or a group. Such a conception inevitably leads to the question, "Who are the power holders?" This question is vacant unless one also asks, "Over whom?" To quote Richard Emerson, "In making these necessary qualifications we force ourselves to face up to the obvious—power is a property of the social relation; it is not an attribute of the actor." (pp. 27–28)

French and Raven (1959) argued for five bases of relational power: legitimate, coercive, reward, expert, and referent. Notably, these power bases are rooted in relational perceptions. The agent (the individual trying to exert power) must be perceived as powerful or influential by the target (the person to whom the influence is directed).

Legitimate power is anchored in the perception that the agent has the right to prescribe and/or proscribe behavior for the target. The power that the target yields to the agent is not necessarily rooted in the relationship, but in the title or position that the agent holds. The agent's power stems from his or her assigned title or position, more so than the interpersonal relationship that the target has with the agent. In a classroom, students generally perceive the teacher as having the authority, because of his or her position, to require students to attend class, complete assignments, participate during class, and take exams.

Coercive power occurs when the target perceives the agent as being able to punish him or her, or being able to withhold a reward that the target deems desirable. In the classroom, students are more likely to yield coercive power to their teacher when they perceive their teacher as having the authority to punish. Additionally, students are more likely to yield coercive power if they perceive their teacher as being able to scrutinize between students who comply and those who resist their influence attempts.

Reward power occurs when the target perceives the agent as being able to reward him or her or being able to withhold punishment. The target must perceive the agent as having the authority to reward the target and the reward must be deemed desirable by the target for this type of relational power to be yielded. For example, students may grant their teacher power knowing that the teacher has the ability to write them a glowing letter of recommendation for a prestigious job or to overlook excessive absences.

Expert power occurs when a target perceives the agent as having competence or expertise in a particular area. For students to yield expert power to their teacher, they must perceive the teacher as being an expert in his or her field of study. Although many teachers are qualified experts, students often fail to yield expert power to them because they perceive the teacher as not having expertise. This might be because of the teacher's inability to communicate his or her knowledge to students. Conversely, many students may yield expert power to an amateur teacher because of the teacher's ability to communicate course content clearly.

Referent power occurs when the target identifies with the agent. The target perceives the agent as being a role model. There are times when people comply with a tough or disliked request if it comes from a leader they respect. In fact, in a military context, soldiers will follow a respected and loved commander into very dangerous situations and will respond compliantly to requests that will put their very lives at risk. In a classroom context, it is important that students respect their teachers, see them as credible, and, to some degree, as role models.

With an understanding of power as a relational phenomenon and French and Raven's (1959) five bases of power, we next examine some of the seminal research on teachers' influence messages, which originated in the organizational context.

Seminal Research on Teacher Influence

In the late 1970s and early 1980s, researchers began to examine how communication was used to influence others in organizational contexts. Research projects focused on management communication style (MCS) and how it influenced organizational outcomes such as employee motivation and satisfaction. Management communication style is presumed to be the product of an organization's leadership style and supervisor's communication style (Richmond & Roach, 1992). Results from the studies indicated that a supervisor's communication style is relatively constant across time within a given organization; however, it may change sharply if the supervisor moves into a new organization or is assigned a new supervisor (Richmond & McCroskey, 1979; Richmond, McCroskey, & Davis, 1982).

The MCS studies also indicated significant relationships between management communication style and employee satisfaction. Specifically, more positive satisfaction outcomes were noted when managers used an "employee-centered" or participative style of communication rather than a "manager-centered" or an authoritative style of communication. Other studies examined management communication style in terms of the power bases from which the styles operated. Examining MCS in conjunction with French and Raven's (1959) power bases indicated that managers should strive to use less negative influence strategies, such as coercion, and use more positive strategies, such as referent and expert influence strategies, where managers influence others based on their valuing and respecting the relationship (Richmond, McCroskey, Davis, & Koontz, 1980; Richmond, Wagner, & McCroskey, 1983).

In 1984, this line of research was expanded by examining the behavior alteration techniques (BATs) that superiors and subordinates used in organizational contexts (Richmond, Davis, Saylor, & McCroskey, 1984). From the subordinate's perspective, results indicated more positive outcomes and more internalization, or long-term influence, when supervisors used positive or prosocial behavioral alteration techniques (i.e., rewarding, valuing), than when they used more negative or antisocial behavioral alteration techniques (i.e., punishing, threatening). Richmond, McCroskey, and Davis (1986) added to this research by noting the link between supervisor power and affinity-seeking strategies with employee satisfaction. These initial studies examining management communicator style, interpersonal power, and behavioral alteration techniques in organizational settings were important in laying the foundation for examining power and influence messages in the instructional context (Richmond & Roach, 1992).

Communication researchers next examined how relational power and influence functions in the instructional context. A number of research questions guided their research: How do teachers and students perceive a teacher's use of relational power and influence in the classroom? How is relational power communicated in the classroom? How does a teacher's use of relational power influence student motivation and learning? How does a teacher's use of immediacy behaviors mediate his or her use of relational power and student learning? These research questions guided what has become known as the "Power in the Classroom" program of research (Plax & Kearney, 1992). According to Plax and Kearney (1992), a program of research meets two rudimentary criteria.

> First, each investigation should be a logical extension of a systematic line of investigation that follow some definable research topic or set of topics. Second, the results of each investigation should serve the heuristic function of stimulating a consideration of additional, related, and worthy issues for further examination. (pp. 68–69)

The first study in this program of research, Power I, examined how teachers and students perceived teachers' use of power in the classroom. After describing French and Raven's (1959) five bases of power, McCroskey and Richmond (1983) asked students and teachers to indicate how frequently teachers used each of the five bases of relational power. Overall, teachers and students reported similar perceptions. Both teachers and students perceived that reward, referent, and expert power were used with greater frequency than the legitimate and coercive bases of power. Two perceptual differences did emerge from the study. Teachers perceived themselves as using more expert power than their students perceived them using. Also, students perceived their teachers as using more coercive power than teachers perceived themselves using.

The second study, Power II, examined how a teacher's use of power as perceived by both the teacher and the student influenced students' affective and cognitive learning. Again, using general descriptions of French and Raven's (1959) five bases of power, Richmond and McCroskey (1984) found that teachers' perceptions of their power use were unrelated to students' self-reports of affective and cognitive learning. Students' perceptions of teacher power, however, were significantly related to their learning. Specifically, coercive and legitimate power were negatively related with student learning and referent and expert power were positively related with student learning. Reward power was not significantly related to either affective or cognitive learning.

Whereas Power I and II focused on teachers' perceived use of the five bases of relational power, Power III examined how power was communicated in the classroom. Kearney, Plax, Richmond, & McCroskey (1985) examined the specific influence techniques and influence messages that teachers used in the classroom to manage student behavior. Data from this study produced a set of 18 behavioral alteration techniques (BATs) and representative behavioral alteration messages (BAMs). This typology of BATs and BAMs was augmented and validated in Power IV, where Kearney, Plax, Richmond, and McCroskey (1984) asked elementary and secondary teachers to generate a list of techniques and messages they used to manage student behavior. The data resulted in a revised typology of 22 BATs and representative BAMs. It is also important to note that the typology represents fully French and Raven's (1959) five bases of relational power. For a complete list of these BATs and BAMs, refer to Figure 6.1.

In the same study, Kearney et al. (1985) asked another group of primary and secondary teachers to indicate how frequently they used each of the techniques to control student behavior. Kearney et al. concluded that teachers' reported use of the 22 BATs was limited. Although all 22 BATs were used, most of the teachers, on average, used only about 6 of them in the classroom. Teachers reported using more frequently prosocial BATs (expert, referent, reward) than antisocial BATs (legitimate, coercive). Although teachers self-reported using antisocial BATs infrequently, they perceived other teachers (their colleagues) as using antisocial BATs with greater frequency.

Power V examined the relationships between teachers' use of the 22 techniques and student affective learning. Additionally, Power V examined the impact of instructional communication training on teachers' use of BATs in the classroom. McCroskey, Richmond, Plax, and Kearney (1985) found a significant relationship between students' perceptions of teachers' BAT use and affective learning. Prosocial BATs (expert, referent, reward) were positively related to affective learning. Antisocial BATs (legitimate, coercive) were negatively related to affective learning. This study also found that teachers who had training in instructional communication were less likely to be perceived by students as using antisocial BATs when compared to teachers with no training in instructional communication. It appears that training in instructional communication benefits both teachers and students.

Power VI departed from the earlier studies in that it tested a theoretical model that emerged from the preceding five studies. All of the prior studies (Power I–Power V) were conducted using an inductive or a discovery-based approach to empirical research. Rather than testing research hypotheses, the first five power studies answered research questions. Having answered a number of important research questions, such as how teachers and students perceive power, how power is related to learning, and how power is communicated, researchers were now ready to test deductively-derived hypotheses. These hypotheses also included the immediacy variable, which was the focus of another program of research that was being conducted simultaneously. Immediacy refers to communication behaviors that influence the degree of psychological and/or physical closeness between individuals (Andersen, 1979; Mehrabian, 1967). "Scholars suggest that some common

FIGURE 6.1 ***Behavior Alteration Techniques (BATs) and Behavior Alteration Messages (BAMs).***

1. *Immediate Reward from Behavior (BAT).* You will enjoy it. It will make you happy. Because it's fun. You'll find it rewarding/interesting. It's a good experience (BAM).
2. *Deferred Reward from Behavior.* It will help you later on in life. It will prepare you for getting a job (or going to graduate school). It will prepare you for achievement tests (or the final exam). It will help you with upcoming assignments.
3. *Reward from Teacher.* I will give you a reward if you do. I will make it beneficial to you. I will give you a good grade (or extra credit) if you do. I will make you my assistant.
4. *Reward from Others.* Others will respect you if you do. Others will be proud of you. Your friends will like you if you do. Your parents will be pleased.
5. *Self-Esteem.* You will feel good about yourself if you do. You are the best person to do it. You always do such a good job.
6. <u>*Punishment from Behavior.*</u> You will lose if you don't. You will be unhappy if you don't. You will be hurt if you don't. It's your loss. You'll feel bad if you don't.
7. <u>*Punishment from Teacher.*</u> I will punish you if you don't. I will make it miserable for you. I'll give you an "F" if you don't. If you don't do it now, it will be homework later.
8. <u>*Punishment from Others.*</u> No one will like you. Your friends will make fun of you. Your parents will punish you if you don't. Your classmates will reject you.
9. <u>*Guilt.*</u> If you don't, others will be hurt. You'll make others unhappy if you don't. Your parents will feel bad if you don't. Others (e.g., classmates, friends) will be punished if you don't.
10. *Teacher/Student Relationship: Positive.* I will like you better if you do. I will respect you. I will think more highly of you. I will appreciate you more if you do. I will be proud of you and supportive of you.
11. <u>*Teacher/Student Relationship:*</u> *Negative.* I will dislike you if you don't. I will lose respect for you. I will think less of you if you don't. I won't be proud of you. I'll be disappointed in you.
12. <u>*Legitimate–Higher Authority.*</u> Do it; I'm just telling you what I was told. It is a rule; I have to do it and so do you. It's a rule. It's administrative/school policy.
13. <u>*Legitimate–Teacher Authority.*</u> Because I told you to. You don't have a choice. You're here to work. I'm the teacher, you're the student. I'm in charge/control, not you. Don't ask; just do it.
14. *Personal (Student) Responsibility.* It is your obligation. It is your turn. Everyone has to do his or her share. It's your job. Everyone has to pull his or her own weight.
15. *Responsibility to Class.* Your group needs it done. The class is depending on you. All your friends are counting on you. Don't let your group down. You'll ruin it for the rest of the class. It's your responsibility.
16. *Normative Rules.* The majority rules. All your friends are doing it. Everyone else has to do it. The rest of the class is doing it. It's part of growing up.
17. <u>*Debt.*</u> You owe me one. Pay your debt. You promised to do it. I did it the last time. You said you'd try to do it this time.
18. *Altruism.* If you do this it will help others. Others will benefit if you do. It will make others happy if you do. I'm not asking you to do it for yourself; do it for the good of your classmates and friends.
19. *Peer Modeling.* Your friends do it. Classmates you respect do it. The friends you admire are doing it. Other students you like do it. All your friends are doing it.
20. *Teacher Modeling.* This is the way I always do it. When I was your age I did it. People who are like me do it. I had to do this when I was in school. Teachers you like and respect do it.
21. *Expert Teacher.* From my experience, it is a good idea. From what I have learned, it is what you should do. This has always worked for me. Trust me—I know what I'm doing. I had to do this before I became a teacher.
22. *Teacher Responsiveness.* Because I need to know how well you understand this. To see how well I've taught you. To see how well you can do it. It will help me know your problem areas.

Antisocial BATs are underlined. Typically, the other BATs are seen as prosocial.

From "Power in the Classroom III: Teacher Communication Techniques and Messages," by P. Kearney, T. G. Plax, V. P. Richmond, and J. C. McCroskey, 1985, *Communication Education, 34,* 19–28. Republished with permission by *Communication Education* and Taylor & Francis Ltd. http://www.tandf.co.uk/journals.

immediacy behaviors include smiling, touching on the hand, arm, or shoulder, moving close to another, making eye contact, facing another, using warm vocals, and leaning toward someone" (Richmond, 2002, p. 67). One might reason that the perceived degree of teacher immediacy and the resulting closeness of relationship between teacher and student might moderate the effects and results of teacher influence attempts on students.

Plax, Kearney, McCroskey, and Richmond (1986) tested four hypotheses. First, they hypothesized that students' perceptions of BAT use would be related to students' affective learning. Second, students' perceptions of teacher nonverbal immediacy would be related to students' affective learning. Third, teacher BAT use would be related to nonverbal immediacy. Fourth, the combination of teacher BAT use and nonverbal immediacy would predict students' affective learning. Finally, Plax et al. (1986) wanted to know which set of teacher communication behaviors (BATs, nonverbal immediacy) was more predictive of students' affective learning.

All four hypotheses of Plax et al (1986) were confirmed. Results of their study indicated that "teachers' use of pro-social messages to alter student behavior tends to increase student perceptions of the teacher's immediacy, which in turn leads to greater affective learning." Conversely, results also indicated that "teachers' use of antisocial messages to alter student behavior tends to decrease student perceptions of the teacher's immediacy, which in turn leads to reduced affective learning on the part of the student" (Plax et al., 1986, p. 54). Overall, this study was very important because results indicated that "teachers' selective BAT use was shown to be indirectly related to affective learning as a function of students' perceptions of teacher immediacy" (Plax et al., 1986, p. 52). In other words, immediacy was found to be a moderating factor between teacher BAT use and student affective learning.

In a follow up study to Power VI, Kearney, Plax, Smith, and Sorensen (1988) again confirmed the moderating effects of teacher nonverbal immediacy on teachers' perceived use of BATs/BAMs. In this study, Kearney et al. (1988) found that students' perceptions of how prosocial their teachers' behavioral alteration messages were depended on students' perceptions of teachers' nonverbal immediacy behaviors. Specifically, when teachers were perceived as being nonverbally immediate, students also perceived teachers as using prosocial BATs/BAMs, even when teachers used antisocial BATs/BAMs. This study highlighted how teachers' verbal and nonverbal messages function together to alter students' decoding or interpretation of their teachers' influence messages.

Communication theory and research suggests that verbal and nonverbal messages function differently in social interactions (Burgoon, 1994; Mehrabian, 1971; Watzlawick, Bavelas, & Jackson, 1967). Verbal messages function to convey the content of the message, whereas nonverbal messages function to establish the relationship. Additionally, verbal messages appear to have their primary impact on cognitive responses whereas nonverbal messages have their primary impact on affective responses (Burgoon, 1994). The results of the research of Kearney et al. (1988) demonstrated how teachers' verbal messages (BAMs) and nonverbal messages (nonverbal immediacy) interacted to affect how instructional messages are interpreted. It appears that teachers' nonverbal immediacy behaviors, which tap into the relational dimension of communication and impact students' emotional responses, alter how students interpret and frame teachers' verbal behavior alteration messages, which convey the content of the message and impact students' cognitive responses.

In the final study of the "Power in the Classroom" program of research, Richmond, McCroskey, Kearney, and Plax (1987) examined the relationship between teacher influence messages and student cognitive learning. Study results indicated that about 36% of the variance in student cognitive learning was accounted for by teacher differential use of influence communication. Specifically, it was found that prosocial behavior alteration techniques/messages positively related with students' self-reports of cognitive learning, while antisocial behavior alteration techniques/messages were negatively related to students' self-reports of cognitive learning. Apparently, then, students are more likely to learn on a cognitive level when the teacher influence attempts are positive and prosocial, and less likely to learn when teacher influence communication is negative and antisocial. Therefore, how teachers use communication to influence their students clearly makes a difference in the classroom.

Continuing Research on Teacher Influence

Early studies examining relational power and influence in the instructional context clearly linked teachers' influence messages with students' affective and cognitive learning. This next section details research conducted during the early 1990s to the present. The first part of this section reviews how teacher influence impacts or is impacted by student motivation, time, and student perceptions of teacher humor. The second section examines graduate teaching assistant influence. The third section focuses on student perceptions of student and teacher influence. The fourth section reviews cross-cultural studies examining teacher influence.

With the rich background provided by the "Power in the Classroom" program of research, Richmond (1990) examined the role of teacher communication as it relates to student motivation. Obviously, student motivation is key to success in the classroom and will determine whether students will continue to learn after the course is completed. Results from this study indicated significant relationships between teacher influence communication and students' motivation to learn. Specifically, prosocial teacher influence communication was positively related to student motivation and antisocial teacher influence communication was negatively related to student motivation.

Relationships, communication, and power are not static phenomena. They are dynamic. They happen in time. They develop. In view of this, Roach (1994) conducted a study examining the patterns and effects of perceived instructor power use over time in a semester. Students were surveyed regarding their instructor communication during the third week of class (Time 1), at midterm (Time 2), and during the last three weeks of class (Time 3). Results indicated that overall instructor use of behavior alteration techniques (BATs) and use of prosocial BATs increased significantly between the first and the middle of the semester, and then remained about the same for the rest of the semester. For antisocial BAT use, results indicated significantly more instructor use at the end of the semester as compared to the first of the semester. Although levels of student cognitive learning were relatively consistent throughout the semester, results indicated a significant drop in student affective learning after the mid point of the semester. With the link between BAT use and student learning in place, these matching end-of-semester trends suggested that instructors might want to make special efforts to preserve affective learning toward the end of the semester by using fewer antisocial influence messages.

Pleasant feelings or attitudes toward the source of power generally are associated with a willingness to comply with that person's power or compliance-gaining use. Punyanunt (2000) examined teacher humor as it is used along with teacher use of behavior alteration techniques. Humor, as was discussed in Chapter 5, can be a powerful communication tool, and when used along with power, may function to make compliance-gaining more positive and palatable to the target. Interestingly, Punyanunt's study indicated that teachers recognize this logical connection and use it to reach desired class ends. Study results indicated strong correlations between teacher use of humor and teacher use of the following behavioral alteration techniques: self-esteem, expert teacher, peer modeling, and teacher modeling. When you are making someone smile, it is difficult for them not to like you. If they are laughing or feel favorably toward you relationally, it is likely that they will comply with a request you are making. Again, it appears that a teacher's use of appropriate instructional humor enhances teacher–student relational perceptions, making the teachers' influence messages and compliance gaining requests more palatable to students.

Graduate Teaching Assistant (GTA) Influence

Although some of the power and compliance-gaining research examined public school teachers (K–12), the majority of the research focused on the college and university educator. One group of higher education instructors, which has been overlooked in the research is graduate teaching assistants (GTA). GTAs are graduate students who are employed to teach undergraduate classes while obtaining their graduate degrees. Some teach alongside professors, while others are given their own class. GTAs teach a large portion of the general education courses at American universities, and many of them have little or no teaching experience (McMillen, 1986). Some GTAs receive training in how to teach and some are just given a book and told to cover the chapters (Andrews, 1985). Many GTAs look forward to teaching and others do not. Some of them adjust and learn to teach; others do not (Boyer, 1990; Weimer, 2002). All of these factors make research and training in this area crucial, especially given the influence and effect GTAs have on large numbers of undergraduate students (Nyquist, Austin, Sprague, & Wulff, 2001). Because GTAs are largely beginning teachers with varying motivations, one cannot assume that GTA communication and teaching patterns will be the same as those of university professors (Gaff, 2002; Nelson & Morreale, 2002; Nyquist, Austin, Sprague, & Wulff, 2001).

In 1991, Roach conducted a study examining GTA use of behavior alteration techniques in the classroom. Interestingly, GTAs were found to use Legitimate–Higher Authority, Legitimate–Teacher Authority, Normative Rules, and Teacher Modeling significantly more than university professors. Notably, all of these BATs are typically perceived as antisocial and generally are less effective and productive in terms of student learning; and they are less conducive to positive teacher–student relational development. It is plausible that teachers who have less experience might use these communication strategies significantly more than seasoned and experienced professors. Antisocial influence messages tend to be counterproductive in the classroom. Fortunately, only two of these BATs—Legitimate–Higher Authority and Teacher Modeling—were in the top five used by GTAs.

There are many instructor communication variables that are related to instructor use of power and influence in the classroom. One such variable is that of instructor argumentativeness. Argumentativeness is a trait that predisposes an "individual to advocate positions on controversial issues and to attack verbally the positions which other people take on these issues" (Infante & Rancer, 1982, p. 72). Roach (1995a) found that students perceived low argumentative GTAs to use more power (overall, and specifically—legitimate, referent, and expert power) than GTAs who are high argumentatives. Furthermore, results indicated that student affective learning scores were significantly higher with low argumentative GTAs than they were with high argumentative GTAs. These findings indicate that, though debate and the vigorous discussion of ideas can be productive in educational settings, students tend to perceive argumentative communication behaviors negatively. It appears that when a high argumentative GTA engages students in debate, students feel singled out; the debate may not be fair because of the teacher–student status differential.

In a companion study to Roach (1995a), an additional study exploring GTA argumentativeness and self-perceived power use was conducted (Roach, 1995b). Results from this study indicated that high argumentative GTAs also self-reported using more overall power than low argumentative GTAs. Furthermore, results indicated a significant difference between high argumentative and low argumentative GTAs on use of specific power bases. High argumentative GTAs reported using more referent and expert power than low argumentative GTAs. Interestingly, the Roach (1995a) findings noted that students perceived just the opposite—that low argumentative GTAs use more referent, expert, and power overall than did high argumentative GTAs. This finding reveals a difference between teacher and student perceptions of teacher communication. Evidently, high argumentative GTAs recognize the value of using prosocial power bases and mistakenly think that is what they are doing, while students perceive that it is the low argumentative GTAs who are using these prosocial power bases. These two studies suggest that high argumentative GTAs may not foster positive student results and perceptions and therefore should temper their use of argumentative communication behaviors in the classroom.

Obviously, student misbehavior or off-task behaviors will stimulate most instructors to enact power strategies to get student minds and behaviors back on task. Though this is a normal power response for most instructors, communication apprehension is another communication variable that may mediate teacher power use. Roach (1999) found that GTAs with higher levels of trait-like communication apprehension tended to use significantly less overall power. It was hypothesized that high communication apprehensive GTAs would experience more student misbehaviors than GTAs with moderate to low communication apprehension. It was reasoned that highly apprehensive GTAs would ignore or overlook student misbehavior hoping that it would eventually diminish. Most seasoned instructors recognize that student misbehaviors that go ignored will generally get worse—not better.

Results from Roach (1999) indicated that a GTA's communication apprehension inhibited them from using the necessary instructor power and influence to manage student misbehavior. Interestingly, GTA state-like communication apprehension reflected similar patterns. Study results indicated that GTAs with higher levels of state-like communication apprehension were significantly less likely to use referent, expert, and reward power-base strategies in the classroom (Roach, 1999). These findings are important because the same study indicated strong relationships between GTA reward power use and student affective and cognitive learning, and student ratings of GTA effectiveness. Furthermore, strong relationships were also found between GTA expert power use and student cognitive learning and student ratings of GTA effectiveness. When communication apprehension inhibits needed instructor communication and behavior, it serves as a threat to student learning and to the overall success of the class.

Student Perceptions of Student and Teacher Influence

Golish (1999) added to the power-in-the-classroom literature by taking a different but very important perspective—that of student power use. This research perspective recognizes that power is not exclusively in the domain of the teacher. This topic is addressed in more detail in Chapter 7, which examines students' influence messages. Golish (1999) examined the specific compliance-gaining strategies students use to influence their GTAs. The argument was made that because of their student status and classroom norms, students may not be permitted to use the power strategies that teachers use on students.

Golish (1999) found that students perceived themselves as having more power with graduate teaching assistants (GTAs) than with professors. Specifically, students saw themselves as having prosocial forms of power with their GTAs, including expert, referent, and reward power: expert power, in that GTAs can learn from them; referent power, in that GTAs can more easily identify with them because they, too, are students; and reward power, in that they can reward the GTA with positive teacher evaluations, which will enable the graduate student to remain employed.

Using an inductive methodology, Golish (1999) generated a typology of 19 compliance-gaining strategies that students used to influence their GTAs. Similar to the original teacher BAT/BAM typology (Kearney, Plax, Richmond, & McCroskey, 1984, 1985), this student power typology reflected some strategies that were prosocial (e.g., honesty-sincerity, flattery, group persuasion, private persuasion, evidence of preparation/logic, performance, and utilitarian justice) and some that were antisocial in nature (e.g., blame, complaining, public persuasion, emotional displays, general excuses, punishing the teacher, reference to higher authority, and verbal force/demand). A third category of student BATs/BAMs—Neutral—was defined and included the following strategies: pleading, guilt, play on the teachers' ability to relate, and stress/overload. Students reported using a wide variety of persuasive strategies to influence their GTAs—primarily prosocial messages, and antisocial messages only when necessary. Rather than damaging the student–teacher relationship, students appear to use more caution when exercising their power. Golish argued that teachers have more choice in the influence strategies they use because they occupy more powerful positions than students.

Golish and Olson (2000) examined further student power and its interaction with instructor use of power. The data indicated that students tend to use prosocial compliance-gaining strategies primarily with their professors (specifically, in order of frequency: private persuasion, flattery, group persuasion, evidence of preparation, and honesty–sincerity). A strong positive correlation was found between student and instructor power use. In fact, student power use was positively related with teacher power use for all power bases (coercive, reward, legitimate, referent) except for expert power (which was unrelated). Interestingly, the highest correlation between student power use and teacher power use was with referent power. Analysis of the relationship between teacher power and student power use revealed that the more instructors use coercive power (antisocial) on students, the more likely students are to use antisocial influence messages on their instructors. Similarly, the more that instructors use reward and referent power (prosocial) on their students, the more likely students are to use prosocial influence messages on their instructors. Although causation cannot be determined at this point, it is important to note that prosocial and antisocial behavior alteration strategies tend to be reciprocated between teachers and students. Which comes first—teacher antisocial influence messages or student antisocial influence messages—may be an important direction for future research.

Although initial influence studies focused exclusively on how teachers communicated power in the classroom, it is important for instructional communication researchers to continue examining how students communicate power in the classroom. Another important consideration for instructional influence is the role that culture plays in communication processes. As one might expect, there are different norms and rules for communication in different cultures. This is true of cultures in different nations as well as different cultures within one nation. One cannot ignore the role of culture in the process of influencing others.

Cross-Cultural Studies Examining Teacher Influence

The "Power in the Classroom" program of research and other related instructional power/compliance-gaining research has produced a wealth of knowledge on how teacher influence messages operate in classrooms in the United States. Although very useful, the generalizability of these findings are limited to the American culture. When one considers the different communication norms and expectations in other countries, the need for research in other cultures becomes very apparent. It is possible that teacher influence messages may operate and function similarly across cultures. It is also very likely, however, that there will be significant differences in how influence messages are used and in how these messages affect student behaviors and learning in different cultures. In addition to researching students from various cultures within American classrooms, researchers are also examining similarities and differences in how instructor power and influence messages are used across cultures. Several studies, for instance, have examined nonverbal immediacy and how it impacts students' cognitive and affective learning in different cultures (e.g., McCroskey, Fayer, Richmond, Sallinen, & Barraclough, 1996; McCroskey, Richmond, Sallinen, Fayer, & Barraclough, 1995; McCroskey, Sallinen, Fayer, Richmond, & Barraclough, 1996). Notably in these studies, nonverbal immediacy and its effects were found to vary somewhat across cultures.

Other studies have found that cross-cultural variation is also present in terms of how teachers communicate power and use influence messages. Lu (1997) conducted a study comparing BAT use by Chinese instructors. Chinese graduate students and scholars at a large Eastern U.S. university were interviewed and surveyed to ascertain the type, likelihood of use, and effectiveness of BAT use in Chinese college classrooms. Differences in cultural norms, expectations, and communication for Chinese classrooms were discussed in the study. In view of these cultural differences, results from the study were very interesting and useful. Figure 6.2 provides a fascinating comparison of the most and least used behavioral alteration techniques by Chinese college instructors as compared to those used by U.S. college instructors (Lu, 1997; Roach, 1991).

This figure reveals an interesting contrast. To understand this contrast, one must realize that the Chinese culture places high value on respect for the teacher, respect for authority, firm discipline, moral education, cooperation, groupness, collectivism, and harmony (Hofstede, 1984). Notably, "Chinese teachers do not see it appropriate . . . to 'please students . . . or boost students' self-esteem' by using reward-based BATs; teachers doing this in the Chinese context will be considered incapable or incompetent" (Lu, 1997, p. 25). "Chinese teachers not only use BATs much more frequently than their U.S. counterparts, but they are more likely to employ antisocial BATs and admonish students in authoritarian and moralist tones" (Lu, 1997, p. 25). In contrast, the United States is a more individualistic culture, placing high value on equality, lower power distance, self-actualization, personal freedom and choice, and independence (Hofstede, 1984). Chinese and U.S. cultural values are readily manifested in the use and effectiveness of instructor BAT use in the classroom.

Roach and Byrne (2001) compared instructor communication behaviors in the American and German university classrooms. Specifically, the study examined

FIGURE 6.2 ***Comparison of Behavior Alteration Technique Use between Chinese and American Instructors.***

CHINESE INSTRUCTORS	AMERICAN INSTRUCTORS
Most Frequently Used in Descending Order	
Punishment from Behavior	Teacher Feedback
Deferred Reward from Behavior	Expert Teacher
Guilt	Immediate Reward from Behavior
Legitimate-Higher Authority	Deferred Reward from Behavior
Person (Student) Responsibility	Teacher Modeling
Least Frequently Used In Descending Order	
Debt	Reward from Others
Legitimate-Teacher Authority	Peer Modeling
Punishment from Others	Debt
Reward from Others	Guilt
Immediate Reward from Behavior	Punishment from Others

From "Culture and Compliance Gaining in the Classroom: A Preliminary Investigation of Chinese College Teachers' Use of Behavior Alteration Techniques," by S. Lu, 1997, *Communication Education, 46,* 10–28, and "Graduate Teaching Assistant's Use of Behavior Alteration Techniques in the University Classroom," by K. D. Roach, 1991, *Communication Quarterly, 39,* 178–188.

students' perceptions of instructor power use, affinity-seeking, and nonverbal immediacy. Survey data assessing student perceptions of instructor behavior were collected from American students in America and from German students in Germany. American instructors were found to use significantly more coercive, legitimate, referent, reward, and overall power when compared to German instructors. In American classrooms, instructor coercive power use was negatively related to student affective and cognitive learning as well as student ratings of instructor effectiveness. However, in German classrooms, instructor coercive power use was negatively related only with student ratings of instructor effectiveness. In American classrooms, instructor use of reward power was positively associated with student affective learning, whereas in German classrooms, this variable was not significantly related. Instructor use of referent power was positively related to student cognitive learning and ratings of instructor effectiveness in American classrooms. Interestingly, in German classrooms instructor use of referent power was *negatively* related to student cognitive learning. In American classrooms, instructor expert power was positively related with student affective learning, student cognitive learning, and student ratings of instructor effectiveness. In contrast, German instructor use of expert power had no significant relationship with any of these variables.

Analysis of these differences between American and German instructor communication is aided by an awareness of how American and German cultures vary on Hofstede's (1984) cultural dimensions. In a study of 39 countries, Hofstede (1984) found that America is slightly higher on the power distance index than is Germany (40 vs. 35; mean score for all surveyed countries = 51). America has lower scores on uncertainty avoidance than does Germany (46 vs. 65; mean score for all surveyed countries = 64). America scores on the individualism index were much higher than those for Germany (91 vs. 67; mean for all surveyed countries = 51). America scored lower on the masculinity index than did Germany (62 vs. 66; mean for all surveyed countries = 51). With variability in these cultural dimensions as a backdrop, it is interesting to note that instructor power use plays a bigger role in student affective and cognitive learning, and satisfaction with instructor for American students (in America) than it does for German students (in Germany). Hofstede's (1984) cultural dimension scores reveal significant differences in American and German cultures. These findings, coupled with the results from Roach and Byrne (2001) where instructors' use of affinity-seeking strategies and nonverbal immediacy behaviors have a stronger influence on American students than German students, demonstrate how important it is for instructors to be aware of and to respond to the cultural norms for appropriate and effective instructional communication.

In a similar study, Roach, Cornett-DeVito, and DeVito (2003) compared American and French teachers' use of instructional communication. Specifically, the study examined students' perceptions of instructor power use, affinity-seeking, and nonverbal immediacy. U.S. students were surveyed regarding their college instructors' communication and French students (in France) were surveyed regarding their college instructors' communication. Results indicated that though there was little difference in American and French instructor overall power use, American instructors were perceived as using significantly more reward, referent, and expert power. French instructors were perceived as using significantly more legitimate power. Interestingly, American instructor use of reward, referent, and expert powers was positively related to student affective learning. For French students, only instructor referent power use was positively related to affective learning. For American students, instructor use of coercive power was negatively related to student ratings of instructor effectiveness, whereas for French students there was no relationship between these two variables.

In each of these cross-cultural studies, significant differences were noted in the use, effectiveness, and influence of teacher power in the classroom. The cross-cultural research suggests that instructors' relational power is culturally situated. What works in one culture may be less effective or possibly offensive in another culture. Educators working across cultures are encouraged to study cultural norms of a given culture, and then to adapt his or her power use strategies accordingly.

Knowledge Claims

Several conclusions or knowledge claims can be drawn from the results of the research summarized in this chapter.

1. Although teachers and students perceive teachers' use of overall power similarly, two important perceptual differences emerged from the research: (1) Teachers perceived themselves as using more expert power than their students perceived them using; and (2) students perceived their teachers as using more coercive power than their teachers perceived them using (McCroskey & Richmond, 1983).

2. Student perceptions of their teachers' use of power are significantly related to their affective and cognitive learning. Specifically, teachers' perceived use of prosocial forms of power (expert, referent, reward) are positively related to students' self-reports of affective and cognitive learning. Conversely, teachers' perceived use of antisocial forms of power (legitimate, coercive) are inversely related to students' self-reports of affective and cognitive learning (Richmond & McCroskey, 1984).

3. Kearney, Plax, Richmond, & McCroskey's (1984, 1985) typology of 22 BATs/BAMs serve as one form of relational power measurement. The BAT/BAM typology also reflects French and Raven's (1959) five bases of social or relational power. While some have challenged the validity of the BAT/BAM typology (Waltman, 1994, 1995; Waltman & Burleson, 1997a, 1997b), others argue for its validity (Kearney & Plax, 1997; Plax & Kearney, 1992). Regardless, the BAT/BAM typology of instructional power continues to serve as the primary form of relational power measurement in the instructional context (Waldeck, Kearney, & Plax, 2001a).

4. Teachers who have training in instructional communication are less likely to be perceived by students as using antisocial BATs when compared to teachers with no training in instructional communication. Instructional communication training benefits teachers and students (McCroskey, Richmond, Plax, and Kearney 1985).

5. Teachers' use of prosocial messages increase students' perceptions of teacher immediacy, which in turn leads to greater student affective learning. Conversely, teachers' use of antisocial messages decrease students' perceptions of teacher immediacy, which in turn leads to reduced student affective learning (Plax, Kearney, McCroskey, & Richmond 1986). Students' perceptions of teacher immediacy moderate the effects of teacher BAT use and student affective learning (Plax, Kearney, McCroskey, & Richmond 1986).

6. Student perceptions of the prosocialness of their teachers' BATs/BAMs are dependent on student perceptions of teacher nonverbal immediacy behaviors. Nonverbally immediate teachers are *perceived* as using prosocial BATs/BAMs, even when they use antisocial BATs/BAMs (Kearney, Plax, Smith, & Sorensen, 1988).

7. Students perceive graduate teaching assistants (GTAs) as using antisocial BATs/BAMs and therefore are less effective and productive in terms of student learning (Roach, 1991).

8. Students perceive low argumentative GTAs as using higher forms of relational power (referent, expert) than GTAs who are perceived as high argumentative. Student affective learning scores are significantly higher with low argumentative GTAs than with high argumentative GTAs (Roach, 1995a). Interestingly, high argumentative GTAs *self-reported* using higher forms of relational power (expert, referent) than low argumentative GTAs (Roach, 1995b).

9. GTAs with higher levels of communication apprehension are significantly less likely to use referent, expert, and reward power-base strategies in the classroom

(Roach, 1999). This finding is important because, in the same study, GTAs' use of prosocial power and student affective and cognitive learning, and student ratings of GTA effectiveness were positively related (Roach, 1999).

10. Students perceived themselves as having more power with graduate teaching assistants (GTAs) than with professors—specifically, prosocial forms of power, including expert, referent, and reward power (Golish, 1999).

11. The relationship between teacher power and student power use reveals that the more instructors use coercive power (antisocial) on students, the more likely students are to use antisocial influence messages on their instructors. The more that instructors use reward and referent power (prosocial) on their students, the more likely students are to use prosocial influence messages on their instructors (Golish and Olson, 2000).

12. Chinese teachers not only use BATs much more frequently than teachers from the United States, but they are also more likely to employ anti- rather than pro-social forms of BATs/BAMs (Lu, 1997).

13. In a study comparing American and German instructors' use of BATs/BAMs, the data suggest that American instructors use significantly more overall power when compared to German instructors (Roach & Byrne, 2001). Additionally, it appears that many of the positive relationships between instructors' use of pro-social power and student outcomes are either insignificantly or inversely related in the German classroom (Roach & Byrne, 2001). Fewer differences in power use were noted between American and French instructors' use of BATs/BAMs (Roach, Cornett-DeVito, & DeVito, 2003).

Directions for Future Research

Although a number of conclusions can be drawn from the research reviewed in this chapter, many questions remain unanswered and may serve as directions for future research.

1. How should teacher power and influence be measured? There are a number of approaches to measuring relational power, including instruments that assess perceptions of relational power developed by Student (1968), Richmond, McCroskey, Davis, and Koontz (1980), and Roach (1994). Additionally, Kearney, Plax, Richmond, and McCroskey's (1984, 1985) typology of behavioral alteration techniques (BATs) and messages (BAMs) has been shown to reflect French and Raven's (1959) five bases of relational power. Do these measures continue to remain valid and reliable in the instructional context? (Waltman & Burleson, 1997a, 1997b). Do these measures remain valid and reliable in primary, secondary, higher, and nontraditional educational contexts, such as the corporate training classroom?

2. What effect does teacher power and influence have on nontraditional students and in nontraditional classrooms? The bulk of the research examining teachers' influence messages has focused on traditional students, or students in primary, secondary, and higher education under the age of 25 (Houser, 2004). Citing the U. S. Department of Education's National Center for Education Statistics, Houser (2004) reports that over 42% of undergraduate students in 1999–2000 were above the age of 24 and 12% were over the age of 40. Houser found that many of the prescriptions yielded from instructional communication research impact nontraditional students differently than traditional students. Additionally, many of today's corporations are becoming "learning organizations" (Senge, 1994), where employees are encouraged to continue their education in the corporate training classroom. If instructional communication researchers want research results that are generalizable, they are encouraged to conduct research that focuses on nontraditional students in nontraditional educational and training classrooms, as well as in traditional classrooms.

3. What effects do electronic delivery systems have on teacher power use in the classroom? The definition of "what is a classroom?" is changing rapidly with the advent of electronic and virtual instructional delivery systems. Regardless of classroom "place" or "instructional medium," teachers will still need to exert influence in the classroom. How will this power be received by virtual or distance students? Will teacher influence be perceived by students in different ways in these contexts? How will teachers need to alter influence attempts to operate successfully in these classroom conditions?

4. Does an instructor's use of technology, such as e-mail, presentational software, or Internet platforms, impact a teacher's influence in the classroom? It could be that an instructor's influence varies as a consequence of using instructional technology. Also, the teacher's influence might depend on *how* the teacher uses the instructional technology. For example, Waldeck, Kearney, and Plax (2001b) found that instructors who used e-mail messages with imbedded immediacy messages (i.e., inclusive language, emotions) enhanced students' willingness to engage in mediated out-of-class communication significantly more than teachers who did not use these embedded immediacy messages.

5. How do societal changes (in prevailing thoughts, attitudes, and beliefs) influence how power is perceived and how it operates in a classroom? Societies are not static. They change, and along with them, the communication norms and expectations change. Perceptions of power, how it should be used, and who can use it change over time. As societies change, one must question if research completed in years past is still relevant, meaningful, or accurate in classrooms of today and tomorrow.

6. How is power perceived, how does it function, and what are its effects in other cultures? As technology and travel bring different cultures together, it is important that instructional communication researchers continue conducting research across cultures. This cross-cultural research will identify differences and similarities and will allow teachers and trainers to work more effectively with diverse groups of students.

Summary

This chapter focused on the rhetorical perspective by examining how teachers use information from audience, source, and message to influence students. First, we defined power as a relational phenomenon. For a teacher (source) to have and use power in the classroom, students (target) must yield power to the teacher. In short, students give teachers permission to influence them. Second, we examined the seminal research on teacher power, which focused specifically on teachers' behavior alteration techniques and messages (BATs/BAMs). This section detailed the results from the "Power in the Classroom" program of research. Third, we examined how the "Power in the Classroom" program of research has been extended by reviewing how graduate teaching assistants (GTAs) use relational power and influence, how students perceive their own use of influence, and how teacher power and influence are perceived and used across cultures. Fourth, we reviewed issues related to how teacher influence messages are measured. Finally, we summarized what we have learned from the research and offered a few directions for instructional communication researchers who want to continue research in this area.

Teaching effectiveness is often synonymous with a teacher's ability to influence his or her students. Although administrators often reward teachers for their ability to influence students' cognitive learning or their ability to keep students focused on specific learning objectives, a teacher's ultimate reward comes from his or her ability to influence students' lives or their affective learning. In order to enhance instructional effectiveness, teachers must recognize their rhetorical influence in the classroom, while at the same time understanding that their rhetorical influence stems from the quality of the teacher–student relationship and the verbal and nonverbal messages that comprise the relationship.

References

Andersen, J. F. (1979). Teacher immediacy as a predictor of teaching effectiveness. In D. Nimmo (Ed.), *Communication yearbook 3* (pp. 543–559). New Brunswick, NJ: Transaction Books.

Andrews. J. D. W. (1985). Why TA training needs instructional innovation. In J. D. W. Andrews (Ed.), *Strengthening the teaching assistant faculty* (pp. 47–82). New Directions for Teaching and Learning, no. 22. San Francisco: Jossey-Bass.

Boice, R. (1996). Classroom incivilities. *Research in Higher Education, 37,* 453–486.

Boice, R. (2000). *Advice for new faculty members.* Boston: Allyn & Bacon.

Boyer, E. L. (1990). *Scholarship reconsidered: Priorities of the professoriate.* The Carnegie Foundation for the Advancement of Teaching. San Francisco: Jossey-Bass.

Burgoon, J. K. (1994). Nonverbal signals. In M. L. Knapp & G. R. Miller (Eds.), *Handbook of interpersonal communication* (pp. 229–285). Thousand Oaks, CA: Sage.

Chory-Assad, R. M., & Paulsel, M. L. (2004). Antisocial classroom communication: Instructor influence and interactional justice as predictors of student aggression. *Communication Quarterly, 52,* 98–114.

French, J. R. P., Jr., & Raven, B. (1959). The bases for social power. In D. Cartwright (Ed.) *Studies in social power* (pp. 150–167). Ann Arbor, MI: Institute for Social Research.

Gaff, J. G. (2002). The disconnect between graduate education and faculty realities: A review of recent research. *Liberal Education, 88,* 6–13.

Golish, T. D. (1999). Students' use of compliance-gaining strategies with graduate teaching assistants: Examining the other end of the power spectrum. *Communication Quarterly, 47,* 12–32.

Golish, T. D., & Olson, L. N. (2000). Students' use of power in the classroom: An investigation of student power, teacher power, and teacher immediacy. *Communication Quarterly, 48,* 293–310.

Hartnett, R. T. (1971). Trustee power in America. In H. L. Hodgkinson & L. R. Meeth (Eds.), *Power and authority* (pp. 25–38). San Francisco: Jossey-Bass.

Hofstede, G. (1984). *Culture's consequences: International differences in work-related values.* London: Sage.

Houser, M. L. (2004). We don't need the same things! Recognizing differing expectations of instructor communication behavior for nontraditional and traditional students. *Journal of Continuing Higher Education, 52,* 11–24.

Infante, D. A., & Rancer, A. S. (1982). A conceptualization and measure of argumentativeness. *Journal of Personality Assessment, 46,* 72–80.

Kearney, P., & Plax, T. G. (1997). Item desirability bias and the BAT checklist: A reply to Waltman and Burleson. *Communication Education, 46,* 95–99.

Kearney, P., Plax, T. G., Richmond, V. P., & McCroskey, J. C. (1984). Power in the classroom IV: Alternatives to discipline. In R. Bostrom (Ed.), *Communication yearbook 8* (pp. 724–746). Beverly Hills, CA: Sage.

Kearney, P., Plax, T. G., Richmond, V. P., & McCroskey, J. C. (1985). Power in the classroom III: Teacher communication techniques and messages. *Communication Education, 34,* 19–28.

Kearney, P., Plax, T. G., Smith, V. R., & Sorensen, G. (1988). Effects of teacher immediacy and strategy type on college student resistance. *Communication Education, 37,* 54–67.

Kearney, P., Plax, T. G., Sorensen, G., & Smith, V. R. (1988). Experienced and prospective teachers' selections of compliance-gaining messages for "common" student misbehaviors. *Communication Education, 37,* 150–164.

Kelsey, D. M., Kearney, P., Plax, T. G., Allen, T. H., & Ritter, K. J. (2004) College students' attributions of teacher misbehaviors. *Communication Education, 53,* 40–55.

Kerlinger, F. N. (1986). *Foundations of behavioral research.* New York: Holt, Rinehart & Winston.

Lu, S. (1997). Culture and compliance gaining in the classroom: A preliminary investigation of Chinese college teachers' use of behavior alteration techniques. *Communication Education, 46,* 10–28.

McCroskey, J. C., Fayer, J. M., Richmond, V. P., Sallinen, A., & Barraclough, R. A. (1996). A multicultural examination of the relationship between nonverbal immediacy and affective learning. *Communication Quarterly, 44,* 297–307.

McCroskey, J. C., & Richmond, V. P. (1983). Power in the classroom I: Teacher and student perceptions. *Communication Education, 32,* 175–184.

McCroskey, J. C., Richmond, V. P., Plax, T. G., & Kearney, P. (1985). Power in the classroom V: Behavior alteration techniques, communication training, and learning. *Communication Education, 34,* 214–226.

McCroskey, J. C., Richmond, V. P., Sallinen, A., Fayer, J. M., & Barraclough, R. A. (1995). A cross-cultural and multi-behavioral analysis of the relationship between nonverbal immediacy and teacher evaluation. *Communication Education, 44,* 281–291.

McCroskey, J. C., Sallinen, A., Fayer, J. M., Richmond, V. P., & Barraclough, R. A. (1996). Nonverbal immediacy and cognitive learning: A cross-cultural investigation. *Communication Education, 45,* 200–211.

McMillen, R. (1986). Teaching assistants get increased training: Problems arise in foreign student programs. *Chronicle of Higher Education, 33,* 9–11.

Mehrabian, A. (1967). Orientation behaviors and nonverbal attitude communication. *Journal of Communication, 16,* 324–332.

Mehrabian, A. (1971). *Silent messages.* Belmont, CA: Wadsworth.

Nelson, P. D., & Morreale, S. P. (2002). Disciplinary leadership in preparing future faculty. *Liberal Education, 88,* 28–33.

Nyquist, J. D., Austin, A. E., Sprague, J., & Wulff, D. H. (2001). *The development of graduate students as teaching scholars: A four-year longitudinal study, final report.* Seattle: University of Washington.

Paulsel, M. L., & Chory-Assad, R. M. (2004). The relationships among instructors' antisocial behavior alteration techniques and student resistance. *Communication Reports, 17,* 103–112.

Plax, T. G., & Kearney, P. (1992). Teacher power in the classroom: Defining and advancing a program of research. In V. P. Richmond and J. C. McCroskey (Eds.), *Power in the classroom: Communication, control, and concern* (pp. 67–84). Hillsdale, NJ: Lawrence Erlbaum.

Plax, T. G., Kearney, P., McCroskey, J. C., & Richmond, V. P. (1986). Power in the classroom VI: Verbal control strategies, nonverbal immediacy and affective learning. *Communication Education, 35,* 43–55.

Plax, T. G., Kearney, P., & Sorensen, G. (1990). The strategy selection–construction controversy II: Comparing pre- and experienced teachers' compliance-gaining message constructions. *Communication Education, 39,* 128–141.

Punyanunt, N. M. (2000). The effects of humor on perceptions of compliance-gaining in the college classroom. *Communication Research Reports, 17,* 30–38.

Richmond, V. P. (1990). Communication in the classroom: Power and motivation. *Communication Education, 39,* 181–195.

Richmond, V. P. (2002). Teacher nonverbal immediacy. In J. L. Chesebro & J. C. McCroskey (Eds.). *Communication for teachers* (p. 67). Boston: Allyn & Bacon.

Richmond, V. P., Davis, L. M., Saylor, K., & McCroskey, J. C. (1984). Power strategies in organizations: Communication techniques and messages. *Human Communication Research, 11,* 85–108.

Richmond, V. P., & McCroskey, J. C. (1979). Management communication style, tolerance for disagreement, and innovativeness as predictors of employee satisfaction: A comparison of single-factor, two-factor, and multiple-factor approaches. In D. Nimmo (Ed.). *Communication yearbook 3* (pp. 359–373). New Brunswick, NJ: Transaction Books.

Richmond, V. P., & McCroskey, J. C. (1984). Power in the classroom II: Power and learning. *Communication Education, 33,* 125–136.

Richmond, V. P., & McCroskey, J. C. (Eds.). (1992). *Power in the classroom: Communication, control, and concern.* Hillsdale, NJ: Lawrence Erlbaum.

Richmond, V. P., McCroskey, J. C., & Davis, L. M. (1982). Individual differences among employees, management communication style, and employee satisfaction: Replication and extension. *Human Communication Research, 8,* 170–188.

Richmond, V. P., McCroskey, J. C., & Davis, L. M. (1986). The relationship of supervisor use of power and affinity-seeking strategies with subordinate satisfaction. *Communication Quarterly, 34,* 178–193.

Richmond, V. P., McCroskey, J. C., Davis, L. M., & Koontz, K. A. (1980). Management communication style and employee satisfaction: A preliminary investigation. *Communication Quarterly, 28,* 37–46.

Richmond, V. P., McCroskey, J. C., Kearney, P., & Plax, T. G. (1987). Power in the classroom VII: Linking behavior alteration techniques to cognitive learning. *Communication Education, 36,* 1–12.

Richmond, V. P., & Roach, K. D. (1992). Power in the classroom: Seminal studies. In V. P. Richmond and J. C. McCroskey (Eds.), *Power in the classroom: Communication, control, and concern* (pp. 47–66). Hillsdale, NJ: Lawrence Erlbaum.

Richmond, V. P., Wagner, J. P., & McCroskey, J. C. (1983). The impact of perceptions of leadership style, use of power, and conflict management style on organizational outcomes. *Communication Quarterly, 31,* 27–36.

Roach, K. D. (1990). A reliability assessment of the Kearney, Plax, Richmond, and McCroskey (1984) BATs and BAMs model. *Communication Research Reports, 7,* 67–74.

Roach, K. D. (1991). Graduate teaching assistant's use of behavior alteration techniques in the university classroom. *Communication Quarterly, 39,* 178–188.

Roach, K. D. (1994). Temporal patterns and effects of perceived instructor compliance-gaining use. *Communication Education, 43,* 236–245.

Roach, K. D. (1995a). Teaching assistant argumentativeness: Effects on affective learning and student perceptions of power use. *Communication Education, 44,* 15–29.

Roach, K. D. (1995b). Teaching assistant argumentativeness and perceptions of power use in the classroom. *Communication Research Reports, 12,* 94–103.

Roach, K. D. (1999). The influence of teaching assistant willingness to communicate and communication anxiety in the classroom. *Communication Quarterly, 47,* 166–182.

Roach, K. D., & Byrne, P. R. (2001). A cross-cultural comparison of instructor communication in American and German classrooms. *Communication Education, 50,* 1–14.

Roach, K. D., Cornett-DeVito, M. M., & DeVito, R. (November, 2003). *A cross-cultural comparison of instructor communication in American and French classrooms.* Paper presented at the annual convention of the National Communication Association, Miami, FL.

Senge, P. M. (1994). *The fifth discipline.* New York: Doubleday.

Sorensen, G., Plax, T. G., & Kearney, P. (1989). The strategy selection–construction controversy: A coding scheme for analyzing teacher compliance-gaining message constructions. *Communication Education, 38,* 102–118.

Student, K. R. (1968). Supervisory influence on work-group performance. *Journal of Applied Psychology, 52,* 188–194.

Waldeck, J. H., Kearney, P., & Plax, T. G. (2001a). Instructional and developmental communication theory and research in the 1990s: Extending the agenda for the 21st century. In W. B. Gudykunst (Ed.), *Communication yearbook 24* (pp. 206–229). Thousand Oaks, CA: Sage.

Waldeck, J. H., Kearney, P., & Plax, T. G. (2001b). Teacher e-mail message strategies and students' willingness to communicate online. *Journal of Applied Communication Research, 29,* 54–70.

Waltman, M. (1994). An assessment of the convergent validity of the checklist of behavior alteration techniques: The association between teachers' likelihood-of-use ratings and informants' frequency-of-use ratings. *Journal of Applied Communication Research, 22,* 295–308.

Waltman, M. (1995). An assessment of the discriminant validity of the checklist of behavior alteration techniques: A test of the item desirability bias in prospective and experienced teachers' likelihood-of-use ratings. *Journal of Applied Communication Research, 23,* 201–211.

Waltman, M. S., & Burleson, B. R. (1997a). Explaining bias in teacher ratings of behavior alteration techniques: An experimental test of the heuristic processing account. *Communication Education, 46,* 75–94.

Waltman, M. S., & Burleson, B. R. (1997b). The reliability of item desirability and heuristic processing in BAT ratings: Respecting the data. *Communication Education, 46,* 100–103.

Watzlawick, P., Bavelas, J. B., & Jackson, D. D. (1967). *Pragmatics of human communication.* New York: W.W. Norton.

Weimer, M. (2002). *Learner-centered teaching: Five key changes to practice.* San Francisco: Jossey-Bass.

Wheeless, L. R., Barraclough, R., & Stewart, R. (1983). Compliance-gaining and power in persuasion. In R. Bostrom (Ed.) *Communication yearbook 7* (pp. 105–145). Beverly Hills, CA: Sage.

Unit III

Relational Perspectives

7

Students' Influence Messages

Timothy P. Mottet
Texas State University–San Marcos

Steven A. Beebe
Texas State University–San Marcos

Cathy A. Fleuriet
Texas State University–San Marcos

Introduction

It was a simple experiment hatched at recess. When the teacher moved to the right side of the classroom, students responded to the teacher's questions. However, when the teacher stood on the left side of the room, the teacher's questions went unanswered. It did not take long for one of your author's eighth-grade teachers to find himself standing on the right side of the room unaware of why he was standing there. We enjoyed this prank for a few minutes, but soon we could not contain our cleverness. We revealed our plot. Fortunately, the teacher had a good sense of humor and joined in the laughter, somewhat amazed at our scheme. What we intuitively tested is now a well-documented fact: Students have the power to influence their teachers' behaviors and, in turn, affect the learning environment. Although in the case of this impromptu eighth-grade experiment, our class was deviously conscious of what we were doing and the teacher was unaware of our influence, ideally, both teachers and students should be aware of how students' verbal and nonverbal messages affect the teaching and learning process.

There is no question that students influence teachers (Brophy & Good, 1974; Cantor & Gelfand, 1977; Klein, 1971; Mottet & Richmond, 2002). In every school and during virtually every class period, students seek extensions on homework assignments, ask for additional help on an assignment, petition to get out of class early, cajole for extra-credit points, or try to find out "What's going to be on the exam." Some students' requests are welcomed and indicate that students are engaged in the learning process (Astin, 1984). Yet other requests may violate teachers' expectations of what is appropriate within typical educational norms (e.g., asking to waive attendance requirements or making a special plea for a higher grade). Many teachers consciously inoculate themselves against students' influence attempts, while other instructors more readily agree to students' requests (Brophy & Good, 1974). Some instructors have learned how to negotiate the power dynamics that are inherent in any teacher–student relationship. Yet other teachers are unaware of how skillfully their students craft messages to which they acquiesce (Brophy & Good, 1974).

Whether intentional or unintentional, *student influence messages are those messages that change or reinforce teachers' attitudes, beliefs, values, and behaviors.* Such subtle nonverbal behaviors as notetaking, forward body leans, head nods, smiling, making eye contact, and appropriately asking and responding to questions may signal to teachers that students are engaged and paying attention. These behaviors have been shown to influence teacher perceptions of their students, their teaching, and their anticipated teaching behaviors (Mottet, Beebe, Raffeld, & Paulsel, 2004, 2005). Although many students, and some teachers, are not aware of how influential these indirect and unintentional (nonverbal) messages are, it has been shown that such messages may be *more* influential than direct and intentional influence attempts (Mottet, Beebe, Raffeld, & Paulsel, 2004, 2005).

At first glance, a chapter focusing on student influence may seem more appropriate in Unit Two, which examined instructional communication from the rhetorical perspective, than in Unit Three, which considers instructional communication from a relational perspective. We discuss student influence messages here because, as has been articulated by many researchers, teaching and learning is a relational partnership (Frymier & Houser, 2000; Richmond & McCroskey, 1992). Student influence messages are one of the strategies students use within the context of the relationship to meet their own instructional and interpersonal goals (Golish & Olson, 2000). Relational communication messages are often about power and influence (Burgoon & Hale, 1984). According to Berger (1996), "during the 1950s and 1960s, the study of interpersonal communication was coterminous with the study of communication and social influence processes" (p. 277). Contemporary communication perspectives continue to focus on the role of influence in relational development (Greene & Burleson, 2003).

This chapter examines how students' verbal and nonverbal messages influence teachers and their teaching in four sections. First, we provide a rationale for why researchers should focus on students' influence messages. Second, we review instructional communication research on the student-to-teacher relationship, or from the student-centered perspective. Third, we summarize the research and discuss the implications for teachers and students. And fourth, we provide instructional communication researchers with directions for future research that explore how students influence their teachers.

Rationale for Examining Students' Influence Messages

There are three reasons why instructional communication researchers should examine how students' verbal and nonverbal messages influence teachers and their teaching: (1) The student–teacher communication process is transactional; (2) student influence messages affect learning; and (3) student influence messages affect how teachers perceive their teaching effectiveness and satisfaction.

The Student–Teacher Communication Process Is Transactional

Communication is defined as a process that is mutually influential and reciprocal (Watzlawick, Bavelas, & Jackson, 1967). It is a transactional process whereby meaning is cocreated by the sender and receiver of a message. Yet, for the past three decades, instructional communication research has been anchored in a linear or "communication as action" paradigm. The overwhelming majority of instructional communication research has focused on how teachers use communication to influence student learning (Waldeck, Kearney, & Plax, 2001a). Missing from the research literature is extensive evidence of how students influence teachers and their teaching (Nussbaum, 1992).

Because teachers and students are "relational partners," in which each mutually meets the other's needs, it is difficult to examine students and their learning without also examining teachers. Similarly, it is equally problematic to examine teachers and their teaching without also examining students. In short, the teacher–student relationship, like most interpersonal relationships, is interdependent. Examining how students influence teachers provides a more complete and accurate understanding of the teacher–student relationship. Therefore, by acknowledging the transactional nature of instructional influence, we remain more true to contemporary conceptualizations of human communication. It should be noted, however, that examining instructional influence only from the student-to-teacher perspective continues to treat communication as a linear rather than as a transactive process. Nonetheless, focusing on the often neglected other half of the teacher–student communication process is a step forward in our understanding the transactional nature of the classroom communication process.

Student Influence Messages Affect Learning

Student influence messages may impact the content and amount of what students learn. For example, some students may find classroom learning to be challenging and at times painful; their natural inclination is to avoid learning. Research suggests that, because of their discomfort with learning or the amount of work assigned, these students intentionally seek to influence their teachers to reduce the amount of work required in the course, work that is specifically designed to enhance their learning (Astin, 1984; Martin, Mottet & Myers, 2000; Pascarella & Terenzini, 1991). Depending on how susceptible they are to student influence, teachers may not always make pedagogical decisions that are in the best interest of their students' learning. For example, teachers may comply with student requests to reduce homework as a way of getting their own needs met (e.g., getting students to like them or to respond positively to them). In some instances, teachers may get their own needs met at the expense of student learning.

Students also learn quickly that if they use indirect influence attempts, such as not responding to a teacher's questions or refusing to participate in class, they may get out of class early, thus jeopardizing their learning (Pascarella & Terenzini, 1991). Many teachers may not be aware that by dismissing class early they reinforce student disengagement rather than engagement. In addition, anecdotal evidence suggests that talkative and responsive students are the unintended victims of disengaged students because they are often punished or sanctioned for keeping the class going for the entire duration (Homans, 1950). Understanding student influence and how it impacts teachers, their teaching, and ultimately student learning, may enable teachers to learn more about how to negotiate power and influence in the classroom in such a way that both teachers' and students' instructional and relational needs can be met.

Student Influence Messages Affect Teacher Self-Perceptions

With increasing student enrollments and teacher retirements, the United States is facing a teacher shortage at all levels of education (Archer, 1999; Coffin, 2002; DeFleur, 1993; Evelyn, 2001). Two factors contributing to teacher attrition are teacher self-efficacy (Soodak & Podell, 1997) and teacher job satisfaction (Ingersoll, 2001).

Teacher self-efficacy is "the extent to which the teacher believes he or she has the capacity to affect student performance" (Berman, McLaughlin, Bass, Pauly, & Zellman, 1977). Teacher job satisfaction is a "state of mind determined by the extent to which the individual perceives his/her job-related needs being met" (Evans, 1997, p. 833). Research suggests that student behaviors directly influence teachers' perceptions of self-efficacy and job satisfaction and therefore may indirectly influence teacher attrition and turnover (Bandura, 1997; Kim & Loadman, 1994; Shann, 1998).

Ross (1998) found teacher self-efficacy to predict such student outcomes as achievement and motivation. Teacher self-efficacy also has been shown to predict teachers' adoption of innovation (Fuchs, Fuchs, & Bishop, 1992), professional commitment (Coladarci, 1992), absenteeism (Imants & Van Zoelen, 1995), and teacher retention (Glickman & Tamashiro, 1982). According to Bandura (1997), an individual's beliefs about self-efficacy are the result of learning processes in which social relationships play an integral role. We have every reason to believe that the quality of the teacher–student relationship influences teacher self-efficacy beliefs (Mottet, Beebe, Raffeld, & Medlock, 2004).

Dinham and Scott (2000) found that teachers were most satisfied in their career because of factors that are intrinsic to the role of teaching, such as helping students achieve, modifying students' attitudes and behaviors, and developing positive relationships with students. According to Shann (1998) and Kim and Loadman (1994), the quality of the teacher–student relationship was the number-one predictor of teacher job satisfaction among primary and secondary educators. Teacher–student relationship quality also plays an important role in how satisfied teachers are at the college level (Pena & Mitchell, 2000). Again, it is believed that students' verbal and nonverbal messages may influence teachers' perceptions of teaching satisfaction (Mottet, Beebe, Raffeld, & Medlock, 2004).

Despite the reasons discussed above for examining the student-to-teacher influence perspective, the majority of instructional communication research has focused on the teacher-to-student influence perspective. One reason for favoring this perspective may be related to research methodology. Getting students to participate in research projects is easier than getting teachers to participate. Another reason may be that teacher-centered models of instruction acknowledge the teacher as the primary agent of influence (Brophy & Good, 1986). More contemporary models of instruction, such as the student-centered pedagogical model or the adult learning androgogical model, acknowledge learners, in addition to teachers, as being agents of influence (Knowles, 1990; Knowles, Holton, & Swanson, 1998; Weimer, 2002). The next section of this chapter more closely examines instructional communication research from the student-to-teacher perspective.

Review of Student-Centered Instructional Communication Research

Four domains of instructional communication research are reviewed in this section: (1) how students' communication traits have been shown to influence teachers; (2) how students' nonverbal immediacy behaviors influence how teachers perceive their students; (3) how students' verbal and nonverbal responsiveness affects teachers and their teaching; and (4) the reciprocal nature of student–teacher classroom interaction and how students and teachers mutually influence each other.

How Student Communication Traits Influence Teachers

A communication trait is "any distinguishable, relatively enduring way in which one individual differs from another" (Daly & Bippus, 1998, p. 2). Communication traits attempt to define the meaningful ways in which people differ. Trait research examines communication behavior as being a manifestation or an expression of one's personality. For example, people who have an extroverted personality are often characterized by how much they express themselves. Extroverts are described as talkative and outgoing. Conversely, people who have an introverted personality are often characterized by how little they express themselves. Introverts are described as quiet or shy, and they are often loners. Such communication traits will have an effect upon the content and number of messages students express toward their teacher.

Quiet Students. Some students are talkative, while others are silent. In Chapter 3, McCroskey and Richmond examined student willingness to communicate and communication apprehension traits. Willingness to communicate refers to an individual's preference to initiate or avoid communication (McCroskey, 1992; McCroskey & Richmond, 1998). Communication apprehension, on the other hand, is an individual's level of fear or anxiety associated with either real or anticipated communication with another person or persons (McCroskey, 1977; McCroskey & Beatty, 1998). The willingness-to-communicate trait addresses an individual's communication preference, whereas the communication apprehension trait addresses an individual's communication fear. The focus in Chapter 3 was on helping teachers better understand their students' communication behaviors. In this section, we would like to briefly review how quiet or shy students, who have a low willingness to communicate and/or a high level of communication apprehension, influence teacher perceptions.

In America, teachers perceive quiet children to be less competent than more talkative students (Richmond & McCroskey, 1998). According to Richmond and McCroskey (1998), teachers expect quiet students to do less well in school and, as a result, treat them as being less intelligent. Quiet students are less likely to be called upon in the classroom, to ask for assistance, to participate in classroom activities, and to engage their teachers in conversations about course content. Consequently, quiet students are less likely to learn from their mistakes and are less likely to receive positive reinforcement from their teachers.

Instructional research also suggests that the quiet college student's grade-point average is significantly below the more talkative college student at the end of the first year of college (Richmond & McCroskey, 1998). While quiet students tend to achieve at levels lower than their aptitudes would suggest, talkative students may achieve at levels above what their aptitudes would suggest (Richmond & McCroskey, 1998).

The trait research that examines quiet students and how teachers perceive them remains particularly salient in terms of Rosenthal and Jacobson's (1968) seminal research examining the effects of teacher expectations on student performance. In the initial study examining what would become known as the "Pygmalion" effect, elementary school teachers were told that a new IQ test administered to their students revealed that certain students labeled as "late bloomers" should show marked increase in intellectual competence over the course of the school year. In actuality, the "late bloomer" label was assigned randomly to the students by the researchers. All students were given an IQ test at the beginning and end of the school term.

The results from Rosenthal and Jacobson's (1968) study revealed that the "late blooming" students improved their IQ scores dramatically compared to other students who were not labeled. This study suggested that teachers form expectations for their students and communicate in a manner that remains consistent with those expectations. For example, if a teacher expects a student to be intelligent, the teacher communicates as though the student is intelligent. The teacher engages the student in conversation. The teacher probes the student's responses. The teacher helps clarify the student's thoughts. Important to this chapter is the role that student communication plays in the formation of teacher perceptions and expectations for how students will perform in the classroom. It is clear that students are rewarded for being verbally responsive. Teachers perceive talkative students more favorably and interact with them in a manner that remains consistent with these more favorable impressions (McCroskey & Daly, 1976; Richmond & McCroskey, 1998).

Student Humor. Humor orientation, according to Booth-Butterfield & Booth-Butterfield (1991), is a communication-based personality trait that assesses an individual's predisposition to use humor frequently and in a number of different situations, as well as their self-perceived effectiveness in producing humorous communication. The influence of teacher humor and humor orientation on student learning was reviewed in Chapter 5. Here we examine the influence of student humor and humor orientation on teachers and their teaching.

Manos (2001) examined the effects of perceived student humor orientation on teachers' perceptions of student credibility, interpersonal attraction, and anticipated leniency behaviors. Her hypotheses tested the principle of homophily, or similarity, where it was predicted that teachers would form more favorable impressions, be more attracted to, and be more lenient with similar rather than dissimilar students in terms of humor orientation. Her hypotheses were not supported. In terms of perceived student credibility, Manos found that high humor-oriented teachers perceived low humor-oriented students as having significantly more credibility, meaning that they were perceived as having more character and competence, than high humor-oriented students. Conversely, she found that low humor-orientated teachers perceived high humor-oriented students as having significantly more credibility (character and competence) than low humor-oriented students.

In terms of perceived interpersonal attraction, Manos (2001) found that, regardless of a teacher's humor orientation, high humor-oriented students were perceived by teachers as being significantly more socially attractive than low humor-oriented students. Student humor orientation did not affect teacher perceptions of student task attraction or a teacher's desire to work with a particular student.

In terms of anticipated leniency behaviors, or a teacher overlooking student misbehaviors, Manos (2001) found that, rather than student humor orientation influencing a teacher's anticipated leniency behavior, it was the teacher's humor orientation that was most influential. High humor-oriented teachers anticipated themselves as being significantly more lenient in overlooking high and low humor-oriented students' misbehaviors than did low humor-oriented teachers.

How Student Nonverbal Immediacy Influences Teachers

Mehrabian's (1971) immediacy principle states that "people are drawn toward persons and things they like, evaluate highly, and prefer; and they avoid or move away from things they dislike, evaluate negatively, or do not prefer" (p. 1). According to Mehrabian, immediacy is a perception of physical or psychological closeness that engenders liking and pleasure in others. "Immediacy is an increase in the sensory stimulation between two persons" (Mehrabian, 1971, p. 3). Additionally, immediacy and liking are recursive, meaning that immediacy enhances feelings of liking, and liking, in turn, enhances perceptions of immediacy (Mehrabian, 1971).

Perceiving someone as immediate or nonimmediate helps individuals to determine whether they should approach or avoid an individual; this initial perception often serves as the basis for relational development (Mehrabian, 1971). Nonverbal communication behaviors, such as forward body leans, relaxed posture and use of gestures, smiling, eye contact, and head nods have been shown to enhance perceptions of closeness between teachers and students (McCroskey & Richmond, 1992). Although perceptions of immediacy can be enhanced by using verbal messages, or what is known as *verbal immediacy* (Mehrabian, 1966), this type of immediacy has limited utility in the instructional context (Mottet & Richmond, 1998).

The impact of teacher immediacy on students and their learning has been studied extensively in the instructional communication context and continues to be one of the more powerful predictors of student learning. This program of research is reviewed in detail in Chapter 8. The paragraphs that follow review the impact of student immediacy on teachers and their teaching.

Rosoff (1978) and Persi (1998) were two of the first researchers to examine the influence of student nonverbal immediacy on teachers. Rosoff's (1978) study was replicated and extended by Baringer and McCroskey (2000) in which they examined the influence of student nonverbal immediacy on teachers' perceptions of student credibility and interpersonal attraction—two variables that have been shown to enhance relational development. Not surprising, all of the relationships were statistically significant and positive. As teachers perceived their students as being more nonverbally immediate, teachers also perceived their students as being more credible or believable. Specifically, student nonverbal immediacy accounted for 25% of the variance in the competence dimension of credibility, 28% of the variance in the character dimension, and 29% of the variance in the goodwill or caring dimension. In short, teachers perceived responsive students to be smart, trustworthy, and caring. Additionally, as teachers perceived their students as using more nonverbal immediacy behaviors, teachers perceived them as being more interpersonally attractive in both social and task roles, with student nonverbal immediacy accounting for 19 and 27% of the variance in each of the respective dimensions. These findings suggest that teachers find responsive students to be more personally rewarding than nonresponsive students. Teachers are more likely to spend more time working and socializing with responsive than nonresponsive students.

Baringer and McCroskey (2000) also examined how student nonverbal immediacy influenced teachers' motivation to teach and teachers' projections of student success. Again, student nonverbal immediacy was statistically significant and positively related to both variables. Teachers reported being more motivated to teach nonverbally immediate students than nonimmediate students, with 34% of the variance being attributed to students' nonverbal immediacy behaviors. Additionally, between 22 and 25% of the variance in students' projected success in the current course and in life beyond college was attributed to students' nonverbal behavior in the classroom. Teachers perceive nonverbally immediate students to be more successful in school as well as in their future professional careers than nonimmediate students.

Mottet (2000) studied the influence of student nonverbal immediacy on teachers in both traditional face-to-face and distance education classrooms that used interactive television technology to bridge the distance between teachers and students. In both conditions, Mottet found statistically significant and positive relationships between student nonverbal immediacy and teacher perceptions of student quality, teaching effectiveness, teaching satisfaction, and quality of teacher–student interpersonal relationships.

In the traditional face-to-face classroom, Mottet (2000) found that 35% of the variance in teachers' perceptions of student competence was attributed to students being nonverbally responsive in the classroom. Additionally, he found 35, 36, and 34% of the variance in teachers' perceptions of their teaching effectiveness, teaching satisfaction, and quality of teacher–student relationships, respectively, were attributed to students being nonverbally responsive in the classroom.

In the interactive television classroom, Mottet (2000) found that 42% of the variance in teachers' perceptions of student competence was attributed to students being nonverbally responsive in the classroom. Additionally, he found 42, 24, and 41% of the variance in teachers' perceptions of their teaching effectiveness, teaching satisfaction, and quality of teacher–student relationships, respectively, were attributed to students being nonverbally responsive in the classroom. With the exception of teaching satisfaction, student nonverbal immediacy behaviors accounted for *more* of the variance in the interactive television classroom than in the traditional face-to-face classroom in terms of how teachers perceived their students and their teaching.

When comparing the traditional face-to-face and distance education classrooms, Mottet (2000) found that teachers in the interactive television classroom perceived their teaching effectiveness, satisfaction, and the quality of the teacher–student relationship *less positively* than when making similar evaluations in the traditional face-to-face classroom. He attributed these less positive perceptions, in part, to the reduction or blurring of nonverbal cues that teachers perceive in their students' behavior. Interactive television technology fails to capture and transmit students' subtle nonverbal cues that remain important to teachers.

To summarize the nonverbal immediacy research, it appears that student nonverbal immediacy influences teachers and their teaching in many of the same ways that teacher nonverbal immediacy influences students and their learning. Student nonverbal immediacy not only positively influences teachers' perceptions of students and the quality of the teacher–student relationship, but also their perceptions of their teaching motivation, effectiveness, and satisfaction, three variables that have been shown to affect student learning (Ross, 1998; Shann, 1998).

How Student Verbal and Nonverbal Responsiveness Influences Teachers

The first two authors of this chapter and a research team from Texas State University–San Marcos examined the effects of student verbal and nonverbal responsiveness on teachers and their teaching using a 2 X 2 experimental research design (Mottet, Beebe, Raffeld, & Medlock, 2004; Mottet, Beebe, Raffeld, & Paulsel, 2004, 2005). Approximately 120 faculty members from the university participated in this study. University educators who volunteered for this study were exposed to one of four treatment conditions. The first independent variable manipulated student nonverbal responsiveness, such as head nods, forward body leans, and eye contact. The second independent variable manipulated student verbal responsiveness, such as initiating questions and responding to the teacher's questions. Both independent variables had high and low conditions.

To create the four treatment conditions that manipulated student nonverbal and verbal responsiveness, four, ten-minute simulated classroom videos were produced showing an instructor teaching seven students how to conduct library research and how to critically evaluate library sources. The teacher and students who appeared in the video were actors. After viewing the video, faculty members were asked to complete a questionnaire containing a number of survey instruments. This data set yielded three different studies, which will be reviewed in the following section.

Effects of Student Responsiveness on Teacher Self-Efficacy and Job Satisfaction. Teacher self-efficacy and teacher job satisfaction have been shown to predict student achievement and motivation (Ross, 1998; Shann, 1998) and teacher retention (Coladarci, 1992; Glickman & Tamashiro, 1982; Shin & Reyes, 1995). With the current teacher shortage, which is occurring at all levels of education (Archer, 1999; DeFleur, 1993; Evelyn, 2001), teacher commitment and retention are becoming more important to administrators who are responsible for staffing classrooms with qualified teachers.

Mottet, Beebe, Raffeld, and Medlock (2004) hypothesized that because teacher self-efficacy and teaching job satisfaction are sensitive to the relational dynamics involved with teaching, and because nonverbal messages have been shown to have their primary impact on people's affective, versus cognitive, responses (Burgoon, 1994, Mehrabian, 1972), student nonverbal responsiveness would have a greater effect on how teachers perceive their effectiveness and satisfaction than student verbal responsiveness (Bandura, 1997; Kim & Loadman, 1994; Shann, 1998). Both hypotheses were supported. Student nonverbal responsiveness accounted for 17%, and verbal responsiveness accounted for 9% of the variance in teacher self-efficacy. In terms of teacher job satisfaction, student nonverbal responsiveness accounted for 51% of the variance, and student verbal responsiveness accounted for only 2% of the variance. The effect size for the nonverbal responsiveness independent variable was 25 times larger than that for the verbal independent variable.

Based on the results of their research, Mottet, Beebe, Raffeld, and Medlock (2004) concluded that student nonverbal responsiveness had a greater effect on teacher perceptions of self-efficacy and job satisfaction than verbal responsiveness. That is, teachers were affected more by their students' eye contact, forward body leans, and head nods than by their students asking and answering questions in the classroom. Additionally, the results suggested that teacher job satisfaction was more susceptible to student nonverbal and verbal responsiveness than teacher self-efficacy and particularly sensitive to student nonverbal responsiveness. Anecdotal evidence suggests that most teachers are not externally motivated or attracted to the teaching profession because of the salaries they make but rather are intrinsically motivated by the quality of the relationships they develop and maintain with their students (Dinham & Scott, 2000). As theorized, student nonverbal responsiveness appears to tap into the relational needs that teachers have to enhance their teaching satisfaction.

Effects of Student Responsiveness on Student Liking and Teacher Compliance. Because affinity for a teacher has been shown to influence student learning (McCroskey & Richmond, 1992) and student compliance (Plax & Kearney, 1992), Mottet, Beebe, Raffeld, and Paulsel (2004) investigated whether student verbal and nonverbal responsiveness interacted to influence how much teachers like their students and their willingness to comply with student requests. They found that, rather than student verbal and nonverbal responsiveness interacting, only student nonverbal responsiveness significantly affected how much teachers like their students and their willingness to comply with student requests, accounting for 66 and 31% of the variance in each respective variable. Again, it appears that student nonverbal responsiveness, rather than verbal responsiveness, is responsible for affecting how much teachers like their students and their willingness to comply with student requests, such as excusing absences, overlooking errors on assignments, and raising a grade if it falls on the cusp of a higher grade. Although some students may allege that teachers are showing preferential treatment toward responsive students, teachers will argue that they are simply reinforcing competent student communication behaviors.

Effects of Student Responsiveness on Teachers' Evaluation of Student Work. Since 41% of the variance in teachers' perceptions of student competence and 66% of the variance in teachers' liking of students were attributable to student responsiveness, Mottet, Beebe, Raffeld, and Paulsel (2005) investigated whether student verbal and nonverbal responsiveness interacted to influence the *relational power* that teachers grant students and whether this power influences how teachers evaluate student essays.

As noted in Chapter 6, French and Raven (1959) argued for five bases of social power (legitimate, coercive, reward, expert, referent) all of which are rooted in relational perceptions. The agent (the individual trying to exert power) must be perceived as powerful or influential by the target (the person to whom the influence is directed). Unlike most instructional communication studies where teachers are the agents of power and students are their targets (Plax & Kearney, 1992), this study examined students as the agents of power and teachers as their targets.

The data suggested that teachers yield relational power to their students based on how responsive students remain in the classroom. Approximately 9 to 18% of the variance in student power was attributable to students' responsive behaviors. With the exception of expert power, students' nonverbal responsiveness impacted the relational power that teachers yield to their students significantly more than students' verbal responsiveness. Teachers' perceptions of students' expert power was impacted by students' verbal and nonverbal responsiveness (eye contact, forward body leans, head nods, answering questions, initiating questions), making this power base the most susceptible to students' responsive behaviors. Additionally, student referent power significantly impacted how teachers evaluated student essays, accounting for 11% of the variance. Students who were yielded referent power received essay grades that were significantly higher than students who were not yielded this form of relational power.

In summary, teachers are clearly not immune from the influence of their students' verbally and nonverbally responsive behaviors. Like other types of relationships, the teacher–student relationship remains interdependent, in that teachers have the ability to influence students and their learning and, similarly, students have the ability to influence teachers and their teaching. Student responsiveness meaningfully affects teacher self-efficacy, teaching satisfaction, teachers' liking of students, and teachers' willingness to comply with student requests. Additionally, student responsive behaviors affect the relational power that teachers grant to students, and this power, to some degree, impacts how teachers evaluate student essays.

How Students and Teachers Influence Each Other

Comstock (1999) examined the reciprocal nature of instructional communication. She tested the theory of interaction adaptation (Burgoon, Stern, & Dillman, 1995), which suggests that communication between people is transactional. Unlike linear conceptualizations of communication, where teacher messages influence student behavior or where student messages influence teacher behavior, communication as transaction is where both teacher and student communication simultaneously affects the other's behavior. The theory of interaction adaptation predicts that both parties adapt to the other's communication behaviors and both are responsible for relational outcomes.

Interaction adaptation theory stipulates that there are three interrelated levels of behavior for any given functional set of interaction behaviors: *required, expected,* and *desired.* When people enter communication transactions with others, they do so with *required* needs, or needs that will drive subsequent interaction patterns. In the classroom, many teachers have required safety and comfort needs that influence their communication with students. When people interact with others, they have certain *expectations* for how the interaction will occur. In the classroom, teachers expect students to remain responsive to their instruction. Finally, when people interact with others, they hope to achieve a *desired* level of behavior. For example, in the classroom, teachers have a desire to explain concepts clearly and accurately and to keep their students focused and on task. This desired level of behavior allows teachers to reach their learning objectives.

The theory suggests that future communicative behavior is determined by what is needed (required), anticipated (expected), and preferred (desired) in any given interaction. Burgoon et al. (1995) referred to this as the *interactional position.* If teachers' and students' classroom interactions provide them with what is needed, anticipated, and preferred, then the interactional patterns are *reciprocated* between the two. However, if the behavior that a teacher expects from students does not match actual student behaviors, then the teacher compensates by *diverging* or *converging* their behaviors to bring about the required, expected, and desired levels of behavior. If this attempt fails, then the teacher reciprocates students' *actual* behavior.

Comstock (1999) tested only a part of this theory. She hypothesized that when students increased their level of nonverbal involvement in the classroom, teachers would reciprocate by increasing their own involvement. Conversely, she hypothesized that when students decreased and maintained a lower level of nonverbal involvement in the classroom, teachers would reciprocate by decreasing involvement. To test her hypotheses, Comstock set up an experiment where she invited 56 randomly assigned professors to present guest lectures to a class of students who were a part of the experiment. Some of the students were assigned the increased-involvement condition and were instructed to increase their nonverbal involvement after two minutes of the professor's lecture. The other students were assigned the decreased-involvement condition and were instructed to decrease their nonverbal involvement after two minutes of the professor's lecture.

The theory of interaction adaptation was partially supported in this first experimental study examining the transactional nature of classroom interaction. Although the professors' nonverbal involvement behaviors decreased in both conditions, which was *not* predicted, their behaviors in the increased involvement condition remained significantly and substantially more involved and expressive than for their counterparts in the decreased involvement condition. Comstock (1999) offered several plausible explanations for why the theory was only partially supported, some of which involved the limitations of the experimental design.

In summary, Comstock (1999) reported that, even during a single, 10-minute class presentation to a group of students, teachers' role performances were, in part, directed by their students. "Taken together with previous research on the effects of teacher involvement behaviors on student motivation and learning, results suggest that teacher–student interaction is transactional and that teacher–student relationships involve mutual influence, with each partner partially responsible for the other's role performance and important relational outcomes" (p. 22).

Knowledge Claims

Several conclusions or knowledge claims may be drawn from the results of the research summarized here. We are going to restate these knowledge claims briefly and then turn our attention to some of the implications for teachers and students.

What Do We Know?

1. Students' low willingness to communicate and/or high communication apprehension negatively influence how teachers perceive them. Teachers perceive quiet or shy students as being less intelligent, treat them as though they are less intelligent, and consequently, quiet students are less likely to learn from their mistakes and to receive positive reinforcements from their teachers (McCroskey & Daly, 1976; Richmond & McCroskey, 1998).

2. Student humor influences how teachers perceive their students; however, its effects are dependent on the humor orientation of the teacher. Three effects emerged from the study conducted by Manos (2001): (a) High humor-oriented teachers perceive low humor-oriented students as being more credible than high humor-oriented students. Conversely, low humor-oriented teachers perceive high humor-oriented students as being more credible than low humor-oriented students; (b) High and low humor-oriented teachers perceive high humor-oriented students as being more socially attractive than low humor-oriented students; and (c) High humor-oriented teachers are more willing to be lenient with both high and low humor-oriented students in terms of overlooking their misbehaviors than low humor-oriented teachers (Manos, 2001).

3. Student nonverbal immediacy positively influences teacher perceptions of student credibility and interpersonal attraction. Specifically, increased student nonverbal immediacy results in increased teacher perceptions of student competence, character, and caring or goodwill (Baringer & McCroskey, 2000). Increased student nonverbal immediacy also results in increased teacher perceptions of task and social attraction (Baringer & McCroskey, 2000).

4. Student nonverbal immediacy positively influences teacher motivation and teachers' belief that their students will be more successful in the course, as well as in life in general (Baringer & McCroskey, 2000).

5. Student nonverbal immediacy positively influences instructor perceptions of student competence, teacher self-efficacy, teaching satisfaction, and quality of the teacher–student relationship in both traditional and interactive television classrooms (Mottet, 2000).

6. Student nonverbal responsiveness affects teacher self-efficacy and teaching satisfaction significantly more so than student verbal responsiveness. Additionally, student nonverbal responsiveness more strongly affects teaching satisfaction than teacher self-efficacy (Mottet, Beebe, Raffeld, & Medlock, 2004).

7. Student nonverbal responsiveness affects teachers' liking of students and their willingness to comply with student requests (Mottet, Beebe, Raffeld, & Paulsel, 2004).

8. Student responsive behaviors affect the relational power that teachers grant to their students, and referent power impacts how teachers evaluate student essays. Students who were yielded referent power received essay grades that were significantly higher than students who were not yielded this form of relational power (Mottet, Beebe, Raffeld, & Paulsel, 2005).

9. Student nonverbal involvement affects teacher nonverbal involvement. Specifically, students' decreased nonverbal involvement in the classroom causes a significant decrease in their teachers' nonverbal involvement, suggesting that teacher behaviors are, in part, directed by their students' behaviors (Comstock, 1999).

What Are the Implications for Teachers and Students?

There are four major implications of the research reviewed in this chapter. Students' verbal and nonverbal messages influence (1) how teachers perceive students, (2) how teachers comply with student requests, (3) how teachers feel about teaching, and (4) how teachers and students mutually influence classroom interaction patterns.

1. Students' influence messages affect teachers' perceptions of students. It is important for teachers to acknowledge that student communication behaviors influence how they perceive and communicate with their students. Knowing that some students prefer not to communicate and/or are fearful of communication, teachers must find ways to enhance their perceptual accuracy of students, using information other than that which is orally communicated. We believe that most teachers are unaware that student talk behavior influences their perceptions of student competence. Additionally, we believe that teachers will be surprised to learn that approximately one quarter of their student competence perceptions and one quarter of their perceptions of students' projected success are attributed to student nonverbal responsive cues, such as smiling, head nodding, forward body leans, and eye contact, rather than to student verbal responsive cues, such as asking questions and responding to their teacher's questions.

2. Students' influence messages affect teachers' willingness to comply with student requests. It is important for teachers to acknowledge that student responsive behaviors influence their willingness to comply with student requests. Some students may perceive teachers' willingness to comply with their requests as showing favoritism or preferential treatment toward responsive or sociable students than toward nonresponsive or nonsociable students. Some teachers, however, may use their willingness to comply with student requests as a way to reward or reinforce what they consider to be effective student communication behaviors.

3. Students' influence messages affect teachers' affective responses toward teaching. It is important for teachers to acknowledge teaching and learning as a partnership. Like any relationship, both partners are responsible for helping the other meet his or her needs. Most teachers are not attracted to teaching because of the high salaries. Instead, teachers are attracted to teaching because they know that teaching will enable them to help students learn and will enable them to get some of their interpersonal needs meet. Student responsiveness plays an important role in how teachers feel about teaching in terms of their motivation to teach, their self-efficacy, and their teaching satisfaction. Teachers must continuously find ways of letting students know they are partially culpable, as in any interdependent relationship, for the quality of instruction they receive in the classroom by helping teachers meet their instructional and relational needs.

4. Students' influence messages affect teacher and student interaction patterns. It is important for teachers to acknowledge the reciprocal nature of teacher and student communication behaviors. Teachers who understand the transactional nature of teacher and student communication can use this knowledge to influence classroom interaction patterns in the desired direction. Informed teachers can guard against student disengagement or passiveness by inoculating themselves against such contagious behaviors. Instead, teachers can infect or elicit student engagement or activeness through their own expressive and animated communication behaviors.

These four implications provide a starting point for helping teachers understand how students' verbal and nonverbal messages influence teachers and their teaching. Teachers who question their effectiveness or have concerns about their level of satisfaction in the classroom should do more than examine their own teaching methods and behaviors for possible clues as to why their classroom experiences are less than positive and fulfilling. They should also look at and listen to their students to consider whether student messages are influencing their affective responses to teaching. Teachers should be cautious, however, in determining the cause and effect relationship between student behaviors and personal effectiveness. Teachers are encouraged to consider whether their students' lack of responsiveness is a reflection or a response to their own lack of teaching responsiveness, or whether students are independently communicating their low interest in the teaching and learning process. By increasing their awareness of the student–teacher communication dynamic, teachers can more skillfully adapt their teaching style to enhance learning. Additional implications stemming from the research examining the effects of student communication on teachers and their teaching are reviewed in Mottet and Richmond (2002) and Richmond and McCroskey (1998).

Directions for Future Research

Although a limited number of conclusions can be drawn from the research reviewed in this chapter, the following questions remain unanswered and may guide the direction of future research.

1. How is teacher–student communication mutually created or transacted in the classroom? Although the research reviewed in this chapter examines the other side of instructional influence (student-to-teacher vs. teacher-to-student), the research fails to capture what Nussbaum (1992) referred to as the "circular nature" of teaching and learning. One reason why researchers may have yet to examine the circular nature of instructional communication is because of the complex research designs that are needed to measure communication as a transactional process. One way that researchers may want to proceed is by finding ways to test Burgoon, Stern, and Dillman's (1995) theory of interpersonal adaptation. Researchers can begin this process by referring to Comstock (1999), who partially tested this theory.

2. What interpersonal and instructional needs do teachers have, and what roles do students play in meeting those needs? Over three decades of instructional communication research has revealed much about the instructional and interpersonal needs of students and how teachers meet those needs (Waldeck, Kearney, & Plax, 2001a). Little research, however, has focused on the instructional and interpersonal needs of teachers. How do students meet, or fail to meet, their teachers' needs for control, inclusion, and affection? What are the effects on teachers and their teaching when these needs are met or unmet? What are the effects on students and their learning when teacher needs are met or unmet? What role does teaching context (i.e., face-to-face classroom vs. distance-education classroom) play in how well students are able to meet the instructional and interpersonal needs of teachers?

3. How do student communication behaviors influence a teacher's style of teaching? Is a teacher's style of teaching more dependent on his or her own personality and communication traits, or is it influenced more by students and their communication behaviors in the classroom? Manos (2001) found that teachers' individual differences and student communication behaviors interacted to influence how teachers perceived their students. Some teachers may be more susceptible to certain student behaviors than others because of the communication and personality traits they possess. For example, teachers who are more susceptible to others' emotional expression or what Hatfield, Cacioppo, and Rapson (1994) referred to as "emotional contagion," or how susceptible a person is to catching others' emotions, may be more willing to comply with student requests than teachers who are less susceptible to emotional contagion (Mottet & Beebe, 2000; Mottet & Beebe, 2002).

4. Does a student's use of technology, such as e-mail, presentational software, or the Internet, impact the influence that the student has on the teacher? For example, Waldeck, Kearney, and Plax (2001b) found that instructors who used e-mail messages with embedded immediacy messages (i.e., inclusive language "us" vs. "you," emoticons) enhanced students' willingness to engage in mediated out-of-class communication significantly more than teachers who did not use these embedded immediacy messages. Can students influence their teachers' willingness to communicate in out-of-class communication by using similar immediacy message strategies? Also, do students' use of presentational software influence how teachers evaluate student presentations? Downing and Garmon (2001) suggest that students who use presentation software may not always be rewarded for their use of technology during their presentation.

5. Can students be taught to engage in nonverbal immediacy behaviors that ultimately influence the quality of instruction they receive from their teachers? Richmond, McCroskey, Plax, and Kearney (1986) found that students were able to discriminate between trained and untrained teachers in terms of teacher nonverbal immediacy behaviors in the classroom. Can teachers discriminate between trained and untrained students in terms of student nonverbal immediacy behaviors in the classroom?

6. Do teachers reward students who engage in responsive communication behaviors? Do teachers reward engaged and responsive students more so than disengaged and unresponsive students by complying with their requests and by being more lenient with them in terms of overlooking their misbehaviors? Are teachers aware of how they reward students? Precisely, how do teachers reward students? Are teacher compliance and leniency behaviors perceived by teachers and students as preferential treatment, or are teachers simply reinforcing what they consider to be effective and appropriate student communication behaviors?

7. How can teacher education programs help preservice teachers use student communication behaviors as information to enhance their teaching effectiveness? How can teacher educators train preservice teachers to inoculate themselves against automatically adapting or converging with students' passive and disengaged behaviors? How can preservice teachers be taught to strategically infect students with active and engaged communication behaviors that have been shown to enhance the affective responses in students? How can teacher educators teach preservice teachers to properly decode or interpret student nonverbal behaviors, ensuring that teachers make the appropriate attributions for such behavior? Answers to these questions would provide teachers with additional strategies that they can use in the classroom to enhance their teaching effectiveness.

8. What other instruments can be used to assess student immediacy or responsiveness? Although not ideal, the nonverbal immediacy behaviors instrument, which was originally designed to assess teacher immediacy (Richmond, Gorham, & McCroskey, 1987), can be modified to assess student immediacy (Baringer & McCroskey, 2000). To address some of the shortcomings of modifying the existing nonverbal immediacy behaviors instrument, Mottet (2000) developed the Nonverbal Responsiveness Measure that assesses teachers' perceptions of student nonverbal responsiveness. This measure was shown to be internally consistent and captured student nonverbal responsiveness in both traditional face-to-face and distance-education classrooms mediated by interactive television technology. The Measure of Nonverbal Responsiveness is included in Figure 7.1.

Instructional communication researchers are encouraged to continue developing or adapting existing instruments that will allow researchers to assess the influence of students' verbal and nonverbal messages on teachers and their teaching in a valid and reliable manner.

FIGURE 7.1 ***Measure of Student Nonverbal Responsiveness.***

(Scale: Never = 0, Rarely = 1, Occasionally = 2, Often = 3, and Very Often = 4)

How often did you *see* your students. . . .

1. raising their hands to talk.
2. displaying facial expressions that reflected their positive attitude.
3. showing interest by taking notes on what you were saying.
4. smiling while talking to you.
5. nodding their heads while you were talking to them.
6. looking at you while they were talking to you.
7. smiling while you were talking to them.
8. sitting up and leaning forward in their chairs.
9. gesturing with their hands and arms while they were talking to you.

(Scale: Never = 0, Rarely = 1, Occasionally = 2, Often = 3, and Very Often = 4)

How often did you *hear* your students. . . .

10. using vocal inflections that suggested their positive attitude.
11. using vocal starters that suggested they wanted to say something.
12. responding quickly to your questions or comments.
13. using vocal variety such as tone, pitch, rate, and volume that suggested their interests.
14. using vocal assurances that suggested they had received and understood your message.

From "Interactive Television Instructor Perceptions of Students' Nonverbal Responsiveness and Their Influence on Distance Teaching," by T. P. Mottet, 2000, *Communication Education, 49,* 146–164. Republished with permission by *Communication Education* and Taylor & Francis Ltd. http://www.tandf.co.uk/journals.

Summary

The purpose of this chapter was to show the side of instructional influence that is rarely discussed or examined in instructional communication research: the "student-to-teacher" side of instructional influence, which acknowledges the interdependent nature of the teacher–student relationship. The research clearly suggests that teachers are as susceptible to student influence as students are to teacher influence. The first section of the chapter provided a rationale for why researchers should continue examining student influence. The second section reviewed the research examining instructional influence from the student-to-teacher perspective. The third section reviewed the knowledge claims yielded from the research, as well as the implications for teachers and students, and the fourth and final section reviewed directions for future research.

References

Archer, J. (1999, March 17). New teachers abandon field at high rate. *Education Week,* p. 20.

Astin, A. W. (1984). Student involvement: A developmental theory for higher education. *Journal of College Student Personnel, 25,* 297–307.

Bandura, A. (1997). *Self-efficacy: The exercise of control.* New York: W. H. Freeman.

Baringer, D., & McCroskey, J. C. (2000). Immediacy in the classroom: Student immediacy. *Communication Education, 49,* 178–186.

Berger, C. R. (1996). Interpersonal communication. In M. B. Salwen & D. W. Stacks (Eds.), *An integrated approach to communication theory and research* (pp. 277–296). Mahwah, NJ: Lawrence Erlbaum.

Berman, P., McLaughlin, M., Bass, G., Pauly, E., & Zellman, G. (1977). *Federal programs supporting educational change: Vol. VII. Factors affecting implementation and continuation* (Rep. No. R-1589/7-HEW). Santa Monica, CA: RAND. (ERIC Document Reproduction Service No. 140–432)

Booth-Butterfield, M., & Booth-Butterfield, S. (1991). Individual differences in the communication of humorous messages. *Southern Communication Journal, 56,* 32–40.

Brophy, J. E., & Good, T. L. (1974). *Teacher–student relationships: Causes and consequences.* New York: Holt, Rinehart & Winston.

Brophy, J. E., & Good, T. L. (1986). Teacher behavior and student achievement. In M. Wittrock (Ed.), *Handbook of research on teaching* (3rd ed.) (pp. 328–375). New York: Macmillan.

Burgoon, J. K. (1994). Nonverbal signals. In M. L. Knapp & G. R. Miller (Eds.), *Handbook of interpersonal communication* (pp. 229–285). Thousand Oaks, CA: Sage.

Burgoon, J. K., & Hale, J. L. (1984). The fundamental topoi of relational communication. *Communication Monographs, 51,* 193–214.

Burgoon, J. K., Stern, L. A., & Dillman, L. (1995). *Interpersonal adaptation: Dyadic interaction patterns.* New York: Cambridge University Press.

Cantor, N. L., & Gelfand, D. M. (1977). Effects of responsiveness and sex of children on adults' behavior. *Child Development, 48,* 232–238.

Coffin, C. (2002). *Touching the future: Final report.* Washington DC: American Council on Education.

Coladarci, T. (1992). Teachers' sense of efficacy and commitment to teaching. *Journal of Experimental Education, 60,* 323–337.

Comstock, J. (1999, November). *Mutual influence in teacher–student relationships: Applying IAT to access teacher adaptation to student classroom involvement.* Paper presented at the annual meeting of the National Communication Association, Chicago, IL.

Daly, J. A., & Bippus, A. M. (1998). Personality and interpersonal communication: Issues and directions. In J. C. McCroskey, J. A. Daly, M. M. Martin, & M. J. Beatty (Eds.), *Communication and personality: Trait perspectives* (pp. 1–40). Cresskill, NJ: Hampton Press.

DeFleur, M. L. (1993). *The forthcoming shortage of communications Ph.D.s: Trends that will influence recruiting.* Working Paper Series from the Freedom Forum Media Studies Center. Arlington, VA: The Freedom Forum.

Dinham, S., & Scott, C. (2000). Moving into the third, outer domain of teacher satisfaction. *Journal of Educational Administration, 38,* 379–392.

Downing, J., & Garmon, C. (2001). Teaching students in the basic course how to use presentation software. *Communication Education, 50,* 218–229.

Evans, L. (1997). Understanding teacher morale and job satisfaction. *Teaching and Teacher Education, 13,* 831–845.

Evelyn, J. (2001, June 15). The hiring boom at 2-year colleges: Faculty slots—with tenure—are available, but not to those who boast about their dissertations. *Chronicle of Higher Education, A8.*

French, J. R. P. Jr., & Raven, B. H. (1959). The bases of social power. In D. Cartwright (Ed.), *Studies in social power* (pp. 150–167). Ann Arbor, MI: University of Michigan Press.

Frymier, A. B., & Houser, M. L. (2000). The teacher–student relationship as an interpersonal relationship. *Communication Education, 49,* 207–219.

Fuchs, L. S., Fuchs, D., & Bishop, N. (1992). Instructional adaptation for students at risk. *Journal of Educational Research, 86,* 70–84.

Glickman, C., & Tamashiro, R. (1982). A comparison of first-year, fifth-year, and former teachers on efficacy, ego development, and problem solving. *Psychology in Schools, 19,* 558–562.

Greene, J. O., & Burleson, B. R. (Eds.). (2003). *Handbook of communication and social interaction skills.* Mahwah, NJ: Lawrence Erlbaum.

Golish, T. D., & Olson, L. N. (2000). Students' use of power in the classroom: An investigation of student power, teacher power, and teacher immediacy. *Communication Quarterly, 48,* 293–310.

Hatfield, E., Cacioppo, J. T., & Rapson, R. L. (1994). *Emotional contagion.* New York: Cambridge University Press.

Homans, G. (1950). *The human group.* New York: Harcourt, Brace, & World, Inc.

Imants, J., & Van Zoelen, A. (1995). Teachers' sickness absence in primary schools, school climate and teachers' sense of efficacy. *School Organization, 15,* 77–86.

Ingersoll, R. M. (2001). Teacher turnover and teacher shortages: An organizational analysis. *American Educational Research Journal, 38,* 499–534.

Kim, I., & Loadman, W. (1994). *Predicting teacher job satisfaction.* Columbus, OH: Ohio State University. (ERIC Document Reproduction Service No. ED383707)

Klein, S. S. (1971). Student influence on teacher behavior. *American Educational Research Journal, 8,* 403–421.

Knowles, M. S. (1990). *The adult learner: A neglected species.* Houston, TX: Gulf Professional.

Knowles, M. S., Holton, E. F., & Swanson, R. A. (1998). *The adult learner: The definitive classic in adult education and human resource development* (5th ed.). Houston, TX: Gulf Professional.

Manos, A. B. (2001). *Students' humor and its influence on teachers' perceptions and anticipated leniency behaviors toward students.* Unpublished master's thesis, Southwest Texas State University, San Marcos, TX.

Martin, M. M., Mottet, T. P., & Myers, S. A. (2000). Students' motives for communicating with their instructors and affective and cognitive learning. *Psychological Reports, 87,* 830–834.

McCroskey, J. C. (1977). Oral communication apprehension: A summary of recent theory and research. *Human Communication Research, 4,* 78–96.

McCroskey, J. C. (1992). Reliability and validity of the willingness to communicate scale. *Communication Quarterly, 40,* 16–25.

McCroskey, J. C., & Beatty, M. J. (1998). Communication apprehension. In J. C. McCroskey, J. A. Daly, M. M. Martin, & M. J. Beatty (Eds.), *Communication and personality: Trait perspectives* (pp. 215–232). Cresskill, NJ: Hampton Press.

McCroskey, J. C., & Daly, J. A. (1976). Teachers' expectations of the communication apprehensive child in the elementary school. *Human Communication Research, 3,* 67–72.

McCroskey, J. C., & Richmond, V. P. (1992). Increasing teacher influence through immediacy. In V. P. Richmond & J. C. McCroskey (Eds.), *Power in the classroom: Communication, control, and concern* (pp. 101–119). Hillsdale, NJ: Lawrence Erlbaum.

McCroskey, J. C., & Richmond, V. P. (1998). Willingness to communicate. In J. C. McCroskey, J. A. Daly, M. M. Martin, & M. J. Beatty (Eds.), *Communication and personality: Trait perspectives* (pp. 119–131). Cresskill, NJ: Hampton Press.

Mehrabian, A. (1966). Immediacy: An indicator of attitudes in linguistic communication. *Journal of Personality, 34,* 26–34.

Mehrabian, A. (1971). *Silent messages.* Belmont, CA: Wadsworth.

Mehrabian, A. (1972). *Nonverbal communication.* Chicago: Aldine-Atherton.

Mottet, T. P. (2000). Interactive television instructors' perceptions of students' nonverbal responsiveness and their influence on distance teaching. *Communication Education, 49,* 146–164.

Mottet, T. P., & Beebe, S. A. (2000, November). *Emotional contagion in the classroom: An examination of how teacher and student emotions are related.* Paper presented at annual conference of the National Communication Association, Seattle, WA. (ERIC Document Reproduction Service No. ED447522)

Mottet, T. P., & Beebe, S. A. (2002). Relationships between teacher nonverbal immediacy, student emotional response, and perceived student learning. *Communication Research Reports, 19,* 77–88.

Mottet, T. P., Beebe, S. A., Raffeld, P. C., & Medlock, A. L. (2004). The effects of student verbal and nonverbal responsiveness on teacher self-efficacy and job satisfaction. *Communication Education, 53,* 150–163.

Mottet, T. P., Beebe, S. A., Raffeld, P. C., & Paulsel, M. L. (2004). The effects of student verbal and nonverbal responsiveness on teachers' liking of students and willingness to comply with student requests. *Communication Quarterly,* 52, 27–38.

Mottet, T. P., Beebe, S. A., Raffeld, P. C., & Paulsel, M. L. (2005). The effects of student responsiveness on teachers granting power to students and essay evaluation. *Communication Quarterly, 53.*

Mottet, T. P., & Richmond, V. P. (1998). An inductive analysis of verbal immediacy: Alternative conceptualization of relational verbal approach/avoidance strategies. *Communication Quarterly, 46,* 25–40.

Mottet, T. P., & Richmond, V. P. (2002). Student nonverbal communication and its influence on teachers and teaching. In J. L. Chesebro & J. C. McCroskey (Eds.), *Communication for teachers* (pp. 47–61) Boston: Allyn & Bacon.

Nussbaum, J. F. (1992). Effective teaching behaviors. *Communication Education, 41,* 167–180.

Pascarella, E. T., & Terenzini, P. T. (1991). *How college affects students: Findings and insights from twenty years of research.* San Francisco: Jossey-Bass.

Pena, D., & Mitchell, D. (2000). The American faculty poll. *NEA Higher Education Research Center Update, 6,* 1–8.

Persi, N. C. (1998, April). *Effects of student nonverbal and verbal immediacy behaviors on teachers' behaviors and perceptions.* Paper presented at the meeting of the Eastern Communication Association, Saratoga Springs, NY.

Plax, T. G., & Kearney, P. (1992). Teacher power in the classroom: Defining and advancing a program of research. In V. P. Richmond & J. C. McCroskey (Eds.), *Power in the classroom: Communication, control, and concern* (pp. 67–84). Hillsdale, NJ: Lawrence Erlbaum.

Richmond, V. P., Gorham, J. S., & McCroskey, J. C. (1987). The relationship between selected immediacy behaviors and cognitive learning. *Communication yearbook 10,* 574–590.

Richmond, V. P., & McCroskey, J. C. (Eds.). (1992). *Power in the classroom: Communication, control, and concern.* Hillsdale, NJ: Lawrence Erlbaum.

Richmond, V. P., & McCroskey, J. C. (1998). *Communication: Apprehension, Avoidance, and Effectiveness* (5th ed.). Boston: Allyn & Bacon.

Richmond, V. P., McCroskey, J. C., Plax, T. G., & Kearney, P. (1986). Teacher nonverbal immediacy training and student affect. *World Communication, 15,* 181–194.

Rosenthal, R., & Jacobson, L. (1968). *Pygmalion in the classroom.* New York: Holt.
Rosoff, J. M. (1978). *The effects of positive feedback on teachers' perceptions of students.* Unpublished master's thesis, West Virginia University, Morgantown, WV.
Ross, J. A. (1998). Antecedents and consequences of teacher efficacy, In J. Brophy (Ed.), *Advances in research on teaching* (Vol. 7, pp. 49–74). Greenwich, CT: JAI Press.
Shann, M. H. (1998). Professional commitment and satisfaction among teachers in urban middle schools. *Journal of Educational Research, 92,* 67–73.
Shin, H. S., & Reyes, P. (1995). Teacher commitment and job satisfaction: A causal analysis. *Journal of School Leadership, 5,* 22–39.
Shulman, L. S. (1986). Paradigms and research programs in the study of teaching: A contemporary perspective. In M. Wittrock (Ed.), *Handbook of research on teaching* (3rd ed.) (pp. 3–36). New York: Macmillan.
Soodak, L. C., & Podell, D. M. (1997). Efficacy and experience: Perceptions of efficacy among preservice and practicing teachers. *Journal of Research and Development in Education, 30,* 214–221.
Waldeck, J. H., Kearney, P., & Plax, T. G. (2001a). Instructional and developmental communication theory and research in the 1990s: Extending the agenda for the 21st century. In W. B. Gudykunst (Ed.), *Communication yearbook 24* (pp. 206–229). Thousand Oaks, CA: Sage.
Waldeck, J. H., Kearney, P., & Plax, T. G. (2001b). Teacher e-mail message strategies and students' willingness to communicate online. *Journal of Applied Communication Research, 29,* 54–70.
Wanzer, M. (2002). Use of humor in the classroom: The good, bad, and the not-so-funny things that teachers say and do. In J. L. Chesebro & J. C. McCroskey (Eds.), *Communication for teachers* (pp. 116–126). Boston: Allyn & Bacon.
Watzlawick, P., Bavelas, J. B., & Jackson, D. D. (1967). *Pragmatics of human communication.* New York: W.W. Norton.
Weimer, M. (2002). *Learner-centered teaching: Five key changes to practice* (2nd ed.). San Francisco: Jossey-Bass.

8

Teacher Immediacy and the Teacher-Student Relationship

Virginia P. Richmond
West Virginia University

Derek R. Lane
University of Kentucky

James C. McCroskey
West Virginia University

Introduction

The principal purpose of formal education in America is to help students acquire or modify cognitive, affective, and behavioral competencies through recognition, recall, and short- and long-term learning. The central role of the teacher is to create instructional environments in which the probability of achieving the intended educational objectives are met and student learning outcomes are enhanced (Anderson & Krathwohl, 2001; Bloom, 1956; Krathwohl, Bloom, & Masia, 1964). Effective teacher behaviors and the accompanying appropriate use of power are directly related to increased student learning outcomes and to positive student evaluations of teaching (Nussbaum, 1992). Arguably, one of the most influential teacher behaviors, as reflected in the unsurpassed wealth of interrelated research, and the subsequent progress made over the past 25 years—not to mention the 10 years since the publication of the first edition of this monograph—is teacher immediacy (Richmond & McCroskey, 1992). In fact, we have argued elsewhere that teacher immediacy is one of the most important bodies of research to both communication and education scholars interested in understanding the variables that impact classroom learning (Chesebro & McCroskey, 1998, 2000, 2001).

Enhancing a teacher's ability to strategically employ different types of verbal and nonverbal immediacy behaviors will increase teacher influence and positively impact student learning outcomes and the teacher–student relationship. Clear evidence for this assertion is provided by Ambady and Rosenthal (1993) in their landmark study titled "Half a Minute: Predicting Teacher Evaluations from Thin Slices of Nonverbal Behavior and Physical Attractiveness." These researchers conducted three studies. In studies one and two, subjects were asked to rate college teachers' and high school teachers' nonverbal behavior and physical attractiveness based on silent video clips that were 10 seconds in length. In study three, they investigated whether strangers' ratings of teachers would predict nonverbal behavior and physical attractiveness consistent with results from studies one and two if shorter video clips were shown. The clips were reduced from 10 seconds to 5 and 2 seconds respectively. The results were astonishing and revealed the following:

> There were no significant differences in the accuracy of judgments based on video clips 10s, 5s, and 2s in length. In addition, there were no significant differences in the accuracy of judgments for the two samples of teachers. . . . Moreover, judgments based on 30s exposures (three 10s clips of each teacher) were not significantly more accurate than judgments based on 6s exposures (three 2s clips of each teacher). (pp. 437–438)

Ambady and Rosenthal (1993) suggest that the human ability to form impressions is strongly supported by their studies. In fact, as has always been suggested in the nonverbal literatures, impression formation takes place very early in the relationship. Often, these initial impressions determine the communication that follows. They conclude that based on nonverbal behaviors shown in very brief (less than 30 seconds) silent video clips, we evaluate our teachers as accepting, active, attentive, competent, confident, dominant, empathic, enthusiastic, honest, likeable, not anxious, optimistic, professional, supportive, and warm. Subjects observed specific nonverbal behavior, such as symmetrical arms, frowning, head nodding, head shaking, pointing, sitting, smiling, standing, strong gestures, head touching, upper torso touching, walking, and weak gestures. They conclude the following:

> Teachers with higher ratings tended to be more nonverbally active and expressive. They were more likely to walk around, touch their upper torsos, and smile. Less effective teachers were more likely to sit, touch their heads, and shake rather than nod their heads. These results suggest that teachers with higher ratings showed more nonverbal expressiveness and involvement than less effective teachers. (pp. 436–437)

They also suggest that teachers "should be made aware of the possible impact of their nonverbal behavior and perhaps even trained in nonverbal skills" (p. 440). The researchers caution, however, that these judgments are most accurate for the affective side of teaching.

We have argued for years that the primary function of teachers' verbal behavior in the classroom is to give content to improve students' cognitive learning. The primary function of teachers' nonverbal behavior in the classroom is to improve affect or liking for the subject matter, teacher, and class, and to increase the desire to learn more about the subject matter. One step toward that is the development of a positive affective relationship between the student and teacher. When the teacher improves affect through effective nonverbal behavior, then the student is likely to listen more, learn more, and have a more positive attitude about school. Effective classroom communication between teacher and student is the key to a positive affect toward learning. As communication improves between teacher and student, so does affect. When teachers are trained to use verbal and nonverbal communication in the classroom more effectively, student–teacher relationships improve and so do the students' affective and cognitive learning. When positive affect is present, learning increases.

This chapter presents an overview of the immediacy construct, introduces the origins of the research program, details contemporary research for understanding significant contributions of immediacy research, provides a summary of the impact of both verbal and nonverbal immediacy on student learning, proposes special concerns associated with immediacy research, presents knowledge claims that are derived from immediacy research, and concludes by proposing directions for future research.

Overview of the Immediacy Construct

Within the instructional context, immediacy is the degree of perceived physical or psychological closeness between teachers and students. Immediacy represents sets of verbal and nonverbal communication behaviors that indicate a teacher's willingness to approach and be approached by students and is influential in reducing the perceived physical or psychological distance between communicators (Andersen, 1979; Mehrabian, 1969). Nonverbal immediacy behaviors include demonstrating variety in vocal pitch, loudness, and tempo; smiling; leaning toward a person; face-to-face body position; decreasing physical barriers (such as a podium or a desk) between themselves and their students, overall relaxed body movements and positions, spending time with students, and informal but socially appropriate attire. Gorham (1988) explained that teachers' use of humor, praise, actions and/or comments that indicate willingness to converse with students both in and out of the classroom, teacher self-disclosure, using inclusive pronouns (i.e., "we", "us", "our") when referring to coursework, willingness to provide feedback, and asking students about their perceptions about assignments, due dates, and so on, all contribute to the notion of verbal immediacy. If we use effective nonverbal and verbal behaviors with our students to increase perceptions of immediacy, our students feel closer to us.

The contemporary view of immediacy has evolved from the work of Mehrabian (1967, 1969, 1971) who was the first to advance the immediacy principle, which asserts: "People are drawn toward persons and things they like, evaluate highly, and prefer; they avoid or move away from things they dislike, evaluate negatively, or do not prefer" (Mehrabian, 1971, p. 1). Expressed simply, "liking causes immediacy." Several studies have been conducted over the past 40 years that have consistently found immediacy behaviors to be associated with more positive affect as well as increased cognitive learning and more positive student evaluations of teachers (Richmond & McCroskey, 2000a). This research has suggested the appropriateness of the following *immediate communication principle:*

> The more communicators employ immediate behaviors, the more others will like, evaluate highly, and prefer such communicators; and the less communicators employ immediate behaviors, the more others will dislike, evaluate negatively, and reject such communicators. We prefer to call this the "principle of immediate communication." (p. 86)

As referenced in other chapters in this book, instructional researchers have provided decades of evidence to support the overall claim that *what* (and *how*) teachers *do* and *say* directly affect student learning outcomes. Teacher influence can be increased through immediacy. Several important generalizations can be drawn from the large body of research on teacher immediacy:

1. Teacher immediacy behaviors can be used effectively to reduce challenge behavior and get students to do what teachers want them to do, so long as they are truly engaging immediacy behaviors, and they continue to use appropriate verbal and nonverbal immediacy behaviors throughout the course.
2. Students are drawn to teachers they trust and perceive as responsive, competent, and caring but avoid teachers they perceive as incompetent, apathetic, and nonresponsive.

3. Teacher immediacy behavior gives the teacher positive forms of behavior control, which enhances their referent power and eliminates the need to use coercive or other antisocial teacher strategies.
4. Immediacy behaviors determine the amount of power students grant teachers (see Chapter 6) and the degree of liking or affinity (see Chapter 9) that a teacher has with students.
5. Students usually will comply with, rather than resist, reasonable teacher requests, if the teacher is liked, respected, and admired by her or his students.

The central discussion in human communication of immediacy as liking was first articulated by McCroskey and Wheeless (1976, pp. 21–22) when they advanced the development of affinity as the first function of communication and discussed its central role in conflict management and avoidance. Bell and Daly (1984) went far beyond the initial attempt of McCroskey and Wheeless to identify ways in which people might use communication to develop affinity with others. Their typology of affinity-seeking techniques included 25 ways people might try to get others to like them. Later work based on their efforts suggest a central role for affinity in the classroom (see Chapter 9).

Of particular importance to the present discussion is the fact that Bell and Daly (1984) included use of nonverbal immediacy cues as one of their 25 affinity-seeking techniques. This inclusion is not coincidental and corresponds with arguments presented by French and Raven (1960), suggesting that referent power is the most influential of the power bases.

Origins of the Immediacy Research Program

The early work on immediacy in instruction was an outgrowth of efforts by faculty and students at West Virginia University to bring together the research literature in the field of communication with research in the field of education, which was specifically directed toward identifying teacher behaviors associated with effective classroom instruction. Janis F. Andersen attempted to explain, in terms familiar to researchers in communication, what was then (early to mid-1970s) available in the education literature concerning communication behaviors believed to be associated with effective teaching.

This was not a simple task, and Andersen spent several months reading without overcoming a growing feeling of frustration. She felt there was a common thread in much of the literature, but identification of that thread was most difficult. Finally, as a function of her then-current work in nonverbal communication, she proposed the construct of "nonverbal immediacy" as representing what she believed the research in education was finding to be important. This construct was an outgrowth of work by Mehrabian (1971) in the interpersonal arena.

Andersen (1978) chose to define immediacy as behaviors that "enhance closeness to and nonverbal interaction with another," a definition first employed by Mehrabian (1969). She then drew on literature from the fields of communication and education to elaborate on that definition and demonstrate that research already existed to indicate positive impact of several nonverbal immediacy behaviors of teachers on classroom outcomes (Andersen, 1978, 1979; Andersen & Andersen, 1982).

Andersen's dissertation was the seminal research effort in this area, not only because she presented the basic theoretical explanation for the impact of immediacy in instruction, but also because she developed an observational methodology for measuring immediacy levels of teachers, the Behavioral Indicants of Immediacy (BII) Scale. She found this measure to be reliable and to have predictive validity and, of considerable importance to later work, she found that carefully trained observers' scores on the instrument correlated highly with scores provided by untrained students enrolled in the targeted courses.

The importance of the BII scale cannot be overemphasized. It was composed of low-inference items relating to teacher behaviors. Hence, the face validity of the measure is extremely high. She also employed two sets of bipolar scales (one composed of five items, the other four items, which McCroskey had used as measures of attitude and beliefs previously) as an alternate measure of immediacy, a Generalized Immediacy (GI) Scale. Although scores on this measure were highly reliable and highly correlated with scores on the BII, it was a very high-inference scale, assessing global perceptions such as closeness and distance, cold and warm, and friendly and unfriendly. The GI Scale was used in many later studies because of its ease of administration. Only after extended use was it generally recognized that the high-inference nature of this instrument made it subject to potential redundancy of measurement when other affective measures were included in the data collection, as they virtually always were.

Most of the results of Andersen's (1978, 1979) study were clear and highly supportive of her hypotheses. Approximately 20% of the variance in student affect toward the subject matter and 46% of the variance in affect toward the teacher were predictable from teachers' scores on nonverbal immediacy. About 18% of the variance in students' behavioral commitment toward taking another course in the subject matter (interpersonal communication) and engaging in the communication practices recommended in the current course in which they were enrolled, were predictable from the teachers' nonverbal immediacy scores. Clearly, nonverbal immediacy was most closely associated with student affect toward the teacher. That was not unanticipated. After all, it is the teacher who is engaging in the behaviors that are viewed as positive. Thus, if any impact on affect is to be observed, it certainly must be expected that it would be affect toward the teacher. This must not, however, be allowed to overshadow the very strong association of nonverbal immediacy with the other affect variables. Clearly, what the teacher does in terms of immediacy has a general impact on student affect, one that goes well beyond simply increasing liking for the teacher.

One hypothesis in Andersen's study was not supported. There were no significant relationships observed between teachers' nonverbal immediacy scores and the test scores used to operationalize cognitive learning. Much has been made of this finding by later writers, particularly those critical of research in this area. This is unfortunate because the nature of the course and the test predicted the failure to find a significant relationship.

The students and teachers in this study all were drawn from a single course (in interpersonal communication). The course employed a common textbook, a common workbook that guided instruction in each class period, a common syllabus, learning objectives that were provided to the students, and tests based on those objectives. With those objectives and the textbook it was quite possible for a student to have mastered the content tested *without ever attending the class.* Hence, the impact of teacher behaviors (immediacy and all others) was virtually prohibited. It is ironic that in the attempt to find a way that a common cognitive test could be employed to test the related hypothesis, it was decided to use students and teachers in a class where every effort had been made to make the tests "teacher proof." Several other studies related to instructional communication were conducted in this same course before it was recognized that the nature of the course design was producing the observed results. The understanding of cognitive objectives was still primitive in the field of communication at that time. As that understanding increased, this type of class ceased to be used for research purposes.

Two other early studies contributed to the recognition of the potential importance of immediacy in instruction. In the first of these, Kearney (Kearney Knutson, 1979; Kearney & McCroskey, 1980) directed attention to the impact on learning of aspects of teachers' communication styles. Among a number of other concerns, she investigated the association of a style variable she called "responsiveness" with affective learning of students. In her discussion of the responsiveness construct, she made clear that it was primarily composed of behaviors related to nonverbal immediacy. Her results indicated a very high association of teacher responsiveness (immediacy) with student affect for both the teacher and the subject matter.

In her dissertation, Sorensen (1980) made the first attempt to extend the study of immediacy to include an aspect of verbal behavior. She manipulated the appropriateness of teacher self-disclosure statements and measured their impact on student perceptions of the teacher's immediacy. Because this study employed a laboratory simulation methodology, the students did not actually see or hear the teacher. They were only exposed to the experimental statements. Even under these circumstances, the variability in self-disclosure statements accounted for 28% of the variance in ratings of teacher immediacy. Clearly, as Mehrabian (1971) had indicated previously, immediacy has verbal as well as nonverbal components, and both can have an impact on learning in the classroom.

Contemporary Research on Immediacy in Instruction

The Importance of Immediacy to the Teacher–Student Relationship

Early research sought to determine the importance of immediacy in the classroom. Initial findings suggested the probability that immediacy might be a central aspect of effective teaching. During the period between 1980 and 1987, a number of studies relating to immediacy were reported. However, for our purposes here, only one study is reviewed before directing attention to the more recent studies. That is the study reported by Plax, Kearney, McCroskey, and Richmond in 1986. Although this study was most concerned with the role of power in the classroom as a function of verbal behavior alteration techniques (BATS; this is discussed in more detail in Chapter 6), the portion of concern here was the theoretical model proposed in that study, suggesting that the impact of verbal control strategies may be mediated by students' perceptions of teacher immediacy.

The results of the Plax et al. (1986) study provided extremely strong support for the theoretical model. Although immediacy and use of BATs each had unique impact on students' affective learning, the overwhelming majority of the impact of BATs was found to be mediated by immediacy. In short, as communication theorists had argued for many years before this study, the nonverbal behaviors of teachers served as mediators for teachers' verbal behaviors. Thus, it is not simply a matter of a teacher using reward, punishment, or some other verbal influence strategy. What the teacher uses as a verbal strategy has a differential impact based on her or his nonverbal immediacy. On balance, in this study of several hundred secondary school students and replicated with several hundred college students, it was found that immediacy could best be described as overpowering verbal control strategies in terms of impact on affective learning. This conclusion has been strongly reinforced by the work of Burroughs (1990) and other work related to student resistance of influence.

Teven and McCroskey (1997) provided one of the first attempts to investigate the teacher–student relationship by focusing on how teacher behavior patterns affect behavior patterns of students. They concluded, "perceived caring is associated with increased affective and perceived cognitive learning in the classroom" (p. 8). They failed, however, to investigate specific student–teacher interaction and relied primarily on self-report measures of student perceptions. In a follow-up study, Teven (2001) argued that "in order to maximize learning, it is essential for teachers to develop a good relationship with their students, because the rapport established between teachers and students, in part, determines the interest and performance level of students" (p. 159). By focusing on specific teacher characteristics and behavior patterns that include caring, nonverbal immediacy, sociocommunicative style (e.g., responsiveness and assertiveness) and verbal aggression, Teven (2001) was also able to determine how some types of teacher behaviors were related to student perceptions. His research, however, did not investigate how specific student interactions influence teacher perceptions and ultimately the student–teacher relationship.

The Cognitive Learning Problem

The earliest problem that communication researchers faced when trying to study the impact of teachers' communication behaviors on students' learning was gaining access to observe the full range of teachers. Poor teachers, those with dubious self-concepts, and those who have a low value for social science research on teaching are usually very unwilling to cooperate with research that may involve anyone observing or reporting on their teaching behaviors. This problem finally was solved (Plax et al., 1986) by collecting data from students about "the last class you had before this one." Thus, when data are collected in classes that meet university requirements, data from a wide and representative range of unidentified teachers are available, even though the individual teachers might not be willing to cooperate if asked to do so.

Although this method overcomes the limitations in generalizability concerning affective learning associated with studying sections in a single course, it makes the measurement of cognitive learning even more difficult. Our examination of the literature in education indicated we were not the first to confront this problem, but those preceding us had not found a satisfactory solution either. The study of variables that impact cognitive learning has long been impeded by the difficulty in establishing valid measures of this type of learning. Although standardized measures of cognitive learning within many specific content areas have been developed, comparisons across content areas, particularly across content areas in disparate fields (such as art and chemistry), suffer from lack of comparability of the cognitive learning measures. Use of standard scores would only partially compensate for those differences.

In addition, two other serious problems confront the use of standardized tests—even if we concede their validity as measures of what the student has learned, which many people will not concede. First, there is no assurance, in most circumstances, that the teacher has attempted to teach what is included on the standardized exam. In fact, great care usually is taken to assure that the teacher does not even know what is on the exam in order to prevent her or him for "teaching the test." Thus, the design and execution of these tests intends to make them "teacher proof." Second, administering such tests to students over a wide range of subjects and courses would be extremely expensive, would require cooperation of their teachers (many of whom would not cooperate), and would be very time consuming for the students participating in the research project (hence leading to high subject loss). These two problems make use of standardized exams an unrealistic solution to this difficult problem.

The next approach we considered was use of data already available in the classes in which students are enrolled. The first data considered, and rejected, was the final grade in the course. These data could be obtained from central records with little or no difficulty. Unfortunately, students' grades often have little relation to what students learn in a given class. Students may know the material when they enroll; they may know so little that they cannot catch up with the other students; grades may be based on such irrelevant (to the amount learned, that is) matters as class participation, work turned in late, attendance, or "attitude." The second data considered (which also relate to student grades) are the exams prepared and administered by the teachers of the individual classes. These were rejected because of the obvious difficulty of obtaining the scores from the teachers, the absence of norms from which to generate standard scores for each student, the general incompetence of individual teachers in generating reliable and valid tests, and finally, the fact that many teacher-made tests are not based on publicly stated objectives and are only marginally related to what is taught in the class.

These problems, which are related to measurement of cognitive learning, usually are not present in carefully controlled experiments. Unfortunately, such experiments usually have low ecological validity for generalizing to normal classrooms. As a result, we decided that obtaining a fully valid measure of cognitive learning across a variety of subject matters, teachers, and student levels was not a realistic goal. No such measures currently exist, and it appears that none are likely to appear in the foreseeable future.

The solution we chose is not a fully satisfactory one. We arrived at it by reasoning that what a person learns is a subjective matter no matter how it is measured. Standardized test scores are valid in the minds of those preparing the exams, but have no necessary correspondence to what is taught by a given teacher in a given class, much less what is learned from that teacher. Scores on teacher-made tests are valid in the mind of the teacher making out the test. However, these may have little or no correspondence with what the student thought he or she was supposed to (and did) learn and may have very low reliability or validity internally.

The other person in this learning equation is the student. Few students leave a course without some idea of how much they learned in that course. Hence, our choice was to use student reports of their learning as our measure of cognitive learning when studying the effect of various communication variables in the classroom. We do not argue this is the true, valid measure of cognitive learning. We do argue that this method provides useful information concerning learning, that if compared with other data on cognitive learning from laboratory experiments, will give us insights into teacher behaviors that can contribute to increased cognitive learning of students. Our first use of the measurement approach was in Power VII (Richmond, McCroskey, Kearney, & Plax, 1987), and we have continued its use in several immediacy studies since that time.

The Cognitive Learning Results

The studies reported by Richmond, Gorham, and McCroskey (1987) broke new ground in two ways. First, these were the first immediacy studies to employ the student self-report approach to measuring cognitive learning. The students were asked to respond to two questions: "On a scale of 0–9, how much did you learn in this class, with 0 meaning you learned nothing and 9 meaning you learned more than in any other class you've had?" and "How much do you think you could have learned in the class had you had the ideal instructor?" By subtracting the score on the first scale from the score on the second, a variable labeled "learning loss" was created. This was intended to remove some of the possible bias with regard to estimated learning that could stem from being forced to take a class in a disliked subject. Hence, two scores were taken to represent students' perceptions of their learning. The first was the "raw learning" score and the second was the "learning loss score." It was presumed that immediacy should be correlated positively with the former and negatively with the latter.

The second unique aspect of this research was the introduction of a new observational measure of immediacy. It was based on the original BII, but the items were worded in an absolute fashion ("This teacher gestures when talking to the class.") rather than in the comparative fashion of the original instrument ("This instructor gestures more while teaching than most other instructors."). In addition, instead of the original 1–7, "strongly agree-strongly disagree" response format, the students were asked to respond by circling Yes or No to indicate whether their teacher used a given behavior at all. Then those responding Yes were asked to indicate in a 1–4, "rarely-very often" response format how frequently the teacher used the behavior. This change was made in response to findings reported by Rodgers and McCroskey (1984), which suggested that the comparative approach might introduce invalidity when students enter classes with substantially different experiences, such as students in the hard sciences compared to students in theater. Subsequent research (Gorham & Zakahi, 1990) indicates that this new approach yields more valid data than the previous approach.

Results of the first Richmond, Gorham, & McCroskey (1987) study indicated that when students were asked either to describe the worst or best teacher they could recall, immediacy behaviors alone permitted 95% accuracy in classifying teachers into the two categories. In the second study, students were asked to recall a class they had in the prior semester and report the immediacy behaviors of the teacher in that class and indicate how much they thought they learned. The subjects were classified into low (0–3), moderate (4–6), or high (7–9) learners. Discriminate analysis indicated that the students could be classified in the correct category, based on the reported teacher immediacy level, with an accuracy level of 68%, over twice what would be expected by chance alone.

An additional examination of these data indicated that students categorized as low learners had teachers who, on average, had moderately low immediacy. Those students with high and moderate learning had teachers who, on average, had moderately high immediacy. This suggests the possibility that the relationship between immediacy and cognitive learning may not be linear. That is, a moderate amount of immediacy may be crucial to attain a moderate amount of cognitive learning, but increased immediacy beyond that level may have little more positive impact. It may even be that there is a point at which the teacher can have "too much" immediacy. The data in this study could not completely confirm such an impact, but this appears to be a possibility worthy of exploration in future research.

Gorham (1988) built upon the Richmond, Gorham, & McCroskey (1987) study by developing and testing a measure of verbal behaviors believed to be related to immediacy. In a study employing the methodology of having students complete questionnaires based on "the class you have just before this one," she replicated the decade-long findings of a strong relationship of nonverbal immediacy with affective learning [for the first time using the Richmond et a1. (1987) measure of nonverbal immediacy] and also the cognitive learning findings in the previous study. Her measure of verbal immediacy was found to produce results very similar to those involving nonverbal immediacy.

At this point it became clear that employing the student self-report method of measuring cognitive learning generated data that pointed to a strong impact of both nonverbal and verbal immediacy. Given the known limitations of such a measure, however, participants in the research program were hesitant to advance strong generalizations related to cognitive learning without comparable results employing another methodology. The next study removed that hesitation.

In order to overcome the limitations related to studying cognitive learning in the field, Kelley and Gorham (1988) designed a laboratory experiment in which all content to be learned was novel and could not be known by the student participants in advance. Students were taught individually. They were read, and asked to recall, four groups of six items in each of four conditions. Each group of items consisted of alternating three- to five-letter nouns and two-digit numbers. The word/number sequences provided six unrelated "chunks" for memory storage and recall.

The four teaching conditions were: (1) high physical immediacy with eye contact, (2) high physical immediacy with no eye contact, (3) low physical immediacy with eye contact, and (4) low physical immediacy with no eye contact. High physical immediacy was operationalized as having the teacher sit on the edge of the chair, lean forward, place nothing between teacher and student, and utilize head nods while administering the test. Low physical immediacy was operationalized as having the teacher recline in the chair, sit with crossed legs, use a notebook to create a barrier between teacher and student, and utilize no head nods. "With eye contact" was operationalized as focusing the teacher's eyes on the eye area of the student while administering all six items. "No eye contact" was operationalized as the teacher focusing eye direction on the notebook while administering all items. After each list of six items was read, the teacher supplied the student with a slip of paper to reproduce the list. The accuracy of reproduction served as the measure of cognitive learning.

Analysis of variance indicated that each of the two types of immediacy behaviors increased learning. Physical immediacy accounted for 11.4% of the total learning variance and eye contact accounted for 6.9%. An interaction of the two immediacy conditions accounted for an additional 1.2% of the variance. This came as a function of the very negative impact of the combination of low physical immediacy and no eye contact condition.

Post hoc, or follow-up, analyses indicated additional impact related to eye behavior. In the primary analysis noted earlier, responses were counted as correct even if they were recalled out of order. Simply put, the measure was one of recall of items, not recall of sequence. When sequence errors were examined, it was found that there were 37 instances of incorrect sequencing in the two conditions with no eye contact, but only 11 instances in the two conditions with eye contact. In addition, students correctly recalled the second digit, while incorrectly recalling the first digit of the two-digit numbers in 68 instances in the two conditions that did not involve eye contact but in only 32 instances in the conditions with eye contact. Both of these differences were statistically significant far beyond chance ($p < .0001$).

The results of the Kelley and Gorham (1988) study filled in the important gap in the previous studies of the relationship between immediacy and cognitive learning. Although that study alone would not "prove" such a relationship in a "real" classroom, neither would the earlier studies drawing on student self-reports. In combination, however, they make a strong case for the relationship. The weaknesses in one type of study are overcome by the strengths of the other type. At this point, then, the presumption moves in favor of a meaningful and positive relationship between nonverbal immediacy and cognitive as well as affective learning. It is now the responsibility of one who doubts such a relationship to disprove it rather than simply to demand more evidence.

Explaining Immediacy's Impact

Over the next decade, several studies investigated specific teacher immediacy behaviors that include humor (Gorham & Christophel, 1990; Wrench & Richmond, 2000; Wanzer & Frymier, 1999) teacher disclosure (Sorensen, 1989), and attire (Gorham, Cohen, & Morris, 1997, 1999; Morris, Gorham, Cohen, & Huffman, 1996; Roach, 1997) with consistent findings. At this point, only the morbidly skeptic among us is likely to question whether increased teacher immediacy has a positive impact on student learning—especially when we measure learning as affective changes in student attitudes. Explaining how that impact occurs, however, is quite another matter. Two viable explanations have been advanced: the arousal–attention explanation and the motivation explanation.

Arousal–Attention Explanation

The arousal–attention explanation was advanced by Kelley and Gorham (1988). They restricted their theory to cognitive learning, but this does not preclude impact on affective learning. They argued that immediacy is related to arousal, which is related to attention, which is related to memory, which is related to cognitive learning. They supported this theory by drawing from research reported prior to their own study, then used the results of their study for additional support.

Essentially, their argument is that a mentally inert student cannot learn. Thus, it is initially essential to arouse the student from an inert state (unless that has already occurred). Lively, immediate behaviors are seen as most likely to generate arousal. That which stimulates arousal is seen then as that which will receive attention. Things cannot be remembered (initially learned) unless they receive initial attention. Thus, behaviors that draw attention to the teacher provide the minimal conditions necessary for learning. If things are vividly presented, they are more likely to be remembered by students who attend to their presentation. Hence, immediate teachers arouse students, draw attention to themselves, have that attention directed to the content being taught, and produce more student learning.

Motivation Explanation

The motivation explanation was advanced by both Christophel (1990a, 1990b) and Richmond (1990). Essentially, this view argued that students learn when they *want* to learn. If they want to learn, they will expend extra effort and learn more. Motivated students want to learn and will work at it. It is recognized that some students are generally more motivated to learn than are others, a trait of motivation orientation. Nevertheless, the motivation level of less motivated students can be increased under some circumstances. Thus, some teacher behaviors may increase student motivation. Specifically, teachers engaging in immediate behaviors are seen as likely to increase state motivation by stimulating the students and directing their efforts in the proper directions.

As noted previously, the Kelley and Gorham (1988) research was predicated on the arousal–attention theory, and the results of the study were those predicted from the theory. Unfortunately, however, they measured neither attention nor arousal. Hence, we cannot say their theory was supported. But at least it was not discounted because the results were consistent with the theory.

In the Richmond (1990) study, student motivation was measured along with measures of several other constructs (immediacy, affinity seeking, BATs, relative power use, learning). Results indicated that motivation was substantially associated with both learning and nonverbal immediacy. This is consistent with the motivation theory but, of course, does not confirm the theory because all of the data were collected simultaneously, thus precluding firm causal explanations.

Two studies were reported by Christophel (1990a, 1990b). The primary difference in the two studies was in the methods of data collection. Study 1 used the same general method used in the Richmond (1990) study and several others noted previously. The research method asked students to reference the class they were taking immediately before the one in which the data were collected. Because this design was subject to the criticism that all of the data were collected from the same subjects at the same time and might inflate correlations observed, her second study used a different data collection method. There were 60 intact classes included in the study. The students in each class were randomly assigned to one of two sets of scales. One set included scales related to verbal immediacy, nonverbal immediacy, and motivation. The other set included scales to measure motivation and learning. Mean scores were completed for each class for each of the two sets of scales. All analyses involved the class as the unit of analysis rather than the individual student. Thus, scores on immediacy from one set of students could be correlated with scores on learning from the other set of students. Similar analyses could be computed for questions concerning motivation.

Because the results of both studies were highly similar, we address those employing the new data collection procedure. Immediacy scores of the first set of students were highly correlated with motivation scores of the other set of students. Similarly, motivation scores of the first set of students were highly correlated with learning scores of the other set of students. Not only did these results support the motivation theory, they also indicated that previous research was most likely not contaminated to any significant degree by simultaneous completion of measures among interrelated concepts.

Multiple correlations of nonverbal immediacy and motivation with the various measures of learning were decomposed to identify unique and collinear predictive power. With the exception of the learning loss scores (where nonverbal immediacy and motivation had very similar amounts of unique ability to predict variance) and affect toward the teacher (where nonverbal immediacy predicted far more variance), motivation was a far superior unique predictor of learning than was immediacy. In conjunction with the finding that much of the predictable variance was a function of the two variables' collinear relationships with learning, this was strongly supportive of the motivation theory's ability to explain the relationship between immediacy and learning.

At this point, then, the theory with the best support for explaining the role of immediacy in enhancing student learning is the motivation theory (Frymier, 1993). The arousal–attention theory, however, certainly should not be discounted. What data are available are supportive of the theory, but they are far from conclusive at this point. Also, it is very possible that both theories will ultimately be found to be useful explanations. They are not in conflict with each other, so acceptance of one does not necessitate rejection of the other. Additional studies have been conducted to clarify the relationship between nonverbal immediacy and different types of learning outcomes with mixed and sometimes contradictory results (Hess & Smythe, 2001; Messman & Jones-Corley, 2001; Rodriguez, Plax, & Kearney, 1996; Titsworth, 2001; Violette, 2002; Witt & Wheeless, 2001; Witt, Wheeless, & Allen, 2004). For example, the results reported by Booth-Butterfield, Mosher, and Molish (1992) that teacher immediacy acts as a peripheral cue and thus directly affects student cognitive learning could not be replicated by Lane, McCroskey, and O'Brien (1996). Even if future research demonstrates only indirect relationships between teacher immediacy and cognitive learning, there is considerable evidence that teacher immediacy positively influences a host of desirable instructional behaviors, including student willingness to talk (Menzel, & Carrell, 1999), student ratings of instruction (Moore, Masterson, Chrisophel, & Shea, 1996), and teacher credibility (Thweatt, & McCroskey, 1998).

Special Concerns

Immediacy and Affinity

As we noted before, one way of viewing immediacy is as one of many methods of seeking affinity. From this perspective, teachers engage in immediate behaviors with students and, as a function of the resulting higher affinity between the teacher and students, the students learn more. This is somewhat like a referent–power explanation. If students like and respect the teacher, they will engage in less misbehavior and direct more efforts toward learning what the teacher suggests is important.

This perspective suggests, then, that there is little direct impact of immediacy on learning. Rather, the impact is seen as indirect. Immediacy leads to increased affinity that results in increased learning. Nothing in the studies reported to date in any way would cause us to reject this perspective. In fact, the results of the Richmond (1990) study are quite supportive. In that work, most of the predictive power of immediacy and affinity seeking was collinear—precisely what we should expect if the impact of immediacy results from increased affinity. Chapter 9 considers this type of general role for affinity in additional ways.

Culture and Immediacy

Most empirically based communication theory is heavily biased in the direction of what is normative for the White, middle-class, American culture. Almost all of the research in instructional communication has been conducted within this cultural context, even though students from junior high school through college levels have been studied.

There is a good reason to suspect that the immediate behaviors of teachers might have a different impact in one culture than they have in another. Much of immediacy is a function of nonverbal behavior, and it is very well established that nonverbal behaviors have different norms and impacts in different cultures. Thus, ignoring culture in the generation of theory concerning immediacy in the classroom greatly increases the probability that the resulting theory will have little cross-cultural validity. This, of course, does not put immediacy theory in any different position than other theories related to communication in instruction, or theory about communication in other contents for that matter.

Researchers interested in immediacy in instruction have expended considerable effort in the past 15 years investigating the potential impact of culture. Both Sanders and Wiseman (1990) and Powell and Harville (1990) have sought to determine whether students from different subcultures in California universities differ in their responses to teacher immediacy behaviors.

Powell and Harville (1990) found only small differences among White, Latino, and Asian-American subgroups with regard to the relationships between nonverbal immediacy behaviors and four affect variables. A similar result was observed for the relationship between verbal immediacy behaviors and those same affect variables for White and Latino subgroups. In contrast, the relationships for verbal immediacy and the affect variables were much smaller for the Asian-American subgroup.

Sanders and Wiseman (1990) conducted a somewhat similar study that included four subgroups: White, Asian, Hispanic, and Black. They collected data related to cognitive, affective, and behavioral (intent) learning. The associations between immediacy (a combination of verbal and nonverbal items) and both cognitive and behavioral learning did not differ across the four ethnic subgroups. With regard to affective learning, the association between immediacy was larger for the Hispanic group than for the Asian or Black groups. The White group did not differ from any of the other three groups.

These relatively small differences among ethnic subgroups may be taken to suggest that the overall relationship between immediacy and learning may not be very large. However, when Sanders and Wiseman (1990) compared the ethnic groups on individual items they found some striking differences. Blacks, in particular, appeared in several instances to respond very differently to some items than members of other groups. However, the number of Blacks in the study was so small that the correlation obtained was not very stable and can be expected to be quite different if based on a large sample.

Although we do not wish to make too much of the results from only two studies, we believe the differences observed here are very conservative estimates of what might be found in comparisons between more clearly different cultures. It can be argued, for example, that all groups of Americans are likely to be more like each other than they are to be like Japanese, Saudis, or Somalians. More recent studies, from this perspective, go beyond examining differences within a given culture to present a true intercultural perspective.

We have conducted (along with colleagues from other countries) several studies of teacher immediacy and learning in cultures outside the United States with consistent findings suggesting relationships in at least some cultures may be very similar to those in the United States (Hinkle, 1998; McCroskey, Fayer, Richmond, Sallinen, & Barraclough, 1996; McCroskey, Richmond, Sallinen, Fayer, & Barraclough, 1995; McCroskey, Sallinen, Fayer, Richmond, & Barraclough, 1996; Myers, Zhong, & Guan, 1998; Neuliep, 1995; 1997; Roach & Byrne, 2001). Although there is still more work to be done, we are encouraged by recent cross-cultural comparisons of nonverbal immediacy, motivation, and cognitive learning among Japanese students and American students in a cultural context outside the United States, which suggest that the relationships are similar to those found among American college students (Pribyl, Sakamoto, & Keaten, 2004). One of the problems we have confronted, and have yet to overcome, is that in many cultures anything that might be seen as student evaluation of a teacher is considered completely unacceptable, and the kind of social science research represented in the work on immediacy is seen to fall into that category. Likewise, isolated research demonstrates the need for continued research to clarify the relationship between gender, gender expectations, and teacher immediacy behaviors that may differentially impact student learning outcomes (Menzel & Carrell, 1999; Violette, 2002).

Immediacy and Training

One concern that always must be addressed by instructional communication researchers is whether their findings can be translated into real improvements in the classroom. Finding that immediate teachers produce more learning in students is an interesting outcome of 30 years of intensive research. But it is a relatively meaningless finding if immediacy is purely personality based and cannot be changed.

Fortunately, a number of studies have found that teacher nonverbal behaviors are subject to change through appropriate instructional intervention. The one most directly related to our present concerns was reported by Richmond, McCroskey, Plax, and Kearney (1986). Teachers in grades 7–12 who were trained in nonverbal communication generally, and nonverbal immediacy behaviors specifically, were paired with teachers in their same school (pairs of teachers in several different schools were involved) who taught the same subject but had no nonverbal communication training. Measures of nonverbal immediacy (BII) and affective learning were administered to the students of both groups of teachers. The students of the trained teachers were seen as significantly more immediate than those of the untrained teachers, and the students of the trained teachers reported higher affect for both the teacher and the subject matter than did the students of the untrained teachers.

Based on this, and other research reviewed by Richmond et al. (1986), it would appear that the results of the research on immediacy in the classroom can be translated into real improvements in teacher behaviors and real increases in student learning. In recent years, studies have been conducted to refine self-report measures of verbal and nonverbal immediacy (McCroskey, 1997; Richmond, McCroskey, & Johnson, 2003; Robinson & Richmond, 1995). For example, Mottet and Richmond (1998) inductively analyzed an alternative measure of verbal immediacy to conceptualize relational verbal approach–avoid strategies. While many of the results reported were not significant, the heuristic value of their research ultimately led to an improved measure of verbal immediacy and a new nonverbal immediacy scale (NIS) (Richmond, McCroskey, & Johnson, 2003). Please see Chapter 13 for a preview of the revised nonverbal immediacy scale (NIS).

Knowledge Claims

Several knowledge claims and conclusions may be drawn from the results of the research summarized in this chapter. Obviously, the immediate teacher is perceived more positively than the nonimmediate teacher, but there are other significant advantages to be gained from teacher immediacy in the classroom. Let us examine these briefly and then turn our attention to directions for future research.

1. Increased teacher immediacy results in increased liking, affiliation, and positive affect on the part of the student. Immediate teachers are liked far more than nonimmediate teachers.

2. Increased teacher immediacy results in an increased student affect for the subject matter. Students who become motivated to learn the subject matter because of the immediate teacher will do well in the content and continue to learn long after the teacher who motivated them is out of the picture.

3. Increased teacher immediacy results in increases in students' cognitive learning. Students with immediate teachers attend more to the subject matter, concentrate more on the subject, retain more of the content, and when challenged can correctly recall more of the subject matter than students with nonimmediate teachers.

4. Increased teacher immediacy results in increased student motivation. It seems that the primary way that immediacy produces learning effects may be as a function of it increasing student motivation.

5. Increased teacher immediacy results in reduced student resistance to teachers' influence attempts or teachers' behavior modification attempts. Immediate teachers seem to have more referent, respect, or liking power; hence students tend to comply with or conform to the wishes of the more immediate teachers. Nonimmediate teachers have more difficulty getting students to comply with or conform to their wishes.

6. Increased teacher immediacy results in the teacher being perceived as a more competent communicator, one who listens and cares. Nonimmediate teachers are usually perceived as ineffective, if not incompetent communicators.

7. Increased teacher immediacy results in the teacher being able to reduce or alleviate student anxiety about the classroom situation. A more immediate teacher is perceived as a more caring, sensitive teacher, hence the student feels less apprehensive about the overall instructional environment.

8. Increased teacher immediacy results in an increased student-to-teacher communication and interaction. Some teachers might see this aspect as a negative. It is not. If students communicate more with their teachers, then the student is more likely to get the information he or she needs (Frymier, 1994; Frymier & Houser, 2000).

9. Increased teacher immediacy results in a reduced status differential between student and teacher. This does not mean the teacher is on the same level as the student. It simply means the student won't be so intimidated by the teacher's higher status. Therefore, the student might be more willing to ask clarifying questions about the content with no fear of the teacher.

10. Increased teacher immediacy results in higher evaluations from one's immediate supervisor. While this may seem unusual at first, it is really very simple to understand. Administrators like teachers who have good classes with few problems. Immediate teachers have good classes with fewer problems than nonimmediate teachers. Hence, administrators will find immediate teachers to be the more effective teachers.

Directions for Future Research

Nonverbal immediacy behaviors are some of the most valuable communication tools instructors have available to them. These nonverbal immediacy skills can help teachers and students have happier, more productive, classroom experiences. Although we can confidently draw a number of conclusions relating to immediacy in instruction, we should not take this fact as indicative of the lack of need for additional research. Research is needed to explore many questions, including the following:

1. May we generalize the just cited conclusions to teachers and students from cultures other than the one that has received primary attention to this point? With the dramatic increase in students from minority cultures confronting schools at all levels in most areas of the United States, answers to this question are critical. There has been increased interest in instructional research recently, which involves students in cross-cultural and multicultural classrooms. McCroskey, Sallinen, Fayer, Richmond, and Barraclough (1996) report that higher levels of teacher immediacy are likely to result in greater student involvment and more overall classroom interaction, regardless of student cultural expectations. Increasing cultural diversity in today's educational settings necessitate that more research be conducted from an intercultural perspective. Most current teachers have little training in how to deal with students from the variety of cultures they must face already, or are destined to face in the near future. While considerable progress has been made in this regard (see Hinkle, 1998; McCroskey, Fayer, Richmond, Sallinen, & Barraclough, 1996; McCroskey, Richmond, Sallinen, Fayer, & Barraclough, 1995; Myers, Zhong, & Guan, 1998; Neuliep, 1995; 1997; Roach & Byrne, 2001), we must continue to adapt our teacher training to the variety of cultures in our society if we are to prepare teachers to communicate effectively with all of the students in our schools.

2. Does being immediate have any impact on the teacher? Although some research has focused on the effects of *student* immediacy on teacher behavior (Baringer & McCroskey, 2000), few studies have addressed the effect that immediacy has on teachers engaging in such behaviors. However, we believe that immediate teachers create a much more positive atmosphere for their students, which in turn creates a much more positive atmosphere for the teacher. We have received many, many anecdotal reports that point in this direction. Some teachers even go so far as to say that being more immediate helped them recover from or prevent burnout.

3. To what extent are different immediacy behaviors differentially effective at the various levels of education? We know that kindergarten teachers often hug their students and college professors usually do not. Are there other behavioral differences among the various teaching levels? We know very little about these differences beyond initial research regarding perceptions of teaching-effectiveness criteria reported by secondary teachers (Johnson & Roellke, 1999). Knowing more would help provide a base for training teachers at the different levels.

4. To what extent are different levels of immediacy, or different immediacy behaviors, differentially effective for different class sizes and different subject matters? Some incidental reports have been made about differences in immediacy as a function of class size, but this issue has not been the focus of primary attention in any study to date. One study (Kearney, Plax, & Wendt-Wasco, 1985) has reported that immediacy appears to have more impact in some subject-matter areas than it does in others, but this finding has not been replicated. We have conducted research to investigate the impact of supervisor and subordinate immediacy on relational and organizational outcomes (Richmond & McCroskey, 2000b) as well as the impact of nonverbal immediacy on physician/patient communication in medical contexts (Richmond, Heisel, Smith, & McCroskey, 1998; Richmond, Smith, Heisel, & McCroskey, 2000), but more research is needed so we can refine our generalizations and adjust to different kinds of classes and contexts. Limited research has also been conducted to investigate immediacy in out-of-class environments with optimistic but inconclusive results (Fusani, 1994; Jaasma & Koper, 1999; Nadler & Nadler, 2000).

5. What is the nature of the relationship between immediacy and cognitive learning? Although we know that a positive relationship exists, it is not yet known whether this is a linear or nonlinear relationship. For example, Comstock, Rowell, and Bowers (1995) and Titsworth (2004) suggest a curvilinear relationship between teacher nonverbal immediacy and student learning, whereas Christensen and Menzel (1998) report a linear relationship between student reports of teacher immediacy behaviors and perceptions of state motivation and of cognitive, affective, and behavioral learning. Which is it? Does cognitive learning continue to increase at very high levels of immediacy? Or does increased immediacy cease to produce more learning at a certain point? Can we reach a point of too much immediacy with resulting reductions in cognitive learning (O'Mara, Allen, Long, & Judd, 1996; Thweatt, & McCroskey, 1996)? Grant that the two are compatible but that this relationship requires additional attention, especially in light of recent meta-analyses that report consistently low effect sizes for the relationship (Witt, Wheeless, & Allen, 2004). One ongoing change in the immediacy research literature is a trend toward increasingly complex conceptions of learning (Hess & Smythe, 2001; Witt & Wheeless, 2001) and their place in our understanding of which verbal and nonverbal teacher behaviors are most effective.

6. To what extent are different levels of verbal immediacy, or different immediacy behaviors, differentially effective for online distance education and computer-mediated classrooms (Lane & Shelton, 2001)? Does technology and medium enhance or detract from the usefulness of teacher immediacy behaviors? Shelton, Lane, and Waldhart (1999) support the need for instructional research that addresses issues of how teacher immediacy behaviors interact with technology to influence student learning outcomes. Some incidental reports have suggested that verbal immediacy may impact student self-reports of learning and satisfaction in distributed learning classrooms (Freitas, Myers, & Avtgis, 1998; Hackman & Walker, 1990). Likewise, Messman and Jones-Corley (2001) report that because environment can interact with student communication apprehension and teacher immediacy to improve student learning outcomes, more research centered on technology and environment is needed. In their review of instructional communication research, Waldeck, Kearney, and Plax (2001), voice concern for the increasing ubiquity of technology and call for research that leads to a better understanding of the impact of new technologies on student learning, as well as the need for more substantive research to understand the impact of computer and video-aided instruction and distance learning on student outcomes (p.224). Witt (1997) echos a similar concern and argues for investigations of teacher immediacy behaviors in the context of distance learning. Because teacher immediacy behaviors may differ in instruction that occurs via the Internet and in other distributed learning contexts, future research in this area is warranted.

7. What theory (theories) can we use to explain effects we already have isolated and predict effects we have not yet studied? There is a substantial base of research on immediacy in the literature. Most of this has been produced in a context of discovery. It is now time to attempt to generate theory from the results available and move on to test the validity of that theory. This process has begun, as we noted earlier in this chapter, but it needs to continue at an increasing rate. Please see Chapter 12 for a more detailed discussion about instructional communication theory development.

8. How do teacher–student interactions ultimately influence student behavioral learning outcomes? Much progress has been made over the past three decades relative to establishing a link between specific teacher immediacy and the subsequent impact on student learning outcomes—especially with regard to affective and cognitive learning. What is noticeably absent from the literature is an investigation of actual classroom interaction and how student–teacher interaction ultimately influences student behaviorial learning outcomes. Waldeck, Kearney, and Plax (2001) in their content analysis of instructional communication research from 1990–1999, argued, "although we know about 'teacher' behaviors and 'student' behaviors independent of one another, we know very little about how teacher-student *interactions* influence learning" (p. 224). Past research conducted by instructional communication scholars attempted to determine which teacher behaviors lead to positive student learning outcomes and how the behaviors effect student–teacher interaction(s). Understanding which combinations of communication behaviors are most effective has been both an interesting and a challenging worthwhile endeavor.

Summary

This chapter has presented an overview of the immediacy construct, introduced the origins of the research program, detailed contemporary research for understanding significant contributions of immediacy research, provided a summary of the impact of both verbal and nonverbal immediacy on student learning, proposed special concerns associated with immediacy research, presented knowledge claims that were derived from immediacy research, and proposed directions for future research.

Great clarity and understanding is possible if instructional communication researchers can continue to refine answers to such fundamental questions as: What is learning? Why does it occur? What role should/does communication play in the learning process? What today is impossible for us to do in education, but if it could be done, would fundamentally change the entire educational process? We are confident in our convictions that learning occurs as a result of communication as students apply knowledge and make connections. If the difference between knowing and teaching is communication (Hurt, Scott, & McCroskey, 1978), then the immediacy research program reviewed in this chapter provides compelling evidence that the teacher–student relationship can be enhanced through verbal and nonverbal immediacy behaviors.

References

Ambady, N., & Rosenthal, R. (1993). Half a minute: Predicting teacher evaluations from thin slices of nonverbal behavior and physical attractiveness. *Journal of Personality and Social Psychology, 64,* 431–441.

Andersen, J. F. (1978). *The relationship between teacher immediacy and teaching effectiveness.* Unpublished doctoral dissertation, West Virginia University, Morgantown, WV.

Andersen, J. F. (1979). Teacher immediacy as a predictor of teaching effectiveness. In D. Nimmo (Ed.), *Communication yearbook 3* (pp. 543–559). New Brunswick, NJ: Transaction Books.

Anderson, L. W., & Krathwohl, D. R. (2001). *A taxonomy for learning, teaching, and assessing: A revision of Bloom's taxonomy of educational objectives.* New York: Addison, Wesley, Longman.

Andersen, P. & Andersen, J. (1982). Nonverbal immediacy in instruction. In L. L. Barker (Ed.) *Communication in the classroom: Original essays* (pp. 98–120). Englewood Cliffs, NJ: Prentice-Hall.

Baringer, D. K., & McCroskey, J. C. (2000). Immediacy in the classroom: Student immediacy. *Communication Education, 49,* 178–186.

Bell, R., & Daly, J. A. (1984). The affinity-seeking function of communication. *Communication Monographs, 51,* 91–115.

Bloom, B. S. (1956). *A taxonomy of educational objectives; Handbook 1: The cognitive domain.* New York: Longmans, Green.

Booth-Butterfield, S., Mosher, N., & Molish, D. (1992). Teacher immediacy and student involvement: A dual process analysis. *Communication Research Reports, 9,* 13–22.

Burroughs, N. F. (1990). *The relationship of teacher immediacy and student compliance resistance with learning.* Unpublished doctoral dissertation, West Virginia University, Morgantown, WV.

Chesebro, J. L., & McCroskey, J. C. (1998). The relationship of teacher clarity and teacher immediacy with students' experiences of state receiver apprehension when listening to teachers. *Communication Quarterly, 46,* 446–456.

Chesebro, J. L., & McCroskey, J. C. (2000). The relationship between students' reports of learning and their actual recall of lecture material: A validity test. *Communication Education, 49,* 297–301.

Chesebro, J. L., & McCroskey, J. C. (2001). The relationship of teacher clarity and immediacy with student state receiver apprehension, affect, and cognitive learning. *Communication Education, 50,* 59–68.

Christensen, L. J., & Menzel, K. E. (1998). The linear relationship between student reports of teacher immediacy behaviors and perceptions of state motivation and of cognitive, affective, and behavioral learning. *Communication Education, 47,* 82–90.

Christophel, D. M. (1990a). *The relationships among teacher immediacy behaviors, student motivation, and learning.* Unpublished doctoral dissertation, West Virginia University, Morgantown, WV.

Christophel, D. M. (1990b). The relationships among teacher immediacy behaviors, student motivation, and learning. *Communication Education, 39,* 323–340.

Comstock, J., Rowell, E., & Bowers, J. W. (1995). Food for thought: Teacher nonverbal immediacy, student learning, and curvilinearity. *Communication Education, 44,* 251–266.

Freitas, F. A., Myers, S. A., & Avtgis, T. A. (1998). Student perceptions of instructor immediacy in conventional and distributed learning classrooms. *Communication Education, 47,* 366–372.

French, J. R. P., Jr., & Raven, B. (1960). The bases of social power. In D. Cartwright & A. Zander (Eds.), *Group Dynamics* (pp. 259–269). New York: Harper & Row.

Frymier, A. B., (1993). The impact of teacher immediacy on students' motivation: Is it the same for all students? *Communication Quarterly, 41,* 454–464.

Frymier, A. B. (1994). A model of immediacy in the classroom. *Communication Quarterly, 42,* 133–144.

Frymier, A. B., & Houser, M. L. (2000). The teacher–student relationship as an interpersonal relationship. *Communication Education, 49,* 207–219.

Fusani, D. S. (1994). "Extra-class" communication: Frequencey, immediacy, self-disclosure, and satisfaction in student–faculty interaction outside the classroom. *Journal of Applied Communication Research, 22,* 232–255.

Gorham, J. (1988). The relationship between verbal teacher immediacy behaviors and student learning. *Communication Education, 37,* 40–53.

Gorham, J., & Christophel, D. M. (1990). The relationship of teachers' use of humor in the classroom to immediacy and student learning. *Communication Education, 39,* 45–62.

Gorham, J., Cohen, S. H., & Morris, T. L. (1997). Fashion in the classroom II: Instructor immediacy and attire. *Communication Research Reports, 14,* 11–23.

Gorham, J. Cohen, S. H., & Morris, T. L. (1999). Fashion in the classroom III: Effects of instructor attire and immediacy in natural classroom interactions. *Communication Quarterly, 47,* 281–299.

Gorham, J., & Zakahi, W. R. (1990). A comparison of teacher and student perceptions of immediacy and learning: Monitoring process and product. *Communication Education, 39,* 354–368.

Hackman, M. Z., & Walker, K. B. (1990). Instructional communication in the televised classroom: The effects of system design and teacher immediacy on student learning and satisfaction. *Communication Education, 39,* 196–206.

Hess, J. A., & Smythe, M. J. (2001). Is teacher immediacy actually related to student cognitive learning? *Communication Studies, 52,* 197–219.

Hinkle, L. J. (1998). Teacher nonverbal immediacy behaviors and student–perceived cognitive learning in Japan. *Communication Research Reports, 15,* 45–56.

Hurt, H. T., Scott, M. D., & McCroskey, J. C. (1978). *Communication in the classroom.* Reading, MA: Addison-Wesley.

Jaasma, M. A., & Koper, R. J. (1999). The relationship of student–faculty out-of-class communication to instructor immediacy and trust and to student motivation. *Communication Education, 48,* 41–47.

Johnson, S. D., & Roellke, C. F. (1999). Secondary teachers' and undergraduate education faculty members' perceptions of teaching-effectiveness criteria: A national survey. *Communication Education, 48,* 127–138.

Kearney Knutson, P. (1979). *Relationships among teacher communication style, trait and state communication apprehension, and teacher effectiveness.* Unpublished doctoral dissertation, West Virginia University, Morgantown, WV.

Kearney, P., & McCroskey, J. C. (1980). Relationships among teacher communication style, trait and state communication apprehension, and teacher effectiveness. In D. Nimmo (Ed.), *Communication yearbook 4* (pp. 533–551). New Brunswick, NJ: Transaction Books.

Kearney, P., Plax, T. G., & Wendt-Wasco, N. J. (1985). Teacher immediacy for affective learning in divergent college classes. *Communication Quarterly, 33,* 61–74.

Kelley, D. H., & Gorham, J. (1988). Effects of immediacy on recall of information. *Communication Education, 37,* 198–207.

Krathwohl, D. R., Bloom, B. S., & Masia, B. B. (1964). *Taxonomy of educational objectives, the classification of educational goals; Handbook II: The affective domain.* New York: David McKay.

Lane, D. R., McCroskey, L. L., & O'Brien, M. W. (1996, May). *Obtaining classroom goals: Revisiting the impact of student involvement and perceived teacher immediacy on affective and cognitive learning.* Paper presented at the annual convention of the International Communication Association, Chicago, IL.

Lane, D. R. & Shelton, M. W. (2001). The centrality of communication education in classroom computer-mediated communication: Toward a practical and evaluative pedagogy. *Communication Education, 50,* 241–255.

McCroskey, J. C. (1997). Self-report measurement. In Daly, J. A., McCroskey, J. C., Ayres, J., Hopf, T., & Ayres, D. M. (Eds.). (2nd ed.). *Avoiding communication: Shyness, reticence, and communication apprehension* (pp. 191–216). Cresskill, NJ: Hampton Press.

McCroskey, J. C., Fayer, J. M., Richmond, V. P., Sallinen, A., & Barraclough, R. A. (1996). A multicultural examination of the relationship between nonverbal immediacy and affective learning. *Communication Quarterly, 44,* 297–307.

McCroskey, J. C., Richmond, V. P., Sallinen, A., Fayer, J., & Barraclough, R. (1995). A cross-cultural and multi-behavioral analysis of the relationship between nonverbal immediacy and teacher evaluations. *Communication Quarterly, 44,* 281–291.

McCroskey, J. C., Sallinen, A., Fayer, J. M., Richmond, V. P., & Barraclough, R. A. (1996). Nonverbal immediacy and cognitive learning: A cross-cultural investigation. *Communication Education, 45,* 200–211.

McCroskey, J. C., & Wheeless, L. R. (1976). *Introduction to human communication.* Boston: Allyn & Bacon.

Mehrabian, A. (1967). Attitudes inferred from neutral verbal communications. *Journal of Consulting Psychology, 31,* 414–417.

Mehrabian, A. (1969). Some referents and measures of nonverbal behavior. *Behavioral Research Methods and Instrumentation, 1,* 213–217.

Mehrabian, A. (1971). *Silent messages.* Belmont, CA: Wadsworth.

Menzel, K. E., & Carrell, L. J. (1999). The impact of gender and immediacy on willingness to talk and perceived learning. *Communication Education, 48,* 31–40.

Messman, S. J., & Jones-Corley, J. (2001). Effects of communication environment, immediacy, and communication apprehension on cognitive and affective learning. *Communication Monographs, 68,* 184–200.

Moore, A., Masterson, J. T., Christophel, D. M., & Shea, K. A. (1996). College teacher immediacy and student ratings of instruction. *Communication Education, 45,* 29–39.

Morris, T. L., Gorham, J., Cohen, S. H., & Huffman, D. (1996). Fashion in the classroom: Effects of attire on student perceptions of instructors in college classes. *Communication Education, 45,* 135–148.

Mottet, T., & Richmond, V. P. (1998). An inductive analysis of verbal immediacy: Alternative conceptualization of relational verbal approach/avoidance strategies. *Communication Quarterly, 46,* 25–41.

Myers, S. A., Zhong, M., & Guan, S. (1998). Instructor immediacy in the Chinese college classroom. *Communication Studies, 49,* 240–254.

Nadler, M. J., & Nadler, L. B. (2000). Out-of-class communication between faculty and students: A faculty perspective. *Communication Studies, 51,* 176–188.

Neuliep, J. W. (1995). A comparison of teacher immediacy in African-American and Euro-American classrooms. *Communication Education, 44,* 267–277.

Neuliep, J. W. (1997). A cross-cultural comparison of teacher immediacy in American and Japanese college classrooms. *Communication Research, 24,* 431–452.

Nussbaum, J. F. (1992). Effective teacher behaviors. *Communication Education, 41,* 167–180.

O'Mara, J., Allen, J. L., Long, K. M., & Judd, B. (1996). Communication apprehension, nonverbal immediacy, and negative expectations for learning. *Communication Research Reports, 13,* 109–128.

Plax, T. G., Kearney, P., McCroskey, J. C., & Richmond, V. P. (1986). Power in the classroom VI: Verbal control strategies, nonverbal immediacy, and affective learning. *Communication Education, 35,* 43–55.

Powell, R. G., & Harville, B. (1990). The effects of teacher immediacy and clarity on instructional outcomes: An intercultural assessment. *Communication Education, 39,* 369–379.

Pribyl, C. B., Sakamoto, M., & Keaten, J. A. (2004). The relationship between nonverbal immediacy, student motivation, and perceived cognitive learning among Japanese college students. *Japanese Psychological Research, 46,* 73–85.

Richmond, V. P. (1990). Communication in the classroom: Power and motivation. *Communication Education, 39,* 181–195.

Richmond, V. P., Gorham, J. S., & McCroskey, J. C. (1987). The relationship between selected immediacy behaviors and cognitive learning. In M. L. McLaughlin (Ed.), *Communication yearbook 10* (pp. 574–590). Newbury Park, CA: Sage.

Richmond, V. P., Heisel, A., Smith, R. S., & McCroskey, J. C. (1998). The impact of communication apprehension and fear of talking with a physician on perceived medical outcomes. *Communication Research Reports, 15,* 344–353.

Richmond, V. P., & McCroskey, J. C. (1992). Increasing teacher influence through immediacy. In V. P. Richmond and J. C. McCroskey (Eds.). *Power in the classroom: Communication, control, and concern.* Hillsdale, NJ: Lawrence Erlbaum.

Richmond, V. P., & McCroskey, J. C. (2000a). *Nonverbal behavior in interpersonal relationships.* Boston: Allyn & Bacon.

Richmond, V. P., & McCroskey, J. C. (2000b). The impact of supervisor and subordinate immediacy on relational and organizational outcomes. *Communication Monographs, 67,* 85–95.

Richmond, V. P., McCroskey, J. C., & Johnson, A. (2003). Development of the nonverbal immediacy scale (NIS): Measures of self- and other-perceived nonverbal immediacy. *Communication Quarterly, 51,* 504–517.

Richmond, V. P., McCroskey, J. C., Kearney, P., & Plax, T. G. (1987). Power in the classroom VII: Linking behavior alteration techniques to cognitive learning. *Communication Education, 36,* 1–12.

Richmond, V. P., McCroskey, J. C., Plax, T. G., & Kearney, P. (1986). Teacher nonverbal immediacy training and student affect. *World Communication, 15,* 181–194.

Richmond, V. P., Smith, R. S., Heisel, A., & McCroskey, J. C. (2000). *Nonverbal immediacy and physician/patient communication.* Paper presented at the Eastern Communication Association, Pittsburgh, PA.

Roach, K. D. (1997). Effects of graduate teaching assistant attire on student learning, misbehaviors, and ratings of instruction. *Communication Quarterly, 45*(3), 125–141.

Roach, K. D., & Byrne, P. R. (2001). A cross-cultural comparison of instructor communication in American and German classrooms. *Communication Education, 50,* 1–14.

Robinson, R. Y, & Richmond, V. P. (1995). Validity of the verbal immediacy scale. *Communication Research Reports, 12,* 80–84.

Rodgers, M. A., & McCroskey, J. C. (1984, March). *Nonverbal immediacy of teachers in classroom environments.* Paper presented at the annual convention of the Eastern Communication Association, Philadelphia, PA.

Rodriguez, J. L., Plax, T. G., & Kearney, P. (1996). Clarifying the relationship between teacher nonverbal immediacy and student cognitive learning: Affective learning as the central causal mediator. *Communication Education, 45,* 293–305.

Sanders, J. A., & Wiseman, R. L. (1990). The effects of verbal and nonverbal teacher immediacy on perceived cognitive, affective, and behavioral learning in the multicultural classroom. *Communication Education, 39,* 341–353.

Shelton, M. W., Lane, D. R., & Waldhart, E. S. (1999). A review and assessment of national educational trends in communication instruction. *Communication Education, 48,* 228–237.

Sorensen, G. A. (1980). *The relationship between teachers' self-disclosure statements on student learning.* Unpublished doctoral dissertation, West Virginia University, Morgantown, WV.

Sorensen, G. A. (1989). The relationships among teachers' self-disclosive statements, students' perceptions, and affective learning. *Communication Education, 38,* 259–276.

Teven, J. J. (2001). The relationship among teacher characteristics and perceived caring. *Communication Education, 50,* 159–169.

Teven, J. J., & McCroskey, J. L. (1997). The relationship of perceived teacher caring with student learning and teacher evaluation. *Communication Education, 46,* 1–9.

Thweatt, K. S., & McCroskey, J. C. (1996). Teacher nonimmediacy and misbehavior: Unintentional negative communication. *Communication Research Reports, 13,* 198–204.

Thweatt, K. S., & McCroskey, J. C. (1998). The impact of teacher immediacy and misbehaviors on teacher credibility. *Communication Education, 47,* 348–358.

Titsworth, S. B. (2001). The effects of teacher immediacy, use of organizational lecture cues, and students' notetaking on cognitive learning. *Communication Education, 50,* 283–297.

Titsworth, S. B. (2004). Students' notetaking: The effects of teacher immediacy and clarity, *Communication Education, 53,* 305–320.

Violette, J. L. (2002). *Immediately clarifying classroom interactions: An examination of teacher immediacy, teacher clarity, teacher gender, and student gender on student affective, cognitive, and behavioral learning.* Unpublished doctoral dissertation, University of Kentucky, Lexington, KY.

Waldeck, J. H., Kearney, P., & Plax, T. G. (2001). Instructional and developmental communication theory and research in the 1990s: Extending the agenda for the 21st century. In W. B. Gudykunst (Ed.). *Communication yearbook 24* (pp. 207–229). Thousand Oaks, CA: Sage.

Wanzer, M. B., Frymier, A. B. (1999). The relationships between student perceptions of instructor humor and students' reports of learning. *Communication Education, 48,* 49–62.

Witt, P. L. (1997). *A study of the relationships among student expectations about teacher nonverbal immediacy, student perceptions of teacher nonverbal immediacy, and affective learning in distance learning and the on-site classroom.* Unpublished master's thesis, University of North Texas, Denton, TX.

Witt, P. L., Wheeless, L. R. (2001). An experimental study of teachers' verbal and nonverbal immediacy and students' affective and cognitive learning. *Communication Education, 50,* 327–342.

Witt, P. L., Wheeless, L. R., & Allen, M. (2004). A meta-analytical review of the relationship between teacher immediacy and student learning. *Communication Monographs, 71,* 184–207.

Wrench, J., & Richmond, V. P. (2000). *The relationship between teacher humor assessment and motivation, credibility, verbal aggression, affective learning, perceived learning, and learning loss.* Paper presented at the annual convention of the National Communication Association, Seattle, WA.

9

Teacher and Student Affinity-Seeking in the Classroom

Ann Bainbridge Frymier
Miami University

Melissa Bekelja Wanzer
Canisius College

Introduction

In this chapter we adopt a relational approach to teaching and research and in doing so operate under the basic premise that teachers and students mutually influence each other to achieve various goals or objectives. As Mottet and Beebe stated in the first chapter of this handbook, a primary goal that many teachers and students hope to obtain is a *quality student–teacher relationship where there is mutual respect and liking.* In an effort to help instructional practitioners understand how to obtain a quality student–teacher relationship, we provide a comprehensive overview of the research on affinity-seeking. Both students and teachers can use affinity-seeking behaviors to gain liking in the classroom. There is a great deal of empirical support for the use of affinity-seeking behaviors in the classroom as a means of increasing affect between teachers and students and, ultimately, facilitating learning. In the following sections of this chapter we will present an overview of the affinity-seeking construct, provide a detailed review of classic and contemporary research on teacher and student affinity-seeking behaviors, offer a detailed list of knowledge claims based on extant research, and, finally, offer suggestions for future research in this area.

Overview of the Affinity-Seeking Construct

According to Schutz's (1966) interpersonal needs theory, we communicate and establish relationships with others to satisfy our most basic human needs for affection, inclusion, and control. To do this we must be willing to expend a great amount of time and effort and, at the same time, utilize a variety of important communication skills. Interpersonal scholars have had a long-standing interest in the variety of ways that individuals establish, maintain, and even terminate their relationships with those around them. The one question that interpersonal scholars seem to keep asking is whether there is a surefire way to increase affect between individuals initially so that they will want to communicate more frequently and eventually establish a relationship. Communication scholars have identified the use of affinity-seeking behaviors as a highly effective means of gaining liking in a variety of contexts.

McCroskey and Wheeless (1976) were the first to introduce the concept of "affinity," defining it as "a positive attitude toward another person" (p. 231). According to McCroskey and Wheeless, when individuals formulate positive or negative attitudes about someone, they often consider the extent to which others are perceived as credible, attractive, and similar. They noted that gaining "affinity" was the single most important reason for why we communicated with those around us. Finally, McCroskey and Wheeless identified seven specific techniques that individuals typically use to gain liking: (1) control physical appearance, (2) increase positive self-disclosure, (3) stress areas of similarity, (4) provide positive reinforcement, (5) express cooperation, (6) comply with other's wishes, and (7) fulfill other's needs. The early research by McCroskey and Wheeless provided communication scholars with a preliminary set of specific behaviors that individuals use to gain liking and facilitate relationships with others.

Later, Bell and Daly (1984) expanded research in this area and defined affinity-seeking as "the active social communicative process by which individuals attempt to get others to like and feel positive toward them" (p. 91). Bell and Daly conceptualized affinity-seeking as a strategic activity with numerous antecedent factors and constraints that influence an individual's strategy choice. Antecedent conditions include an individual's goals, motivations, and level of consciousness. Constraints include social skills, past experiences, personal predispositions, and situational characteristics. Bell and Daly hypothesized that together these factors influence the specific affinity-seeking strategies and tactics a person chooses and that a target's response to affinity-seeking can influence a future strategy choice by the agent.

In summary, Bell and Daly describe the affinity-seeking process as dynamic and emphasize that individuals choose specific behaviors (tactics) to enact affinity-seeking strategies.

A primary focus of Bell and Daly's (1984) research was to identify how people go about gaining affinity. To develop a more comprehensive list of strategies, Bell and Daly asked 22 small groups of adult and traditional college-age students to create a list of all the typical things that people say and do to get others to like them. Responses from the study participants were subjected to content analysis procedures with 25 mutually exclusive categories of affinity-seeking behaviors emerging. The 25 affinity-seeking strategies identified by Bell and Daly are shown in Figure 9.1.

Bell and Daly (1984) confirmed that individuals who use several affinity-seeking strategies were perceived as likeable, socially successful, and satisfied with their lives. Additionally, Bell and Daly found that communicators were more likely to use affinity-seeking strategies with someone of equal rather than higher status. Subsequent research on affinity-seeking sought to determine whether there was a relationship between the status of the source and strategy choices. For example, in the classroom context, where the relationship is asymmetrical, would teachers be more likely to use certain strategies and avoid others? The focus of the next several studies in this area was to examine the extent of teachers' use of affinity-seeking strategies with their students.

FIGURE 9.1 ***Affinity-Seeking Techniques and Descriptions of Classroom Usage.***

1. *Altruism.* The teacher tries to be of help and assistance in whatever the student is currently doing. For example, the teacher may hold the door for the student, assist him or her with studies from getting the needed materials for assignments to assisting with other school-related tasks. The teacher also gives advice when it is requested.
2. *Assume Control.* The teacher presents self as a leader, a person who has control over the classroom. For example, the teacher directs the conversations held by students, takes charge of the classroom activities the two engage in, and mentions examples of where he or she has taken charge or served as a leader in the past.
3. *Assume Equality.* The teacher presents self as an equal of the other person. For example, the teacher avoids appearing superior or snobbish, and does not play "one-upmanship" games.
4. *Comfortable Self.* The teacher acts comfortable in the setting comfortable with her or himself, and comfortable with the students. The teacher is relaxed, at ease, casual, and content. Distractions and disturbances in the environment are ignored. The teacher tries to look as if he or she is having a good time, even if he or she is not. The teacher gives the impression that "nothing bothers" her or him.
5. *Concede Control.* The teacher allows the student to control the relationship and situations surrounding the two. For example, the teacher lets the student take charge of conversations, and so on. The teacher also lets the student influence her or his actions by not acting dominant.
6. *Conversational Rule-Keeping.* The teacher follows closely the culture's rules for how people socialize with others by demonstrating cooperation, friendliness, and politeness. The

(*Continued*)

FIGURE 9.1 ***(Continued)***

teacher works hard at giving relevant answers to questions, saying the right things, acting interested and involved in conversations, and adapting messages to the particular student or situation. The teacher avoids changing the topic too soon, interrupting the student, dominating classroom discussions, and excessive self-references. The teacher tries to avoid topics that are not of common interest to students.

7. *Dynamism.* The teacher presents self as a dynamic, active, and enthusiastic person by acting physically animated and lively while talking with the student, varying intonation and other vocal characteristics, and by being outgoing and extroverted with the students.

8. *Elicit Other's Disclosure.* The teacher encourages the student to talk by asking questions and reinforcing student responses. For example, the teacher inquires about the student's interests, feelings, opinions, views, and so on. The teacher responds as if these are important and interesting, and continues to ask more questions of the student.

9. *Facilitate Enjoyment.* The teacher seeks to make the situations in which the two are involved very enjoyable experiences. The teacher does things the students will enjoy, is entertaining, tells jokes and interesting stories, talks about interesting topics, says funny things, and tries to make the classroom conducive to enjoyment and learning.

10. *Inclusion of Others.* The teacher includes the student in social activities and groups of friends. The teacher introduces the student to her or his friends, and makes the student feel like "one of the group."

11. *Influence Perceptions of Closeness.* The teacher engages in behaviors that lead the student to perceive the relationship as being closer and more established than it has actually been. For example, the teacher uses nicknames of the students, talks about "we," rather than "I" or "you." The teacher also discusses any prior activities that included both of them.

12. *Listening.* The teacher pays close attention to what the student says, listening very actively. The teacher focuses attention solely on the student, paying strict attention to what is said. Moreover, the teacher demonstrates that he or she listens by being responsive to the student's ideas, asking for clarification of ambiguities, being open-minded, and remembering things the student says.

13. *Nonverbal Immediacy.* The teacher signals interest and liking through various nonverbal cues. For example, the teacher frequently makes eye contact, stands or sits close to the student, smiles, leans toward the student, makes frequent head nods, and directs much gaze toward the student. All of the above indicates the teacher is very much interested in the student and what he or she has to say.

14. *Openness.* The teacher is open and discloses information about background, interests, and views. The teacher may even disclose very personal information about insecurities, weaknesses, and fears to make the student feel very special (e.g., "just between you and me").

15. *Optimism.* The teacher presents self as a positive person—an optimist—to appear to be a person who is pleasant to be around. The teacher acts in a "happy-go-lucky" manner, is cheerful, and looks on the positive side of things, avoids complaining about things, talking about depressing topics, and being critical of self and others.

16. *Personal Autonomy.* The teacher presents self as an independent, free-thinking person—the kind of person who stands on their own, speaks their mind regardless of the consequences, refuses to change behavior to meet the expectations of others, and knows where he or she is going in life. For instance, if the teacher finds he or she disagrees with the student on some issue, the teacher states an opinion anyway, is confident that her or his view is right, and may even try to change the mind of the student.

17. *Physical Attractiveness.* The teacher tries to look as attractive and professional as possible in appearance and attire by wearing nice clothes, practicing good grooming, showing concern for proper hygiene, standing up straight, and monitoring their appearance.

FIGURE 9.1 ***(Continued)***

18. *Presenting Interesting Self.* The teacher presents self to be a person who would be interesting to know. For example, the teacher highlights past accomplishments and positive qualities, emphasizes things that make her or him especially interesting, expresses unique ideas, and demonstrates intelligence and knowledge. The teacher may discreetly drop the names of impressive people he or she knows. The teacher may even do outlandish things to appear unpredictable, wild, or crazy.
19. *Reward Association.* The teacher presents self as an important figure that can reward the student for associating with her or him. For instance, the teacher may offer to do favors for a student, and gives information that would be valuable. The teacher's basic message to the student is "if you like me, you will gain something."
20. *Self-Concept Confirmation.* The teacher demonstrates respect for the student, helps the student feel good about how they view themselves. For example, the teacher treats the student like a very important person, compliments the student, says only positive things about the student, and treats what the student says as being very important information. The teacher may also tell other teachers about what a great student the individual is, in hopes that the comment will get back to the student through third parties.
21. *Self-Inclusion.* The teacher may set up frequent encounters with the student. For example, the teacher will initiate casual encounters with the student, attempt to schedule future encounters, tries to be physically close to the student, and puts her or himself in a position to be invited to participate in some of the student's social activities/groups/clubs.
22. *Sensitivity.* The teacher acts in a warm, empathic manner toward the student to communicate caring and concern. The teacher also shows sympathy to the student's problems and anxieties, spends time working at understanding how the student sees life, and accepts what the student says as an honest response. The message is, "I care about you as a person."
23. *Similarity.* The teacher tries to make the student feel that the two of them are similar in attitudes, values, interests, preferences, personality, and so on. The teacher expresses views that are similar to the views of the student, agrees with some things the student says, and points out the areas that the two have in common. Moreover, the teacher deliberately avoids engaging in behaviors that would suggest differences between the two.
24. *Supportiveness.* The teacher is supportive of the student and the student's positions by being encouraging, agreeable, and reinforcing to the student. The teacher also avoids criticizing the student or saying anything that might hurt the student's feelings, and sides with the student in disagreements they have with others.
25. *Trustworthiness.* The teacher presents self as trustworthy and reliable by emphasizing his or her sense of responsibility, reliability, fairness, dedication, honesty, and sincerity. The teacher also maintains consistency among their stated beliefs and behaviors, fulfills any commitments made to the student, and avoids "false fronts" by acting natural at all times.

From "The Affinity-Seeking Function of Communication," by R. A. Bell and J. A. Daly, 1984, *Communication Monographs, 51,* 91–115. Republished with permission by *Communication Monographs* and Taylor & Francis Ltd. http://www.tandf.co.uk/journals.

Teachers' Use of Affinity-Seeking Strategies

In an effort to determine whether Bell and Daly's (1984) affinity-seeking typology was generalizable to the classroom context, McCroskey and McCroskey (1986) asked 311 elementary and secondary school teachers to report the extent to which their peers used the 25 strategies in their classrooms. Both primary and secondary teachers with a broad range of teaching experience participated in this study. Participants were asked to first indicate whether they had ever observed a teacher in their school using the 25 affinity-seeking strategies. Next, the study participants indicated how frequently they had observed the teachers in their school using the strategies. The researchers asked the participants to report on their peers' use of the affinity-seeking strategies to avoid a social desirability effect. The eight strategies that were reportedly used the most often, were *physical attractiveness, sensitivity, elicit other's disclosure, trustworthiness, nonverbal immediacy, conversational rule-keeping, dynamism,* and *listening*. Participants indicated that 90 percent of the teachers at their school used the eight strategies listed above.

In a similar study, Gorham, Kelley, and McCroskey (1989) asked 229 primary and secondary teachers to generate a list of all of the things they do to get students to like them and to like the material they teach. Unlike the McCroskey and McCroskey (1986) study, these teachers were asked about their own use of affinity-seeking behavior. Teachers were asked to generate original examples of affinity-seeking behavior rather than choose from a list of previously generated examples. One of the main objectives of the study was to determine whether new affinity-seeking strategies would emerge. More specifically, the researchers were interested in any differences that existed in the kinds of behaviors that teachers used to gain liking toward themselves and their subject matter. In this study, 229 teachers enrolled in graduate education classes were asked to respond to two questions—"How difficult is it for you to get the students in your class to like you as a teacher?" and "How difficult is it for you to get the students in your class to like the subject matter you teach?"—using Likert-type scales (rate from 0–9). Additionally, teachers were asked to list at least five specific examples of things they did to get a student to like them and to like the subject matter. The examples generated by teachers were submitted to content analytical procedures and Gorham et al. found that the Bell and Daly (1984) typology could be used to interpret the teachers' responses in their study. Thus, they confirmed that the affinity-seeking typology was descriptive of how teachers gain affinity from students. Similar to the McCroskey and McCroskey study, Gorham et al. noted that the typology was generalizable across contexts.

The personal affinity-seeking strategies that teachers used to gain liking for themselves differed significantly from those used to gain liking for their course material. For example, when attempting to get students to like the subject matter, a majority of the teachers used the *facilitate enjoyment* and *concede control* affinity-seeking strategies. When attempting to generate affect toward themselves, teachers indicated they used *eliciting disclosures, inclusion of self,* and *optimism.* These findings indicated that teachers approached the task of generating affinity toward their course material differently than they did in generating affinity toward themselves. Not surprisingly, teachers indicated that it was more challenging to generate affect toward their subject matter than towards themselves. Finally, most teachers seemed to rely on only a few affinity-seeking strategies when attempting to gain liking from students.

While the McCroskey and McCroskey (1986) and Gorham et al. (1989) studies documented primary and secondary teachers' use of affinity-seeking behaviors, subsequent research explored college professors' use of affinity-seeking in the classroom. For example, Roach (1991) compared student perceptions of differences in affinity-seeking use between professors and graduate teaching assistants (GTAs). Professors were reported to use affinity-seeking strategies more frequently than GTAs. Students reported GTAs using *assume equality, conceded control, elicit other's self-disclosure,* and *self-inclusion* more frequently than professors; professors were reported to use *assume control, comfortable self, personal autonomy,* and *trustworthiness* more than GTAs. Roach observed that GTAs, who tended to be younger and less experienced, utilized affinity-seeking strategies that emphasized equality and openness, whereas professors were more likely to employ strategies that exuded self-confidence and control. Regardless of the difference in use, both GTA and professor use of affinity-seeking strategies resulted in greater liking toward the instructor and an increase in both affective and cognitive learning.

Richmond (1990) further examined affinity-seeking in the college classroom by investigating the relationship between teachers' use of affinity-seeking strategies and student learning and motivation. She found that teacher affinity-seeking was significantly and moderately correlated with perceived affective learning (r ranging from .11 to .45) and cognitive learning (r ranging from .12 to .35) as well as student state motivation to study (r ranging from .11 to .40). Richmond reported that the 25 affinity-seeking strategies accounted for 28% of the variance in students' state motivation to study. Additionally, Richmond identified five strategies that had significant correlations (r ranging from .28 to .40) with motivation: *facilitate enjoyment, assume equality, optimism, self-concept confirmation,* and *nonverbal immediacy.* These were not the only strategies positively associated with learning and motivation; however, Richmond identified these five as most important.

Instructional scholars wondered whether there were additional benefits associated with teachers' use of affinity-seeking behaviors. Frymier and Thompson (1992) hypothesized that affinity-seeking strategies could be used to enhance perceptions of credibility. They found that teacher use of affinity-seeking was more strongly associated with the character dimension ($r = .70$) of credibility than the competence dimension ($r = .58$). Affinity-seeking strategies that accounted for unique variance in character were: *assume equality, conversational rule-keeping, optimism, personal autonomy,* and *physical attractiveness.* Strategies that accounted for unique variance in competence were: *assume equality, comfortable self, concede control, dynamism,* and *trustworthiness.* Frymier and Thompson also examined the relationship between affinity-seeking and student motivation to study (similar to Richmond, 1990) and reported that the 25 strategies accounted for 46% of the variance in students' state motivation to study. Four strategies were found that accounted for unique variance and were significant predictors of student motivation. Those strategies were: *assume control, facilitate enjoyment, nonverbal immediacy,* and *trustworthiness.*

Prisbell (1994a) extended Richmond's (1990) and Frymier and Thompson's (1992) work on affinity-seeking in the classroom by examining the relationship between student perceptions of teacher affinity-seeking behaviors and satisfaction with communication in the classroom. He noted that 16 of the 25 Bell and Daly (1984) affinity-seeking strategies were positively and significantly associated with satisfaction with teacher communication. Additionally, Prisbell pointed out that affinity-seeking strategies accounted for 46% of the overall variance in satisfaction with communication ratings.

In a similar study, Prisbell (1994b) examined the relationship between students' perceptions of teacher affinity-seeking behaviors in relationship to student perceptions of teacher competence. As expected, Prisbell found that students perceived their instructors as more competent or able to interact with others effectively when the teacher used affinity-seeking behaviors. There were several affinity-seeking strategies that elicited moderately strong correlations with teacher competence, namely, *altruism, assume equality, dynamism, elicit other's disclosure, listening, sensitivity,* and *trustworthiness.* Based on this data, Prisbell recommends that teachers use these strategies in the classroom as one means of enhancing their competence.

In an effort to extend previous research and to examine the validity of using the affinity-seeking typology in the instructional context, Frymier (1994) conducted a panel study over the course of a semester. Students completed a measure of their motivation to study in a particular class on the first day of the semester before they had attended the class. At the mid-point of the semester, students reported on their instructor's use of affinity-seeking strategies, their liking for the instructor, and their motivation and learning (affective and cognitive). During the last week of the semester, students again completed the same scales they had completed at the mid-point of the semester. To establish validity for the affinity-seeking typology in the instructional context, Frymier examined the 25 strategies in relation to an overall measure of liking. The 25 strategies accounted for 46% of the variance in liking. Sixteen of the 25 strategies were positively associated with liking of the teacher, including *altruism, assume equality, comfortable self, concede control, conversational rule-keeping, dynamism, elicit other's disclosure, facilitate enjoyment, listening, nonverbal immediacy, openness, optimism, physical attractiveness, present interesting self, self-concept confirmation,* and *sensitivity.* This finding confirmed previous research that the affinity-seeking typology was appropriate for the instructional context, but that not all strategies were appropriate or useful in the classroom.

Frymier (1994) also proposed a motivation model of affinity-seeking that hypothesized that affinity-seeking enhanced students' motivation to study, which in turn enhanced students' learning. The motivation model was compared to a direct-effects model that proposed that affinity-seeking had a direct impact on learning. Using path analysis, Frymier found clear support for the motivation model and in the process identified 13 strategies that had the largest impact on learning. These strategies were: *altruism, assume equality, comfortable self, concede control, conversational rule-keeping, dynamism, elicit other's disclosure, facilitate enjoyment, listening, nonverbal immediacy, openness, optimism,* and *sensitivity.* This study provides evidence that affinity-seeking does not have a direct impact on learning, but rather that affinity-seeking impacts students' motivation and enthusiasm for the class and content. Higher levels of motivation most likely result in students putting more time and effort into a class, which in turn results in greater learning.

Myers (1995) examined the relationship between students' perceptions of teacher affinity-seeking behaviors and classroom climate. Myers speculated that if students perceived that their teachers were using more affinity-seeking behaviors in the classroom, they would view their classroom climates more favorably. Not surprisingly, 19 of the 25 Bell and Daly (1984) affinity-seeking strategies were significantly associated with classroom climate. Students also reported that their teachers used 19 of the 25 strategies quite regularly in the classroom. The strategies not correlated or negatively correlated with classroom climate included the following: *concede control, inclusion of others, influence perceptions of closeness, openness, physical attractiveness, reward association,* and *self-inclusion.* These negative or nonsignificant relationships were consistent with previous research (Frymier, 1994; Richmond, 1990). The majority of these strategies (e.g., *concede control, inclusion of others, influence perceptions of closeness, reward association,* and *self-inclusion*) would be inappropriate for teachers to use with their students. For example, students noted that it was uncommon for teachers to give in to their students (e.g., *concede control*) or include themselves in student activities (e.g., *inclusion of other*). Myers suggested that if teachers want to create a supportive classroom climate where students feel comfortable expressing themselves, they should enact many of the affinity-seeking strategies that are strongly associated with climate. Specifically, teachers should concentrate on being dynamic, altruistic, supportive, and trustworthy when interacting with students.

In 2001, Roach and Byrne extended the affinity-seeking research beyond that of the U.S. culture to the German culture. Roach and Byrne had U.S. students and German students (in Germany) report on their instructors' use of affinity-seeking as well as report their levels of affective and cognitive learning. Roach and Byrne found that American students reported their American instructors as using significantly more affinity-seeking strategies in the classroom (M = 82.4) than the German students reported (M = 75.7). Additionally, the researchers noted that "the relationship between instructor affinity-seeking and student cognitive learning was significantly stronger for American students than it was for German students" (Roach & Byrne, 2001, p. 10). However, German students also benefited from teachers who used affinity-seeking strategies in the classroom. Affinity was associated with affective learning at r = .53 and r = .45 in the U.S. and German classrooms respectively. Similarly, affinity was associated with cognitive learning at r = .60 and r = .36 in the U.S. and German classrooms respectively. This research was the first to extend the construct of affinity-seeking beyond U.S. culture. Finding similar relationships in another culture provides evidence of the pervasiveness of the role of affect in the classroom.

Coming from a different perspective than much of the affinity research presented thus far, Cummings and Romano (2002) examined the impact of the presence of an honor code on perceptions of teacher affinity-seeking. Cummings and Romano hypothesized that when a teacher incorporated a formal honor code into class, students would perceive that teacher as using less affinity-seeking. Cummings and Romano used a quasi-experimental design where a single teacher taught two versions of the same class (algebra), one with an honors code and one without. The experiment was repeated the following semester. Cummings and Romano found that students in the honor code sections reported that the teacher used each of the affinity-seeking strategies less frequently than those students in the nonhonor code sections. This research reminds us that affinity-seeking does not operate in a vacuum. How students interpret teachers' affinity-seeking is influenced by their "other" behaviors as well as the context. Perhaps the use of an honor code led the students to perceive the instructor's use of affinity-seeking as insincere, and therefore did not report it being used as frequently.

Research on teachers' use of affinity-seeking behaviors in the classroom has consistently elicited favorable results. More specifically, it has been linked to more favorable student impressions, increases in student motivation and affective learning, and general increases in learning. Strategies such as *dynamism* and *facilitate enjoyment* have consistently accounted for significant amounts of variance in student outcomes.

Students' Use of Affinity-Seeking Strategies

As stated earlier in this chapter, the relationship between the teacher and student is a transactional one. Thus, teachers and students engage in affinity-seeking behaviors in an effort to improve communication inside and outside of the classroom. Wanzer (1995, 1998) studied students' use of affinity-seeking behaviors. As part of her dissertation project she asked college students to generate a list of things students said or did to gain liking from their college instructors. To obtain yet another perspective on student affinity-seeking behaviors, she asked college teachers to compile a list of the things students said or did to gain liking from them. As expected, most of the examples generated by both the students and professors fell into the Bell and Daly typology (22 out of 25 strategies and 23 out of 25 strategies, respectively). Unlike previous research that did not identify any new affinity-seeking strategies, Wanzer's work resulted in the development of four new affinity-seeking behavior *requirements* (i.e., do the schoolwork that is required of the student), achievement (i.e., do well academically in the classes), *gifts* (i.e., buy the professor a gift), and *flirting* (i.e., flirt with the teacher in an effort to gain liking). Interestingly, student and professor perceptions of student affinity-seeking behaviors were very similar (Wanzer, 1995; 1998). This process resulted in a 29-category typology of student affinity-seeking behaviors.

Another important goal of Wanzer's (1995) research was to determine whether students' use of affinity-seeking strategies with their professors resulted in greater liking. To study the impact of student affinity-seeking behavior on liking, Wanzer asked students to approach a current college professor that they knew fairly well and have the professor complete a survey to assess the frequency that the student used the newly generated list of student affinity-seeking strategies and the level of affect toward the student. Professors returned their surveys through campus mail. Students also indicated the extent to which they used affinity-seeking strategies with the professor they approached. Not surprisingly, a total of 17 out of 29 teachers reported student affinity-seeking behaviors that correlated positively and significantly with instructor affect toward the student. A total of 12 out of 29 student-reported, affinity-seeking behaviors correlated positively and significantly with teachers' liking.

Post hoc analysis conducted by Wanzer (1995) attempted to further categorize the student affinity-seeking strategies and compare differences in strategy effectiveness. Wanzer explored differences between groups of student affinity-seeking strategies identified as either active or passive. Wanzer suspected that some strategies required greater effort on the part of the communicator and would, therefore, be recognized more readily by recipients and perhaps be perceived as more effective. Affinity-seeking strategies were labeled "passive" by the researcher when they took minimal effort to execute. Passive strategies included *concede control, listening, physical attractiveness, supportiveness,* and *trustworthiness.* Alternatively, those strategies that required greater effort by the sender were labeled "active." Active strategies included *self-concept confirmation, facilitate enjoyment, dynamism, interesting self,* and *achievement.* Not surprisingly, there was an insignificant relationship between students' reported use of passive strategies and teacher liking and a significant positive relationship between students' reported use of active strategies and teacher liking (r = .32). Interestingly, teachers perceived students' use of both active and passive affinity-seeking strategies favorably. The correlations between teachers' reports of both active and passive student affinity-seeking behaviors and liking were significant and very similar (r = .43, r = .44 respectively). Wanzer noted that as long as the teacher "picks up" on the students' use of either active or passive student affinity-seeking behaviors, liking increases.

From the teacher's perspectives, several of the student affinity-seeking strategies proved to be quite effective in gaining liking. If students want to achieve more positive relationships with their teachers, they should attempt to engage in the affinity-seeking behaviors with the strongest correlation with teacher liking, namely: *conversational rule keeping* (r = .45), *comfortable self* (r = .42) *dynamism* (r = .39) and *facilitate enjoyment* (r = .36). Alternatively, students should probably avoid strategies that were either negatively associated or unrelated to teacher affect such as: *assume control, assume equality, influence perceptions of closeness, inclusion of other, elicit other's disclosure, flirting, reward association,* and *gifts.* When students use strategies such as *assume equality, inclusion of other,* or *influence perceptions of closeness,* they work under the assumption that the student–teacher relationship is an egalitarian one. Because the relationship between teachers and students is typically considered asymmetrical, with teachers being in a more powerful position, use of many of these strategies (e.g., *assume control, assume equality, influence perceptions of closeness, elicit other's disclosure,* etc.) would violate relationship norms.

Knowledge Claims

The last 30 years of affinity-seeking research has provided us with a significant amount of information on the different ways that individuals can gain liking and influence in the classroom. After a thorough review of the literature, it is safe to conclude that instructors' and students' use of affinity-seeking strategies have consistently been associated with increased affect. In the following sections we advance a number of knowledge claims that are based on the primary research findings discussed in this chapter.

1. When teachers use affinity-seeking strategies with students, the classroom climate improves and students appear to be more motivated to study and have greater affective learning (Myers, 1995).

2. Students perceive instructors who use affinity-seeking as more credible (Frymier & Thompson, 1992).

3. As long as teachers "pick up" on students' use of affinity-seeking behaviors, use of both passive and active strategies result in greater teacher affect (Wanzer, 1995).

4. The following teacher perceived student affinity-seeking strategies had the strongest correlation with teacher liking: *conversational rule keeping, comfortable self, dynamism,* and *facilitate enjoyment.* Most of these could be considered *active* affinity-seeking strategies (Wanzer, 1995).

5. College students need to realize that the teacher–student relationship is an asymmetrical one, and so use of affinity-seeking strategies that violate relationship norms could be detrimental to the relationship. Specifically, we recommend that students avoid the following affinity-seeking strategies: *assume control, assume equality, influence perceptions of closeness, inclusion of other, elicit other's disclosure, flirting, reward association,* and *gifts* (Wanzer 1995).

6. Not all of the affinity-seeking strategies are effective for the classroom context. Teachers must consider whether their goal is to increase affect toward themselves or their subject matter and then choose the appropriate strategy for achieving their goals.

7. Across the research on teacher use of affinity-seeking, there are *10 strategies* that have consistently been positively associated with either learning, motivation, credibility, or positive classroom climate.

- *Facilitate enjoyment.* When teachers are able to make classroom activities enjoyable, students appreciate it and respond positively.
- *Optimism.* Being optimistic and having a positive outlook has been consistently related to positive affect in the classroom.
- *Assume equality.* In effect, this is when a teacher de-emphasizes his or her higher status and treats students as equals.
- *Conversational rule-keeping.* This strategy is consistent with *assume equality.* When teachers use *conversational rule-keeping* they are being polite and treating students with respect.
- *Comfortable self.* A teacher using *comfortable self* appears relaxed and confident and may help students to also feel comfortable in the classroom.
- *Dynamism.* Teachers who are dynamic and enthusiastic consistently elicit greater liking from students.

- *Elicit other's disclosures.* When teachers use this strategy they are paying individual attention to students and showing interest in them as individuals. Most people find it confirming and complimentary to have someone of higher status show interest in them.
- *Altruism.* When teachers are altruistic and attempt to be helpful, students like them better. Students may not expect teachers to go out of their way to be helpful, so when they do, it is particularly appreciated.
- *Listening.* Listening goes hand-in-hand with *elicit other's disclosures* in terms of communicating confirmation to the student. When a teacher is listening to a student, he or she is focusing attention on the student.
- *Sensitivity.* Sensitivity involves expressing empathy and caring toward the student. Like *listening,* this strategy involves focusing attention on the student.

These 10 strategies provide a teacher with several options for gaining affinity from students. A teacher should not feel pressured to use all 10 strategies. Rather, a teacher should identify strategies he or she is comfortable with and use them regularly while teaching. Use of affinity-seeking strategies also needs to be sincere. Students will most likely notice insincere use of the strategies. Teachers who are insincere will likely be perceived as manipulative, resulting in a reduction of positive affect in the classroom.

A common theme running through these strategies is that when teachers use these behaviors in the classroom they are expressing caring and concern for their students. These strategies do not involve teachers forcing themselves into the students' social circles. The self-inclusion strategy has consistently been found to be ineffective and infrequently used by teachers. Although both teachers and students often want a positive relationship with one another, they do not want to be "buddies." Based on the research discussed in this chapter, there appear to be specific types of affinity-seeking strategies that are available for teachers and students to use for developing positive and appropriate relationships.

Directions for Future Research

The affinity-seeking typology is primarily descriptive in nature. Bell and Daly (1984) sought to understand *how* people go about getting others to like them. Their goal was to describe this phenomenon. The research that has been conducted on affinity-seeking since Bell and Daly published their landmark research has sought to further our understanding of how people use the strategies and how these strategies are associated with perceptions and outcomes. This program of research has remained descriptive for the most part and has not ventured into addressing the *why* question. That is, affinity-seeking scholars have not put forth an in-depth explanation of why affinity-seeking functions as it does. Often we struggle with operationalizing complex constructs. In the case of affinity-seeking, the operationalization is far more developed than the conceptualization. And this is where future research needs to take affinity-seeking. More specifically, we raise several different relevant questions that future research in this area could explore.

1. How should affinity-seeking be measured? One of the valuable aspects of the affinity-seeking typology is that it described 25 specific strategies for gaining affinity. This strength is also a weakness. A typology by nature is cumbersome and difficult to work with in the research context. As a form of measurement, the affinity-seeking typology is essentially a series of 25 single-item measures, each containing multiple behaviors, which violates one of the basic principles of measurement development. Items should not be double-barreled. Efforts to simplify the affinity-seeking typology (Dolin, 1995; Frymier, Houser, & Shulman, 1995; Frymier & Thompson, 1992) have not been particularly useful. For affinity-seeking scholarship to move from description to theory, the affinity-seeking typology must be framed at a conceptual level. While we do not want to discard the typology, we do need a more valid and parsimonious means of measuring the affinity-seeking construct. Once this is accomplished, researchers can more easily examine how affinity functions within the instructional setting, and how it differs conceptually from variables such as immediacy, affective learning, and motivation.

2. What is the relationship between affinity-seeking and immediacy? Immediacy is one of the affinity-seeking strategies in the typology, however, immediacy is a construct in its own right. Immediacy is defined as perceptions of physical or psychological closeness (Richmond, Gorham, & McCroskey, 1987) and has been operationalized as a variety of primarily nonverbal behaviors, such as eye contact, vocal variety, and physical closeness. Bell and Daly (1984) define affinity-seeking "as the active social-communicative process by which individuals attempt to get others to like and to feel positive toward them" (p. 91). These two variables most certainly overlap, at a minimum. Future research needs to determine how these two concepts are related to one another conceptually and operationally. It is possible that affinity-seeking strategies are simply a means of achieving immediacy. This idea needs to be investigated. If the relational result of affinity-seeking is different from the use of immediacy behaviors, what is the difference?

3. How do student affinity-seeking behaviors affect teachers and their teaching? As mentioned previously, the relationship between teachers and students is a transactional one, where each interactant has the ability to influence the other's behavior. If we believe that teachers and students exert mutual influence in the classroom, then why has the majority of instructional research focused almost exclusively on how *teachers'* behaviors affect *students*? There is a very good chance that student behavior, such as affinity-seeking, affects teachers' behaviors. Why, for example, has the role that students play in creating a classroom environment that is conducive for learning been largely neglected? With the exception of the research by Wanzer (1995), all of the studies in this chapter focused on teachers' use of affinity-seeking behaviors and how these behaviors contribute to students' learning experiences. We speculate that students' behaviors have the potential to contribute to or detract from the learning environment. Mottet, Beebe, and Fleuriet review the limited research examining students and their influence on teachers and their teaching in Chapter 7. Perhaps the next logical step in this line of inquiry is for researchers to examine students' use of and proficiency at affinity-seeking behaviors with their professors in relationship to important classroom outcomes. For example, when students use affinity-seeking strategies appropriately with their professors, do the professors "misbehave" (see Chapter 10) less or work harder to create a supportive classroom environment? Another interesting question is whether college students could be trained to use affinity-seeking strategies effectively with their professors? Students could be recruited to participate in a study where one half of the participants would be trained in the appropriate types of affinity-seeking strategies to use in the classroom. Next, researchers could investigate differences in students' grades and perceptions of their classroom experiences with their professors based on whether the student was trained to use affinity-seeking strategies throughout the semester. We suspect that when students are proactive and make frequent appropriate attempts to generate a positive relationship with their professors that they will also have a more positive experience that semester. Are students who are mentored by faculty members more effective affinity-seekers? Perhaps more research should explore how student behaviors, such as affinity-seeking strategies, affect the classroom environment and students' learning experiences.

4. What is the impact of affinity-seeking behaviors in instructional contexts outside the U. S. culture and in racially diverse classrooms? Roach and Byrne's (2001) study has been the only research that explored affinity-seeking outside of U.S. culture. In order to fully understand the construct of affinity-seeking, it needs to be examined in a variety of cultures. Additionally, the affinity-seeking research has almost exclusively been conducted with White Americans. We really do not know if the observed affinity-seeking relationships hold up with non-White American students. Clearly, this is an area where much research could be done.

Summary

In this chapter we reviewed the affinity-seeking construct from its beginning in 1976 with McCroskey and Wheeless's conceptualization and Bell and Daly's (1984) development of the affinity-seeking typology through the most recent application of the typology (Cummings & Romano, 2002). The program of research examining affinity-seeking is less developed than many of the other programs reviewed in this book. As was discussed in areas for future research, the typology structure has been somewhat of a hindrance. Despite the limitations of the typology, the research has consistently found that use of affinity-seeking in the classroom is beneficial for students' learning and motivation. Most research has focused on teacher use of affinity-seeking rather than on student use of affinity-seeking. The typology provides a useful description of specific behaviors teachers and students alike can perform to facilitate liking between teachers and students. The research has also provided some description of the boundaries of teacher–student relationships. Strategies such as *self-inclusion* and *reward association* have consistently had nonsignificant or negative relationships with student learning and motivation. Strategies such as *conversational rule-keeping* and *facilitate enjoyment* have consistently had significant positive relationships with student learning and motivation. These consistent relationships indicate that effective teacher–student relationships are characterized by mutual respect and liking while maintaining a certain respectful distance.

Existing research provides us with a good understanding of how affinity-seeking is related to classroom outcomes. Future research needs to further develop the operationalization of affinity-seeking and to examine how the construct of affinity-seeking is related to other instructional constructs, particularly immediacy.

References

Bell, R. A., & Daly, J. A. (1984). The affinity-seeking function of communication. *Communication Monographs, 51,* 91–115.

Cummings, K., & Romano, J. (2002). Effect of an honor code on perceptions of university instructor affinity-seeking behavior. *Journal of College Student Development, 43,* 862–875.

Dolin, D. J. (1995). An alternative form of teacher affinity-seeking measurement. *Communication Research Reports, 12,* 220–226.

Frymier, A. B. (1994). The use of affinity-seeking in producing liking and learning in the classroom. *Journal of Applied Communication Research, 22,* 87–105.

Frymier, A. B., Houser, M. L., & Shulman, G. M. (1995, April). *A measure of affinity-seeking: An alternative to the Bell and Daly typology.* Paper presented at the Eastern Communication Association annual convention, Pittsburgh, PA.

Frymier, A. B., & Thompson, C. A. (1992). Perceived teacher affinity-seeking in relation to perceived teacher credibility. *Communication Education, 41,* 388–399.

Gorham, J., Kelley, D. H., & McCroskey, J. C. (1989). The affinity-seeking of classroom teachers: A second perspective. *Communication Quarterly, 37,* 16–26.

McCroskey, J. C., & McCroskey, L. L. (1986). The affinity-seeking of classroom teachers. *Communication Research Reports, 3,* 158–167.

McCroskey, J. C., & Wheeless, L. R. (1976). *Introduction to human communication.* Boston: Allyn & Bacon.

Myers, S. A. (1995). Students perceptions of teacher affinity-seeking and classroom climate. *Communication Research Reports, 12,* 192–199.

Prisbell, M. (1994a). Affinity-seeking strategies associated with students' perceptions of satisfaction with communication in the classroom. *Perceptual and Motor Skills, 79,* 33–34.

Prisbell, M. (1994b). Students' perceptions of teachers' use of affinity-seeking and its relationship to teachers' competence. *Perceptual and Motor Skills, 78,* 641–642.

Richmond, V. P. (1990). Communication in the classroom: Power and motivation. *Communication Education, 39,* 181–195.

Richmond, V. P., Gorham, J., & McCroskey, J. C. (1987). The relationship between selected immediacy behaviors and cognitive learning. In M. McLaughlin (Ed.), *Communication yearbook 10* (pp. 574–590). Beverly Hills, CA: Sage.

Roach, K. D. (1991). The influence and effects of gender and status on university instructor affinity-seeking behavior. *Southern Communication Journal, 57,* 73–80.

Roach, K. D., & Byrne, P. R. (2001). A cross-cultural comparison of instructor communication in American and German classrooms. *Communication Education, 50,* 1–14.

Schutz, W. (1966). *The interpersonal underworld.* Palo Alto, CA: Science and Behavior Books.

Wanzer, M. B. (1995). *Student affinity-seeking messages and teacher liking: Subordinate initiated relationship building in superior-subordinate dyads.* Unpublished doctoral dissertation, West Virginia University, Morgantown, MV.

Wanzer, M. B. (1998). An exploratory investigation of student and teacher perceptions of student-generated affinity-seeking behaviors. *Communication Education, 47,* 373–382.

10

College Teacher Misbehaviors

Mary B. McPherson
California State University, Long Beach

Patricia Kearney
California State University, Long Beach

Timothy G. Plax
California State University, Long Beach

Introduction

Teachers are quick to recount both good and bad experiences in their classrooms. Some classes are remembered as particularly vibrant. These experiences make teachers feel good about themselves and what they do. Then there are those classes teachers recall as problematic. Students were disruptive, arrived late to class, engaged in unrelated activities during lecture, and appeared unresponsive and indifferent. With these experiences, even the most devoted teachers can become discouraged and disheartened about what they do.

An age-old question remains: Why do some classes seem to go well and others do not? College teachers lament that some students are overloaded with other classes and obligations. They may conclude that students have short attention spans or lack essential study skills. Teachers may believe that students' expectations about school are misguided, expecting their classes to be entertaining, easy, and requiring little or no effort on their part. Whatever the explanation, teachers continue to blame students for the problems they have teaching and managing the classroom (e.g., Gorham & Millette, 1997). Years of research reflect that view by concentrating almost exclusively on student disruptions, or misbehaviors, that interfere with classroom instruction with little or no consideration of teachers as the potential problem source (Kearney, Plax, & Allen, 2002). What teachers may fail to realize, is that what they say and do may trigger students' misbehaviors.

Kearney, Plax, Hays, and Ivey (1991) challenged the assumption that problem ownership for student disruptions lies solely with the student. They initiated a program of research based on the premise that teachers are an important source of student misbehaviors. In this landmark study, the label *misbehaviors,* was extended to include those behaviors that teachers say and do that interfere with instruction. College students identified a number of their teachers who lacked basic teaching skills, humiliated students, showed up late for class, returned paper and exams late, and overwhelmed students by making their classes too difficult. Understandably, such teacher misbehaviors could stimulate student disruption, resistance, and other problems.

Even with data validating these and other teacher misbehaviors, the use of the label, *misbehavior,* continues to be misunderstood. Critics of this label point to specific misbehaviors, like foreign or regional accents, as unintentional teacher attributes or personal traits that cannot be defined as misbehaviors. We disagree. Even though we may prefer our students to appreciate or accept our individual and cultural differences, students may continue to label those behaviors as disruptive to their learning. Importantly, teacher misbehaviors are those behaviors identified by *students* that irritate, demotivate, or substantially distract them from learning (Kearney et al., 1991). Essentially, teacher misbehaviors reflect student perceptions of teacher actions that interfere with learning, even if those teacher behaviors are unintentional or reflect personal attributes.

Rationale for Examining Teacher Misbehaviors

Teachers spend time preparing lectures, developing experiential learning activities, carefully crafting assignments, conferencing with students, and evaluating or giving feedback. With this much effort, most teachers want their energy to result in positive outcomes for students and for them. As teachers, we hope our labors enhance students' cognitive and affective learning. In spite of our best efforts, students report that teachers say and do things that interfere with their learning. In fact, students believe that teachers are their primary source of demotivation (Gorham & Christophel, 1992; Gorham & Millette, 1997). Even though students indicate that most teachers misbehave infrequently, when they do, those behaviors likely affect student behaviors and perceptions.

When it comes to misbehaving, college students apparently follow their teachers' leads. For instance, students are more likely to engage in aberrant behaviors when teachers misbehave early in the semester (Boice, 1996). Specifically, students are more distracted, noisier in class, and engage in inefficient and less note-taking when teachers set the tone by engaging in misbehaviors themselves. Over time, these student misbehaviors become more pronounced. With misbehaving teachers, students become increasingly uninvolved, oppositional, and/or combative. For example, one college student complained, "[The teacher] starts off by telling us that he won't be talking to us outside class, only his TAs will. He tells us that his lectures won't count on tests. Why bother?" (Boice, 1996, p. 466).

Teacher misbehaviors not only affect students, but indirectly affect teachers as well. When comparing end-of-term teacher evaluations, students rate teachers who misbehave lower than those who do not (Boice, 1996; Schrodt, 2003). Similarly, students perceive misbehaving teachers as less credible (Schrodt, 2003). Regrettably, teacher misbehaviors are often associated with new teachers (Boice, 1996) who are untenured and rely most heavily on receiving positive evaluations as part of their tenure review documentation. The pressure to receive good teaching evaluations is perhaps highest for new teachers, yet they are the very ones most likely to suffer the consequences of their own misbehaviors.

In addition to negative teacher evaluations, teacher misbehaviors adversely influence students' affective learning (McPherson & Bippus, 2003; McPherson, Kearney, & Plax 2003; Wanzer & McCroskey, 1998). Recognizing the relationship between affective and cognitive learning, we can argue further that teacher misbehaviors should negatively influence students' cognitive learning as well. Several studies provide direct tests of that influence. Boice (1996) found that students demonstrate lower levels of comprehension with teachers who misbehave. Furthermore, Myers (2002) reported that verbally aggressive teachers negatively affected students' motivation and self-reports of their own cognitive learning. In addition, Gill (1994) discovered that teacher accents, one of the teacher misbehaviors identified by students (Kearney et al., 1991), negatively interfered with students' comprehension. These studies indicate that teachers do, in fact, misbehave and when they do, they interfere with the teaching and learning process.

Origins of the Research Program

Until the early 1990s, student behaviors were the focus for researchers attempting to understand classroom disruption. Students were studied as the primary source of interference with learning. Teachers, on the other hand, were represented as custodians or managers, responsible for students' academic engagement in on-task behaviors. From this perspective, researchers identified power-based teacher strategies for modifying students' actions (Kearney, Plax, Richmond, & McCroskey, 1985). Researchers assumed that because students misbehaved, they needed to be managed and their behavior controlled. Years of research verified that students misbehave, and when they do, teachers can initiate behavior alteration techniques to control that behavior and motivate students to engage in alternative behaviors more conducive to learning. Yet, this perspective fails to illustrate the full picture. Apparently, students are not the only source of instructional interference.

Departing from the traditional perspective of students as the source of learning interference, Kearney, Plax, Hays, and Ivey (1991) initiated a research program investigating what *teachers* say and do that interferes with their teaching and students' learning. These researchers argued that not only do teachers misbehave, but those misbehaviors can influence how students think about, feel, and act toward the teacher, school, and themselves. Essentially, they reasoned that teacher misbehaviors are important antecedents to student misbehaviors.

Kearney, Plax, and their colleagues (1991) contend that when teachers misbehave, students are likely to become demotivated, dissatisfied, and resist teacher attempts to keep them on task. A large body of literature documents a relationship between what teachers say and do with students' behaviors. Teacher behaviors are known to influence student achievement, time spent on-task, compliance, affect, work habits, motivation, the development of social skills, and a number of other student reactions. We know, then, that what teachers say and do can significantly affect how students think and behave.

To investigate the potential influence of teacher misbehaviors on student responses, Kearney, Plax, Hays, and Ivey (1991) launched their program of research with two studies. Study one was designed to inductively derive types of teacher misbehaviors from college students' reports. To answer their research question, *"What do college teachers say and do that students perceive as misbehaviors?"* students were asked to think back over their college careers and recall specific instances where teachers had said or done something during a course that had irritated, demotivated, or substantially distracted them in an aversive way. Students were then asked to provide brief, but specific, written descriptions of as many teacher misbehaviors as they could. Of the 250 students sampled, almost 2,000 descriptions of teacher misbehaviors emerged. These descriptions were then content analyzed and coded into 28 different categories of misbehavior. Of the inductively derived categories of misbehaviors, the five most frequently cited types of misbehaviors were teachers' use of sarcasm or putdowns, absenteeism from class or early dismissals, failure to stay on subject, unfair testing practices, and boring lectures.

In study two, another 261 students completed questionnaires that validated the original 28 misbehavior categories. (Figure 10.1 provides a complete list of all 28 misbehavior categories with sample descriptions of each.) Students reported how frequently their target teacher engaged in each of the misbehavior types. Delivering boring lectures, straying from the subject matter, employing unfair testing procedures, presenting confusing and unclear lectures, and returning students' work late were the most frequently reported teacher misbehaviors. Interestingly, the top three rated misbehaviors from their second study correspond with three of the top five identified in Study one.

The second study was also designed to determine whether the 28 categories could be meaningfully and reliably reduced. Factor analyses revealed three underlying dimensions of teacher misbehavior that can be profiled as incompetence,

FIGURE 10.1 ***Teacher Misbehavior Categories with Sample Descriptions.***

Misbehavior	Description
Absent	Does not show up for class, cancels class without notification, and/or offers poor excuses for being absent.
Tardy	Is late for class or tardy.
Keeps Students Overtime	Keeps class overtime, talks too long or starts class early before all the students are there.
Early Dismissal	Lets class out early, rushes through the material to get done early.
Strays From Subject	Uses the class as a forum for her/his personal opinions, goes off on tangents,talks about family and personal life, and/or generally wastes class time.
Confusing/Unclear Lectures	Unclear about what is expected, lectures are confusing and vague, contradicts him/herself, jumps from one subject to another, and/or lectures are inconsistent with assigned readings.
Unprepared/Disorganized	Is not prepared for class, unorganized, forgets test dates, and/or makes assignments but does not collect them.
Deviates From Syllabus	Changes due dates for assignments, behind schedule, does not follow the syllabus, changes assignments, and/or assigns books but does not use them.
Late Returning Work	Late in returning papers, late in grading and turning back exams, and/or forgets to bring graded papers to class.
Sarcasm and Putdowns	Is sarcastic and rude, makes fun of and humiliates students, picks on students, and/or insults and embarrasses, students.
Verbally Abusive	Uses profanity, is angry and mean, yells and screams, interrupts and/or intimidates students.
Unreasonable and Arbitrary Rules	Refuses to accept late work, gives no breaks in 3-hours classes, punishes entire class for one student's misbehavior, and/or is rigid, inflexible, and authoritarian.
Sexual Harassment	Makes sexual remarks to students, flirts with them, makes sexual innuendos, and/or is chauvinistic.
Unresponsive to Students' Questions	Does not encourage students to ask questions, does not answer questions or recognize raised hands, and/or seems "put out" to have to explain or repeat him/herself.
Apathetic to Students	Doesn't seem to care about the course or show concern for students, does not know the students' names, rejects students' opinions, and/or does not allow for class discussion.
Inaccessible to Students Outside of Class	Does not show up for appointments or scheduled office hours, is hard to contact, will not meet with students outside of office time, and/or doesn't make time for students when they need help.
Unfair Testing	Asks trick questions on tests, exams do not relate to the lectures, tests are too difficult, questions are too ambiguous, and/or teacher does not review for exams.
Unfair Grading	Grades unfairly, changes grading policy during the semester, does not believe in giving A's, makes mistakes when grading, and/or does not have a predetermined grading scale.

(Continued)

FIGURE 10.1 ***(Continued)***

Boring Lectures	Is not an enthusiastic lecturer, speaks in monotone and rambles, is boring, too repetitive, and/or employs no variety in lectures.
Information Overload	Talks too fast and rushes through the material, talks over the students' heads, uses obscure terms and/or assigns excessive work.
Information Underload	The class is too easy, students feel they have not learned anything, and/or tests are too easy.
Negative Personality	Teacher is impatient, self-centered, complains, acts superior, and/or is moody.
Negative Physical Appearance	Teacher dresses sloppy, smells bad, clothes are out of style, and cares little about his/her overall appearance.
Does Not Know Subject Matter	Doesn't know the material, unable to answer questions, provides incorrect information, and/or isn't current.
Shows Favoritism or Prejudice	Plays favorites with students or acts prejudiced against others, is narrow-minded or close-minded, and/or makes prejudicial remarks.
Foreign or Regional Accents	Teacher is hard to understand, enunciates poorly, and has a strong accent that makes it difficult to understand.
Inappropriate Volume	Doesn't speak loudly enough or speaks too loud.
Bad Grammar/Spelling	Uses bad grammar, writes illegibly, misspells words on the exam (or on the board), and/or generally uses poor English.

From "College Teacher Misbehaviors: What Students Don't Like about What Teachers Say or Do," by P. Kearney, T. G. Plax, E. R. Hays, and M. J. Ivey, 1991, *Communication Quarterly, 39,* 309–324. Republished with permission by the Eastern Communication Association.

offensiveness, and indolence. *Incompetent* teachers engage in a cluster of misbehaviors that indicate to students that they don't care about either the course or the student. These teachers don't bother to learn their students' names, make their tests too difficult, and are unable or unwilling to help their students succeed. Above all, incompetent teachers are simply bad lecturers. They either bore or confuse their students; some overload them with too much information; and still others mispronounce words or engage in accented speech that the students cannot understand.

The cluster of misbehaviors associated with *offensive* teachers characterizes them as "mean," "cruel," and "ugly." They humiliate students, play favorites, intimidate, and are generally condescending, rude, and self-centered. In addition, offensive teachers are sarcastic, verbally abusive, arbitrary, and unreasonable. Finally, the misbehaviors associated with *indolent* teachers are reminiscent of the absent-minded professor. They fail to show up for class and often arrive late when they do, forget test dates, neglect to grade homework, constantly readjust assignments, and underwhelm students by making their classes and tests too easy.

The resulting factor-based profiles of teacher misbehaviors stimulated a number of additional research questions, providing the foundation for a program of research. Looking to theory to frame or ground subsequent research, Kearney et al. (1991) relied on two theoretical perspectives, attribution theory and norms violation theory. What follows is a systematic and chronological review of that research.

Theoretical Perspectives Guiding the Research

Attribution Theory

Attribution theory provides a framework for understanding how we explain others' behaviors as well as our own in order to predict and control the world around us (Heider, 1958). Essentially, we attempt to make sense of our own and others' behaviors through a process of observation and perception formation. Once we do make sense of those behaviors, our attributions allow us to respond appropriately to our social environment (Kelley, 1967; Weiner 1979). The processes that guide or determine the attributions that people make are all linked to the context in which the behaviors occur. In the classroom context, students attempt to make sense of their teachers' behaviors. Kelsey, Kearney, Plax, Allen, and Ritter (2004) recognized that attribution theory affords a meaningful framework for investigating how students interpret and react to teacher misbehaviors. Before we describe the details of this study, we examine first the tenets of attribution theory in the context of the classroom.

The classroom context defines specific roles and behaviors for students and teachers. For instance, students may presume that their teacher will be prepared for class with organized materials. If a teacher forgets to bring essential materials to class, students might interpret that behavior as disorganized and conclude that the teacher is absent-minded (i.e., attributing the behavior to the teacher's personality). As a result, students may respond by *slacking off* on their own work. This pattern of attribution and response can be explained by the core assumptions of attribution theory.

Three assumptions underlie this theoretical perspective. First, people seek to interpret or understand self and others' behavior in terms of its causes. Second, people assign causes systematically. Third, attributed causes play an important role in determining reactions to those behaviors (Heider, 1958; Jones & Davis, 1965; Kelley, 1967; Kelley & Michela, 1980; Shaver, 1975). Assuming that people assign causes and they do so in some systematic way, attribution theory outlines three types of information that perceivers utilize when assigning causes to others' behaviors. Specifically, when perceivers are faced with the necessity of interpreting the behavior of others, perceivers choose among three possible explanations: the situation, intentionality or disposition, and unintentionality or chance.

Behaviors explained by the *situation* occur when we conclude that a person's conduct was caused by particular circumstances or environmental factors. These situational explanations are called *external* attributions; the cause of the behavior is considered to be outside of the individual enacting the behavior. The behavior may be counter to a person's "typical" actions and one that is displayed occasionally, and in a particular situation. The second type of explanation, *intentionality* or *disposition,* refers to actions or behaviors attributed to an individual's personality. As a rule, we attribute intentionality or disposition when behaviors are characterized as stable over time, consistent across situations, and typical. Dispositional explanations are called *internal* attributions; the individual is held responsible for the behavior. We describe behaviors as *unintentional* or *chance* when the causes are neither due to the situation nor to the person's disposition. Such behaviors are perceived as less controlled or more spontaneous. With such chance behaviors, we are unable to predict the likelihood of their reoccurrence in the future (Heider, 1958; Kelley, 1950).

Although researchers describe these attributional explanations separately, they work in combination. For instance, behaviors that are consistent over time and viewed as intentional are likely to be assigned internal attributions. Conversely, behaviors that are rarely displayed and perceived as unintentional are associated with external attributions (Kelley, 1950). Applied to the classroom context, a teacher may misbehave by failing to show up for class. Students may attribute that misbehavior to either external or internal causes. Externally, the student may explain the teacher's one-time failure to attend as a function of some family emergency or a car accident. Internally, the student may explain the same behavior of a chronically late teacher as a function of some persistent trait or characteristic, like laziness, apathy, or thoughtlessness. How students attribute causes to teacher misbehaviors may influence their motivation to learn, willingness to comply, and evaluation of their teachers' effectiveness (Kelsey et al., 2004).

Apparently, both teachers and students appear to make biased attributions about what they do. Consistent with the fundamental attribution error (Heider, 1958), students should over-attribute internal causes to their teachers' negative behaviors and over-attribute external causes to their own shortcomings. In an effort to determine how students cope with teachers who misbehave, Kelsey et al. (2004) investigated explanations or attributions that students assign to misbehaving teachers. They began by arguing that negative behaviors of others are likely to be viewed as internal or dispositional in origin. Moreover, they reasoned that, when faced with misbehaving teachers in the classroom context, students would be more likely to assign more internal than external causes to teacher misbehaviors. Following Kelley's (1950) work on attributions, these researchers also argued that students are likely to associate more internal attributions with teachers who consistently or regularly misbehave, but more external attributions with teachers who only occasionally misbehave. Because earlier research established that teacher immediacy (i.e., behaviors that communicate closeness) can neutralize the impact of teacher misbehaviors on students' perceptions (Thweatt & McCroskey, 1996), Kelsey et al. (2004) also examined whether immediacy would have a similar neutralizing effect on students' attributions.

Undergraduate students ($N = 619$) were asked to focus on the teacher of the class that meets immediately before or after the class in which data were collected. With that teacher in mind, students completed a series of measures targeting their perceptions of their teachers' nonverbal immediacy and likelihood of engaging in a variety of teacher misbehavior types. An open-ended question asked them to provide reasons why they think their teacher would engage in those particular misbehaviors that are identified on the scale. Students were further asked to respond to scales assessing attributions about their target teacher's misbehaviors, including consistency and causality.

As expected, the findings from this study revealed that students more readily assign causal attributions of internality, rather than externality, when their teachers misbehave. When teachers misbehaved, students were likely to view those behaviors as rooted in dispositional or personal characteristics, more so than with situational or environmental forces. Moreover, the reliance on internal attributions for teacher misbehaviors was similar across offensive, indolent, and incompetent teacher misbehavior profiles. Further, students associated internal or dispositional attributions with teachers who misbehaved consistently. The association between external attributions and occasional or infrequent misbehaviors was much weaker. Once again, when attributing causes of teacher misbehavior, students relied primarily on internal or dispositional factors.

Most surprising was the finding that teacher immediacy failed to neutralize or mediate students' attributions of misbehaving teachers. Teacher misbehaviors, not immediacy, contributed substantively to students' ascriptions of causality, and then primarily for attributions of internality rather than externality. Apparently, teachers who misbehave can expect students to assign dispositional attributions, regardless of their level of immediacy.

This study made important contributions to our understanding of students' reactions to teachers' behaviors. First, we know how students attribute causes to teachers who misbehave, particularly for those teachers reported to be incompetent, offensive, or indolent. Second, even though teacher immediacy may be a salient and powerful mediator of some students' perceptions, immediacy does not impact the types of attributions students assign to teacher misbehaviors. Prior claims that implied that immediate teachers could escape assignments of negative attributions (Kearney, Plax, & Burroughs, 1991; Thweatt & McCroskey, 1996; 1998) were not supported in this investigation.

Third, Kelsey et al. (2004) demonstrated that internal and external attributions function independently. Students can attribute causes either internally (a predisposition) or externally (situational factors). Fourth, with teacher misbehaviors, students are likely to attribute primarily internal attributions. This finding follows directly from the fundamental attribution error. Overall, this study suggests that students are not very forgiving of their instructors when those teachers misbehave. Students hold teachers responsible for their own misbehaviors and appear to be relatively inattentive to issues and concerns that teachers often view as important mitigating factors for their misbehaviors. Students care less about teacher demeanor than they do about how professionally and consistently they behave in their classes. On those occasions when teachers mess up, they can't make up for it simply by being friendly or immediate. Even those teachers who employ all the right moves (e.g., eye-contact, close proximity, smiling) are not immune to students' tendencies to attribute internal causality to aberrant behaviors.

Students not only assign more internal attributions to teachers who engage in general misbehaviors, but also do so for particular misbehaviors. Rather than examining global displays of teacher misbehaviors, McPherson and Young (2003, 2004) investigated students' attributions of teacher displays of a specific misbehavior: anger. Anger expressions are closely related to those teacher misbehaviors categorized previously as "offensive" (e.g., putdowns, verbal abuse) in the original Kearney et al. (1991) study. McPherson and Young reasoned that the way in which teachers display anger will influence students' attributions. When teachers become angry, they may express that anger aggressively by shouting at students, calling them names, slamming books, or glaring at them. Alternatively, teachers may show their anger assertively by discussing their dissatisfaction with the students and working collaboratively to correct a problem. McPherson and Young hypothesized that students would assign higher levels of internality to teachers displaying antisocial or aggressive anger, and lower levels to teachers expressing their anger in more prosocial or assertive ways.

Undergraduate students (N = 300) were asked to describe a time when a teacher became angry in one of their college classes. They were then asked to provide a reason for their teacher's anger and complete survey items measuring type of anger expression and attributions of internality. As predicted, students assigned greater internal attributions to teachers who expressed their anger more aggressively than assertively. Paradoxically, when asked to provide specific reasons for teacher anger, students generated more external reasons (e.g., student misbehaviors, lack of student effort and motivation, and student–teacher power challenges) than internal reasons (e.g., teacher personality and lack of teaching skill). In effect, students saw themselves as responsible for causing their teachers to become angry. Yet, they appear to blame teachers primarily for the expression of that anger.

As with previous research, McPherson and Young (2003, 2004) verified that students do, indeed, make causal attributions about their teachers' misbehaviors (in this case, teacher expressions of anger). For aggressive or threatening displays of anger, students described the teacher as yelling, screaming, calling students stupid, blowing his or her top, or losing control. In these cases of aggression, students blamed the teacher for the anger display by assigning greater internal attributions. Other students described their teachers' anger as nonthreatening. Although these teachers still communicated their anger, they did so by calmly discussing the problem. Students assigned fewer internal attributions to these more assertive displays.

Why do students perceive these two styles of anger displays so differently? Perhaps students perceive aggression as more egregious than assertiveness. Alternatively, students might not view assertive anger as a misbehavior at all. Importantly, though, the display of anger (i.e., aggressive or assertive) was the impetus for the attribution, not the act of becoming angry. The causal attribution process is a complex one. Students clearly differentiated the experience of anger from the expression of anger. Students also distinguished between anger expressed in a reasonable way (assertively) from anger that is not (aggressively).

Adding to this line of programmatic research, McPherson and Bippus (2003) focused on student attributions of another type of teacher misbehavior, classroom embarrassment. If you'll recall, students in the original Kearney et al. (1991) study ranked embarrassment as one of the top five most frequently cited teacher misbehaviors. Classroom embarrassment typically occurs when teachers draw attention to particular students in front of the entire class. For example, teachers may publicly discount students' ideas or criticize their work, accuse them of cheating, reveal a grade to the rest of the class, comment on students' appearance, or even point out a student who is violating a classroom rule (e.g., being tardy or talking in class). McPherson and Bippus investigated the attributions students make about teachers who embarrass them in these and other ways and how those attributions influence students' affect toward the teacher.

College students ($N = 208$) were asked to think of a specific incident in which they were significantly embarrassed by a teacher in the classroom. They were asked to describe the embarrassing event and offer an explanation of why they thought the teacher embarrassed them (i.e., identify the teacher's goal). Students also described what they said or did in their efforts to cope with that embarrassing event and completed a survey measuring their attributions about the teacher's embarrassment-inducing behavior and their resulting affect.

All students in this study were able to recall a time when a teacher engaged in this misbehavior. By the looks of it, teacher-initiated embarrassment is a salient experience for students. Further, as many as a third of the students believed that their teacher used embarrassment as a strategy to gain their compliance (e.g., get the students to follow class rules, encourage them to study harder). Still, slightly more than a quarter of the students didn't know why their teachers embarrassed them. Regardless of their ability to determine their teachers' goals, students had no trouble making judgments about offending teachers. The attribution analysis revealed that affective learning decreased when students believed their teachers intentionally embarrassed them (even if they were unable to determine the goal). In other words, students who believed their teachers intentionally embarrassed them liked their teachers less and were less likely to enroll in another course with that teacher. The extent to which students perceived teachers' behaviors as internal to the teacher or stable over time resulted in higher affective learning.

This study confirms that when teachers engage in embarrassment as a type of misbehavior, attributions influence students' assessment of teachers. As expected, students evaluated teachers more highly when they saw their teacher's embarrassment of them as less intentional. However, the more students attributed internality to their teacher's use of embarrassment and saw their teacher's behavior as consistent or stable over time, the higher their evaluations of the teacher. One explanation is that students generally see embarrassing students as a classroom management strategy. Teachers "hold the floor" more often than students and generally have more power over what occurs in the classroom. Therefore, teachers who tend to say or do things that cause students embarrassment may elicit respect for performing their expected role. Nonetheless, a teacher who is seen as trying to embarrass students—not doing so simply as a function of the job but as an intentional and perhaps vindictive act—would not garner the same positive evaluations from students. To understand how students cope with deviations from anticipated teacher behaviors, a growing body of research is utilizing norm violation explanations to understand student evaluations of misbehaving teachers.

Norm Violations Model

In addition to attribution theory, researchers have used the norm violations model (Levine, Anders, Banas, Baum, Endo, Hu, & Wong, 2000) as a framework for studying teacher misbehaviors. Norms are situationally-based standards for behavior that prescribe certain actions. Norm violations occur when a person's behavior falls outside the range of acceptable behavior and is deemed inappropriate or deviant relative to the context. In other words, while persons often expect normative behavior from others, it is also possible to expect (based on information from a third party or prior interaction) inappropriate, deviant, or nonnormative behavior from others. Because norms specify the range of socially acceptable behavior in particular contexts, behaviors that violate norms should be evaluated negatively by others, whether the inappropriate behavior is expected or not.

By definition, teacher misbehaviors represent a type of classroom norm violation. Because teacher misbehaviors hinder learning, students are likely to perceive these behaviors as inappropriate and unacceptable. By examining teacher misbehaviors as violations of normative classroom behavior, researchers focused their studies on students' reactions to those violations.

Berkos, Allen, Kearney, and Plax, (2001) were interested in how students process and then manage, or cope with, these norm violations. One way we process information is through imagined interactions (IIs). *Imagined interactions* are defined as a social cognitive process in which individuals imagine themselves communicating with others (Edwards, Honeycutt, & Zagacki, 1988). Specifically, IIs are a type of conversational daydream in which individuals imagine what they might say to another person, or reflect on what they should have said in a conversation that has already taken place. Imagined interactions serve three primary functions. They help us to (1) rehearse what we'll say in future encounters, (2) release built-up emotions and tension, and (3) analyze and clarify our thinking.

Berkos et al. (2001) examined whether teacher norm violations (operationalized as teacher misbehaviors) provoke students' imagined interactions. Imagined interactions allow students to replay violation events, identify teacher norm violations or misbehaviors, decide on their responses, and thus, cope with those deviations. Arguing that teacher norm violations should stimulate students' cognitive processing, Berkos and her associates reasoned that students are likely to use IIs following teacher misbehaviors. Recognizing the improbability that students would actually confront their teachers, they further reasoned that student IIs would not be used for rehearsal. Instead, they predicted that students would rely on IIs primarily as a substitute for interacting with their misbehaving teacher or as a way to manage their frustrations with the teacher.

College students ($N = 237$) were given one of three teacher misbehavior (norm violation) profiles derived from the original misbehavior study (Kearney et al., 1991)—an offensive, indolent, or incompetent teacher profile. After reading their assigned profile, students were asked to provide an example of an actual teacher who fit the profile of the norm-violating teacher targeted. In this way, subsequent participants' responses would be anchored to an actual violating teacher.

Participants then responded to survey items assessing their imagined interactions with the target teacher and their likelihood of engaging in actual interactions with (confronting) the teacher.

An important by-product of this study was that students were able to recall specific examples of teachers who fit each of the three norm violations profiled. This procedure substantiated the validity of the teacher misbehavior profiles. (Figure 10.2 provides sample descriptions that students supplied for actual teachers who were offensive, incompetent, or indolent.) Results indicated that, regardless of the norm violation profiled, students reported using imagined interactions. Students indicated the greatest likelihood of relying on IIs to process norm violations with offensive teachers and least with indolent teachers. Students further reported a greater reliance on IIs as a way to deal with their norm-violating teachers rather than interacting with or confronting them. Particularly with offensive teachers, students preferred to use IIs as a substitute for and a means of avoiding actual contact with their teachers who misbehave. Of the three types of norm violations, or misbehaviors, offensiveness represented the most directly threatening to students. Predictably, this teacher misbehavior profile elicited the greatest amount of avoidance and IIs from students.

As you will see with this next study, students not only react to teacher norm violations with imagined interactions, they also respond to violations in their evaluations of their teachers. McPherson, Kearney, and Plax (2003) utilized the norm violations model to investigate students' perceptual and affective reactions to a specific teacher misbehavior. This study investigated teacher expressions of anger that students define as appropriate or inappropriate. By definition, teacher expressions of anger that students consider inappropriate are norm violations; those that are considered appropriate are not. Additionally, we examined how students evaluate teachers who express anger in these normative and nonnormative ways. We argued that anger alone does not constitute a misbehavior. Rather, the intensity and the manner in which the anger is expressed determine whether students perceive the expression as a misbehavior or norm violation. Rules govern both the intensity and display of emotions. These rules or norms specify what emotion expressions are appropriate and inappropriate for specific situations.

Recall the two expressions of anger (McPherson & Young, 2003; 2004) discussed earlier—aggressive and assertive displays. Aggressiveness represents threatening presentations of anger that are often hostile and represent little or no respect for the target of the anger. Aggressive anger can be characterized as either direct or indirect, but both forms are threatening. The more direct expression, *distributive aggression,* is often displayed as shouting, criticizing, threatening, using abusive language, throwing objects, and trying to "get even." *Passive aggression* is more indirect and includes displays like, giving the silent treatment, communicating cold/dirty looks, and leaving the room. Unlike aggressive forms of anger expressions, *assertive anger* consists of nonthreatening (but direct) displays. Assertive anger is characterized as honestly articulating thoughts and feelings without assigning blame and taking into account others' needs and rights. Assertive anger is expressed by trying to be fair, listening to the other's side of the story, discussing the problem, and trying to "patch things up."

FIGURE 10.2 ***Students' Characterizations of the Three Teacher Misbehavior Profiles.***

Misbehavior Profile	Student Characterization
Offensive Teacher	He only tells them their way of doing work is wrong.
	He said things like, "Don't bother coming to class because you are doing terrible anyway."
	She would always talk down or belittle those she did not like by using sarcastic or rude comments.
	My teacher was offensive because he was constantly promoting his religion while putting others down. This was very inappropriate, especially for an anatomy class.
	He cursed for emphasis and became very aggressive in [his] discipline. His "in-your-face" teaching style did spur some to work harder, but some rebelled and did not complete the work.
	He used pick-up lines on pretty female students.
Incompetent Teacher	Actually he didn't lecture, but he read us material from the book. In many cases, lectures were like, "Open to page . . . " and so on, "On the bottom part is a definition you need to know." He never demonstrated any interest in students.
	The teacher would talk too fast and tried to cover too much material. The teacher would assign too much homework and never would allow time for students' questions.
	He just gave homework and tests and didn't lecture or teach at all.
	He told us that the next test was going to be too difficult to pass.
	[She] talked and lectured to herself. She didn't want to be asked questions.
Indolent Teacher	She never stuck to due dates and was very lax in grading. The entire semester was basically spent reading a newspaper while she was at her desk. When we finally got our assignments back, they were so tardy the corrections were no longer helpful.
	He was totally unprepared for class and also was consistently late. Sometimes he never showed up.
	The teacher lost our homework.
	[He/she was] consistently 5–10 minutes late, blaming traffic! Repeated topics already lectured.
	He missed a lot of class and would play videos.
	[She/he] encouraged group work, even on exams.
	We didn't have to take the final.
	We never got our assignments back.

From "When Norms Are Violated: Imagined Interactions as Processing and Coping Mechanisms, by K. M. Berkos, T. H. Allen, P. Kearney, and T. G. Plax, 2001, *Communication Monographs, 68,* 289–300. Republished with permission by *Communication Monographs* and Taylor & Francis Ltd. http://www.tandf.co.uk/journals.

The ways in which we express anger affect our relationships and the judgments others make about us. Research consistently shows that aggressive anger displays are viewed more negatively than assertive ones (Guerrero, 1994; Sereno, Welch, & Braaten, 1987). Undoubtedly, the way in which anger is expressed influences how the anger is perceived. Therefore, we predicted that students perceive aggressive and intense anger as less appropriate teacher behavior (and thus, norm violating) and assertive, low intensity anger as more appropriate (McPherson, Kearney, & Plax, 2003).

Violations of normative behavior are not only considered inappropriate, but can also stimulate individuals to assign valence, or value, to the violation and the source. For instance, if a teacher unexpectedly gives students extra-credit points, students are likely to perceive that violation as positive ("positively valenced violation") and perceive the teacher more positively as well. In the instructional context, valence is subsumed within affective learning, which refers to positively or negatively valenced attitudes regarding the teacher and the course. Studies show that students report high affect for teachers and the course when their teachers engage in friendly, open, and caring behaviors. Norm violation theory would suggest then, that students will assign positively valenced affect when teachers express their anger in more caring ways than when teachers are more hostile with their anger. Therefore, we predicted that aggressive and intense expressions of teacher anger should be negatively associated with affect, and that assertive and less intense displays should be positively associated with affect.

We asked undergraduate students (N = 301) to recall a teacher who became angry in one of their college classes and describe the angry episode or event. With that teacher and episode in mind, students then responded to measures of anger intensity, anger expression, appropriateness, and affect. Results indicated that teacher anger, alone, did not necessarily constitute a norm violation or misbehavior. As expected, how the anger was expressed influenced students' reactions. Intense and aggressive anger, like those displayed by offensive teachers, were reported by students as inappropriate and resulted in lower student affect. Teachers who expressed anger in less intense and more assertive ways were perceived to be appropriate and resulted in higher student affect. Only normative expressions of anger were associated with positive student affect. Consequently, effective teachers can feel and express their anger, but they are advised to display their anger in ways their students perceive as appropriate or normative.

Related Studies

Although a number of important studies examining teacher misbehavior are theory driven, other studies are more atheoretical. In general, these studies fall into two categories: (1) factors that influence student perceptions of misbehaviors and (2) the resulting consequences of teacher misbehaviors. The first set of studies investigates variables that influence students' perceptions of teachers who misbehave.

Researchers in the first two studies presented here argue that perceptions of teacher misbehaviors are influenced heavily by other teacher characteristics, particularly teacher immediacy and sociocommunicative style.

Teacher immediacy is one of the most examined concepts in instructional communication and has been consistently associated with outcomes of student affective and cognitive learning. Immediacy refers to the perception of physical and/or psychological closeness. As noted earlier, the behaviors that define immediacy are primarily nonverbal and include smiling, eye contact, forward body lean, head nodding, and other similar approach behaviors. To examine the potential mediating effects of immediacy on student perceptions of teacher misbehaviors, Thweatt and McCroskey (1996) designed a simulation study, providing students with one of four scenarios of hypothetical teachers. Teachers were characterized as either immediate or nonimmediate and engaging in either appropriate or inappropriate (i.e., misbehaving) behaviors. After reading the scenarios, students ($N = 382$) were asked to rate their perceptions of the target teacher's level of immediacy and misbehaviors.

What the researchers found was noteworthy. Results indicated that students were unable to differentiate between misbehaving and nonmisbehaving teachers when the profiled teacher was nonimmediate. Not so for the immediate teacher conditions; students were, in fact, able to discriminate between the immediate teacher who misbehaved and the immediate teacher who did not. In essence, students perceived nonimmediate teachers as misbehaving, even when the teacher was characterized as engaging in appropriate or positive teacher behaviors. In fact, teachers described as nonimmediate with no misbehaviors were judged to be misbehaving as much as nonimmediate teachers who were misbehaving. These findings suggest that nonimmediacy behaviors are capable of being defined or explained as a type of misbehavior. Apparently, teachers who are unenthusiastic, stand behind the podium, and seem tense are judged by students as misbehaving.

Wanzer and McCroskey (1998) argued that teachers' sociocommunicative style (i.e., combined perceptions of assertiveness and responsiveness) would mediate perceptions of teacher misbehaviors. Assertive teachers are highly task-oriented, proactive, independent, and effective classroom managers. Responsive teachers are empathetic, caring, friendly, sociable, and warm. Hypothesizing an inverse relationship between assertive and responsive teachers and student perceptions of teacher misbehaviors, these researchers asked college students ($N = 189$) to complete measures assessing these variables. As predicted, students reported that teachers who possess these qualities were not perceived as misbehaving. In other words, assertive and responsive teachers were seen as "well-behaved." To avoid student perceptions of misbehaving, the findings across these two studies would suggest that teachers should be immediate, assertive, and responsive.

In the same study described above, Wanzer and McCroskey (1998) also examined potential consequences of teacher misbehaviors. In addition to asking about their teachers' misbehaviors, students also rated their liking for the teacher and their affect toward the course. As expected, teachers who are seen as misbehaving were less liked and their courses were evaluated negatively. The consequences of misbehaving, or the perceptions of misbehaving, are the focus of the next set of studies.

Two related studies examine those factors that motivate or demotivate students in the college classroom. Gorham and Christophel (1992) asked college students (*N* = 308) to list teacher behaviors that motivated and demotivated them to do their course work. Coincidentally, many of the demotivators students listed were similar to those teacher misbehaviors students identified in the original teacher misbehavior study (Kearney, Plax, Hays, & Ivey, 1991). Typical demotivators (or teacher misbehaviors) cited were boring or confusing lectures, dissatisfaction with grading and assignments, and poor organization of the course or learning material. One of the more important associated consequences of teacher misbehaviors, then, may very well be student demotivation.

In their follow-up study, Gorham and Millette (1997) asked college teachers (*N* = 224) to identify those factors that motivated or demotivated students to learn. Their lists coincided with those identified by students in the previous study. However, teachers attributed student demotivation more to student factors and less to their own teacher misbehaviors. In other words, these teachers perceived student demotivation to be primarily the students' fault and responsibility.

In addition to reduced student affect and motivation, misbehaving teachers are faced with other unwanted outcomes. Thweatt and McCroskey (1998) examined the impact of teacher immediacy and misbehavior on teacher credibility. Teacher credibility refers to students' perceptions of teacher competence, trustworthiness, and caring. Employing a two-study, replicated design, college students (*N* = 385) were given one of four scenarios, manipulating levels of teacher immediacy and misbehavior. After reading their respective scenarios, students completed measures of teacher credibility. As might be expected, the immediate teacher who did not misbehave was perceived to be the most credible. Students perceived the least credible teacher as both nonimmediate and misbehaving. However, it was teacher immediacy and *not* misbehavior that appeared to be most closely associated with students' perceptions of teacher credibility. Apparently, when the teacher was immediate, the impact of other negative teacher misbehaviors became less important—at least when it came to perceptions of credibility. Even so, misbehaving teachers are likely to suffer from perceptions of lower credibility overall. This consequence becomes even more critical for novice, rather than experienced, teachers who are more likely to misbehave and face greater challenges of establishing credibility with their students.

Whereas this set of studies examined the entire spectrum of classroom misbehaviors, other research focused on specific teacher misbehaviors. For instance, teacher accent was identified by students as a misbehavior in the original investigation (Kearney et al., 1991) and verified in subsequent studies. Although not generally considered by teachers to be a misbehavior, accents have the potential to carry with it multiple unwanted results. Gill (1994) reasoned that the degree of similarity or discrepancy between teacher and student accents would influence students' comprehension and teacher evaluations. College students (*N* = 90) were randomly assigned to one of six conditions, manipulating three levels of teacher accents (and two different lectures). After listening to their respective lectures, students completed recall tests and other measures. Results indicated that teachers with accents more similar to those of their students were viewed more favorably than teachers who held discrepant accents. Additionally, students scored lower on comprehension or recall tests when their teachers exhibited discrepant accents, even when the teacher's accent was not all that discrepant. Although scholars have argued that unintentional teacher traits, such as accents, should not be considered misbehaviors, Gill's study supports students' perceptions that accented teachers are, by definition, misbehaving.

Roach (1997) examined yet another possible consequence of teacher misbehavior: attire. In the original misbehavior study, students included *negative physical appearance* as one of the 28 categories of teacher misbehaviors. Roach questioned whether graduate teaching assistants' (GTA) level of professional attire influenced students' perceptions of their own learning and other related outcomes. College students ($N = 355$) were asked to rate their GTA's professional dress and respond to a set of evaluation measures. Results indicated that with their less professionally attired GTAs, students reported lower cognitive and affective learning and lower teacher evaluations. Moreover, students reported a greater likelihood of misbehaving themselves with those teachers who also "misbehaved" by wearing unprofessional attire.

Taken together, the research suggests that teacher misbehaviors have a considerable impact on students and teachers. Since the original teacher misbehavior study, we know more about what influences students' perceptions of teacher misbehaviors and the multiple consequences of those misbehaviors. Over time, the research program on teacher misbehaviors has moved forward substantially. Research verifies that teachers do misbehave, and that those misbehaviors can have detrimental effects on teachers, students, and the teaching/learning process.

Knowledge Claims

In reviewing over a decade of teacher misbehavior research, several conclusions can be drawn.

1. Not so unlike the complaints teachers allege about their students, students report that their teachers misbehave, and they do so in a variety of ways. Although teachers might not view their behaviors as similarly problematic, students can easily identify teacher behaviors that interfere with their learning. College students were able to generate thousands of misbehavior samples that could be coded into 28 specific types of teacher misbehaviors (Kearney et al., 1991). These 28 types can be further reduced into three broad categories or profiles: incompetent, offensive, and indolent.

2. In spite of what critics may claim, a number of teacher behaviors are perceived by their students as disruptive to their learning. Teacher accents, for instance, have been shown to interfere with students' comprehension (Gill, 1994). By definition, then, this and other teacher characteristics or disruptive behaviors are appropriately termed *misbehaviors*.

3. Misbehaviors are often associated with inexperienced teachers who are untenured and who rely heavily on positive teaching evaluations for their employment permanence (Boice, 1996).

4. Teacher misbehaviors are contagious. More student disruptions and aberrant behaviors occur with misbehaving teachers (Boice, 1996).

5. Students assign both internal and external attributions to teachers who misbehave. Students' attributions, however, are biased in favor of internality (Kelsey et al., 2004; McPherson & Young, 2003). Consistent with the fundamental attribution error, students are more likely to blame their teachers, holding teachers fully responsible for their actions. This bias exists across all three teacher misbehavior profiles of incompetence, indolence, and offensiveness (Kelsey et al., 2004).

6. Even though other research indicates that immediacy is a salient and powerful mediator of students' perceptions, teacher immediacy fails to overwhelm the effects of teacher misbehaviors (Kelsey et al., 2004). Whether immediate or nonimmediate teachers misbehave, students continue to assign attributions of internality. Teachers can't simply make up for their misbehaviors, then, by being immediate.

7. Teacher anger alone does not sufficiently constitute a misbehavior. Rather, the intensity and manner in which the anger is expressed determines whether or not students perceive it as a norm violation (McPherson et al., 2003). Intense and aggressive displays of teacher anger are perceived as misbehaviors and stimulate negative affect. On the other hand, normative (i.e., assertive) displays of anger are associated with positive student affect.

8. Teacher-initiated embarrassment, in and of itself, is not a misbehavior. When teachers are perceived to intentionally or arbitrarily embarrass their students, they can expect students to evaluate them and the course negatively. Even so, when teachers intentionally embarrass and they appear to do so consistently over time, students are more likely to evaluate them less negatively (McPherson & Bippus, 2003). Apparently, when embarrassment is seen as a teacher misbehavior, students respond aversively, but when embarrassment is seen as an instructional or classroom management strategy, students are more open to its use.

9. Teacher misbehavior can be conceptualized as a type of classroom norm violation (Berkos et al., 2001; McPherson et al., 2003). Consistent with norm violation models, classroom norms for teacher behavior dictate what is appropriate and what is not. Violations of those norms via misbehaviors are associated with negatively-valenced student responses.

10. When faced with a misbehaving teacher, students employ imagined interactions (IIs) as a way to cope with the classroom norm violation (Berkos et al., 2001). Rather than using the imagined interactions as a rehearsal for eventual encounters with the teacher, students rely on IIs as a substitute for confrontation. Teachers who engage in offensive misbehaviors, more than the other types, are associated with greater student use of IIs and avoidance.

11. Teacher characteristics influence students' perceptions of misbehaviors. We know that even when teachers misbehave, students' perceptions of that misbehavior can be managed. Teachers can get away with some misbehaviors if they also happen to be assertive and responsive communicators (Wanzer & McCroskey, 1998). However, some teacher behaviors actually enhance perceptions of misbehaviors. Nonimmediate teachers don't seem to get a break. Even when they engage in appropriate, normative classroom behaviors, their nonimmediacy behaviors provoke the perception of misbehaving (Thweatt & McCroskey, 1996).

12. Students of misbehaving teachers are negatively affected when it comes to learning. Not only are misbehaving teachers less liked than their behaving counterpart, but students also report lower affect toward the course (Wanzer & McCroskey, 1998), less motivation to do coursework (Gorham & Christophel, 1992), and, with specific misbehaviors, less cognitive learning (Gill, 1994; Roach, 1997).

13. Teachers who misbehave receive more negative evaluations from their students. Misbehaving teachers receive lower teacher ratings on affect (Wanzer & McCroskey, 1998) and credibility (Thweatt & McCroskey, 1998). Their misbehaviors are seen as inappropriate, and students hold them accountable for what they do or fail to do.

14. For the most part, large and small teacher misbehaviors affect students negatively. This remains true regardless of whether teachers display a cluster of misbehaviors (e.g., offensive, indolent, and incompetent teachers) or a specific misbehavior (e.g., speaking with an accent or expressing anger aggressively).

Directions for Future Research

The research on teacher misbehaviors has come a long way since the publication of the original article (Kearney, Plax, Hays, & Ivey, 1991). Theory has been integrated into the research program. Both attribution and norm violation theories have strengthened the knowledge claims derived from research findings. We have made an effort to contextualize our projects within explicit theoretical frameworks and to steadily advance a 10-year program of research in this area of instructional communication. Only when scholars initiate and sustain research programs are we able to draw sound, generalizable conclusions about communication and learning (Waldeck, Kearney, & Plax, 2001). So, where do we go from here? Questions remain, including, but not limited to, the following:

1. What instructional consequences of their own misbehaviors do teachers acknowledge?
2. How do teachers justify their use of misbehaviors?

3. What salient teacher characteristics mediate students' perceptions of teacher misbehaviors?
4. In addition to attribution and norm violation theories, what other theories might help us understand and predict the occurrence and consequences of teacher misbehaviors?
5. To what extent are teacher misbehaviors contagious?
6. Why do teachers engage in misbehaviors? How effective are teacher misbehaviors as classroom management strategies?
7. What overriding theory or model of classroom misbehavior might be generated from the existing research?

References

Berkos, K. M., Allen, T. H., Kearney, P., & Plax, T. G. (2001). When norms are violated: Imagined interactions as processing and coping mechanisms. *Communication Monographs, 68,* 289–300.

Boice, R. (1996). Classroom incivilities. *Research in Higher Education, 37,* 453–486.

Edwards, R., Honeycutt, J. M., & Zagacki, K. S. (1988). Imagined interactions as an element of social cognition. *Western Journal of Speech Communication, 52,* 23–45.

Gill, M. M. (1994). Accent and stereotypes: Their effect on perceptions of teachers and lecture comprehension. *Journal of Applied Communication Research, 22,* 348–361.

Gorham, J., & Christophel, D. M. (1992). Students' perceptions of teacher behaviors as motivating and demotivating factors in college classes. *Communication Quarterly, 40,* 239–252.

Gorham, J., & Millette, D. M. (1997). A comparative analysis of teacher and student perceptions of sources of motivation and demotivation in college classes. *Communication Education, 46,* 245–261.

Guerrero, L. K. (1994). "I'm so mad I could scream": The effects of anger expression on relational satisfaction and communication competence. *Southern Communication Journal, 59,* 125–141.

Heider, F. (1958). The psychology of interpersonal relations. New York: Wiley.

Jones, E. E., & Davis, K. E. (1965). From acts to dispositions: The attribution process in person perceptions. In L. Berkowitz (Ed.), *Advances in experimental social psychology.* (pp. 219–266). New York: Academic Press.

Kearney, P., Plax, T. G., & Allen, T. H. (2002). Understanding student reactions to teachers who misbehave. In J. L. Chesebro & J. C. McCroskey (Eds.), *Communication for teachers* (pp. 127–140). Boston: Allyn & Bacon.

Kearney, P., Plax, T. G., & Burroughs, N. F. (1991). An attributional analysis of college students' resistance decisions. *Communication Education, 40,* 325–340.

Kearney, P., Plax, T. G., Hays, E. R., & Ivey, M. J. (1991). College teacher misbehaviors: What students don't like about what teachers say or do. *Communication Quarterly, 39,* 309–324.

Kearney, P., Plax, T. G., Richmond, V. P., & McCroskey, J. C. (1985). Power in the classroom III: Teacher communication techniques and messages. *Communication Education, 34,* 19–28.

Kelley, H. H. (1950). The warm–cold variable in first impressions of persons. *Journal of Personality, 31,* 457–501.

Kelley, H. H. (1967). Attribution theory in social psychology. In D. Levine (Ed.), Nebraska symposium on motivation (Vol. 15). Lincoln, NE: University of Nebraska Press.

Kelley, H. H., & Michela, J. L. (1980). Attribution theory and research. *Annual Review of Psychology, 31,* 457–501.

Kelsey, D. M., Kearney, P., Plax, T. G., Allen, T. H., & Ritter, K. J. (2004) College students' attributions of teacher misbehaviors. *Communication Education, 53,* 40–55.

Levine, T. R., Anders, L. N., Banas, J., Baum, K. L., Endo, K., Hu, A. D. S., & Wong, N. C. H. (2000). Norms, expectations, and deception: A norm violation model of veracity judgments. *Communication Monographs, 67,* 123–137.

McPherson, M. B., & Bippus, A. M. (2003, February). *Student responses to teacher-initiated embarrassment.* Paper presented at the annual meeting of the Western States Communication Association, Salt Lake City, UT.

McPherson, M. B., Kearney, P. & Plax, T. G. (2003). The dark side of instruction: Teacher anger as norm violations. *Journal of Applied Communication Research, 31,* 76–90.

McPherson, M. B., & Young, S. L. (2003, May) Students' explanations of teacher anger: *The attribution of teachers' emotional expressions.* Paper presented at the annual meeting of the International Communication Association, San Diego, CA.

McPherson, M. B., & Young, S. L. (2004). What students think when teachers get upset: Fundamental attribution error and student-generated reasons for teacher anger. *Communication Quarterly, 52,* 357–369.

Myers, S. A. (2002). Perceived aggressive instructor communication and student state motivation, learning, and satisfaction. *Communication Reports, 15,* 113–121.

Roach, K. D. (1997). Effects of graduate teaching assistant attire on student learning, misbehaviors, and ratings of instruction. *Communication Quarterly, 45,* 125–141.

Schrodt, P. (2003). Students' appraisals of instructors as a function of students' perceptions of instructors' aggressive communication. *Communication Education, 52,* 106–121.

Sereno, K. K., Welch, M., & Braaten, D. (1987). Interpersonal conflict: Effects of variations in manner of expressing anger and justification for anger upon perceptions of appropriateness, competence, and satisfaction. *Journal of Applied Communication Research, 15,* 128–143.

Shaver, K. G. (1975). *An introduction to attribution processes.* Cambridge, MA: Winthrop.

Thweatt, K. S., & McCroskey, J. C. (1996). Teacher nonimmediacy and misbehavior: Unintentional negative communication. *Communication Research Reports, 13,* 198–204.

Thweatt, K. S., & McCroskey, J. C. (1998). The impact of teacher immediacy and misbehaviors on teacher credibility. *Communication Education, 47,* 348–358.

Waldeck, J. H., Kearney, P., & Plax, T. G. (2001). Instructional and developmental communication theory and research in the 90s: Extending the agenda for the 21st century. In W. Gudykunst (Ed.), *Communication yearbook 24* (pp. 207–230). Newbury Park, CA: Sage.

Wanzer, M. B., & McCroskey, J. C. (1998). Teacher socio-communicative style as a correlate of student affect toward teacher and course material. *Communication Education, 47,* 43–52.

Weiner, B. (1979). A theory of motivation for some classroom experiences. *Journal of Educational Psychology, 71,* 3–25.

11

Student Incivility and Resistance in the Classroom

Patricia Kearney
California State University, Long Beach

Timothy G. Plax
California State University, Long Beach

Mary B. McPherson
California State University, Long Beach

Introduction

A colleague recently recounted an instance in which a student was talking during a lecture. When she asked the student to stop, the student ignored the request and continued her conversation. Disruptive, unruly student behaviors and general student disobedience are experiences none of us want to encounter in our classrooms. From displays of rudeness and outbursts to incidences of inattentiveness and tardiness, student misbehaviors can dominate instructional time and undermine our objectives. Whether rooted in reality or not, teachers may come to believe that students are becoming more demanding, aggressive, and ill-mannered. College students may insist on higher grades or bargain with teachers to cancel tests or postpone assignments. Although instances of student disrespect and disregard for learning might only represent a small portion of classroom experiences, the effects of these behaviors are powerful. The constant demands to manage even a few uncivil students can make teaching challenging, frustrating, and unpleasant.

Common student incivilities and misbehaviors, such as talking during a lecture, cutting class, inattentiveness, and leaving class early are not only irritating for teachers, but also hinder student learning. In fact, incivilities (Boice, 2000) or misbehaviors are defined as things students say or do that impede learning. Thus, managing these misbehaviors is a concern for virtually all teachers. In fact, an entire discipline has developed around the study of classroom management (Emmer, Evertson, & Worsham, 2000; Evertson, Emmer, & Worsham, 2000). One way teachers respond to student misbehaviors is to employ compliance-gaining techniques or strategies to either discourage student off-task behavior or encourage on-task behavior (see Chapter 6). Specifically, teachers utilize a variety of behavior alteration techniques (BATs) to modify students' actions (Kearney, Plax, Richmond, & McCroskey, 1984). And yet, when teachers try to get students to behave appropriately, students sometimes resist the compliance-gaining attempts.

Student resistance becomes destructive when students act in opposition to teachers' on-task appeals. Students can resist teachers' compliance-gaining attempts by failing to do homework, sleeping during a lecture, or coming to class unprepared. Clearly these behaviors would interfere with their learning. Still, student resistance is not necessarily destructive or harmful; some student resistance can result in positive outcomes. Burroughs, Kearney, and Plax (1989) define resistance as either constructive or destructive oppositional behavior.

Burroughs et al. (1989) explain that, by definition, constructive resistance results in greater on-task behavior. Student resistance may help us discover which assignments are unhelpful or when a lecture is unclear. Student inattentiveness can tell us when we need to do a better job of making the material relevant to our students. In this way, student resistance can be helpful for teaching and learning. Resistance is also productive when students act in opposition to teachers who do things that might inhibit learning (i.e., teacher misbehaviors). At times, teachers encourage distractions, employee arbitrary rules, or assign "busy work." For these reasons and others, students can benefit from resisting their teachers.

Why Study Student Incivility and Resistance?

Student misbehaviors do not necessarily depict the majority of student behaviors. In a typical college classroom of 30 students, only 5 or 6 students actually avoid or resist doing something the teacher wants them to do (Burroughs, 1990). Although that number may seem small, we know that only a few students can disrupt an entire class. Just one or two students who misbehave can substantially impact the classroom culture or environment. Teachers, especially new ones, can mistakenly assume that the most vocal or disruptive students represent the behavior or attitudes of the entire class. Moreover, new teachers often fail to appreciate the audience effect associated with how they handle the misbehaving student. How and when teachers respond to student disruptions influences the other students' impressions of their teachers' ability to effectively manage.

The importance of managing the classroom effectively became obvious to one of the authors of this chapter, Mary, during her first year teaching as a new professor. Mary made several errors common to beginning instructors. In one class, several students regularly made sarcastic comments and complained about assignments and tests. After a few unsuccessful attempts to manage the misbehaving students, Mary gave up. She began to believe that all students in that class were problematic. Overestimating the representativeness of the problem onto the rest of her students was a mistake. The remaining "behaving" students eventually became frustrated with Mary's inability and unwillingness to control the class, and took matters into their own hands. In an effort to solve the problem themselves, a physical altercation erupted among the students and the misbehaviors ceased. Understanding student misbehaviors and resistance, then, is important for helping teachers manage those few disruptive (and often unrepresentative) students. Moreover, managing misbehaviors helps us to meet the normative expectations that other students hold for us in our role as teacher.

In addition to overestimating the representativeness of student misbehaviors, teachers may also mistakenly assume that student incivility and resistance is due to students' dispositions. Not so unlike the fundamental attribution error, teachers often attribute negative behaviors to students' internal states, dispositions, and intentions. For example, Gorham and Millette (1997) found that teachers perceive students to be responsible for their own demotivation, rather than the teacher. Likewise, teachers may believe that student misbehaviors reflect negatively on the student, but not on themselves. In a chronicle of rudeness in America, Caldwell (1999) argues that manners or civilities echo our morals. In other words, our behaviors mirror our principles and values. If this is true, then student misbehaviors in the classroom communicate more than their lack of manners or poor socialization. Teachers might assign to misbehaving students more fundamental negative attitudes and values toward their teaching, the class, and learning more generally.

Student resistance also reveals something about our own teaching. We know, for instance, that students are more likely to engage in misbehaviors with teachers who, themselves, engage in misbehaviors (see Chapter 10). Students are also more likely to misbehave when teachers are nonimmediate (Kearney, Plax, & Burroughs, 1991; Kearney, Plax, Smith, & Sorensen, 1988; Lee, Levine, Cambra, 1997). The likelihood of resistance increases further when nonimmediate teachers employ punishment-based influence attempts (Kearney et al., 1988; Plax, Kearney, Downs, & Stewart, 1986) rather than reward-based ones. In some cases, then, student resistance serves as feedback about our teaching. Therefore, understanding how and why students misbehave and resist can help teachers make more effective choices with their students.

What follows is a review of research investigating student incivility, misbehaviors, and resistance. We begin by discussing how and why students misbehave.

Next, we review the seminal literature on students' compliance-resistance strategies and what factors influence students' resistance.

What Does the Research Tell Us?

Student Incivilities or Misbehaviors

Managing the classroom is a common and ongoing teacher activity. Most teachers endeavor to manage their classes in such a way that students are interested in the topic and are involved in learning by doing their assignments, paying attention during lectures, and offering insightful comments in class. When students do not conduct themselves in these productive ways, teaching can become a daunting experience. Especially for new teachers, unruly or defiant students can be intimidating. We noted earlier that for the average class, approximately 5 or 6 students out of 30, or about 18%, will resist what the teacher wants them to do (Burroughs, 1990). Yet many courses that service general education requirements are taught as large lecture classes. Extending this finding to a large lecture of about 250 students, we might expect about 45 (18%) students to misbehave.

Importantly, students do not misbehave in the same ways. Student misbehaviors can be described as active or passive (Plax & Kearney, 1999). Active misbehaviors are *overt* attempts to disrupt learning and include cheating, asking counterproductive questions, challenging the teacher's authority, diverting classroom talk from the lesson, interrupting, leaving class early or coming to class late, and talking to friends during lecture. Passive misbehaviors, on the other hand, involve *covert* behaviors that interrupt learning. Examples of passive misbehaviors involve inattentiveness, turning in late assignments (or not turning them in at all), sleeping during class, reading the newspaper, or doing other homework in class.

Students display both active and passive misbehaviors. However, active misbehaviors are the more disruptive and upsetting to teachers and other students in the class. In an effort to better understand classroom misbehaviors, Boice (1996) visited 10 class meetings and interviewed both teachers and students in those classes. Based on classroom observations and interviews, Boice discovered that both novice teachers and their students ranked the same three active misbehaviors as the most disturbing of all the classroom incivilities noted:

> 1) students conversing so loudly that lecturers and student discussants could not be heard throughout a third or more of class meetings, 2) students confronting teachers with sarcastic comments or disapproving groans, and 3) the presence of one or perhaps two "classroom terrorists" whose unpredictable and highly emotional outbursts made the entire class tense. (p. 463)

After these initial three rankings, teachers and students began to differ in their perceptions. Teachers identified additional student incivilities next on their list, including students' reluctance to talk, coming to class unprepared, demanding make-up exams or extending assignments, and arriving late or leaving early. Not surprisingly, students identified teacher, not student, misbehaviors next on their list of classroom incivilities. Teacher nonimmediacy behaviors, surprise exams, and teachers' arriving late or canceling class ranked high on their list of disturbing classroom incivilities. Regardless of the type of misbehavior indicated, though, students were more likely to act in uncivil ways when they observed the teacher engaging in misbehaviors (Boice, 1996).

Misbehaving students can be particularly unsettling to a novice teacher. At the same time, student misbehaviors can give teachers helpful clues for when they need to improve their teaching. Boice (1996) observed that teachers' responses to student misbehaviors can be fruitful. Immediate teachers who respond to students in a socially skilled, positive way can help calm unruly students. Additionally, Boice observed that teachers can interpret misbehaviors as feedback to help them determine when to change teaching strategies and reengage students. Misbehaviors can cue teachers when to provide breaks or change the pacing. In this way, students indirectly exert power over their own learning environment.

Although student behaviors can serve as potential feedback for teachers, students may not be skilled at effectively and appropriately providing that feedback. Simonds (1997) argued that students challenge their teachers as a way to exert influence in the classroom. Based on her previous research, Simonds created an instrument to measure student behaviors that serve to challenge teachers. Rather than ask students about their own behavior, however, Simonds reasoned that faculty would be better able to recall and generate more challenge behaviors than students. Thus, she asked 397 full-time college teachers to complete the survey with their students' behaviors in mind.

Teachers identified a number of student challenge behaviors, with the most frequently cited classified into four categories. *Procedural challenges* include student behaviors that challenge both explicit and implicit rules and norms. Examples of procedural challenges include wanting to make up work after excessive absences, wanting to receive full credit for late work, coming to class late, talking during class, and offering "off the wall" examples in class discussion. *Evaluation challenges* are used when students question testing procedures or grades. Evaluation challenges include questioning the grade on an assignment, begging for a higher grade, comparing scores with other students, questioning the fairness of grading, and arguing over test questions. *Power challenges* are displayed when students try to influence the teacher's or other students' behaviors in class. Students attempt to challenge a teacher's power by questioning the instructor's knowledge of specific content, attempting to control when a task will be done, not participating in class discussions, attempting to embarrass the instructor, and interrupting the instructor to reinforce their own opinions. *Practicality challenges* occur when students question the relevance of the course or tasks. These challenges include questioning the relevance of tasks to everyday life, questioning the importance of subject matter, complaining that theories are not applicable to real life, questioning why class should be required, and disputing the relevance of concepts being discussed in lecture.

The Simonds (1997) study reveals which behaviors *teachers* report that students use most frequently to challenge them in class. Many of those challenges referenced are often interpreted by teachers as negative or aversive. But should they be? Student challenges can be helpful by providing teachers with meaningful feedback about their students' learning needs and wants. Additionally, students might engage in challenging behaviors for reasons other than subverting teacher control. After all, the attributions teachers assign to student behaviors may differ from students' explanations of their own behavior. Research shows that students' and teachers' perceptions often conflict. Recall from Chapter 10, for instance, how students and teachers differ in their attributions of student motivation and demotivation (Gorham & Christophel, 1992; Gorham & Millette, 1997). From students' perspectives, challenges may be employed to express their confusion and frustration over assignments that require clarification, to point out inequities or perceived favoritism, or to question the teacher's content credibility over a specific issue. In these ways, student challenges become strategies to elicit help and direction from their teachers.

Student Resistance

Student resistance is often coupled with student misbehavior. In both cases the student's behavior is in opposition to what the teacher usually desires. Student *misbehaviors* encompass those student actions that interfere with learning (Kearney et al., 1984). Student *resistance,* on the other hand, is a *reaction* to teachers' compliance-gaining attempts and can be either constructive or destructive to the learning process. Thus, Kearney and Plax (1992) argue that not all resistance attempts should be considered as misbehaviors or treated as problems. As stated earlier, resistance can be constructive when students resist teacher behaviors that inhibit on-task behavior, or destructive when the resistance obstructs learning. Consequently, it is destructive, not constructive, resistance that manifests itself as misbehavior. To understand the resistance literature, we will begin by reviewing what we know about teacher compliance gaining.

Within the teacher compliance-gaining research, teacher *power* is defined as a teacher's capacity to influence students to do something they would not have done had they not been influenced (McCroskey & Richmond, 1983). Through their program of research, Kearney et al. (1984) identified 22 behavior alteration techniques (BATs) and representative behavior alternation messages (BAMs) that teachers report using in managing student behavior (see Chapter 6). These techniques and corresponding messages can be described as either prosocial or antisocial. Prosocial BATs include those messages that are designed to be helpful and beneficial to students. These techniques encourage students and are reward-based. Antisocial or punishment-based BATs refer to those strategies that foster competitiveness, exclude students, and undermine students' self-esteem. Regardless of the specific strategy, though, students do not always do what teachers want them to do by complying with the BAM. As an extension of the power research, Burroughs, Kearney, and Plax (1989) investigated those instances when students resist teachers' compliance-gaining attempts.

Burroughs, Kearney, and Plax (1989) began by eliciting student-generated strategies for classroom resistance. Students were given one of four scenarios of a hypothetical teacher asking them to comply with a specific request. Two scenarios described an immediate teacher (friendly, expressive, eye contact) who used either a prosocial or an antisocial BAT. The other two scenarios described a nonimmediate teacher (tense, reserved, avoids eye contact) who used either a prosocial or an antisocial BAT. After reading the scenarios, students were asked to indicate their willingness to comply with or resist that request and describe what strategies they would use to resist that target teacher. The 574 students included in the sample generated nearly 3,000 compliance-resistance messages. These messages were then coded into categories of similar messages resulting in 19 compliance-resistance techniques (see Figure 11.1). Moreover, categories were characterized as either active or passive techniques. Active resistance strategies are more direct and include *challenge the teacher's basis of power, direct communication,* and *hostile defensive.* Passive strategies are more indirect and include "reluctant compliance," *ignoring the teacher,* and *deception.*

Reviewing the Burroughs et al. (1989) study, Kearney and Plax (1992) concluded that teachers and students would rather use passive, nonconfrontational strategies, such as giving excuses, than rely on aggressive confrontational techniques. They offer two reasons why. First, they argue that passive strategies enable students to resist without the teacher immediately recognizing the resistance as resistance. Active resistance, being more public, may force the teacher to react. Second, passive, as opposed to active, strategies are more likely to be considered socially acceptable forms of resistance. Kearney and Plax reasoned that students have been socialized to behave, to a large extent, as compliers. Unable or unwilling to comply, students who choose to resist are probably better off selecting passive strategies. Such passive resistance attempts are less likely to disrupt the entire class and provoke a power struggle with the teacher.

Consistent with this reasoning, other research reveals that when confronted with norm-violating or misbehaving teachers, students are more likely to rely on imagined interactions than to actually confront their teachers (Berkos, Allen, Kearney, & Plax, 2001). Students reported using imagined interactions as coping mechanisms, not to take action, but to replace action, in their efforts to deal with misbehaving teachers. In other words, students imagined or reflected on what they would say or do when faced with a misbehaving teacher. In this way, they employed more passive, than active strategies for coping.

Factors Influencing Resistance

So far, we've shown that students do occasionally resist teachers' compliance-gaining attempts. We have also explained how students resist using specific resistance strategies. We now turn to a discussion of those factors that influence student resistance decisions and strategy choices. Resistance decisions and strategy selections do not occur in a vacuum. Student resistance is part of a complex interaction of factors involved in teacher–student exchanges. The most important stimulus to

FIGURE 11.1 ***Student Resistance Techniques.***

Technique	Description
Teacher Advice	I would offer the teacher advice: Prepare yourself better so you give better lectures. Be more expressive: Everything will work out to your advantage. You should relate more with students before trying to give any advice. If you open up, we'll tend to be more willing to do what you want.
Teacher Blame	I would resist by claiming that the teacher is boring. The teacher makes me feel uneasy. It is boring; I don't get anything out of it. You don't seem prepared yourself. If you weren't so boring, I would do what you want.
Avoidance	I would simply drop the class. I won't participate as much. I won't go to class. I'll sit in the back of the room.
Reluctant Compliance	I'll do only enough work to get by. Although I would comply with the teacher's demands, I would do so unwillingly. I'll come more prepared, but not be interested at all. Grudgingly, I'll come prepared.
Active Resistance	I won't come prepared at all. I'll leave my book at home. I'll continue to come unprepared to get on the teacher's nerves. I'll keep coming to class, but I won't be prepared.
Deception	I'll act like I'm prepared for class even though I may not be. I may be prepared, but play dumb for spite. I might tell the teacher I would make an effort, but wouldn't. I'll make up some lie about why I'm not performing well in this class.
Direct Communication	I'll go to the teacher's office and try to talk to him/her. After class I would explain my behavior. I would talk to the teacher and explain how I feel and how others perceive him/her in class.
Disruption	I'll disrupt the class by leaving to get needed materials. I would be noisy in class. I'll ask questions in a monotone voice without interest. I'll be a wise-guy in class.
Excuses	I would offer some type of excuse: I don't feel well. I don't understand the topic. I can remember things without writing stuff down. I forgot. My car broke down. The class is so easy I don't need to stay caught up.
Ignoring the Teacher	I would simply ignore the teacher's request, but come to class anyway. I probably wouldn't say anything; just do what I was doing before. I would simply let the teacher's request go in one ear and out the other.
Priorities	I would tell the teacher I had other priorities: I have other homework so I can't prepare well for this one. I have kids, and they take up my time. I'm too busy. This class is not as important as my others. I only took this class for general education requirements.
Challenge the Teacher's Basis of Power	I would challenge the teacher's authority by asserting: Do others in class have to do this? No one else is doing it, so why should I? Do you really take this class seriously? If it's such a good idea, why don't you do it?

FIGURE 11.1 (*Continued*)

Rally Student Support	I would rally up student support. I would talk to others in class to see if they feel the same. I would tell my classmates not to go to class. I might get others to go along with me in not doing what the teacher wants.
Appeal to Powerful Others	I would talk to someone in higher authority. I might complain to the department chair that this instructor is incompetent and can't motivate the class. I would make a complaint to the dean about the teacher's practices. I would talk to my advisor. I would threaten to go to the dean.
Modeling Teacher Behavior	I would indicate to the teacher that I would participate more if he/she were more enthusiastic about what he/she is doing. I might say: You aren't enjoying it, so how can I? If you're not going to make the effort to teacher well, I won't make an effort to listen. You don't do it, so why should I?
Modeling Teacher Affect	I would tell the teacher that if he/she doesn't care about us students, why should I care about what he/she wants? I would say: You don't seem to care about this class, why should I? You have no concern for this class yourself.
Hostile Defensive	I'd take a more active stance and tell the teacher that I'm old enough to know how I can do in this class. Right or wrong, that's the way I am. I'm surprised you even noticed I'm in your class. Lead your own life. My behavior is my business.
Student Rebuttal	I would argue that I know what works for me; I don't need your advice. I don't need this grade anyway. I'm doing just fine without changing my behavior. We'll see when the test comes up.
Revenge	I'll get even by expressing my dissatisfaction with the teacher/course on evaluations at the end of the term. I won't recommend this teacher/class to others. I'll write a letter to put in the teacher's personnel file. I'll steal or hide the teacher's lecture notes or test.

From "Compliance-Resistance in the College Classroom," by N. F. Burroughs, P. Kearney, and T. G. Plax, 1989, *Communication Education, 38,* 214–229. Republished with permission by *Communication Education* and Taylor & Francis Ltd. http://www.tandf.co.uk/journals.

students' resistance decisions is likely to be the teacher. What teacher characteristics or behaviors are most likely to influence those decisions?

Teacher immediacy, a salient teacher characteristic, is one of the most widely documented predictors of teacher communication effectiveness (see Chapter 8). Recall that immediacy behaviors are those that communicate closeness and warmth, whereas, nonimmediacy behaviors communicate distance and detachment. Essentially, immediacy is the perception of physical or physiological closeness. Using the immediacy principle that people approach or behave positively with people they like and avoid those they dislike, Kearney, Plax, Smith, and Sorensen (1988) reasoned that teacher immediacy should influence student resistance decisions.

Additionally, the researchers argued that the type of teacher compliance-gaining strategy employed should also influence those resistance decisions.

Relying on hypothetical scenarios, Kearney, Plax, Smith and Sorensen (1988) simulated teachers who were immediate or nonimmediate and who used either prosocial or antisocial BAMs to gain students' compliance. Faced with one of the four different teacher scenarios, students were asked to indicate their willingness to resist or comply. As predicted, Kearney and her colleagues found that students demonstrated a greater willingness to comply with teachers who were perceived as immediate than with teachers who were nonimmediate. Students were also more likely to resist compliance with teachers who used antisocial rather than prosocial compliance strategies. However, when taken together, immediacy had a more powerful effect on likelihood of resistance than did compliance strategy (prosocial or antisocial). Interestingly, the results of the manipulation check revealed that when students read the scenario describing the immediate teacher, they also perceived the teacher as using prosocial BAMs even when the teacher was described as using antisocial messages. These findings demonstrate that immediacy is a salient teacher attribute for mitigating the impact of antisocial compliance-gaining strategies on student resistance. We might conclude, then, that immediate teachers not only face fewer resistance attempts by students than nonimmediate teachers, but also are potentially immune to the negative effects of using antisocial BATs.

To further understand the nature of student resistance, Kearney, Plax, and Burroughs (1991) investigated *why* college students resist. Using attribution theory as a potential explanation for those strategies students select in their resistance attempts, these researchers argued that students would choose whether or not to resist and how they would resist based on the attributions they make about their teachers. In overview, attribution theory focuses on the process by which we construct, interpret, and identify causes of our own and others' behavior (Heider, 1958; Kelley, 1967). Students enter the classroom with preconceived notions of what constitutes acceptable or normative teacher behaviors. Teacher behaviors out of line with these normative perceptions are likely to stimulate the process of making sense or attributing causes to that behavior. Students will search for reasons why the teacher behaves the way she or he does. Once the attribution of causality has been cast, the newly constructed interpretation will dominate students' assessments of that teacher. It turns out that not all attributions are created equal. That is, some attributes are more salient or critical to forming perceptions than others (e.g., Kelley, 1950). Important to students' perceptions of their teachers, salient teacher attributes tend to overwhelm other, less relevant characteristics. Such attributes often suppress or confound students' recognition and regard for other teacher characteristics.

The question then becomes, which teacher characteristics are more salient than others? Past instructional research on compliance resistance indicates that teacher immediacy and teachers' compliance strategy type (prosocial and antisocial) are two attributes that influence students' reactions. Recall that students' perceptions of teachers' prosocial and antisocial compliance techniques were distorted by teachers' level of immediacy (Kearney et al., 1988). In that study, students were unable to accurately differentiate prosocial from antisocial BAT types when the strategy was imbedded within the context of immediacy. Indeed, students either disregard antisocial BATs or misperceive them as prosocial when the teacher is immediate. Immediacy provides an antecedent attribution to the specific behavior of compliance-gaining strategy choice.

To test the salience of immediacy in students' resistance decisions and strategy selections, Kearney et al. (1991) once again asked students to read and respond to one of four teacher compliance scenarios. Like earlier research in this series, the scenarios included descriptions of an immediate (or nonimmediate) teacher using a prosocial (or antisocial) BAT to obtain student compliance. However, unlike previous studies in which students were asked to construct resistance messages, almost 400 students were given sample messages of each of the 19 resistance categories derived from earlier research. Students were asked to indicate how likely they would be to use these or similar statements to resist the teacher in the given scenario. Analyses of those responses validated the original typology and revealed that the categories could be reduced to two dimensions, but the strategies comprising each dimension could be considered passive or active strategy types. Consistent with attribution theory, two very different conceptual dimensions emerged: teacher-owned and student-owned. To better understand these conceptual labels, it's a good idea to examine the strategies that make up each of those dimensions.

Strategies representing the first factor, *teacher-owned,* are those in which students consider the teacher as the problem source. This dimension included these strategies: *teacher advice, teacher blame, appeal to powerful others, modeling teacher behavior,* and *modeling teacher affect. Student-owned* strategies are those that presume the student should be held accountable for the problem. This dimension includes these strategies: *deception, ignoring the teacher, priorities, hostile defensive,* and *student rebuttal.* (Interestingly, active and passive strategies were represented across both dimensions of teacher- and student-owned problems. The prior scheme of active/passive simply would not fit as discriminators between the two dimensions of teacher and student ownership.)

The strategy labels selected represent a focus based on the student's perspective. Thus, *teacher-owned* problems include those teacher behaviors that interfere with the student's needs and objectives. When the problem is *teacher-owned,* student resistance strategies reflect the student's opinion that the teacher is responsible for the student's resistance decision. Kearney et al. (1991, p. 334) found that students were more likely to resist *teacher-owned* problems by saying to the teacher, "If you weren't so boring, I would do what you want," or "I would participate more if you were more enthusiastic about what you're doing." On the other hand, *student-owned* resistance strategies show that students justify their resistance by holding themselves primarily responsible for their own behavior. When students own the reasons for their resistance, they are likely to say, "I have other homework so I can't prepare well for this one," or "Right or wrong, that's the way I am" (p. 334).

These dimensions indicate that students choose strategies of resistance based on causal attributions. For *teacher-owned* strategy selections, students assign blame to the teacher; for *student-owned* strategy selections, students assign blame to themselves. When the researchers factored in the salient attribute of teacher immediacy into these strategy selections, findings indicated that students were significantly more likely to use *student-owned* techniques with immediate teachers and *teacher-owned* techniques with nonimmediate instructors. As you might expect, teachers' use of BAT types (prosocial or antisocial) had no effect on students' resistance decisions/selections. In other words, teacher immediacy, not compliance-gaining strategy type, was the salient attribute for students' resistance decisions.

To more fully appreciate these findings, Kearney and her colleagues (1991) also examined a variety of student responses when asked to briefly explain why they selected the particular resistance strategies that they did. Whether the teacher BATs employed were prosocial or antisocial, students by and large liked the teacher depicted in the two immediate conditions more than the teacher referenced in the nonimmediate conditions. Immediate teachers who were portrayed as using prosocial BATs, produced one of the most interesting reactions. Students felt that these teachers were telling them to comply for their own good (p. 336). Students who were exposed to both the prosocial and antisocial immediate teacher scenario were consistently more likely to choose student-owned strategies to resist teacher compliance attempts. Essentially, students are more likely to blame themselves, rather than their immediate teachers, for their noncompliance. Conversely, students exposed to the nonimmediate teacher conditions blamed the teacher, not themselves, for their resistance. Thus, students hold nonimmediate teachers accountable for students' selecting teacher-owned techniques. Students described the nonimmediate teachers as cold and uncaring, incompetent, and unenthused about their jobs. Students believed that their own resistance could make the nonimmediate teachers more self-aware of their inadequacies as instructors.

As expected, Kearney, Plax and Burroughs (1991) found that student attributions of immediate teachers were tremendously positive, but attributions of nonimmediate teachers were more negative. Thus, students chose strategies of resistance that coincide with those perceptions. Research informs us that students are more likely to comply with immediate teachers (Kearney, Plax, Smith, & Sorensen, 1988). However, when students do not, or cannot, comply with those immediate teachers, they are more likely to blame themselves for the resistance. Students are not only more likely to resist compliance with nonimmediate teachers, but when they do, they will blame the teacher for the resistance. Nonimmediate teachers have the worst-case scenario.

Teacher immediacy is obviously important in establishing students' attributions about their teachers and in determining students' compliance or resistance decisions. Other researchers argue that how teachers ask for or demand compliance may influence how students choose to resist. Paulsel and Chory-Assad (2004) examined the relationship between teachers' use of antisocial BATs and students' reliance on teacher-owned resistance techniques. In their study, students rated their teacher's likelihood of using each of the different BAMs that represented only those associated with antisocial BATs. Similarly, students rated their likelihood of using each of the resistance messages that represented only the teacher-owned resistance techniques. As expected, results revealed that in response to anticipated antisocial compliance-gaining attempts, students were likely to resort to teacher-owned resistance strategies.

Intercultural researchers consistently argue that cultural background should be also considered in students' resistance decisions. Lee, Levine, and Cambra (1997) investigated the influence of culture manifested through students' independent and interdependent "self-construals" on their resistance. *Independent self-construal* is normally associated with those from more individualistic cultures. People with an independent self-construal view themselves as autonomous persons and whose behavior stems from internal feelings, thoughts, and actions. *Interdependent self-construal* is typically associated with those from more collectivistic cultures. People who adopt an interdependent self-construal focus on their connection with other people and are usually less direct. They highlight external features such as status, roles, relationships, and belonging. Based on these descriptions, Lee et al. predicted that students with interdependent self-construals would be less likely to resist teachers' compliance attempts, and that students with independent self-construals would be more likely to resist.

The researchers presented a sample of 420 elementary and secondary multicultural students with one of four hypothetical scenarios in which a teacher was described as either liked or disliked and used either prosocial or antisocial strategies to get the student to stop talking. After reading the scenarios, students completed a series of questions that would assess their self-construals and likelihood of resisting the compliance attempt. Like previous research, their results indicated that students were less likely to resist liked teachers and those who relied on prosocial compliance strategies. But how did cultural self-construal fare? Self-construal had an inverse, but negligible, effect on students' resistance. Interdependent self-construals reported less likelihood of resistance overall. Virtually no association was obtained between independent self-construals and resistance. Apparently, multicultural self-construals have little or no impact on students' decisions to resist their teachers.

While a number of factors may influence students' resistance decisions, teacher immediacy is still the primary salient attribute affecting those decisions. The type of compliance-gaining strategy that teachers employ is less important. Attribution theory offers a powerful explanation for why students resist some teachers and not others. Moreover, the theory provides insight into the reasons why students choose particular strategies to resist some teachers and different strategies for others. What we don't know are those other salient teacher and student characteristics or behaviors that influence students' resistance. Teacher immediacy may be criterial, but it does not provide the complete picture of how and why students resist.

Other classroom-relevant factors might also influence students' resistance decisions. In particular, grading practices and classroom procedures may affect student perceptions of instructor fairness and students' subsequent resistance choices. Investigating fairness, Chory-Assad and Paulsel (2004) define classroom justice as "perceptions of fairness regarding outcomes or processes that occur in the instructional context" (p. 256). Chory-Assad and Paulsel (2004) argued that students' perceptions of justice should be negatively related to student resistance. These researchers asked students to complete a series of measures designed to assess classroom justice, student behavioral choices, and resistance. Results indicated that classroom injustices surrounding procedural issues of fairness in grading, scheduling, and other practices were associated with students' likelihood of resistance. Understanding students' perceptions of justice helps us to better understand students' resistance decisions.

Knowledge Claims

This chapter reviewed the research on student incivility and student resistance that spans the last 15 years. What do we now know about student resistance? What have we really learned?

1. Students' resistance to teachers' compliance-gaining attempts can be active or passive. *Active resistance* is more direct and is potentially perceived as more threatening to teachers. *Passive resistance* is covert, but can be equally disruptive. Of the classroom resistance strategies observed, Boice (1996) found that both students and teachers identify the most disturbing classroom incivilities as active student resistance.

2. Student misbehaviors and incivilities are both defined as things students say or do to impede learning. Important to students' learning and teachers' effectiveness, then, is the teachers' ability to manage student misbehaviors. Teachers rely on a variety of compliance-gaining strategies, called behavior alteration techniques (BATs), to encourage students to stay on task and to discourage them from remaining off task (Kearney, Plax, Richmond, & McCroskey, 1984).

3. Resistance to teachers' compliance attempts are often considered potential misbehaviors. When resistance results in off-task activity, learning is jeopardized. In this way, students' resistance is destructive. However, Kearney and Plax (1992) explain that not all student resistance should be defined as destructive. There are times when students resist their teachers as a way of staying on task. In this way, resistance becomes constructive. Constructive resistance occurs when students act in opposition to teachers who do things that might inhibit their learning.

4. Student resistance often provides teachers with feedback about their own teaching. Increased incidences of student resistance signal problems with teaching. Teachers should reevaluate their own instructional behavior in light of their students' resistance (Boice, 1996).

5. Students challenge teachers as a way to gain control over their own learning environment. Students challenge teachers in four primary ways (Simonds, 1997): procedural, evaluation, power, and practicality challenges. Most challenges are perceived by teachers as punishing, and yet we argue that student challenges may actually function like constructive resistance.

6. Students resist teachers' compliance-gaining attempts in a variety of ways. Students report 19 common strategies that can be further categorized as either active or passive (Burroughs, Kearney, & Plax, 1989). Both teachers and students prefer passive resistance strategies.

7. Teachers who display immediacy behaviors are less likely to encounter student resistance than teachers who do not (Kearney, Plax, Smith, & Sorensen, 1988). Moreover, teacher immediacy often overwhelms the negative effects of teachers who rely on antisocial BATs. In fact, students do not perceive immediate teachers as using antisocial techniques, even when they do!

8. Students' resistance choices are determined, in part, by the attributions they assign to their teachers and to themselves (Kearney, Plax, & Burroughs, 1991). Students choose particular resistance strategies when they believe their teacher owns the problem and select different strategies when they hold themselves responsible for the problem.

9. Once again, immediacy plays an important role in students' behavioral choices. Students are more likely to use student-owned resistance techniques with immediate teachers and teacher-owned strategies with nonimmediate teachers (Kearney, Plax, & Burroughs, 1991). Attribution theory explains the critical importance of teacher immediacy in students' resistance decisions and selections.

10. Although teacher immediacy proved to be an important variable in understanding student misbehaviors and resistance, students' cultural identity is not a particularly useful predictor of their resistance (Lee, Levine, and Cambra, 1997). Other classroom factors may be important to understanding students' resistance decisions, including perceptions of classroom procedural injustices (Chory-Assad & Paulsel, 2004).

Directions for Research

Although we seem to have a better grasp of college student misbehavior and resistance, many questions remain unanswered. Our students continue to resist and teachers continue to be frustrated. Some teachers may argue that student incivility has reached an all-time high. With the prevalence of student incivility in the classroom and the associated negative consequences on learning, more research in this area is warranted. We suggest a number of ways to reinvigorate research in this important area of instructional communication.

1. Research should begin by asking whether or not students are becoming more uncivil in the classroom. Alternatively, are teachers becoming sensitive to and intolerant of student resistance?

2. We now have a better understanding of teacher misbehaviors and student misbehaviors. Evidence suggests that teacher behaviors influence choices students make in the classroom and vice versa. Thus, our question becomes, how do teacher and student misbehaviors mutually influence each other?

3. We know how teachers define student challenge behaviors (Simonds, 1997), and yet, we do not know how students would define those same behaviors. We suspect that what teachers consider to be challenging would not be similarly perceived by students themselves. What behaviors do students identify as challenges? What reasons do teachers and students provide for students' use of challenge strategies? What goals do student challenges accomplish?

4. Lee, Levine, and Cambra (1997) make a good argument for culture as a factor in determining student resistance and yet, their research yielded only minimal effects. Perceptions of classroom injustices may direct students' resistance decisions (Chory-Assad & Paulsel, 2004). What other classroom factors might influence student incivilities and constructive or destructive resistance?

5. Although Kearney, Plax, and Burroughs (1991) rely on attribution theory in their efforts to explain and predict students' resistance decisions, no other investigation has been based in theory. Researchers must make every effort to contextualize their projects within a theoretical framework in order to advance this important area of instructional communication (Waldeck, Kearney, & Plax, 2001). Without theory, this line of research will remain fragmented and underdeveloped.

References

Berkos, K. M., Allen, T. H., Kearney, P., & Plax, T. G. (2001). When norms are violated: Imagined interactions as processing and coping mechanisms. *Communication Monographs, 68,* 289–300.

Boice, R. (1996). Classroom incivilities. *Research in Higher Education, 37,* 453–486.

Boice, R. (2000). *Advice for new faculty members.* Boston: Allyn & Bacon.

Burroughs, N. F. (1990). *The relationship of teacher immediacy and student compliance-resistance with learning.* Unpublished doctoral dissertation, West Virginia University, Morgantown, WV.

Burroughs, N. F., Kearney, P., & Plax, T. G. (1989). Compliance-resistance in the college classroom. *Communication Education, 38,* 214–229.

Caldwell, M. (1999). *A short history of rudeness: Manners, morals, and misbehaviors in modern America.* New York: Picador USA.

Chory-Assad, R. M., & Paulsel, M. L. (2004). Classroom justice: Student aggression and resistance as reactions to perceived unfairness. *Communication Education, 53,* 255–275.

Emmer, E. T., Evertson, C. M., & Worsham, M. E. (2000). *Classroom management for secondary teachers* (5th ed.). Boston: Allyn & Bacon.

Evertson, C. M., Emmer, E. T., & Worsham, M. E. (2000). *Classroom management for elementary teachers* (5th ed.). Boston: Allyn & Bacon.

Gorham, J., & Christophel, D. M. (1992). Students' perceptions of teacher behaviors as motivating and demotivating factors in college classes. *Communication Quarterly, 40,* 239–252.

Gorham, J., & Millette, D. M. (1997). A comparative analysis of teacher and student perceptions of sources of motivation and demotivation in college classes. *Communication Education, 46,* 245–261.

Heider, F. (1958). *The psychology of interpersonal relations.* New York: Wiley.

Kearney, P., & Plax, T. G. (1992). Student resistance to control. In V. Richmond & J. C. McCroskey (Eds.), *Power in the classroom: Communication, control, and concern* (pp. 85–100). Hillsdale, NJ: Lawrence Erlbaum.

Kearney, P., Plax, T. G., & Burroughs, N. F. (1991). An attributional analysis of college students' resistance decisions. *Communication Education, 40,* 325–342.

Kearney, P., Plax, T. G., Richmond, V. P., & McCroskey, J. C. (1984). Power in the classroom IV: Teacher communication techniques as alternatives to discipline. *Communication yearbook, 8,* 724–746.

Kearney, P., Plax, T. G., Smith, V. R., & Sorensen, G. (1988). Effects of teacher immediacy and strategy type on college student resistance to on-task demands. *Communication Education, 37,* 54–67.

Kelley, H. H. (1950). The warm–cold variable in first impressions of persons. *Journal of Personality, 31,* 457–501.

Kelley, H. H. (1967). Attribution theory in social psychology. In D. Levine (Ed.), *Nebraska symposium on motivation* (Vol. 15). Lincoln, NE: University of Nebraska Press.

Lee, C. R., Levine, T. R., & Cambra, R. (1997). Resisting compliance in the multicultural classroom. *Communication Education, 46,* 28–43.

McCroskey, J. C., & Richmond, V. P. (1983). Power in the classroom I: Teacher and student perceptions. *Communication Education, 32,* 176–184.

Paulsel, M. L., & Chory-Assad, R. M. (2004). The relationships among instructors' antisocial behavior alteration techniques and student resistance. *Communication Reports, 17,* 1–10.

Plax, T. G., & Kearney, P. (1999). Classroom management: Contending with college student discipline. In A. L. Vangelisti, J. A. Daly, & G. W. Friedrich (Eds.), *Teaching communication: Theory, research, and methods* (pp. 269–285). Mahwah, NJ: Lawrence Erlbaum.

Plax, T. G., Kearney, P., Downs, T. M., & Stewart, R. A. (1986). College student resistance toward teachers' use of selective control strategies. *Communication Research Reports, 3,* 20–27.

Simonds, C. J. (1997). Challenge behavior in the college classroom. *Communication Research Reports, 14,* 481–492.

Waldeck, J. H., Kearney, P., & Plax, T. G. (2001). Instructional and developmental communication theory and research in the 90s: Extending the agenda for the 21st century. In W. Gudykunst (Ed.), *Communication yearbook 24* (pp. 207–230). Newbury Park, CA: Sage.

Unit IV

Theory and Assessment

12

Theorizing About Instructional Communication

Timothy P. Mottet
Texas State University–San Marcos

Ann Bainbridge Frymier
Miami University

Steven A. Beebe
Texas State University–San Marcos

Introduction

Making sense out of the unknown world begins early for most people. It is not uncommon to hear children asking their parents: What is that? How does it work? and Why does it work? In short, children are theorizing about their world. Similarly, instructional communication researchers try to make sense out of the communication that occurs in instructional settings by asking the same three questions in an effort to explain and predict classroom behavior. A theory helps manage the uncertainty of our world. As summarized by Dubin (1978), "The need for theories lies in the human behavior of wanting to impose order on unordered experiences" (p. 6).

According to Kerlinger (1986), a theory is a set of interrelated concepts, definitions, and propositions that present a systematic view of phenomena. A theory also specifies the relationships among the concepts with the objective of explaining and predicting the phenomenon being studied. In short, a theory helps individuals organize their experiences (Shaw & Costanzo, 1970). Although volumes have been written about teaching and learning, instructional communication researchers continue to search for theoretical explanations to help them answer the *what, how,* and *why* questions in instructional settings.

This chapter is a rudimentary effort to examine selected issues surrounding theory development in instructional communication. Our intent is not to create or advocate a single theory of instructional communication, but to provide a framework or a scaffolding for instructional communication theory development. In short, we consider this chapter to be a point of departure rather than a destination. It is organized around three key questions:

1. What are the essential elements of instructional communication theory development?
2. What is the current state of instructional communication theory development?
3. What are new directions for instructional communication theory development?

Essential Elements of Theory Development

One application of this chapter is to provide a blueprint to assist others in developing instructional communication theory. To begin this process, we discuss three essential elements of theory development. Expanding on the work of Dubin (1978), Whetten (1989) discussed these elements by asking three questions: (1) *What* variables, constructs, and concepts should be considered as part of the logical explanation of the phenomenon under study? (2) *How* are these variables, constructs, and concepts related? and (3) *Why* are these variables, constructs, and concepts related? We will attempt to answer these three questions and show how they apply to theory development in the study of instructional communication.

What Variables, Constructs, and Concepts Should Be Included?

In our study of instructional communication, the phenomenon under study is communication that links teaching with learning and learning with teaching. A theory examining this phenomenon might include a number of variables that fall into one of three clusters: teaching, learning, and communication. In the teaching cluster, the variables might include teacher self-efficacy, teaching satisfaction, and motivation to teach. In the learning cluster, the variables might include student learning, compliance, and motivation. In the communication cluster, the variables might include teacher and students use of verbal and nonverbal message variables, such as nonverbal immediacy, affinity-seeking, humor, clarity, and compliance gaining strategies.

How Are These Variables, Constructs, and Concepts Related?

This is where researchers begin putting the pieces of a theoretical model together. Researchers develop theoretical models by diagramming variables using arrows that indicate how the variables should be related. This phase adds order to the theory development process by explicitly delineating patterns. How do teachers' communication behaviors impact students and their learning? How do students' communication behaviors impact teachers and their teaching? Are the effects direct or indirect? What variables moderate or mediate the relationships between teachers and students or students and teachers? Are the effects caused by variables acting independently of each other or are the effects the result of two or more variables interacting together?

Why Are These Variables, Constructs, and Concepts Related?

Finally, what logic explains the proposed causal relationships? Why should a teacher's use of certain verbal and nonverbal messages affect student learning, motivation, and compliance? Why should a student's use of certain verbal and nonverbal message variables affect teacher self-efficacy, teaching satisfaction, and motivation to teach? Why is it that in some situations nonverbal messages appear to be more potent in terms of affecting teaching and learning outcomes while in other situations, verbal messages appear to be more powerful? According to Bacharach (1989), a theory is useful if it can both explain and predict. "An explanation establishes the substantive meaning of constructs, variables, and their linkages, while a prediction tests that substantive meaning by comparing it to empirical evidence" (p. 501).

To summarize, answers to the *what* and *how* questions describe, whereas answers to the *why* question explains. The *what* and *how* questions provide a scaffolding for how researchers should interpret patterns and explain discrepancies in their observations of communication in the instructional context. Answering the *why* question provides a plausible and cogent explanation for why researchers should expect certain relationships to exist. Together, answers to these three questions lay the foundation for an instructional communication theory that describes, explains, and predicts. With the theory development framework in place, we turn our attention to a review of the role of theory in instructional settings in the past, with an emphasis on two mature instructional communication theories.

Current State of Instructional Communication Theory Development

Each decade since 1972, when the International Communication Association formed the Instructional Development Division, an article has been published that reviews and summarizes instructional communication theory and research. In 1977, Scott and Wheeless's *Communication Yearbook* article, titled "Instructional Communication Theory and Research: An Overview," opened with this caveat:

> The richness of the term instructional communication, as well as the ill-defined parameters for theory and research in the area, make this overview difficult to write. There are too many interpretations of the field, too many potential theory bases to consider, and too many investigations, which could legitimately be labeled instructional communication research. (p. 495)

Despite this difficulty, Scott and Wheeless (1977) reviewed various programs of research, which they classified as falling into one of the following domains of research: teachers as sources and receivers, students as sources and receivers, message variables, learning strategies, media, and feedback and reinforcement. They also reviewed the two dominant theories that were tested and used to explain research findings in instructional communication research including cognitive-field theory and stimulus-response associationism.

Seven years later, Staton-Spicer and Wulff's (1984) *Communication Education* article, titled "Research in Communication and Instruction: Categorization and Synthesis," provided researchers with a way to organize instructional communication research. The rationale for their review included the following:

> Every discipline needs to examine its product periodically by scrutinizing the research it is producing. A descriptive examination of the research of a discipline is important from two perspectives. First, it seems that an appropriate way to define an area of study is to examine the research produced within the parameters of the area. . . . Second, a descriptive examination is a critical step in theory building. (p. 377)

Reviewing research from 1974 to 1982, Staton-Spicer and Wulff's (1984) systematic efforts yielded six major categories of research: teacher characteristics, student characteristics, teaching strategies, speech criticism and student evaluation, speech content, and speech communication programs. Staton-Spicer and Wulff concluded their review by complimenting researchers for the "quality and distinctiveness" of their work, however, they also cautioned researchers about the numerous "isolated studies that cannot be placed into a coherent framework" (p. 384). They closed by suggesting that "[w]hat we need are integrated studies that generate propositions from which we can build theory" (p. 384).

In 2001, Waldeck, Kearney, and Plax's *Communication Yearbook* article, titled "Instructional and Developmental Communication Theory and Research in the

1990s: Extending the Agenda for the 21st Century," commended instructional communication researchers for demonstrating the central role of communication in effective instruction. "We owe a lot to these early efforts—key terms and variables have been defined, processes and effects have been substantiated, and innovative studies have yielded important prescriptive implications for the classroom" (p. 208). While acknowledging the progress, Waldeck et al. (2001) argued that

> few examples of theoretically grounded or programmatic research appear in the literature. If we are to legitimate and develop instructional communication further as an area of research and theory, we need to take time now to pause and reflect on what we have learned and what we still need to do. (p. 208)

Waldeck et al's (2001) systematic review of the research literature yielded 11 theories or categories of theories that had been tested in the instructional context or used to explain the effects and relationships identified in instructional communication research: Arousal Theory, Keller's ARCS Model of Instructional Design, French and Raven's Bases of Power, Attribution Theory, Expectancy Learning/Learned Helplessness, Arousal Valence Theory, Approach/Avoidance, Information Processing Theory, Social Learning/Cognitive Theory, Cultivation Theory, and Developmental Theories. In the same article, Waldeck et al. categorized instructional communication variables and programs of research by identifying the following six categories: student communication, teacher communication, mass-media effects on children, pedagogical methods/technology use, classroom management, and teacher–student interaction.

Although each of these important articles have aided researchers in thinking about instructional communication scholarship, they have fallen short in terms of helping researchers *develop* instructional communication theories. One limitation that runs across the three summary articles is that they are descriptive rather than prescriptive. Bacharach (1989) criticizes the lack of theory development in organization and management, another applied discipline similar to instructional communication, on the grounds that what is intended as theory development is simply description. He argues that description must be distinguished from theory. "While descriptions may be the source material of theories, they are not themselves theoretical statements" (p. 497). He continues by stating that "[w]hile some forms of descriptive analysis are often confused with theory, all researchers agree that categorization of data—whether qualitative or quantitative—is not theory" (p. 497).

Rather than generating authentic instructional communication theory, researchers have a tendency to either test theories from other disciplines in the instructional context or use theories from other disciplines to explain their findings (Waldeck, Kearney, & Plax, 2001). This practice is also quite common in other areas of the communication studies discipline, such as interpersonal and organization communication. Although the communication discipline has a tradition of adapting and using other disciplines' theories very successfully (Cohen, 1994), some researchers believe that after three decades of instructional communication research, theories of instructional communication should be emerging from the research (Waldeck, Kearney, & Plax, 2001). Waldeck et al. suggested that

> [w]e know very little about the theoretical bases or implications of instructional communication research. Although the theoretical implications of some studies may be evident to sophisticated readers, researchers have made very little effort to contextualize their projects in explicit theoretical frameworks. (p. 224)

While agreeing with this criticism, we also argue that two theories of instructional communication have emerged from communication research: (1) communication apprehension (refer to Chapter 3) and (2) nonverbal immediacy (refer to Chapter 3). Although neither of these theories can be considered *pure* instructional communication theory, or in the case of immediacy, which comes from social psychology, even pure communication theory, both constructs have been studied and tested extensively in the instructional communication context.

New Directions for Instructional Communication Theory Development

The emotional response of learners to instruction, whether students' and teachers' goals are met, and the role of relational power in instructional settings may provide new vantage points for explaining and predicting the role of communication in the classroom. Each of these theoretical points of departure examines essential elements of instructional communication theory development. Emotional response theory examines the role of emotions in instructional communication. Rhetorical and relational goal theory focuses on the rhetorical and relational goals that teachers and students have and how these goals guide the instructional communication that is transacted in the classroom. Finally, the theory of relational power and instructional influence explains and predicts effective instructional communication in terms of the power that is cultivated and eventually yielded within the teacher–student relationship. Each theoretical framework attempts to better explain previous research findings in a new theoretical light.

Emotional Response Theory

Since Aristotle's nomination of pathos as one of the available means of persuasion, researchers have been both fascinated and perplexed by the role emotions play in explaining, predicting, and controlling human behavior (Damasio, 1994; LeDoux, 1996). From the seminal work of Darwin (1872) to contemporary interest in emotional intelligence, popularized by Goleman (1995), emotions are a powerful force in influencing human behavior. Communication researchers have explored the central role emotions play in the communication process (Andersen & Guerrero, 1998; Planalp, 1999).

In instructional settings, social psychologists have explored how students *feel about* the learning context (Cohen, Steele, & Ross, 1999; Dweck, 2002; Gilbert, Driver-Linn, & Wilson, 2002; Grant & Dweck, 2003; Spencer, Steele, & Quinn, 2002; Steele,

1999) as well as how students *feel in* the learning context (Ashby, Isen, & Turken, 1999; Mathews & Macleod, 1994; Reisberg & Heuer, 1995; Revelle & Loftus, 1992; Rusting, 1999). Instructional communication researchers have explored relationships between students and emotions in the learning context through an examination of such emotion-related variables and theories as nonverbal immediacy (Andersen, 1979; Christophel, 1990; Frymier, 1994), affinity seeking (Frymier & Thompson, 1992; McCroskey & McCroskey, 1986), motivation (Christophel, 1990; Frymier, 1994), arousal-attention theory (Kelley & Gorham, 1988), motivation theory (Christophel, 1990; Richmond, 1990; Frymier, 1994), and affective learning theory (Rodriguez, Plax, & Kearney, 1996). Each of these theoretical frameworks implicitly or explicitly acknowledges the role that emotions play in explaining and predicting student learning. What is emerging from these theoretical threads is a comprehensive framework that may explicate more precise relationships between student emotional responses in the classroom to instruction and learning.

An Overview. The theory of emotional response has it origins in the work of Mehrabian (1971) and his conceptualization of implicit communication (nonverbal communication). It is presented here as a comprehensive instructional communication theory based upon several research streams (Beebe & Biggers, 1986; Biggers & Masterson, 1983; Buck, 1984; Mottet & Beebe, 2002; Russell & Barrett, 1999).

Emotional response theory posits that human emotional response is an accurate predictor of whether an individual approaches or avoids a person, place, idea, or thing, including whether someone approaches or avoids learning (Mehrabian, 1981; Russell & Barrett, 1999; Vinson & Biggers, 1993). Mehrabian (1981) suggested that all emotional states may be adequately described in terms of (1) pleasure–displeasure, (2) arousal–nonarousal, and (3) dominance–submissiveness. Each dimension is of a continuous nature and has within its range positive and negative values as well as a neutral point. Combinations of various values on each dimension characterize different emotions. An emotional response of pleasure (increased liking), arousal (increased intensity), and dominance (increased permission to approach) would predict approach behavior. An emotional response of displeasure (decreased liking), nonarousal (decreased intensity), and submissiveness (decreased permission to approach) would predict avoidance behavior.

One of the values of emotional response theory is the increased precision that can be gained by classifying emotional responses on three independent dimensions. The pleasure–displeasure dimension is defined by such adjective pairs as happy–unhappy, pleased–annoyed, or satisfied–unsatisfied. Psychological indication of this dimension is the presence or absence of a longing to approach the subject or object (Mehrabian, 1981). Generally, stimuli that produce greater pleasure elicit greater feelings of liking (Mehrabian, 1981).

The arousal–nonarousal dimension is defined by adjective pairs like stimulated–relaxed, excited–calm, or frenzied–sluggish. Psychological indication of this dimension is mental alertness (Mehrabian, 1981). Behavioral indicators for this dimension are physical activity levels. The arousal dimension modifies emotional reactions to stimuli by exaggerating the reaction of liking or disliking (pleasure).

The dominance–submissive dimension is defined by adjective pairs like controlling–controlled or influencing–influenced. Psychological indicators of this dimension are feelings of power and control. Generally, emotions of greater dominance result in an increased license or permission to behave in a certain way (e.g., to express liking or disliking toward something). Conversely, emotions of submissiveness result in decreased permission to experience liking or disliking.

The Role of Implicit Messages on Emotional Responses. Central to emotional response theory is the role implicit messages play in generating emotional responses in others. Mehrabian (1981) defines implicit communication as "aspects of speech [that] are not dictated by correct grammar but are rather expressions of feelings and attitudes above and beyond the contexts conveyed by speech" (p. 2). Implicit communication is primarily nonverbal. Examples of implicit communication include use of personal space, facial expression, body posture, and head nods, as well as paralinguistic features of communication such as tone, rate, pitch, and volume.

In the explicit communication system (language is the best example), behaviors are primarily symbolic and the rules for their association are externally verifiable. Words may be looked up in a dictionary; grammar rules may be used to evaluate the appropriateness or inappropriateness of explicit communication structure and syntax. The rules of explicit communication are socially shared (Mehrabian, 1981).

Within the implicit communication system, behaviors generally function as signs. The coding rules are not externally verifiable, are less likely to be socially constructed, and are part of a biologically shared signal system (Buck, 1984). Implicit messages are often unintentional expressions of underlying emotions; behaviors are more automatic or reflexive (Mead, 1934).

Predictions. In a review of literature, Biggers and Rankis (1983) reported that emotion accounted for a large percentage (40% or more) of variance in research studies predicting behavior. In the instructional context, students may use their emotions as information to guide what Hatfield, Cacioppo, and Rapson (1994) referred to as *bivalent (approach/withdrawal) behavior.* Put most simply, the theory of emotional response predicts that (1) people pursue things they like, (2) people like things that they feel positive emotions for, and (3) people's emotions are influenced by the implicit messages they receive from others. As shown in Figure 12.1, emotional response theory suggests that teacher communication behaviors (e.g., immediacy, affinity-seeking) engender human emotional responses on three dimensions (pleasure, arousal, and dominance). The exact levels of pleasure, arousal, and dominance are dependent upon such factors as cultural background and the expectations of the learner. It is predicted that enhanced levels of pleasure, arousal, and dominance result in approach behaviors, including increased learning stemming from the increased approach to the information and increased engagement with the content. It is also predicted that decreased levels of pleasure, arousal, and dominance

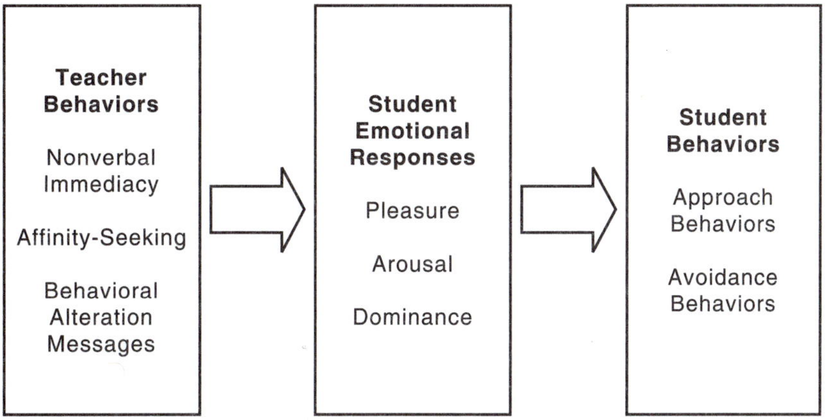

FIGURE 12.1 *Emotional Response Theory.*

would result in disengagement or avoidant behaviors, resulting in decreased levels of motivation and learning.

Applications to Instructional Communication Research. As explained in this chapter, several instructional communication researchers have used Mehrabian's immediacy construct to explain teacher effects upon both student affective and cognitive learning (Andersen, 1979; McCroskey & Richmond, 1992). The immediacy variable, which is integral to emotional response theory, was taken from Mehrabian's original notion of implicit communication and applied to instructional settings by Andersen (1979). Applying the construct of immediacy to the instructional context using emotional response theory results in the following propositions:

- Teachers who use immediacy cues will engender student emotional responses of pleasure, arousal, and dominance that will, in turn, result in more time on task, student attention, and increased learning.
- Students who use more immediacy cues will engender teacher emotional responses of pleasure, arousal, and dominance that will, in turn, result in enhanced self-perceptions of teacher efficacy and job satisfaction.

In addition to explaining the impact of nonverbal immediacy, emotional response theory may be used to explain the effectiveness of other instructional communication variables. Teacher affinity-seeking behaviors may be interpreted as efforts to increase the emotional responses of liking (pleasure) and interest (arousal) while also granting teacher or student permission to approach or learn (dominance). Behavior alteration techniques and messages may be yet another way of coding teacher behaviors that influence the emotional responses of learners. Similarly, a host of other teacher–student constructs and variables, such as teacher enthusiasm, teacher communicator style, use of humor, solidarity, and teacher credibility may be explained using emotional response theory assumptions.

What's Next? Opportunities exist for instructional communication researchers to further explore and validate emotional response theory as an explanatory and predictive framework for assessing relationships between teacher–student and student–teacher classroom communication. Several research questions emerge from the literature.

1. What specific instructional communication behaviors or conditions lead to enhanced student emotional responses, which then result in increased learning? Similarly, what specific behaviors or conditions lead to enhanced teacher emotional responses, which then result in increased teaching effectiveness and thus enhanced student learning (Ross, 1998; Shann, 1998)?

2. What are optimal levels of pleasure, arousal, and dominance that result in enhanced learning? We do not know what levels of emotional response result in optimal learning. For example, is there always a linear relationship between an emotional response of pleasure and learning? Are there situations where displeasure may motivate a student to learn? Previous research suggests that the relationship between arousal and learning may be curvilinear (Burke, Heuer, & Reisberg, 1992; Reisberg & Heuer, 1995; Revelle & Loftus, 1992). Too much or too little arousal can inhibit learning. Additional research is needed to identify relationships between learning, arousal, pleasure, and dominance. The dominance dimension of emotional response theory has been the most challenging to consistently document (Mottet & Beebe, 2002; Russell & Barrett, 1999).

3. How can emotional responses be measured with increased validity and reliability? Currently, emotional responses are measured using pencil and paper self-reports that include semantic differential scales (Mehrabian, 1981). The validity and reliability of emotional response measurement may be enhanced by using physiological measures, such as blood pressure and pulse rate. Valid and reliable measurement may enhance researchers' abilities to predict approach and avoidant behavior using emotional response as the source of such behavior.

4. What are the implications of emotional response theory on teacher and student instructional communication behavior? Emotional response theory suggests that rather than focusing primarily on the behavior of the teacher (immediacy behaviors, affinity-seeking strategies, behavior alteration messages), learning is best explained by how students interpret and respond to teacher behaviors. It is hypothesized that learning occurs not because of what the teacher does, but by how the student responds emotionally to all aspects of the learning experience. In essence, emotional response theory is a student-centered rather than a teacher-centered paradigm. Rather than emphasizing teacher-centered behaviors (such as being more immediate), teacher educators should emphasize how to interpret student emotional responses so that they can best adapt to their students.

In summary, emotional response theory is a conceptual framework that provides a unified theoretical perspective that allows researchers to better explain relationships between teacher–student communication and learning. The essential elements of theory development that opened this chapter included: (1) What constructs are a part of the theory? (2) How are these constructs related? and (3) Why are these constructs related? Figure 12.1 represents three groupings of constructs that address the first essential element of theory development: teacher instructional communication behaviors, student emotional responses (pleasure, arousal, dominance), and student approach/avoidant behaviors.

How are these constructs related? Teacher behavior in the classroom, especially implicit communication behaviors, elicits emotional responses of pleasure, arousal, and dominance in students, which in turn influence their approach/avoidant behaviors. Behaviors that elicit feelings of pleasure should result in feelings of liking. Higher levels of arousal increase the amount of liking or disliking that exists in the teacher–student relationship. Dominance–submissiveness centers on feelings of being in control and having permission to behave as one wishes.

Why are these constructs related? Emotional responses are powerful stimuli that influence how humans respond to their environment, including communication behavior, especially implicit communication behavior. Emotional response theory holds promise in helping to integrate a variety of research streams that have examined such teacher behaviors as immediacy, affinity-seeking, and behavior alteration messages (BAMs). Additional research is needed to further test the applicability and validity of emotional response theory in instructional settings.

Rhetorical/Relational Goal Theory

The classroom is a place where students and a teacher interact. Both teachers and students bring to the classroom their own knowledge, expectations, experiences, culture, personalities, and intelligence, as well as their difficulties. While the teacher is typically the most powerful person in the classroom and sets the tone and procedures for the class, students also impact the teacher. (Chapter 7 is devoted to describing and explaining how students influence teachers.) Additionally, there is research that indicates that students' characteristics interact, to some extent, with teacher communication behaviors. Wanzer and Frymier (1999) found that students' humor orientation interacted with reports of teacher humor orientation on learning. Additionally, Frymier (1993a) found that students beginning the semester with low or moderate motivation benefited the most from having an immediate teacher. Similarly, Frymier (1993b) found high and low communication apprehensive students to be differentially impacted by teacher immediacy. Wooten and McCroskey (1996) found that students' sociocommunicative orientation interacted somewhat with teachers' sociocommunicative style on trust. This research, taken together, provides support for the proposition that teacher communication behaviors interact with student communication behaviors and characteristics, and learning outcomes are influenced by the teacher and the student.

In Chapter 1 Mottet and Beebe described the rhetorical and relational traditions in communication. These two traditions also reflect two of the primary purposes we have when communicating: (1) to influence and/or achieve goals and (2) to develop and maintain relationships. These two goals are present in the instructional context just as they are in any other communication context. Both teachers and students communicate in the classroom context with these purposes, however, their specific goals and needs differ. The result is two driving forces in the classroom—student goals and teacher goals. Student goals may be best understood in terms of their needs. Because students are subordinate to the teacher and dependent on the teacher to achieve their goals, they use communication to insure their needs are met.

Student Needs. Students bring different needs to the classroom. One perspective is that of Milton, Pollio, and Eison (1986) who proposed the constructs of learning orientation and grade orientation. Students differ on what they are seeking from their educational experience. Learning-oriented (LO) students view the classroom as a context in which they expect to encounter new information and ideas that will be both personally and professionally significant (Milton et al., 1986). Grade-oriented (GO) students view the educational experience as a crucible in which they are tested and graded, a necessary evil that they must endure on the way to getting a degree or becoming certified in a profession (Milton et al., 1986). Students who are grade-oriented view the learning experience through a different lens than do learning-oriented students. These two types of students require different things from their instructors to accomplish their educational goals.

Students' academic needs are to achieve educational goals, which are in the form of learning and/or obtaining a certain grade. Consistent with Milton et al.'s (1986) conceptualization of LO and GO, students' academic goals revolve primarily around obtaining a particular grade (grade orientation) and/or learning the content (learning orientation). Students' needs are met through interactions with the instructor, other students, and course materials (such as books, videos, assignments, etc.). When teachers use outlines, relevant examples, clear learning objectives, and other message variables (see Chapter 5) that help students achieve their educational goals, students' academic needs are likely to be met.

A second type of need students have is relational. Students have the need to feel confirmed as a student and often as a person. Hurt, Scott, and McCroskey (1978) suggested that students have interpersonal needs in addition to their academic needs, and recommended that teachers address both types of needs in the classroom. Students meet these needs by interacting with their instructor and with other students. An assumption here is that students want to receive confirmation from their teachers. This is supported by Ellis's (2000) research on confirmation and Frymier and Houser's (2000) finding that the communication skill of ego support (helping students believe in themselves) was viewed as the second most important skill for teachers to have (referential skill—explaining things clearly and facilitating understanding—was first). Additionally, much of the research on immediacy has reaffirmed students' desire or appreciation for a closer relationship with their teachers.

Our first proposition is that students have both relational and academic needs; however, not all students are equally driven by each need. For some students, academic needs will dominate; for others, relationship needs will dominate; and some will be equally driven by the two needs.

Teacher Goals. Teachers also have goals and needs they bring to the classroom. Teacher goals are primarily of two types—rhetorical goals and relational goals. As was discussed in Chapter 1, rhetorical goals coincide with a source or teacher orientation. When emphasizing rhetorical goals, teachers focus on influencing students to learn and understand the content as presented by the teacher. These teachers are often described as more teacher-centered. They have an agenda or a plan for what they want students to do and learn, and direct students along that path. Teacher-centered teachers are described as disseminators of information who rely heavily on the lecture method of teaching (Chall, 2000).

Relational goals involve the type of relationship the teacher wants to have with his or her students. Many teachers may not be cognizant of the relational goals they have with students, however, as discussed by Watzlawick, Bavelas, and Jackson (1967), all communication has a relational element. Therefore, teacher communication with students has a relational element, and some teachers will be more aware of this than others. Gorham and Burroughs (1989) found that teachers make a conscious effort to get students to like them. It is likely that some teachers make an effort to have as little contact with students as possible, with many teachers between the extremes of consciously avoiding knowing their students and consciously seeking affinity and liking with their students. When we refer to teachers emphasizing relational goals, we mean teachers who are seeking a closer relationship with students. When we refer to teachers who deemphasize relational goals, we mean teachers who either do not really care about their relationship with students or who avoid their students. Teachers who emphasize relational goals often view learning as something the teacher and students do together. This has been described as a student-centered approach (Chall, 2000). Teachers using this approach have been described as facilitators who engage students in dialogue.

Although student-centered teaching and teacher-centered teaching have been described as independent approaches at opposite ends of the continuum (Chall, 2000), the two approaches may be relatively independent of one another. A teacher could simultaneously focus on rhetorical and relational goals. An example of this might be a teacher who focuses on rhetorical goals by using lecture to communicate specific source-centered meanings in regards to content that he or she wants students to understand. Throughout the lecture, the teacher might ask students questions that encourage them to apply the content to existing knowledge or to relate their personal experiences to the content. The discussion questions that allow students to express their thoughts and feelings about the content reflect more relational goals and are consistent with what has been termed a student-centered approach to teaching. This leads us to a second proposition: that teachers have both rhetorical and relational goals; however, they differ in the emphasis they put on each goal. Related to this proposition is the question, "Are rhetorical and relational goals really independent of one another?"

A Model of Teacher Goals and Student Needs. Verbal and nonverbal immediacy have received a great deal of attention in the instructional communication research literature and have consistently been found to be positively associated with increased learning and motivation (see Chapter 8 for a review). While in many ways immediacy is a relational construct, it does not necessarily indicate a focus on relational goals. Research suggests that speakers who are dynamic and likeable will be perceived as more credible and therefore more persuasive (Andersen, 2004). Therefore, an effective teacher who emphasizes rhetorical goals will likely be an immediate lecturer to gain and maintain students' attention and to facilitate retention of the information, as well as to enhance his or her credibility. An effective teacher who emphasizes relational goals will also use immediacy, however, as a means to developing interpersonal relationships with students rather than for gaining attention and establishing credibility. Identifying teachers as having a rhetorical focus or a relational focus is based on their intentional goals, rather than on the means they use to achieve those goals. Therefore, rhetorical goals and relational goals must be operationalized as teachers' reports of what their goals are. Similarly, students' academic and relational needs must be operationalized as descriptions of their needs. Needs are internal and cannot be directly observed.

Within any classroom there will likely be an interaction between teacher goals and student needs. What goals teachers emphasize and how they go about achieving them influences how students' needs are met. Additionally, how students interact with the teacher, classmates, and instructional materials will also influence how their needs are met. The expectation is that teachers who emphasize relational goals would meet students' relational needs and that teachers who emphasize rhetorical goals would meet students' academic needs. However, in order to meet students' needs, teachers must effectively accomplish their goals. Just because a teacher has set goals (rhetorical or relational) doesn't mean he or she is able to accomplish those goals. A teacher may have the rhetorical goal of having students know and understand the stages of relational development. However, if the information is poorly presented and disorganized, the teacher's goal will not likely be accomplished and students' academic needs will not likely be met. Many of the teacher communication behaviors discussed in previous chapters, such as immediacy, clarity, relevance, humor, compliance-gaining, and affinity-seeking can be viewed as facilitating factors that allow teachers to meet their rhetorical and relational goals. If a teacher either lacks goals (rhetorical or relational) or is unable to communicate effectively with students, the teacher is unlikely to meet students' relational and academic needs. This leads to another proposition: Effective teaching occurs first when teachers set appropriate rhetorical and relational goals, and second, are able to use appropriate communication strategies to accomplish their goals.

Students are likely to be most satisfied with their classroom experience when their relational and academic needs are met through their interactions with their teachers and classmates. Students who have very low relational needs may become annoyed with a teacher who emphasizes relational goals over rhetorical goals. These students may find discussions and activities that allow the students and teacher to get to know one another or that allow students to express their personal views as a waste of time. They may be anxious to get down to business and cover content. Students with high relational needs may be bored or unmotivated with a teacher who emphasizes rhetorical goals over relational goals. They may have difficulty staying with the content because they feel unimportant to the teacher. These students may not find learning to be intrinsically rewarding enough for interest and enthusiasm to be generated throughout the course. A positive relationship with the teachers and/or classmates may help generate motivation to study and learn the content. Therefore, a fourth proposition is that when students' academic needs and relational needs are met, students will be more satisfied with their classroom experience.

Teachers who emphasize both rhetorical and relational goals and are able to successfully utilize communication behaviors such as immediacy, relevance, clarity, and compliance-gaining to achieve those goals are most likely to meet students' relational and academic needs. Teachers, who emphasize one goal over the other, are likely to meet some students' needs. Figure 12.2 illustrates how student needs and teacher goals impact student outcomes.

The research that this theory is rooted in has primarily been conducted in college classrooms. However, teachers at all levels have goals they want to achieve in their classrooms. At lower grades, teachers are likely to emphasize relational goals. Young children typically have a strong need to receive confirmation and approval from adults. Teachers of young children know they must establish a relationship with each of their students to be effective teachers. At some point in the middle grades, students are expected to be focused on the content and to no longer need someone to hold their hand. At the college level, teachers are traditionally viewed as disseminators of information, and students are expected to be self-motivated consumers of that information. The research on immediacy and related variables has consistently indicated that students of all ages respond positively to teachers who use immediacy behaviors and are approachable (Houser, 2002). It is likely that as students mature and develop, their relational needs lessen, however some students will always desire affirmation from their teachers and need ego support to maintain motivation for the course. As students become more mature and establish mature relationships, they are less likely to have strong relational needs in the classroom.

A proposition of this theory is that teachers at all levels have relational and rhetorical goals, however, the exact nature of those goals and how those goals are accomplished differ with different grade levels and different contexts. Similarly, we propose that students at all levels have relational and academic needs; however, those needs differ in intensity at different stages of development, and how those needs are satisfied differs across contexts and stages of development.

What's Next? The first step in testing this model is to develop instruments to measure teacher goals and student needs. The proposition that teachers have relational goals and rhetorical goals needs to be confirmed, as does the proposition that students have academic and relational needs. This can be accomplished with traditional measurement development, as well as qualitative methods, such as

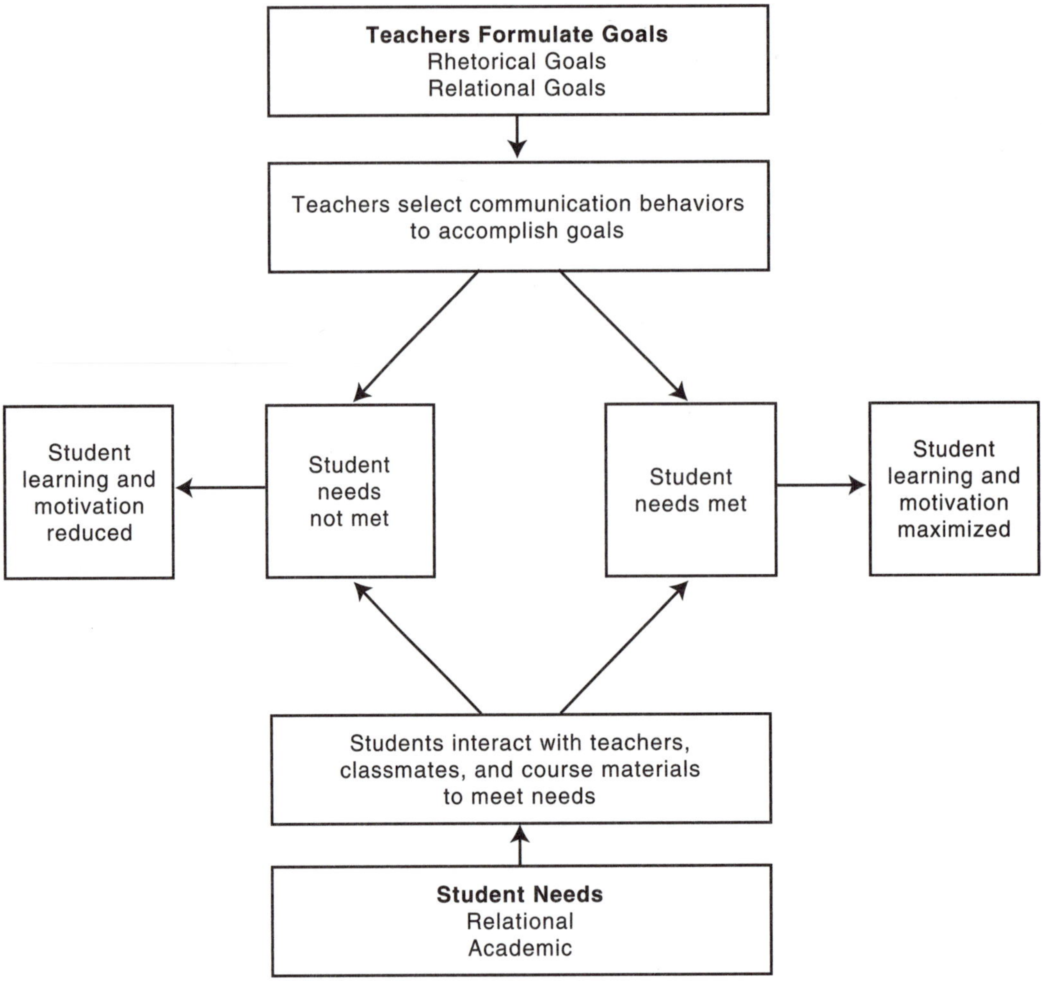

FIGURE 12.2 *Rhetorical/Relational Goal Theory.*

interviews. The relationship between teacher relational goals and rhetorical goals also needs to be examined. Are these two constructs independent or related? If they are related, how are they related to one another? The relationship between teacher goals and students' needs also needs to be explored. We stated earlier that we think teacher goals and student needs interact with one another. We made the prediction that when students' needs are met, they will learn and achieve more in the classroom. Survey research could be conducted initially to explore these relationships. Once there is a more thorough understanding of the variables and how they are related, experimental studies could be designed that allow for greater control in testing the model.

Additionally, the proposition that variables such as immediacy, clarity, and affinity-seeking can be used to achieve both rhetorical and relational goals needs to be tested. Valid measures of teacher goals would need to be developed before this proposition could be tested.

Throughout this chapter we have referred to the three essential questions of theory development: What are the key variables? How are the variables related? and Why are the variables related as proposed? We will summarize the rhetorical/relational goal theory by linking what was discussed to these three essential elements. *What are the key variables?* The key variables of the theory are that teachers have rhetorical and relational goals and that students have relational and academic needs. *How are the variables related?* Teachers enter the classroom with rhetorical and relational goals; however, these goals are not always well developed. Similarly, students enter the classroom with academic and relational needs. How the teacher goes about achieving his or her goals influences students' abilities to meet their needs. When teachers set appropriate goals and use effective communication to achieve their goals, students' needs are more likely to be met.

Why Are the Variables Related as Proposed? The classroom context, like most communication contexts, involves individuals mutually influencing one another in the process of accomplishing their goals and meeting their needs. Research indicates that teacher communication and student communication behaviors interact to influence student outcomes. Because the classroom is transactional in nature, the teacher and the student must collaborate in some fashion for students to have positive learning outcomes. This collaboration does not typically occur in the one-on-one format typical of friendships and other dyadic relationships. Rather, the collaboration plays out over the course of a semester through lectures, discussions, exams, and grades. When the teacher's behavior meets students' needs so that they can accomplish their goals, students are likely to learn more, retain more, and to place greater value on the content.

Relational Power and Instructional Influence Theory

Another new direction for instructional communication theory development integrates the work of French and Raven (1959) and Kelman (1961, 1974). We are referring to this new direction as the Theory of Relational Power and Instructional Influence. This theory explains and predicts how teachers and students influence each other through relational power. According to Hartnett (1971), "power is a property of the social relation; it is not an attribute of the actor" (pp. 27–28). The power that teachers and students need in order to remain influential with each other is a by-product of the teacher–student relationship and is ultimately grounded in the verbal and nonverbal messages that are created and used in the instructional setting. The theory of relational power and instructional influence merges three streams of research, including Kelman's (1974) model of social influence, French and Raven's (1959) five bases of social or relational power, and instructional communication research, which enhances teaching effectiveness (Chesebro & McCroskey, 2002).

The first stream of research centers on the work of Kelman (1958, 1961, 1974), who identified three levels of social influence: compliance, identification, and internalization.

> *Compliance* occurs when an individual accepts influence because the individual hopes to achieve a favorable reaction from another person or group. The individual adopts the induced behavior not because he/she believes in its content but because the individual expects to gain specific rewards or approval and avoids punishments.
>
> *Identification* occurs when an individual accepts influence because he/she wants to establish or maintain a relationship to another person or group. . . . The individual actually believes in the responses which he/she adopts.
>
> *Internalization* occurs when an individual accepts influence because the content of the induced behavior—the idea or action of which it is composed—is intrinsically rewarding. The individual adopts the induced behavior because it is congruent with his value system. (Kelman, 1958, p. 53)

One way to conceptualize Kelman's (1958) three levels of social influence is by placing them on a continuum according to influence strength (McCroskey, 1998). At one end of the continuum is compliance—short-term influence. Students comply with a teacher's request to obtain a particular reward or to avoid punishment. Once obtained, the compliance is short-lived and students return to their usual behavior. At the other end of the continuum is internalization—long-term influence. This level of influence occurs when students internalize the teacher's requested behaviors. Rather than completing homework to obtain a reward or to avoid punishment, students complete the homework because it is what students do. In short, homework behaviors have become habituated and a part of the student's value system. Although instructional communication researchers are more accustomed to examining how teachers influence their students, this model of social influence can also be used to demonstrate the influence that students have on teachers (Mottet, Beebe, Raffeld, & Paulsel, 2004, 2005).

Our first proposition is that the teacher–student relationship is similar to other types of interpersonal relationships in that the relationship involves influence (Berger, 1994). Teachers influence students to ensure that their needs are met. Similarly, students influence teachers to ensure that their needs are met. Although short-term compliance is acceptable in many situations, we believe that most teachers probably desire long-term influence, whereas students internalize their educational experiences to become informed citizens who value lifelong learning.

The second stream of research focuses on French and Raven's (1959) five bases of relational power: legitimate, reward, coercive, expert, and referent. French and Raven's work served as the theoretical foundation for the "Power in the Classroom" program of research conducted by Jim McCroskey, Virginia Richmond, Pat Kearney, and Tim Plax in the 1980s. The "Power in the Classroom" studies, which were reviewed in Chapter 6, yielded a number of important research conclusions and prescriptions for classroom instruction.

Evidence suggests that a teacher's ability to influence students is determined by the relational power that students yield to their teacher (Plax & Kearney, 1992). In short, relational power is not a quality that an individual naturally possesses, but is a quality that is yielded to an individual based on the type and quality of relationship that two people have with each other (Barraclough & Stewart, 1992). Additionally, not all five bases of power have been shown to yield equal influence. The research consistently demonstrates that a teacher's cultivation of expert and referent power, or prosocial forms of power, with students remains more effective in terms of enhancing student motivation and learning (Plax & Kearney, 1992). Prosocial forms of power are reward-based, whereas antisocial forms of power are coercive-based (Plax & Kearney, 1992). Also, there is limited evidence to suggest that a student's ability to influence a teacher is determined by the relational power that teachers yield to their students (Golish & Olson, 2000; Mottet, Beebe, Raffeld, & Paulsel, 2004, 2005).

Our second proposition is that teachers and students influence each other by yielding power to the other, which is a by-product of the teacher–student relationship. Additionally, not all types of relational power yield similar levels of influence. Prosocial forms of power (expert, referent, reward), which are more dependent on relational perceptions of enhanced credibility, interpersonal attraction, similarity, and affinity, are probably more likely to yield long-term influence (i.e., internalization) than antisocial forms of power (legitimate, coercive), which are probably more likely to yield short-term influence (i.e., compliance). Many instructional communication researchers believe that, as the quality of the teacher–student relationship increases, so does the relational power (Barraclough & Stewart, 1992; McCroskey & Richmond, 1992; Plax & Kearney, 1992).

The third stream of research examines a number of important verbal and nonverbal communication variables that have been shown to enhance the teacher–student relationship, and ultimately instructional effectiveness. Many of these communication variables and their corresponding programs of research are reviewed in this book, including instructional humor (Chapter 5), student nonverbal immediacy behaviors (Chapter 7), teacher nonverbal immediacy behaviors (Chapter 8), and teacher and student use of affinity-seeking behaviors (Chapter 9). These verbal and nonverbal communication behaviors have been shown to enhance relational development between teachers and students and students and teachers.

Our third proposition is that the quality of the teacher–student relationship is dependent on the types of verbal and nonverbal messages that are exchanged and created between teachers and students. Relational development is enhanced when teachers and students appropriately use the above-referenced communication behaviors. Similarly, relational development is retarded or diminished when these communication behaviors are not used or inappropriately used.

Figure 12.3 illustrates how these three streams of research and their respective propositions are related. The inverted pyramid reflects the scope of one's influence: Individual verbal and nonverbal communication behaviors yield minimal influence; however, the scope of the influence increases through the relationship that teachers

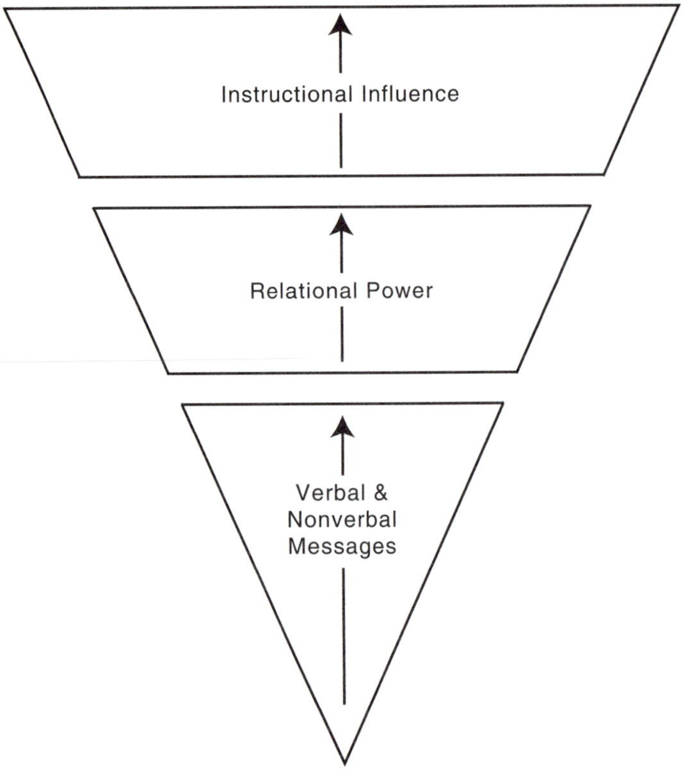

FIGURE 12.3 ***Relational Power and Instructional Influence Theory.***

and students develop with each other and the types of power that teachers and students grant each other. At the bottom of the inverted pyramid are the individual verbal and nonverbal communication behaviors that teachers and students use to enhance relational development, which is the next level of the inverted pyramid. Depending on the quality of the teacher–student relationship, teachers and students yield relational power to each other, which is the next layer of the pyramid. The top tier of the pyramid reflects the potential influence that teachers and students have on each other.

A set of predictions that remains untested in the instructional communication research literature is the relationships between French and Raven's (1959) five bases of power and Kelman's (1961, 1974) three levels of social influence. Figure 12.4 illustrates these predictions.

View the three levels of social or instructional influence (i.e., compliance, identification, internalization) as the dependent variable and the five bases of relational power (i.e., legitimate, coercive, reward, expert, referent) as the independent variable. It is believed that antisocial forms of power (i.e., legitimate, coercive) yield short-term influence (i.e., compliance) whereas prosocial forms of power (expert,

INSTRUCTIONAL INFLUENCE →

RELATIONAL POWER ↑

Bases of Power	Compliance	Identification	Internalization
Referent	X	X	X
Expert	X	X	X
Reward	X		
Coercive	X		
Legitimate	X		

FIGURE 12.4 ***Predicted Relationships Between Relational Power and Instructional Influence.***

referent) yield long-term influence (i.e., internalization). As people cultivate higher forms of relational power (as they move up), they also have more long-term influence such as internalization (moving to the right).

What's Next? Instructional communication researchers who continue to test the theory of relational power and instructional influence are encouraged to address the following three questions that may enhance the development of this theory and its application to the instructional context.

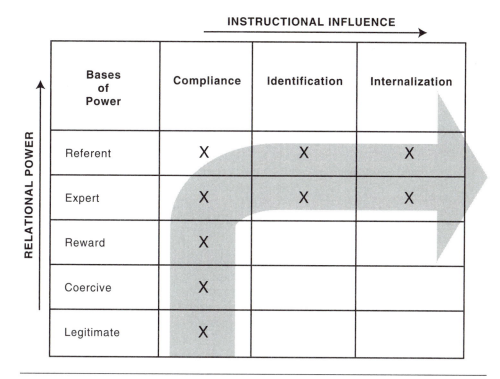

1. How should Kelman's (1961, 1974) conceptualization of social influence be measured in the instructional context? How should researchers measure compliance, identification, and internalization? According to Kelman, compliance is short-term influence, whereas internalization is long-term influence. Researchers may want to consider measuring influence by assessing students' affective learning (refer to Chapter 1 for an affective learning measure). Mottet and Richmond (1998) offer a number of assessment items that have been shown to reflect Krathwohl, Bloom, and Masia's (1964) taxonomy of affective learning, which reflects both short- and long-term forms of affective learning. Researchers are encouraged to examine whether affective learning remains a valid and reliable way to assess Kelman's model of social influence. Additionally, what instruments could be used to assess students' instructional influence (compliance, identification, internalization) on teachers?

2. How should French and Raven's (1959) conceptualization of relational power be measured in the instructional context? There are a number of approaches to measuring relational power, including instruments that assess perceptions of relational power developed by Student (1968), Richmond, McCroskey, Davis, and Koontz (1980), and Roach (1994). Additionally, Kearney, Plax, Richmond, and McCroskey (1985) developed a typology of behavioral alteration techniques (BATs) and messages (BAMs) that assess actual communication behaviors that have been shown to reflect French and Raven's (1959) five bases of relational power. Do these measures continue to remain valid and reliable in the instructional context? Can these measures be used to assess teachers' perceptions of student power? Do these measures remain valid and reliable in nontraditional educational contexts, such as the corporate training classroom?

3. What additional instructional communication behaviors should be assessed to capture the breadth and depth of the teacher–student relationship? Most of the current measures have been used to assess students' perceptions of their teachers' instructional communication behaviors. Can these measures be used to assess teachers' perceptions of their students' instructional communication behaviors?

To summarize, the theory of relational power and instructional influence is another conceptual framework that provides a unified way of explaining and predicting how power and influence affect teaching and learning. Again, using the essential elements of theory development, Kelman's (1961, 1974) model of social influence, French and Raven's (1959) bases of social power, and the instructional communication variables reviewed in this book answer the first question concerning the constructs that are a part of the theory. How are the constructs related? Teachers and students' appropriate use of the verbal and nonverbal communication behaviors enhance relational development. The quality of the teacher–student relationship affects the type of power that teachers and students yield to each other, thereby affecting the degree to which teachers and students influence each other.

Finally, why should these constructs be related as indicated? Although, the predictive power of this theory originates in the verbal and nonverbal communication behaviors that teachers and students exchange with each other, it is the *teacher–student relationship* that ultimately predicts the level of power that is yielded and the degree of influence that occurs. According to McCroskey and Richmond (1992), it is the amount of liking or affinity that relational partners have for each other that determines the amount of power or influence that one person grants to the other. "People usually will comply with, rather than resist, reasonable instructions or requests if they like, respect, and admire their teacher" (McCroskey & Richmond, 1992, p. 102).

Summary

Theory helps us better explain what sometimes baffles us. As noted by Dubin (1978), theory helps us "impose order on unordered experiences" (p. 6). This chapter has "imposed order" on instructional communication findings by: (1) identifying the essential elements of instructional communication theory development, (2) identifying the current state of instructional communication theory development, and (3) proposing new directions for instructional communication theory development.

Expanding on Dubin's (1978) proposals for theory development, Whetten (1989) suggested that theory development address three questions: (1) *What* variables, constructs, and concepts should be considered as part of the logical explanation of the phenomenon under study? (2) *How* are these variables, constructs, and concepts related? and (3) *Why* are these variables, constructs, and concepts related? Using the *What, How,* and *Why* questions as guides, we provided a brief overview of the current state of instructional communication theory development, noting the challenge previous scholars have had in developing a taxonomy of instructional communication theory. Despite these challenges, two theories have emerged from the instructional communication research—communication apprehension and nonverbal immediacy. The theory of communication apprehension and nonverbal immediacy appear to have considerable heuristic value and continue to resonate with instructional communication researchers.

The last half of the chapter focused on three relatively new theoretical points of departure that may provide frameworks for understanding instructional communication research. First, emotional response theory suggests that humans respond to their environments in emotional ways. Mehrabian (1981) suggested that all emotional states may be adequately described in terms of three primary dimensions: pleasure–displeasure, arousal–nonarousal, and dominance–submissiveness. A learner's emotional response may be a good predictor of his or her approach–avoidant instructional behaviors.

A second theory, rhetorical/relational goal theory, suggests that both teachers and students bring their own needs and goals to the learning situation. Among them is the need for relational support as well as for information that assists in influencing others. Both relational and rhetorical needs influence expectations and levels of satisfaction. Teacher and student classroom behaviors operate to address both the needs and goals of providing relational support and rhetorical influence. Such behaviors as immediacy, affinity-seeking, use of humor, and other well-researched instructional communication variables may be better understood by viewing these behaviors as a means of fulfilling rhetorical and relational needs of both students and teachers.

Finally, the theory of relational power and instructional influence explains and predicts how teachers and students influence each other through the teacher–student relationship. It is suggested that teachers and students influence each other by yielding each other power, which is a by-product of the teacher—student relationship and is grounded in the verbal and nonverbal messages that teachers and students create and exchange with one another.

This chapter is not designed to be a close-ended review of extant instructional communication theory. Its ultimate goal is to encourage instructional communication students and scholars to ponder the development and integration of new theoretical frameworks that may help researchers impose order on the sometimes "unordered experiences" of the teaching and learning process. Emotional Response Theory, Rhetorical/Relational Goal Theory, and Relational Power and Instructional Influence Theory are three possibilities that attempt to answer the *What, How,* and *Why* questions of theory development.

References

Andersen, J. F. (1978). *The relationship between teacher immediacy and teaching effectiveness.* Unpublished dissertation, West Virginia University, Morgantown, MV.

Andersen, J. F. (1979). Teacher immediacy as a predictor of teaching effectiveness. In D. Nimmo (Ed.), *Communication yearbook 3* (pp. 543–559). New Brunswick, NJ: Transaction Books.

Andersen, P. A. (2004). Influential actions: Nonverbal communication and persuasion. In J. S. Seiter & R. H. Gass (Eds.), *Perspectives on persuasion, social influence, and compliance gaining* (pp. 165–180). Boston, Allyn & Bacon.

Andersen, P. A., & Guerrero, L K. (1998). *Handbook of communication and emotion: Research, theory, application, and contexts.* San Diego: Academic Press.

Ashby, F. G., Isen, M. M., & Turken, A. U. (1999). A neuropsychological theory of positive affect and its influence on cognition. *Psychological Review, 106,* 529–550.

Bacharach, S. B. (1989). Organizational theories: Some criteria for evaluation. *Academy of Management Review, 14,* 496–515.

Bandura, A. (1973). *Aggression: A social learning analysis.* Englewood Cliffs, NJ: Prentice-Hall.

Barraclough, R. A., & Stewart, R. A. (1992). Power and control: Social science perspectives. In V. P. Richmond & J. C. McCroskey (Eds.), *Power in the classroom: Communication, control, and concern* (pp. 1–18). Hillsdale, NJ: Lawrence Erlbaum.

Beatty, M. J., & McCroskey, J. C. (2001). *The biology of communication: A communibiological perspective.* Cresskill, NJ: Hampton Press.

Beatty, M. J., McCroskey, J. C., & Heisel, A. D. (1998). Communication apprehension as temperamental expression: A communibiological paradigm. *Communication Monographs, 65,* 197–219.

Beebe, S. A., & Biggers, T. (1986). The relationship of trait and state emotion: Emotional responses to "The Day After." *World Communication Journal, 15.*

Berger, C. R. (1994). Power, dominance, and social interaction. In M. L. Knapp & G. R. Miller (Eds.), *Handbook of interpersonal communication* (2nd ed.) (pp. 450–507). Thousand Oaks, CA: Sage.

Biggers, T., & Masterson, J. T. (1983). A reconceptualization of communication apprehension in terms of the emotional-eliciting qualities of communication situation. *Communication, 12,* 93–105.

Biggers, T., & Rankis, O. (1983). Dominance–submissiveness as an affective response to situations and as a predictor of approach–avoidance. *Social Behavior and Personality, 11,* 61–69.

Buck, R. (1984). *The communication of emotion.* New York: Guilford Press.

Burke, A., Heuer, F., & Reisberg, D. (1992). Remembering emotional events. *Memory & Cognition, 20,* 277–290.

Chall, J. S. (2000). *The academic achievement challenge: What really works in the classroom?* New York: Guilford Press.

Chesebro, J. L. & McCroskey, J. C. (Eds.) (2002). *Communication for teachers.* Boston: Allyn & Bacon.

Christophel, D. M. (1990). The relationship among teacher immediacy behaviors, student motivation, and learning. *Communication Education, 39,* 323–340.

Cohen, H. (1994). *The history of speech communication: The emergence of a discipline, 1914–1945.* Annandale, VA: Speech Communication Association.

Cohen, G. L., Steele, C. M., Ross, L. D. (1999). The mentor's dilemma: Providing critical feedback across the racial divide. *Personality & Social Psychology Bulletin, 25,* 1302–1318.

Damasio, A. (1994). *Descartes' error: Emotion, reason, and the human brain,* New York: Avon Books.

Darwin, C. (1872). *The expression of the emotions in man and animals.* London: Murray.

Dubin, R. (1978). *Theory building.* New York: Free Press.

Dweck, C. S. (2002). Beliefs that make smart people dumb. In R. J. Sternberg (Ed.), *Why smart people can be so stupid* (pp. 24–41). New Haven, CT: Yale University Press.

Ellis, K. (2000). Perceived teacher confirmation: The development and validation of an instrument and two studies of the relationship to cognitive and affective learning. *Human Communication Research, 26,* 264–291.

Fremouv, W. J. (1984). Cognitive-behavioral therapies for modification of communication apprehension. In J. C. McCroskey & J. A. Daly (Eds.), *Avoiding communication: Shyness, reticence, and communication apprehension* (pp. 209–215). Beverly Hills, CA: Sage.

French, J. R. P., Jr., & Raven, B. (1959). The bases of social power. In D. Cartwright (Ed.), *Studies in social power.* Ann Arbor, MI: University of Michigan Press.

Frymier, A. B. (1993a). The impact of teacher immediacy on students' motivation: Is it the same for all students? *Communication Quarterly, 41,* 454–464.

Frymier, A. B. (1993b). The relationship among communication apprehension, immediacy and motivation to study. *Communication Reports, 6,* 8–17.

Frymier, A. B. (1994). A model of immediacy in the classroom. *Communication Quarterly, 42,* 133–144.

Frymier, A. B., & Houser, M. L. (2000). The teacher–student relationship as an interpersonal relationship. *Communication Education, 49,* 207–219.

Frymier, A. B., & Thompson, C. A. (1992). Perceived teacher affinity-seeking in relation to perceived teacher credibility. *Communication Education, 41,* 388–399.

Gilbert, D. T., Driver-Linn, E., & Wilson, T. D. (2002). The trouble with Vronsky: Impact bias in the forecasting of future affective states. In L. F. Barrett & P. Salovey (Eds.), *The wisdom in feeling: Psychological processes in emotional intelligence* (pp. 114–143). New York: Guilford.

Goleman, D. (1995). *Emotional intelligence: Why it can matter more than IQ.* New York: Bantam Books.

Golish, T. D., & Olson, L. N. (2000). Students' use of power in the classroom: An investigation of student power, teacher power, and teacher immediacy. *Communication Quarterly, 48,* 293–310.

Gorham, J., & Burroughs, N. F. (1989, May). *Affinity-seeking in the classroom: Behaviors perceived as indicators of affinity gained.* Paper presented at the annual meeting of the Eastern Communication Association, Ocean City, MD.

Grant, H. & Dweck, C. S. (2003). Clarifying achievement goals and their impact. *Journal of Personality & Social Psychology, 85,* 541–553.

Hartnett, R. T. (1971). Trustee power in America. In H. L. Hodgkinson & L. R. Meeth (Eds.), *Power and authority* (pp. 25–28). San Francisco: Jossey-Bass.

Hatfield, E., Cacioppo, J. T., & Rapson, R. L. (1994). *Emotional contagion.* New York: Cambridge University Press.

Houser, M. L. (2002). *Communication expectations for college instructors: Do traditional and nontraditional students want the same things?* Unpublished doctoral dissertation, University of Tennessee, Knoxville.

Hurt, H. T., Scott, M.D., & McCroskey, J. C. (1978). *Communication in the classroom.* Reading, MA: Addison-Wesley.

Kearney, P., Plax, T. G., Richmond, V. P., & McCroskey, J. C. (1985). Power in the classroom III: Teacher communication techniques and messages. *Communication Education, 34,* 19–28.

Kelley, D. H., & Gorham, J. (1988). Effects of immediacy on recall of information. *Communication Education, 37,* 198–207.

Kelly, L. (1997). Skills training as a treatment for communication problems. In J. A. Daly, J. C. McCroskey, J. Ayres, T. Hopf, & D. M. Ayres (Eds.), *Avoiding communication: Shyness, reticence, and communication apprehension* (2nd ed.) (pp. 331–366). Cresskill, NJ: Hampton Press.

Kelly, L., & Keaten, J. A. (2000). Treating communication anxiety: Implications of the communibiological paradigm. *Communication Education, 49,* 45–57.
Kelman, H. C. (1958). Compliance, identification, and internalization: Three processes of attitude change. *Journal of Conflict Resolution, 2,* 51–60.
Kelman, H. C. (1961). Processes of opinion change. *Public Opinion Quarterly, 25,* 57–78.
Kelman, H. C. (1974). Further thoughts on the processes of compliance, identification, and internalization. In J. T. Tedeschi (Ed.), *Perspectives on social power* (pp. 125–171). Chicago: Aldine.
Kerlinger, F. N. (1986). *Foundations of behavioral research* (3rd ed.). New York: Holt, Rinehart and Winston.
Krathwohl, D. R., Bloom, B. S., & Masia B. B. (1964). *Taxonomy of educational objectives, Handbook II: Affective domain.* New York: McKay.
LeDoux, J. (1996). *The emotional brain: The mysterious underpinnings of emotional life.* New York: Touchstone.
Matthews, A., & Macleod, C. (1994). Cognitive approaches to emotion. *Annual Review of Psychology, 45,* 25–50.
McCroskey, J. C. (1972). The implementation of a large-scale program of systematic desensitization for communication apprehension. *Speech Teacher, 21,* 255–264.
McCroskey, J. C. (1977). Oral communication apprehension: A summary of recent theory and research. *Human Communication Research, 4,* 78–96.
McCroskey, J. C. (1978). Validity of the PRCA as an index of oral communication apprehension. *Communication Monographs, 45,* 192–203.
McCroskey, J. C. (1998). *An introduction to communication in the classroom.* Acton, MA: Tapestry Press.
McCroskey, J. C., & Beatty, M. J. (1998). Communication apprehension. In J. C. McCroskey, J. A. Daly, M. M. Martin, & M. J. Beatty (Eds.), *Communication and personality: Trait perspectives* (pp. 215–232). Cresskill, NJ: Hampton Press.
McCroskey, J. C., & Beatty, M. J. (2000). The communibiological perspective: Implications for communication in instruction. *Communication Education, 49,* 1–6.
McCroskey, J. C., & McCroskey, L. L. (1986). The affinity-seeking of classroom teachers. *Communication Research Reports, 3,* 158–167.
McCroskey, J. C., & Richmond, V. P. (1992). Increasing teacher influence through immediacy. In V. P. Richmond & J. C. McCroskey (Eds.), *Power in the classroom: Communication, control, and concern* (pp. 101–119). Hillsdale, NJ: Lawrence Erlbaum.
McCroskey, L. L., & McCroskey, J. C. (2002). Willingness to communicate and communication apprehension in the classroom. In J. L. Chesebro & J. C. McCroskey (Eds.), *Communication for teachers* (pp. 19–34). Boston: Allyn & Bacon.
Mead, G. H. (1934). *Mind, self, and society.* Chicago: University of Chicago Press.
Mehrabian, A. (1971). *Silent messages.* Belmont, CA: Wadsworth.
Mehrabian, A. (1968). Inference of attitudes from the posture, orientation, and distance of a communicator. *Journal of Consulting and Clinical Psychology, 32,* 296–308.
Mehrabian, A. (1981), *Silent messages: Implicit communication of emotions and attitudes.* Belmont, CA: Wadsworth.
Meichenbaum, D. (1976). Toward a cognitive theory of self-control. In G. Schwartz & D. Shapiro (Eds.), *Consciousness and self-regulation: Advances in research* (pp. 113–132). New York: Plenum.
Milton, O., Pollio, H. R., & Eison, J. A. (1986). *Making sense of grades: Why the grading system does not work and what can be done about it.* San Francisco: Jossey-Bass.
Mottet, T. P., & Beebe, S. A. (2002). Relationships between teacher nonverbal immediacy, student emotional response, and perceived student learning. *Communication Research Reports, 19,* 77–88.
Mottet, T. P., Beebe, S. A., Raffeld, P. C., & Paulsel, M. L. (2004). The effects of student verbal and nonverbal responsiveness on teachers' liking of students and willingness to comply with student requests. *Communication Quarterly, 52,* 27–38.
Mottet, T. P., Beebe, S. A., Raffeld, P. C., & Paulsel, M.. L. (2005). The effects of student responsiveness on teachers granting power to students and essay evaluation. *Communication Quarterly, 53.*

Mottet, T. P., & Richmond, V. P. (1998). New is not necessarily better: A re-examination of affective learning measurement. *Communication Research Reports, 15,* 370–378.

Planalp, S. (1999). *Communicating emotion: Social, moral, and cultural processes.* New York: Cambridge University Press.

Plax, T. G., & Kearney, P. (1992). Teacher power in the classroom: Defining and advancing a program of research. In V. P. Richmond & J. C. McCroskey (Eds.), *Power in the classroom: Communication, control, and concern* (pp. 67–84). Hillsdale, NJ: Lawrence Erlbaum.

Reisberg, D., & Heuer, F. (1995). Emotion's multiple effects on memory. In J. L. McGaugh, N. Weinberger, & G. Lynch (Eds.), *Brain and memory: Modulation and mediation on neuroplasticity* (pp. 84–92). New York: Oxford University Press.

Revelle, W., & Loftus, D. A. (1992). The implications of arousal effects for the study of affect and memory. In S. A. Christianson (Ed.), *Handbook of emotion and memory.* Hillsdale, NJ: Lawrence Erlbaum.

Richmond, V. P. (1990). Communication in the classroom: Power and motivation. *Communication Education, 39,* 181–195.

Richmond, V. P., Martin, M. M., & Cox, B. (1997). A bibliography of related practice, theory, and research. In J. A. Daly, J. C. McCroskey, J. Ayres, T. Hopf, & D. M. Ayres (Eds.) *Avoiding communication: Shyness, reticence, and communication apprehension,* 2nd ed. (pp. 401–488) Cresskill, NJ: Hampton Press.

Richmond, V. P., McCroskey, J. C., Davis, L. M., & Koontz, K. A. (1980). Perceived power as a mediator of management communication style and employee satisfaction: A preliminary investigation. *Communication Quarterly, 28,* 37–46.

Roach, K. D. (1994). Temporal patterns and effects of perceived instructor compliance-gaining use. *Communication Education, 43,* 236–245.

Rodriguez, J. I., Plax, T. G., & Kearney, P. (1996). Clarifying the relationship between teacher nonverbal immediacy and student cognitive learning: Affective learning as the central causal mediator. *Communication Education, 45,* 293–305.

Ross, J. A. (1998). Antecedents and consequences of teacher efficacy, In J. Brophy (Ed.), *Advances in research on teaching* (Vol. 7, pp. 49–74). Greenwich, CT: JAI Press.

Russell, J. A., & Barrett, L. F. (1999). Core affect, prototypical emotional episodes, and other things called emotion: Dissecting the elephant. *Journal of Personality and Social Psychology, 76,* 805–819.

Rusting, C. L. (1999). Interactive effects of personality and mood on emotion-congruent memory and judgment. *Journal of Personality and Social Psychology, 77,* 1073–1086.

Scott, M. D., & Wheeless, L. R. (1977). Instructional communication theory and research: An overview. In B. D. Rubin (Ed.), *Communication yearbook 1* (pp. 495–511). New Brunswick, NJ: Transaction.

Shann, M. H. (1998). Professional commitment and satisfaction among teachers in urban middle schools. *Journal of Educational Research, 92,* 67–73.

Shaw, M. E., & Costanzo, P. R. (1970). *Theories of social psychology.* New York: McGraw-Hill.

Spencer, S. J., Steele, C. M., Quinn, D. M. (2002). Stereotype threat and women's math performance. In A. E. Hunter & C. Forden (Eds.), *Readings in the psychology of gender: Exploring our differences and commonalities* (pp. 54–68). Boston: Allyn & Bacon.

Staton-Spicer, A. Q., & Wulff, D. H. (1984). Research in communication and instruction: Categorization and synthesis. *Communication Education, 33,* 377–391.

Steele, C. M. (1999). Thin ice: "Stereotype threat" and black college students. *The Atlantic Monthly, 284,* 44–47, 50–54.

Student, K. R. (1968). Supervisory influence on work-group performance. *Journal of Applied Psychology, 52,* 188–194.

Vinson, L., & Biggers, J. T. (1993). Emotional Response as a predictor of compliance-gaining message selection. *Southern Communication Journal,* 192–206.

Waldeck, J. H., Kearney, P., & Plax, T. G. (2001). Instructional and developmental communication theory and research in the 1990s: Extending the agenda for the 21st century. In W. B. Gudykunst (Ed.), *Communication yearbook 24* (pp. 206–229). Thousand Oaks, CA: Sage.

Wanzer, M. B., & Frymier, A. B. (1999). The relationship between student perceptions of instructor humor and students' reports of learning. *Communication Education, 48,* 48–62.

Watzlawick, P., Bavelas, J. B., & Jackson, D. D. (1967). *Pragmatics of human communication.* New York: W.W. Norton.

Whetten, D. A. (1989). What constitutes a theoretical contribution? *Academy of Management Review, 14,* 490–495.

Wooten, A. G., & McCroskey, J. C. (1996). Student trust of teacher as a function of socio-communicative style of teacher and socio-communicative orientation of student. *Communication Research Reports, 13,* 94–100.

Zimbardo, P. G., Ebbesen, E. B., & Maslach, C. (1977). *Influencing attitudes and changing behavior* (2nd ed.). Reading, MA: Addison-Wesley.

13

Assessing Instructional Communication

Timothy P. Mottet
Texas State University–San Marcos

Virginia P. Richmond
West Virginia University

James C. McCroskey
West Virginia University

Introduction

Although instructional assessment has become a common practice for some educational leaders, it remains a mystery to others for at least two reasons. First, educational leaders disagree as to what constitutes effectiveness (Shulman, 1986).

Many educational leaders do not know or cannot agree on what teaching effectiveness looks and sounds like. In short, what behaviors comprise teaching effectiveness? Second, many educational leaders are not aware of the vast array of assessment instruments that are available to measure teaching effectiveness.

The purpose of this chapter is to take the mystery out of instructional assessment by identifying key principles and practices of effective instructional communication. This chapter is directed to those interested in careers as teachers and trainers, as well as educational administrators and instructional leaders who are responsible for quality teaching and learning outcomes, such as directors of corporate training and development, teaching and learning centers, corporate education, and continuing education programs.

There are several reasons why this chapter remains important to instructional leaders. First, instructional leaders are responsible for modeling effective instructional communication behaviors (McCroskey & Richmond, 1991). If they want others to use effective instructional communication in the classroom, then they, too, should be effective teachers and trainers. In short, instructional leaders must be able to "walk the talk." They must be able to demonstrate the communication behaviors and practices they want members of their teaching and training teams to use on the front line.

Second, instructional leaders are responsible for developing effective teachers and trainers (McCroskey & Richmond, 1991). Instructional leaders must be able to coach and develop teachers and trainers by helping them modify or change ineffective instructional practices. Instructional leaders must be prepared to explain why some instructional communication behaviors and practices are more effective than others.

Third, instructional leaders are responsible for ensuring that quality learning outcomes occur (McCroskey & Richmond, 1991). Instructional leaders are typically accountable for guaranteeing that their organizations and institutions are getting a return on their instructional investments (Phillips, 1997). To teach and train well, organizations and institutions invest large sums of money in teachers/trainers, equipment, and facilities to guarantee quality instruction. Instructional leaders are responsible for ensuring that the investments yield a return that is considered valuable and competitive. Superintendents are responsible for ensuring the taxpayers' investments are put to good use by educating children and young adults who are able to function in a complex world. Similarly, directors of training and development in service companies are responsible for ensuring that customer service representatives can manage customer queries in a timely and efficient manner.

This chapter examines strategies that instructional leaders may want to use to enhance instructional assessment. We begin by briefly reviewing the rhetorical and relational perspectives that have been used to structure this handbook. Next, we identify some of the instructional communication practices or behaviors that reflect these perspectives, along with suggested assessment instruments that can be used to evaluate the behaviors. Finally, we conclude the chapter with caveats for instructors who remain effective in the classroom.

Using the Rhetorical and Relational Perspectives

Mottet and Beebe argued in Chapter 1 that effective instructional communication is *both* a rhetorical and a relational communication process. Depending on the instructor's learning objectives, rhetorical forms of communication may be most appropriate for some learning objectives, while at other times relational forms of communication may be most appropriate. These communication processes are not polar opposites; they simply reflect different strategies for achieving a common goal—to facilitate student learning.

From a rhetorical communication perspective, the instructional communication is teacher-directed. Instructors use verbal and nonverbal messages with the intention of influencing or persuading students. Teachers persuade or influence student learning through the message. From a relational perspective, the communication process is more collaborative. Instructors and students mutually cocreate and use verbal and nonverbal messages to influence learning outcomes; instructors and students mutually influence each other through the relationship.

As a starting point, instructional leaders are encouraged to structure their assessment plan so that it reflects both the rhetorical and relational perspectives anchored in these two rich theoretical and research traditions. We next describe ways to identify and measure instructional communication practices.

Evaluating Instructional Communication Practices

There is evidence that instructional leaders typically rely on poorly developed evaluation instruments to assess instructional effectiveness (Rubin, 1999; Shulman, 1986; Vangelisti, 1999). Unfortunately these instruments, which often lack adequate validity and reliability, are used to determine instructors' salary increases and promotions. Rather than relying on inadequate measures, we encourage instructional leaders to develop an evaluation plan that includes instructional communication research measures that are both valid and reliable.

There are two additional reasons why we advocate using instructional communication research measures to evaluate and assess instruction. First, instructional leaders and practitioners can easily use the items from the measures to address specific communication deficiencies. Many of the recommended instructional communication instruments are considered low-inference measures, meaning that they are comprised of multiple items that reflect discrete communication behaviors. Rather than relying on a single-item measure or on a global perception of the communication behavior, low-inference measures assist instructional leaders, as well as teachers and trainers, by identifying specific behaviors that may need enhancing. Second, with slight modification, the measures can be used as both a self-report assessment and as an other-report assessment. In some situations, it may be beneficial to see how the instructor's self-report of instructional communication behaviors differ

FIGURE 13.1 ***Instructional Communication Perspectives, Instructor Practices, Instructional Outcomes, and Assessment Instruments.***

Perspectives	Instructor Practices	Instructional Outcomes
Rhetorical	Teacher Clarity (Fig 13.2) (Chesebro & McCroskey, 1998) Content Relevance Behaviors (Fig 13.3) (Frymier & Shulman, 1995) Measure of Compliance-Gaining Messages (Fig 13. 4) (Kearney, Plax, Richmond, & McCroskey, 1985) Teacher Credibility (Fig 13. 5) (McCroskey & Teven, 1999)	**Student Outcomes** Affective Learning (Fig 13.9) (McCroskey, 1994) Cognitive Learning (Fig 13. 10) (Richmond, Gorham, & McCroskey, 1987) Behavioral Learning (Morreale, 1994) (Spitzberg, 1995) (Beebe & Barge, 2003) **Teacher Outcomes**
Relational	Nonverbal Immediacy Behaviors (Fig 13. 6) (Richmond, McCroskey, & Johnson, 2003) Affinity-Seeking Behaviors (Fig 13. 7) (Bell & Daly, 1984) (McCroskey & McCroskey, 1986) Instructor Misbehaviors (Fig 13. 8) (Kearney, Plax, Hays, & Ivey, 1991)	Teacher Self-Efficacy (Figs 13.11, 13.12) (Gibson & Dembo, 1984) (Mottet, Beebe, Raffeld, & Medlock, 2004) Teacher Satisfaction (Figs 13.13, 13.14) (Plax, Kearney & Downs, 1986) (Mottet, Beebe, Raffeld, & Medlock, 2004) Teacher Motivation (Fig 13.15) (Baringer & McCroskey, 2000)

from students' reports of the same behavior. In addition to having students complete the other-report assessment instruments, instructional leaders or other experts can use the measure to assess the instructor's use of instructional communication.

What follows are selected instruments that reflect both the rhetorical and relational perspectives of instructional communication. Figure 13.1 organizes the instruments by perspectives and instructor communication practices. This figure also features a list of assessment instruments that can be used to measure instructional outcomes for both students and teachers.

Assessing Rhetorical Communication Behaviors

Instructor Clarity Behaviors. Instructor clarity has been defined as "the process by which an instructor is able to effectively stimulate the desired meaning of course content and processes in the minds of students through the use of appropriately structured verbal and nonverbal messages" (Chesebro & McCroskey, 1998, p. 448). The Teacher Clarity Short Inventory (TCSI), developed by Chesebro & McCroskey (1998), contains 10 items. A review of this assessment instrument is available in Chapter 5. A copy of the inventory is featured in Figure 13.2.

FIGURE 13.2 ***Teacher Clarity Short Inventory.***

Instructions: Please indicate your level of agreement with the following items as they refer to your feelings towards this course. Please respond to the following sentences on a 1 to 7 scale, with 1 representing Completely Disagree and 7 representing Completely Agree.

Completely Disagree 1 2 3 4 5 6 7 Completely Agree

___ My teacher clearly defines major concepts.
___ My teacher's answers to student questions are unclear.*
___ In general, I understand the teacher.
___ Projects assigned for the class have unclear guidelines.*
___ My teacher's objectives for the course are clear.
___ My teacher is straightforward in his lecture.
___ My teacher is not clear when defining guidelines for out-of-class assignments.*
___ My teacher uses clear and relevant examples.
___ In general, I would say that my teacher's classroom communication is unclear.*
___ My teacher is explicit in his instruction.

* Reverse code for scoring

From "The Development of the Teacher Clarity Short Inventory (TCSI) to Measure Clear Teaching in the Classroom," by J. L. Chesebro and J. C. McCroskey, 1998, *Communication Research Reports, 15,* 262–266. Republished with permission by the Eastern Communication Association.

Instructor Content Relevance Behaviors. Content relevance refers to students' perceptions of whether instructional course content satisfies students' personal needs, personal goals, and/or career goals (Keller, 1983). Frymier and Shulman (1995) developed a 12-item scale to measure students' reports of their teachers' use of relevance strategies in the classroom. This instrument is reviewed in Chapter 5 and a copy of the measure is featured in Figure 13.3.

FIGURE 13.3 ***Content Relevance Scale.***

Instructions: Read each statement and use the following scale to indicate how frequently your teacher performs each of the behaviors. There are no right or wrong answers.

Never = 0 Rarely = 1 Occasionally = 2 Often = 3 Very Often = 4

___ Uses examples to make the content relevant to me.
___ Provides explanations that make the content relevant to me.
___ Uses exercises or explanations that demonstrate the importance of the content.
___ Explicitly states how the material relates to my career goals or my life in general.
___ Links content to other areas of content.
___ Asks me to apply content to my own interests.
___ Gives assignments that involve the application of the content to my career interests.
___ Helps me to understand the importance of the content.
___ Uses own experiences to introduce or demonstrate a concept.
___ Uses student experiences to demonstrate or introduce a concept.
___ Uses discussion to help me understand the relevance of a topic.
___ Uses current events to apply a topic.

From "'What's In It for Me?': Increasing Content Relevance to Enhance Students' Motivation," by A. B. Frymier and G. M. Shulman, 1995, *Communication Education, 44,* 40–50. Republished with permission by *Communication Education* and Taylor & Francis Ltd. http://www.tandf.co.uk/journals.

Instructor Compliance-Gaining Messages. The behavioral alteration technique and message (BAT/BAM) typology, reviewed in Chapter 6 and developed and revised by Kearney, Plax, Richmond, and McCroskey (1985), includes a comprehensive list of 22 compliance-gaining techniques and messages that instructors use in their attempts to influence students. This typology reflects French and Raven's (1959) five bases of relational power. A copy of this instrument is featured in Figure 13.4.

FIGURE 13.4 *Measure of Compliance-Gaining Messages.*

Instructions: As a teacher, you will often try to get your students to do things that they may not want to do. Below you'll find a series of statements that a teacher might use in her/his efforts to encourage students to change their behaviors. These statements are grouped into 22 separate categories. Please read all the statements in each category. Then, indicate how likely you would be to use statements of that type for each of the 22 categories to influence your own students. Use a 1–7 scale, with 7 = extremely likely and 1 = extremely unlikely. Respond quickly.

___ 1. *Immediate Reward from Behavior:* You will enjoy it. It will make you happy. Because it is fun. You will find it rewarding/interesting. It is a good experience.

___ 2. *Deferred Reward from Behavior:* It will help you later on in life. It will prepare you for getting a job (or going to graduate school). It will prepare you for achievement tests (or the final exam). It will help you with upcoming assignments.

___ 3. *Reward from Teacher:* I will give you a reward if you do. I will make it beneficial to you. I will give you a good grade (or extra credit) if you do. I will make you my special assistant.

___ 4. *Reward from Others:* Others will respect you if you do. Others will be proud of you. Your friends will like you. Your parents will be pleased.

___ 5. *Self-Esteem:* You will feel good about yourself if you do. You are the best person to do it. You always do such a good job.

___ 6. *Punishment from Behavior:* You will lose if you don't. You will be unhappy if you don't. You will be hurt if you don't. It's your loss. You'll feel bad if you don't.

___ 7. *Punishment from Teacher:* I will punish you if you don't. I will make it miserable for you. I'll give you an "F" if you don't. If you don't do it NOW, it will be homework tonight.

___ 8. *Punishment from Others:* No one will like you. Your friends will make fun of you. Your parents will punish you if you don't. Your classmates will reject you.

___ 9. *Guilt:* If you don't, others will be hurt. You'll make others unhappy if you don't. Your parents will feel bad if you don't. Others will be punished if you don't.

___ 10. *Teacher-Student Relationship: Positive:* I will like you better if you do. I will respect you. I will think more highly of you. I will appreciate you more if you do. I will be proud of you.

___ 11. *Teacher-Student Relationship: Negative:* I will dislike you if you don't. I will lose respect for you if you don't. I will think less of you if you don't. I won't be proud of you. I'll be disappointed in you.

___ 12. *Legitimate-Higher Authority:* Do it—I'm just telling you what I was told. It is a rule, I have to do it and so do you. It's a school policy.

___ 13. *Legitimate-Teacher Authority:* Because I told you to. You don't have a choice. You're here to work! I'm the teacher, you're the student. I'm in charge, not you. Don't ask, just do it.

___ 14. *Personal [Student] Responsibility:* It is your obligation. It's your turn. Everyone has to do his/her share. It's your job. Everyone has to pull her/his own weight.

FIGURE 13.4 ***(Continued)***

___ 15. *Responsibility to Class:* Your group needs it done. The class depends on you. All your friends are counting on you. Don't let your group down. You'll ruin it for the rest of the class.

___ 16. *Normative Rules:* The majority rules. All of your friends are doing it. Everyone else has to do it. The rest of the class is doing it. It's part of growing up.

___ 17. *Debt:* You owe me one. Pay your debt. You promised to do it. I did it the last time. You said you'd try this time.

___ 18. *Altruism:* If you do this, it will help others. Others will benefit if you do. It will make others happy if you do. I'm not asking you to do it for yourself; do it for the good of the class.

___ 19. *Peer Modeling:* Your friends do it. Classmates you respect do it. The friends you admire do it. Other students you like do it. All your friends are doing it.

___ 20. *Teacher Modeling:* This is the way I always do it. When I was your age, I did it. People who are like me do it. I had to do this when I was in school. Teachers you respect do it.

___ 21. *Expert Teacher:* From my experience, it is a good idea. From what I have learned, it is what you should do. This has always worked for me. Trust me—I know what I'm doing. I had to do this before I became a teacher.

___ 22. *Teacher Feedback:* Because I need to know how well you understand this. To see how well I've taught you. To see how well you can do it. It will help me know your problem areas.

Note: Category labels (in *italics*) should be omitted from the actual questionnaire during administration.

From "Power In the Classroom III: Teacher Communication Techniques and Messages," by P. Kearney, T. G. Plax, V. P. Richmond, and J. C. McCroskey, 1985, *Communication Education, 31,* 19–28. Republished with permission by *Communication Education* and Taylor & Francis Ltd. http://www.tandf.co.uk/journals.

Instructor Credibility. Instructor credibility is viewed as "the attitude of a receiver that references the degree to which a source is seen to be believable" (McCroskey, 1998, p. 80) and was reviewed in Chapter 4. Based on Aristotle's conceptualization of ethos (i.e., competence, trustworthiness, goodwill), competence refers to the degree to which a teacher is perceived by students to be knowledgeable about a given subject matter; trustworthiness or character refers to the degree to which a teacher is trusted by students; and goodwill refers to the degree to which a teacher is perceived to be caring (McCroskey, 1992; Teven & McCroskey, 1997). The perceived source credibility measure developed by McCroskey and Teven (1999) includes 18 items and assesses the three dimensions of source credibility: competence, character, and caring. A copy of the instrument is featured in Figure 13.5.

Assessing Relational Communication Behaviors

Instructor Nonverbal Immediacy Behaviors. Nonverbal immediacy behaviors are those nonlinguistic behaviors that enhance relational development and perceptions of physical and psychological closeness. As discussed in Chapter 8,

FIGURE 13.5 ***Teacher Credibility.***

Instructions: Please indicate your impression of your teacher by circling the appropriate number bet ween the pairs of adjectives below. The closer the number is to an adjective, the more certain you are of your evaluation.

Competence								
Intelligent	1	2	3	4	5	6	7	Unintelligent*
Untrained	1	2	3	4	5	6	7	Trained
Inexpert	1	2	3	4	5	6	7	Expert
Informed	1	2	3	4	5	6	7	Uninformed*
Incompetent	1	2	3	4	5	6	7	Competent
Bright	1	2	3	4	5	6	7	Stupid*
Character								
Honest	1	2	3	4	5	6	7	Dishonest*
Untrustworthy	1	2	3	4	5	6	7	Trustworthy
Honorable	1	2	3	4	5	6	7	Dishonorable*
Moral	1	2	3	4	5	6	7	Immoral*
Unethical	1	2	3	4	5	6	7	Ethical
Phony	1	2	3	4	5	6	7	Genuine
Caring								
Cares about me	1	2	3	4	5	6	7	Doesn't care about me*
Has my interests at heart	1	2	3	4	5	6	7	Doesn't have my interests at heart*
Self-centered	1	2	3	4	5	6	7	Not self-centered
Concerned with me	1	2	3	4	5	6	7	Unconcerned with me*
Insensitive	1	2	3	4	5	6	7	Sensitive
Understanding	1	2	3	4	5	6	7	Not understanding*

* Reverse code for scoring

Note: Category labels (in italics) should be omitted from the actual questionnaire during administration.

From "Goodwill: A Reexamination of the Construct and Its Measurement," by J. C. McCroskey and J. J. Teven, 1999, *Communication Monographs, 66,* 90–103. Republished with permission by *Communication Monographs* and Taylor & Francis Ltd. http://www.tandf.co.uk/journals.

nonverbal immediacy behaviors include forward body leans, head nods, eye contact, expressive gestures, and smiling. The nonverbal immediacy scale (NIS), revised by Richmond, McCroskey, and Johnson (2003), contains 26 items. A copy of the instrument is featured in Figure 13.6.

Instructor Affinity-Seeking Behaviors. Extending the seminal work of McCroskey and Wheeless (1976), Bell and Daly (1984) defined affinity-seeking as "the active social communicative process by which individuals attempt to get others to like and feel positive toward them" (p. 91). Bell and Daly identified 25 mutually exclusive categories of affinity-seeking behaviors. This instrument is reviewed in Chapter 9, and a copy of the measure is featured in Figure 13.7.

FIGURE 13.6 ***Nonverbal Immediacy Scale–Observer Report (NIS-O).***

Instructions: The following statements describe the ways some people behave while talking with or to others. Please indicate in the space at the left of each item, the degree to which you believe the statement applies to (fill in the target person's name or description). Please use the following 5-point scale:

1 = Never; 2 = Rarely; 3 = Occasionally; 4 = Often; 5 = Very Often

___ 1. The teacher uses her/his hands and arms to gesture while talking to people.
___ 2. The teacher touches others on the shoulder or arm while talking to them.
___ 3. The teacher uses a monotone or dull voice while talking to people.
___ 4. The teacher looks over or away from others while talking to them.
___ 5. The teacher moves away from people when they touch him/her while talking.
___ 6. The teacher has a relaxed body position when he/she talks to people.
___ 7. The teacher frowns while talking to people.
___ 8. The teacher avoids eye contact while talking to people.
___ 9. The teacher has a tense body position while talking to people.
___ 10. The teacher sits close or stands close to people while talking with them.
___ 11. The teacher's voice is monotonous or dull when he/she talks to people.
___ 12. The teacher uses a variety of vocal expressions when he/she talks to people.
___ 13. The teacher gestures when he/she talks to people.
___ 14. The teacher is animated when he/she talk to people.
___ 15. The teacher has a bland facial expression when he/she talks to people.
___ 16. The teacher moves closer to people when he/she talks to them.
___ 17. The teacher looks directly at people while talking to them.
___ 18. The teacher is stiff when he/she talks to people.
___ 19. The teacher has a lot of vocal variety when he/she talks to people.
___ 20. The teacher avoids gesturing while he/she is talking to people.
___ 21. The teacher leans toward people when he/she talks to them.
___ 22. The teacher maintains eye contact with people when he/she talks to them.
___ 23. The teacher tries not to sit or stand close to people when he/she talks with them.
___ 24. The teacher leans away from people when he/she talks to them.
___ 25. The teacher smiles when he/she talks to people.
___ 26. The teacher avoids touching people when he/she talks to them.

Scoring:
Step 1. Start with a score of 78. Add the scores from the following items:
1, 2, 6, 10, 12, 13, 14, 16, 17, 19, 21, 22, and 25.
Step 2. Add the scores from the following items:
3, 4, 5, 7, 8, 9, 11, 15, 18, 20, 23, 24, and 26.
Total Score = Step 1 minus Step 2.

Norms:

Females	Mean = 96.7	S.D. = 16.1	High = >112	Low = <81
Males	Mean = 91.6	S.D. = 15.0	High = >106	Low = <77
Combined	Mean = 94.2	S.D. = 15.6	High = >109	Low = <79

Authors Note:
This is the most up-to-date measure of nonverbal immediacy as an other- or observer-report. Earlier measures have had problematic alpha reliability estimates. This instrument may be used for any target person (most earlier measures were designed only for observations of teachers). Alpha reliability estimates around .90 should be expected. This measure also has more face validity than previous instruments because it has more and more diverse items. Its predictive validity is also excellent.

(*Continued*)

FIGURE 13.6 (*Continued*)

When using this instrument it is important to recognize that the difference in these observer-reports between females and males is not statistically different. Hence, it is unnecessary to employ biological sex of the person completing the instrument in data analyses involving this instrument. It is recommended that the COMBINED norms be employed in interpreting the results employing this instrument. However, sex differences of the target persons on whom the instrument is completed may be meaningful. This possibility has not been explored in the research to date (Richmond, McCroskey, & Johnson, 2003).

To use the assessment instrument as a self-report (Nonverbal Immediacy Scale-Self Report, NIS-S), use the following instructions:

The following statements describe the ways some people behave while talking with or to others. Please indicate in the space at the left of each item, the degree to which you believe the statement applies TO YOU. Please use the following 5-point scale: 1 = Never; 2 = Rarely; 3 = Occasionally; 4 = Often; 5 = Very Often

Scoring: Remains the same as the Nonverbal Immediacy Scale–Other Report (NIS-O).

Norms:

Females	Mean = 102.0	S.D. = 10.9	High = >112	Low = <92
Males	Mean = 93.8	S.D. = 10.8	High = >104	Low = <83

From "Development of the Nonverbal Immediacy Scale (NIS): Measures of Self- and Other-Perceived Nonverbal Immediacy, by V. P. Richmond, J. C. McCroskey, and A. Johnson, 2003, *Communication Quarterly, 51,* 504–517. Republished with permission by the Eastern Communication Association.

Instructor Misbehaviors. Teacher misbehaviors are those behaviors identified by students that irritate, demotivate, or substantially distract them from learning (Kearney, Plax, Hays, & Ivey, 1991). Teacher misbehaviors reflect student perceptions of teacher actions that interfere with learning, even if those teacher behaviors are unintentional or reflect personal attributes, such as a teacher's dialect or accent. Kearney, Plax, Hays, and Ivey (1991) identified a typology of 28 teacher misbehaviors, which collapse into three factors of teacher misbehaviors: incompetence, offensiveness, and indolence. According to Kearney, Plax, and Allen (2002), *incompetent* teachers engage in a cluster of misbehaviors that indicate to students that they don't care about either the course or the student. *Offensive* teachers are characterized as mean, cruel, and ugly. *Indolent* teachers are characterized as lazy and absent-minded. This instrument is reviewed in Chapter 10 and a copy of the typology is included in Figure 13.8.

Evaluating Instructional Communication Outcomes

With the increasing pressure for accountability at all levels of education (McNeil, 2000; Sacks, 2001), the rhetorical and relational communication practices or *process* variables reviewed above have taken a back seat to the student learning outcomes or *product* variables that will be reviewed in this section. We recommend that instructional communication assessment plans focus on *both* process (instructional communication practices) and product (instructional communication outcome) variables

FIGURE 13.7 ***Measure of Affinity-Seeking Behaviors.***

Instructions: Read each strategy description and then indicate how often you have used the strategy by using the following scale:

1 = Never; 2 = Rarely; 3 = Occasionally; 4 = Often; 5 = Very Often

___ 1. *Altruism:* The teacher attempting to get a student to like him/her tries to be of help and assistance to the student in whatever he/she is currently doing. For example, the person holds the door for the student, assists him/her with his studies, helps him/her get the needed materials for assignments, and helps run errands for the student. The teacher also gives advice when it is requested.

___ 2. *Assume Control.* The teacher attempting to get a student to like him/her presents self as a leader, a person who has control over his/her classroom. For example, he/she directs the conversations held by students, takes charge of the classroom activities the two engage in, and mentions examples of where he/she has taken charge or served as a leader in the past.

___ 3. *Assume Equality.* The teacher attempting to get a student to like him/her presents self as an equal of the other person. For example, he/she avoids appearing superior or snobbish, and does not play "one-upmanship" games.

___ 4. *Comfortable Self.* The teacher attempting to get a student to like him/her acts comfortable in the setting the two find themselves, comfortable with him/herself, and comfortable with the student. He/she is relaxed, at ease, casual, and content. Distractions and disturbances in the environment are ignored. The teacher tries to look as if he/ she is having a good time, even if he/she is not. The teacher gives the impression that "nothing bothers him/ her."

___ 5. *Concede Control.* The teacher attempting to get a student to like him/her allows the student to control the relationship and situations surrounding the two. For example, he/she lets the student take charge of conversations and so on. The teacher attempting to be liked also lets the student influence his/her actions by not acting dominant.

___ 6. *Conversational Rule-Keeping.* The teacher attempting to get a student to like him/her follows closely the culture's rules for how people socialize with others by demonstrating cooperation, friendliness, and politeness. The teacher works hard at giving relevant answers to questions, saying the right thing, acting interested and involved in conversation, and adapting his/her messages to the particular student or situation. He/she avoids changing the topic too soon, interrupting the student, dominating classroom discussions, and making excessive self-references. The teacher using this strategy tries to avoid topics that are not of interest to his/her students.

___ 7. *Dynamism.* The teacher attempting to get a student to like him/her presents him/herself as a dynamic, active, and enthusiastic person. For example, he/she acts physically animated and very lively while talking with the student, varies intonation and other vocal characteristics, and is outgoing and extroverted with the students.

___ 8. *Elicit Other's Disclosure.* The teacher attempting to get a student to like him/ her encourages the student to talk by asking questions and reinforcing the student for talking. For example, the teacher inquires about the student's interests, feelings, opinion, views, and so on. He/she responds as if these are important and interesting, and continues to ask more questions of the student.

___ 9. *Facilitate Enjoyment.* The teacher attempting to get a student to like him/her seeks to make the situations in which the two are involved very enjoyable experiences. The teacher does things the students will enjoy, is entertaining, tells jokes and interesting stories, talks about interesting topics, says funny things, and tries to make the classroom conducive to enjoyment. The teacher attempting to get a student to like him/her includes the student in his/her social activities and groups of friends. He/she introduces the student to his/her friends, and makes the student feel like "one of the group."

(*Continued*)

FIGURE 13.7 ***(Continued)***

___ 10. *Inclusion of Others.* The teacher attempting to get a student to like him/her includes the student in her/his social activities and group of friends. They introduce the students to her/his friends, and make the student feel like "one of the group."

___ 11. *Influence Perceptions of Closeness.* The teacher attempting to get a student to like him/her engages in behaviors that lead the student to perceive the relationship as being closer and more established than it has actually been. For example, she/he uses nicknames of the students, talks about "we", rather than "I" or "you". He/she also discusses any prior activities that included the student.

___ 12. *Listening.* The teacher attempting to get a student to like him/her pays close attention to what the student says, listening very actively. They focus attention solely on the student, paying strict attention to what is said. Moreover, the teacher attempting to be liked demonstrates that he/she listens by being responsive to the student's ideas, asking for clarification of ambiguities, being open-minded, and remembering things the student says.

___ 13. *Nonverbal Immediacy.* The teacher attempting to get a student to like him/her signals interest and liking through various nonverbal cues. For example, the teacher frequently makes eye contact, stands or sits close to the student, smiles, leans toward the student, uses frequent head nods, and directs much gaze toward the student. All of the above indicate the teacher is very much interested in the student and what he/she has to say.

___ 14. *Openness.* The teacher attempting to get a student to like him/her is open. He/she discloses information about his/her background, interests, and views. He/she may even disclose very personal information about his/her insecurities, weaknesses, and fears to make the student feel special and trusted (e.g., "Just between you and me").

___ 15. *Optimism.* The teacher attempting to get a student to like her/him presents self as a positive person—an optimist—so that he/she will appear to be a person who is pleasant to be around. He/she acts in a "happy-go-lucky" manner, is cheerful, and looks on the positive side of things. He/she avoids complaining about things, talking about depressing topics, and being critical of self and others.

___ 16. *Personal Autonomy.* The teacher attempting to get a student to like him/her presents self as an independent, free-thinking person—the kind of person who stands on her/his own, speaks her/his mind regardless of the consequences, refuses to change her/his behavior to meet the expectation of others, and knows where he/she is going in life. For instance, if the teacher finds he/she disagrees with the student on some issue, the teacher states her/his opinion anyway, and is confident that her/his view is right, and may even try to change the mind of the student.

___ 17. *Physical Attractiveness.* The teacher attempting to get a student to like him/her tries to look as attractive as possible in appearance and attire. He/she wears nice clothes, practices good grooming, shows concern for proper hygiene, stands up straight, and monitors appearance.

___ 18. *Present Interesting Self.* The teacher attempting to get a student to like him/ her presents self to be a person who would be interesting to know. For example he/she highlights past accomplishments and positive qualities, emphasizes things that make him/her especially interesting, expresses unique ideas, and demonstrates intelligence and knowledge. The teacher may discretely drop the names of impressive people he/she knows. He/she may even do outlandish things to appear unpredictable, wild, or crazy.

___ 19. *Reward Association.* The teacher attempting to get a student to like him/her presents self as an important figure who can reward the student for associating with him/her. For instance, he/she offers to do favors for the other, and gives the students information that would be valuable. The teacher's basic message to the student is "if you like me, you will gain something."

FIGURE 13.7 ***(Continued)***

___ 20. *Self-Concept Confirmation.* The teacher attempting to get a student to like him/her demonstrates respect for the student, helps the student feel good about how he/she views her/himself. For example, the teacher treats the student like a very important person, compliments the student, says only positive things about the student, and treats the things the student says as being very important information. He/she may also tell other teachers about what a great student the individual is, in hopes that the comment will get back to the student through third parties.

___ 21. *Self-inclusion.* The teacher attempting to get a student to like him/her sets up frequent encounters with the student. For example, the teacher will initiate casual encounters with the student, attempt to schedule future encounters, try to be physically close to the student, and puts him/herself in a position to be invited to participate in the student's social activities.

___ 22. *Sensitivity.* The teacher attempting to get a student to like him/her acts in a warm, empathic manner toward the student to communicate caring and concern. He/she also shows sympathy to the student's problems and anxieties, spends time working at understanding how the student sees her/his life, and accepts what the student says as an honest response. The message is "I care about you as a person."

___ 23. *Similarity.* The teacher attempting to get a student to like him/her tries to make the student feel that the two of them are similar in attitudes, values, interests, preferences, personality, and so on. He/she expresses views that are similar to the views of the student, agrees with some things the student says, and points out the areas that the two have in common. Moreover, the teacher deliberately avoids engaging in behaviors that would suggest differences between the two.

___ 24. *Supportiveness.* The teacher attempting to get a student to like him/her is supportive of the student and the student's positions by being encouraging, agreeable, and reinforcing to the student. The teacher also avoids criticizing the student or saying anything that might hurt the student's feelings, and sides with the student in disagreements he/she has with others.

___ 25. *Trustworthiness.* The teacher attempting to get a student to like him/her presents self as trustworthy and reliable. For example, he/she emphasizes his/her responsibility, reliability, fairness, dedication, honesty, and sincerity. He/she also maintains consistency among her/his stated beliefs and behaviors, fulfills any commitments made to the student, and avoids "false fronts" by acting natural at all times.

From "The Affinity-Seeking Function of Communication," by R. A. Bell and J. A. Daly, 1984, *Communication Monographs, 51,* 91–115 and "The Affinity-Seeking of Classroom Teachers," by J. C. McCroskey and L. L. McCroskey, 1986, *Communication Research Reports, 3,* 158–167. Republished with permission by *Communication Monographs* and Taylor & Francis Ltd. http://www.tandf.co.uk/journals.

for two reasons. First, if an organization is not achieving its intended outcomes, it may be the result of poor teaching or training. By assessing the instructional communication processes or practices, an educational leader better understands the overall impact that teaching and training practices have on learning outcomes. Second, if an organization is reaching its learning outcomes, educational leaders must be able to explain their success and effectiveness. In an article discussing communication competence, Parks (1994) suggests that "to be competent therefore we must not only 'know' and 'know how,' we must 'do' and 'know that we did'" (p. 591). Assessing both process and product variables allow an educational leader to meet the competence criteria outlined by Parks.

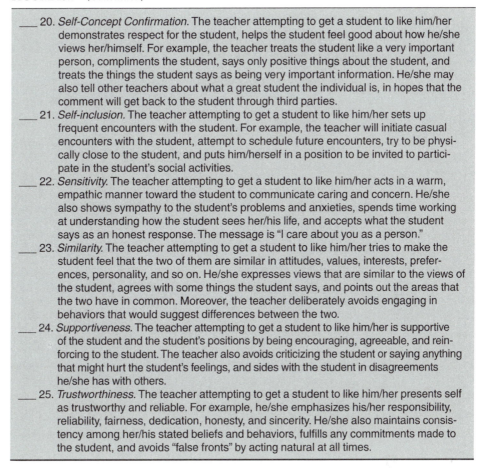

FIGURE 13.8 ***Typology of Instructor Misbehaviors.***

Instructions: The following are descriptions of behaviors teachers have been observed doing or saying in some classes, which students have identified as "teacher misbehaviors." Indicate on a scale from 0–4 how frequently your teacher exhibits the same or similar behaviors. Use the following scale:

0 = Never; 1 = Rarely; 2 = Occasionally; 3 = Often; 4 = Very Often

___ (Absent) Does not show up for class, cancels class without notification, and/or offers poor excuses for being absent.

___ (Tardy) Is late for class or tardy.

___ (Keeps Students Overtime) Keeps class overtime, talks too long or starts class early before all the students are there.

___ (Early Dismissal) Lets class out early, rushes through the material to get done early.

___ (Strays From Subject) Uses the class as a forum for her/his personal opinions, goes off on tangents, talks about family and personal life and/or generally wastes class time.

___ (Confusing/Unclear Lectures) Unclear about what is expected, lectures are confusing and vague, contradicts him/herself, jumps from one subject to another, and/or lectures are inconsistent with assigned readings.

___ (Unprepared/Disorganized) Is not prepared for class, unorganized, forgets test dates, and/or makes assignments but does not collect them.

___ (Deviates From Syllabus) Changes due dates for assignments, behind schedule, does not follow the syllabus, changes assignments, and/or assigns books but does not use them.

___ (Late Returning Work) Late in returning papers, late in grading and turning back exams, and/or forgets to bring graded papers to class.

___ (Sarcasm and Putdowns) Is sarcastic and rude, makes fun of and humiliates students, picks on students, and/or insults and embarrasses students.

___ (Verbally Abusive) Uses profanity, is angry and mean, yells and screams, interrupts and/or intimidates students.

___ (Unreasonable and Arbitrary Rules) Refuses to accept late work, gives no breaks in 3-hours classes, punishes entire class for one student's misbehavior, and/or is rigid, inflexible, and authoritarian.

___ (Sexual Harassment) Makes sexual remarks to students, flirts with them, makes sexual innuendos, and/or is chauvinistic.

___ (Unresponsive to Students' Questions) Does not encourage students to ask questions, does not answer questions or recognize raised hands, and/or seems "put out" to have to explain or repeat him/herself.

___ (Apathetic to Students) Doesn't seem to care about the course or show concern for students, does not know students' names, rejects students' opinions, and/or does not allow for class discussion.

___ (Inaccessible to Students Outside of Class) Does not show up for appointments or scheduled office hours, is hard to contact, will not meet with students outside of office time and/or doesn't make time for students when they need help.

___ (Unfair Testing) Asks trick questions on tests, exams do not relate to the lectures, tests are too difficult, questions are too ambiguous, and/or teacher does not review for exams.

___ (Unfair Grading) Grades unfairly, changes grading policy during the semester, does not believe in giving A's, makes mistakes when grading, and/or does not have a predetermined grading scale.

___ (Boring Lectures) Is not an enthusiastic lecturer, speaks in monotone and rambles, is boring or too repetitive, and/or employs no variety in lectures.

___ (Information Overload) Talks too fast and rushes through the material, talks over the students' heads, uses obscure terms, and/or assigns excessive work.

FIGURE 13.8 ***(Continued)***

___	(Information Underload) The class is too easy, students feel they have not learned anything, and/or tests are too easy.
___	(Negative Personality) Teacher is impatient, self-centered, complains, acts superior, and/or is moody.
___	(Negative Physical Appearance) Teacher dresses sloppy, smells bad, clothes are out of style, and cares little about his/her overall appearances.
___	(Does Not Know Subject Matter) Doesn't know the material, unable to answer questions, provides incorrect information, and/or isn't current.
___	(Shows Favoritism or Prejudice) Plays favorites with students or acts prejudiced against others, is narrow-minded or close-minded, and/or makes prejudicial remarks.
___	(Foreign or Regional Accents) Teacher is hard to understand, enunciates poorly, and has a strong accent that makes it difficult to understand.
___	(Inappropriate Volume) Doesn't speak loudly enough or speaks too loud.
___	(Bad Grammar/Spelling) Uses bad grammar, writes illegibly, misspells words on the exam (or on the board), and/or generally uses poor English.

From "College Teacher Misbehaviors: What Students Don't Like About What Teachers Say or Do," by P. Kearney, T. G. Plax, E. R. Hays, and M. J. Ivey, 1991, *Communication Quarterly, 39,* 309–324. Republished with permission by the Eastern Communication Association.

This section of the chapter, which examines the evaluation of instructional communication outcomes, diverges slightly from more traditional learning outcome approaches by examining instructor outcomes in addition to traditional student outcomes. The assessment literature has become overly focused on student outcomes at the expense of instructor outcomes (McNeil, 2000; Sacks, 2001), when both are needed for instructional effectiveness. As reviewed in Chapter 7, research suggests that students' verbal and nonverbal communication behaviors affect teachers and their teaching in much the same way that teachers' verbal and nonverbal communication behaviors affect students and their learning (Mottet, Beebe, Raffeld, & Medlock, 2004; Mottet, Beebe, Raffeld, & Paulsel, 2004). Students' ability to influence their teachers remains important, especially because many of the instructor outcome variables (self-efficacy, satisfaction, motivation), which are directly impacted by student communication, are also related to student outcomes, such as motivation, achievement, and learning (Caparar, Barbaranelli, Borgogni, & Steca, 2003; Dinham & Scott, 2000; Ross, 1998).

Assessing Student Outcomes

Affective Learning. Affective learning addresses students' attitudes, beliefs, values, and feelings about what they learn (Krathwohl, Bloom, & Masia, 1964). In Chapter 1, we argued that affective learning is a more valid indicator of instructional effectiveness than cognitive learning. Additionally, we argued that the affective learning measure is superior to cognitive learning measures, which continue to be plagued with validity and reliability problems. The Affective Learning Measure is featured in Figure 13.9.

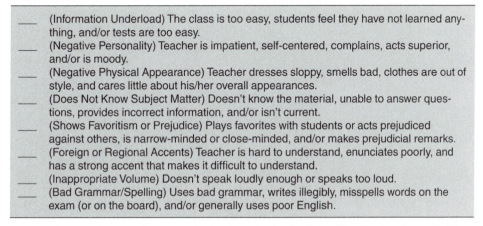

FIGURE 13.9 ***Affective Learning Measure.***

Instructions: Using the following scales, evaluate the class you are taking. Please circle the number for each item that best represents your feelings.

Content/subject matter of the course:

Bad	1	2	3	4	5	6	7	Good
Valuable	1	2	3	4	5	6	7	Worthless*
Unfair	1	2	3	4	5	6	7	Fair
Negative	1	2	3	4	5	6	7	Positive

Your likelihood of actually enrolling in another course of related content if your schedule so permits:

Unlikely	1	2	3	4	5	6	7	Likely
Possible	1	2	3	4	5	6	7	Impossible*
Improbable	1	2	3	4	5	6	7	Probable
Would	1	2	3	4	5	6	7	Would Not*

Note: When behavioral learning is part of a course, then the affective learning measure can be augmented with the following two sets of items.

Behaviors recommended in the course:

Good	1	2	3	4	5	6	7	Bad*
Worthless	1	2	3	4	5	6	7	Valuable
Fair	1	2	3	4	5	6	7	Unfair*
Positive	1	2	3	4	5	6	7	Negative*

In "real life" situations, your likelihood of actually attempting to engage in behaviors recommended in the course:

Likely	1	2	3	4	5	6	7	Unlikely*
Impossible	1	2	3	4	5	6	7	Possible
Probable	1	2	3	4	5	6	7	Improbable*
Would Not	1	2	3	4	5	6	7	Would

* Reverse code for scoring

From "Assessment of Affect Toward Communication and Affect Toward Instruction in Communication," by J. C. McCroskey, 1994, in S. Morreale, M. Brooks, R. Berko, and C. Cooke (Eds.), *1994 SCA Summer Conference Proceedings and Prepared Remarks* (pp. 55–71). Annandale, VA: Speech Communication Association.

Cognitive Learning. Cognitive learning focuses on the acquisition of knowledge and the ability to understand and use knowledge (Bloom, 1956). To evaluate an individual instructor's impact on student cognitive learning, assessors are encouraged to use the instructors' exams as long as they are valid and reliable. Jacobs and Chase's (1992) *Developing and Using Tests Effectively* and Scannell and Tracy's (1975) *Testing and Measurement in the Classroom* will help assessors evaluate the validity and reliability of the instructors' exams. Also, instructional leaders may want to use Richmond, Gorham, and McCroskey's (1987) Cognitive Learning Measure (CLM), which has been used frequently by instructional communication researchers. The Cognitive Learning Measure is featured in Figure 13.10.

Behavioral Learning. Behavioral learning, also referred to as psychomotor learning, focuses on physical action and the development of physical skills (Bloom, 1956). If the instructor's course includes a behavioral component, assessors may want to

FIGURE 13.10 ***Cognitive Learning Measure.***

Instructions: Please answer the following two questions. Please place your response in the space provided.

___ On a scale of 0–9, how much did you learn in this class, with 0 meaning you learned nothing and 9 meaning you learned more than in any other class you've had.

___ How much do you think you could have learned in this class had you had the ideal instructor? (Use the same 0–9 scale.)

Scoring: By subtracting the score on the first question from the score on the second question you can obtain what is called a "learning loss" score. This procedure is recommended, rather than just using the first score, because it is believed that this procedure will remove some of the possible bias that students have when taking a course in a disliked subject matter.

From "The Relationship Between Selected Immediacy Behaviors and Cognitive Learning," by V. P. Richmond, J. S. Gorham, and J. C. McCroskey, 1987, in M. L. McLaughlin (Ed.), *Communication Yearbook 10* (pp. 574–590). Newbury Park, CA: Sage.

evaluate the instructor's instructional communication effectiveness by evaluating students' behavioral learning. If the instructor teaches communication skills, instructional leaders are encouraged to use the following assessment instruments, which have been endorsed by the National Communication Association. Morreale's (1994) *Competent Speaker Form* assesses presentational speaking skills; Spitzberg's (1995) *Conversational Skills Rating Scale* assesses speaking and listening skills; and Beebe and Barge's (2003) *Competent Group Communicator* instrument assesses effective small group communication behaviors. To assess other behaviors, instructional leaders may need to develop their own assessment instrument. Chapter 11 in Beebe, Mottet, and Roach's (2004) *Training and Development: Enhancing Communication and Leadership Skills* may be a useful resource for instructional leaders who have limited experience in developing behavioral learning assessment instruments. Also, instructional leaders may find Christ's (1994) *Assessing Communication Education: A Handbook for Media, Speech, and Theater Educators* a practical and useful guide for assessing students' behavioral learning.

Assessing Teacher Outcomes

Teacher Self-Efficacy. Teacher self-efficacy is "the extent to which the teacher believes he or she has the capacity to affect student performance" (Berman, McLaughlin, Bass, Pauly, & Zellman, 1977, p. 137). To assess teacher self-efficacy, instructional leaders are encouraged to use Gibson and Dembo's (1984) Teacher Efficacy Scale, which is a self-report, 31-item, Likert-type measure that includes two subfactors. The first factor assesses personal teaching efficacy, and the second factor assesses general teaching efficacy. The measure is featured in Figure 13.11. For a global measure of teacher self-efficacy, refer to Mottet, Beebe, Raffeld, and Medlock (2004), which is featured in Figure 13.12.

Teacher Job Satisfaction. Teacher job satisfaction is the "state of mind determined by the extent to which the individual perceives his/her job-related needs

FIGURE 13.11 ***Teacher Efficacy Scale.***

Instructions: Please indicate the degree to which you agree or disagree with each statement below by placing the number from the following scale in the space provided:

1 = Strong Disagree
2 = Moderately Disagree
3 = Disagree Slightly More Than Agree
4 = Agree Slightly More Than Disagree
5 = Moderately Agree
6 = Strongly Agree

___ When a student does better than usual, many times it is because I exerted a little extra effort.
___ The hours in my class have little influence on students compared to the influence of their home environment.
___ If parents comment to me that their child behaves much better at school than he/she does at home, it would probably be because I have some specific techniques of managing his/her behavior, which they lack.
___ The amount that a student can learn is primarily related to family background.
___ If a teacher has adequate skills and motivation, she/he can get through to the most difficult students.
___ If students aren't disciplined at home, they aren't likely to accept any discipline.
___ I have enough training to deal with almost any learning problem.
___ My teacher training program and/or experience has given me the necessary skills to be an effective teacher.
___ Many teachers are stymied in their attempts to help students by lack of support from the community.
___ Some students need to be placed in slower groups so they are not subjected to unrealistic expectations.
___ Individual differences among teachers account for the wide variations in student achievement.
___ When a student is having difficulty with an assignment, I am usually able to adjust it to his/her level.
___ If one of my new students cannot remain on task for a particular assignment, there is little that I could do to increase his/her attention until he/she is ready.
___ When a student gets a better grade than he usually gets, it is usually because I found better ways of teaching that student.
___ When I really try, I can get through to most difficult students.
___ A teacher is very limited in what she/he can achieve because a student's home environment is a large influence on his/her achievement.
___ Teachers are not a very powerful influence on student achievement when all factors are considered.
___ If students are particularly disruptive one day, I ask myself what I have been doing differently.
___ When the grades of my students improve, it is usually because I found more effective teaching approaches.
___ If my principle suggested that I change some of my class curriculum, I would feel confident that I have the necessary skills to implement the unfamiliar curriculum.
___ If a student masters a new math concept quickly, this might be because I knew the necessary steps in teaching that concept.
___ Parent conferences can help a teacher judge how much to expect from a student by giving the teacher an idea of the parents' values toward education, discipline, etc.
___ If parents would do more with their children, I could do more.

FIGURE 13.11 ***(Continued)***

___ If a student did not remember information I have presented in a previous lesson, I would know how to increase his/her retention in the next lesson.
___ If a student in my class becomes disruptive and noisy, I feel assured that I know some techniques to redirect him quickly.
___ School rules and policies hinder my doing the job I was hired to do.
___ The influences of a student's home experiences can be overcome by good teaching.
___ When a child progresses after being placed in a slower group, it is usually because the teacher has had a chance to give him/her extra attention.
___ If one of my students couldn't do a class assignment, I would be able to accurately assess whether the assignment was at the correct level of difficulty.
___ Even a teacher with good teaching abilities may not reach many students.

From "Teacher Efficacy: A Construct Validation," by S. Gibson and M. H. Dembo, 1984, *Journal of Educational Psychology, 76*, 569–582. Republished with permission by Sherri Gibson, PhD.

being met" (Evans, 1997a, p. 833). Assessors interested in evaluating teacher job satisfaction are encouraged to read Evans (1997b), and are referred to the Teacher Satisfaction Scale developed in Plax, Kearney, and Downs (1986), and reviewed in Rubin, Palmgreen, and Sypher (1994). The Plax et al. (1986) Teacher Satisfaction Scale is featured in Figure 13.13. For a global measure of teacher job satisfaction, refer to Mottet, Beebe, Raffeld, and Medlock (2004), which is featured in Figure 13.14.

Teacher Motivation. Teacher motivation is a teacher's internal state of readiness to take action or achieve a goal. Sederberg and Clark (1990) define teacher motivation as "a proponent state that energizes and guides behavior" (p. 5). For a global measure of teacher motivation, refer to Baringer and McCroskey (2000), which is featured in Figure 13.15. For a more comprehensive measure of teacher motivation, instructional leaders are encouraged to obtain the Work Motivation Inventory, which was developed by Blais, Lachance, Vallerand, Briere, and Riddle (1993), and includes 16 items grouped into four subfactors.

FIGURE 13.12 ***Teacher Self-Efficacy.***

Instructions: Please respond to the following word pairs based upon how effective you are as a teacher. Circle one number for *each* set of word pairs that reflects your judgment or evaluation. Note that in some cases the most positive number is a "1" while in other cases it is a "7."

Ineffective	1	2	3	4	5	6	7	Effective
Inefficient	1	2	3	4	5	6	7	Efficient
Unskilled	1	2	3	4	5	6	7	Skilled
Incapable	1	2	3	4	5	6	7	Capable
Successful	1	2	3	4	5	6	7	Not Successful*

* Reverse code for scoring

From "The Effects of Student Verbal and Nonverbal Responsiveness on Teacher Self-Efficacy and Job Satisfaction," by T. P. Mottet, S. A. Beebe, P. C. Raffeld, and A. L. Medlock, 2004, *Communication Education, 53*, 150–163.

FIGURE 13.13 ***Teacher Satisfaction Scale.***

Instructions: Please place a check next to the word that most accurately answers each of the following six questions.

1. Have you ever considered quitting teaching?
___ Never
___ Seldom
___ Sometimes
___ Usually
___ Always

2. Everything considered, how satisfying has teaching been for you?
___ Very Satisfying
___ Satisfying
___ Somewhat Satisfying/Dissatisfying
___ Dissatisfying
___ Very Dissatisfying

3. If you had your life to live over, do you think you would go into teaching as a profession?
___ Definitely
___ Probably
___ Possibly
___ Probably Not
___ Definitely Not

4. Are you generally comfortable with the cooperation exhibited by your students in your classes?
___ Never
___ Seldom
___ Sometimes
___ Usually
___ Always

5. In general, how satisfied are you with the motivation of the students you teach?
___ Very Satisfied
___ Satisfied
___ Somewhat Satisfied/Dissatisfied
___ Dissatisfied
___ Very Dissatisfied

6. How satisfied are you with the general level of students' abilities in your classes?
___ Very Satisfied
___ Satisfied
___ Somewhat Satisfied/Dissatisfied
___ Dissatisfied
___ Very Dissatisfied

Note: Items 1–3 are satisfaction with teaching. Items 4–6 are satisfaction toward students.

From "Communicating Control in the Classroom and Satisfaction with Teaching and Students," by T. G. Plax, P. Kearney, and T. M. Downs, 1986, *Communication Education*, *35*, 379–388.

Instructional Communication Caveats

Before concluding this chapter and this handbook, we offer a few final caveats for those who use and practice the rhetorical and relational instructional communication principles and behaviors reviewed in this handbook, and for those who assess

FIGURE 13.14 ***Teacher Job Satisfaction.***

Instructions: Please respond to the following word pairs based upon how satisfied you are as a teacher. Circle one number for *each* set of word pairs that reflects your judgment or evaluation. Note that in some cases the most positive number is a "1" while in other cases it is a "7."

Unsatisfied	1	2	3	4	5	6	7	Satisfied
Not Pleased	1	2	3	4	5	6	7	Pleased
Sad	1	2	3	4	5	6	7	Happy
Gratified	1	2	3	4	5	6	7	Ungratified*
Unfulfilled	1	2	3	4	5	6	7	Fulfilled

* Reverse code for scoring

From "The Effects of Student Verbal and Nonverbal Responsiveness on Teacher Self-Efficacy and Job Satisfaction," by T. P. Mottet, S. A. Beebe, P. C. Raffeld, and A. L. Medlock, 2004, *Communication Education, 53,* 150–163.

these communication behaviors. Although these caveats are anecdotal rather than empirically grounded, they stem from our multiple interactions with teachers and trainers who have advanced degrees in instructional communication.

Effective Instructors Have Increased Communication Demands

Teachers who use instructional communication well are considered approachable to their students, and this perception creates a demand for the instructor. This demand, if not managed well, may become problematic for several reasons. First, research suggests that students are motivated to communicate with instructors who are relationally effective in the classroom for a variety of reasons (Mottet, Martin, & Myers, 2004). Some of these reasons (i.e., excuse-making, sycophantic) are not always a productive use of the instructor's time. Instructors must find

FIGURE 13.15 ***Teacher Motivation.***

Instructions: Please respond to the following word pairs based upon how motivated you are as a teacher. Circle one number for *each* set of word pairs that reflects your judgment or evaluation. Note that in some cases the most positive number is a "1" while in other cases it is a "7."

Motivated	1	2	3	4	5	6	7	Unmotivated*
Interested	1	2	3	4	5	6	7	Uninterested*
Don't want to teach	1	2	3	4	5	6	7	Want to teach
Inspired	1	2	3	4	5	6	7	Uninspired*
Excited	1	2	3	4	5	6	7	Not excited*
Dreading it	1	2	3	4	5	6	7	Looking forward to it

* Reverse code for scoring

From "Immediacy in the Classroom: Student Immediacy," by D. K. Baringer and J. C. McCroskey, 2000, *Communication Education, 49,* 178–186.

ways to manage the increase in voicemail and e-mail messages, as well as the demand for increased office hours. This increase in communication demand requires considerable time and energy. Additionally, increased teacher–student communication or engagement may not be rewarded, depending on the institution's goals, for example, at a research university where the number of publications and research grants are recognized and rewarded and where increased student–teacher communication is a deterrent to a faculty member getting tenured and promoted (Kennedy, 1999).

Second, if the communication demand is not managed well, instructors may not be able to meet the communication expectations that students have for the instructor. If instructors approach communication in their teaching and training style, but remain communication avoidant outside of the classroom in order to meet their other job duties and obligations (i.e., research, service), there is the chance that they will violate students' expectations. Being unavailable or not as available as an instructor would like, conflicts with the approach perceptions that students have of them. We feel certain that these contradictory messages will eventually erode instructor credibility and other relational perceptions that are needed in order to remain influential in the classroom.

Finally, because of instructors' effective use of instructional communication, there is probably going to be a growing demand for the courses or the training programs they teach. This is only a problem when other courses (and instructors/trainers) do not attract the number of students needed to conduct the courses in a profitable manner. In short, the effective instructor's courses are conducted and others are cancelled because of the lack of interest and, therefore, paychecks are impacted. Depending on the circumstances and the political climate, there may be consequences for an instructor's effectiveness.

Effective Instructors Are Misperceived

Because of the increased demand that is a manifestation of an instructor using rhetorical and relational instructional communication practices effectively, there is the possibility that an instructor and his or her teaching or training may be misperceived. Again, anecdotal evidence suggests that teachers who are in demand (i.e., students wanting to enroll in their classes) are sometimes misperceived as being easy, or their classes are lacking the rigor required in other classes. We argue that, in reality, just the opposite occurs. When an instructor is rhetorically and relational effective, students give him or her permission to challenge them intellectually and to make demands on them that students would consider unrealistic with other instructors who are less effective in the classroom. Rather than being easy, teachers who use instructional communication principles and practices well are probably more rigorous.

The "easy" misperception may also be the result of effective instructors having a nonnormal grade distribution. In some educational organizations and institutions, grade distributions are still used as one criterion for instructional effectiveness. Instructors who remain effective in the classroom, sometimes do not have the bell-shaped distribution of grades that are recognized and rewarded as an indicator of instructional effectiveness. Again, we argue that for the instructor who is rhetorically and relationally effective, the distribution of scores will probably be nonnormal rather than normal. Again, depending on the circumstances and the political climate in which the instructor works, there may be consequences for his or her instructional effectiveness.

Finally, in some institutions of higher education, where producing research is a condition of employment, we believe that effective instructors are sometimes misperceived as not being serious about their research. If instructors are recognized for their teaching, then it is sometimes assumed that these instructors invest little time in their research. This perception is probably rooted in the belief that there are only so many hours in a day, and educators simply do not have time to be effective at both. From our experiences, teachers who use instructional communication principles and practices well are also prolific researchers in their respective fields.

Our goal in reviewing these caveats was not to be cynical, but to acknowledge and address some of the consequences of being an effective instructor. Although much of teaching and training remains an autonomous and private activity, we do not teach in a vacuum. Teachers and trainers are members of complex organizational systems that remain sensitive to relational dynamics that may have ripple effects in the system (McCroskey & Richmond, 1991).

Summary

The purpose of this chapter was to take the mystery out of instructional assessment for instructional leaders by identifying effective teaching and training practices and ways to evaluate these practices. We reviewed the rhetorical and relational perspectives that were used to frame this handbook. We argued that because instructional effectiveness is a teacher or a trainer's effective use of rhetorical *and* relational communication, instructional leaders may want to use these perspectives to structure their assessment plan.

Next, we identified some of the instructional communication practices or behaviors that reflect the perspectives along with suggested assessment instruments that can be used to assess the behaviors. We also identified some of the instructional outcomes that instructional leaders are responsible for, including student learning and teacher outcomes, along with suggested assessment instruments. Finally, we completed the chapter by discussing some of the caveats to being an effective instructor.

References

Baringer, D. K., & McCroskey, J. C. (2000). Immediacy in the classroom: Student immediacy. *Communication Education, 49*, 178–186.

Beebe, S. A., & Barge, J. K. (2003). Evaluating group discussion. In R. Y. Hirokawa, R. S. Cathcart, L. A. Samovar, & L. D. Henman (Eds.), *Small group communication: Theory and practice* (pp. 275–288). Los Angeles: Roxbury.

Beebe, S. A., Mottet, T. P., & Roach, K. D. (2004). *Training and development: Enhancing communication and leadership skills.* Boston: Allyn & Bacon.

Bell, R. A., & Daly, J. A. (1984). The affinity-seeking function of communication. *Communication Monographs, 51,* 91–115.

Berman, P., McLaughlin, M., Bass, G., Pauly, E., & Zellman, G. (1977). *Federal programs supporting educational change: Vol. VII. Factors affecting implementation and continuation* (Rep. No. R-1589/7 HEW). Santa Monica, CA: RAND. (ERIC Document Reproduction Service No. 140–432).

Blais, M. R., Lachance, L., Vallerand, R. J., Briere, N. M., & Riddle, A. S. (1993). L'inventarie des motivations au travail de Blais (The Work Motivation Inventory). *Revue Quebecoise de Psychologie, 14,* 185–215.

Bloom, B. S. (1956). *Taxonomy of educational objectives, Handbook I: Cognitive domain.* New York: McKay.

Caparar, G. V., Barbaranelli, C., Borgogni, L., & Steca, P. (2003). Efficacy beliefs as determinants of teachers' job satisfaction. *Journal of Educational Psychology, 95,* 821–832.

Chesebro, J. L., & McCroskey, J. C. (1998). The development of the teacher clarity short inventory (TCSI) to measure clear teaching in the classroom. *Communication Research Reports, 15,* 262–266.

Christ, W. G. (Ed.) (1994). *Assessing communication education: A handbook for media, speech, and theatre educators.* Hillsdale, NJ: Lawrence Erlbaum.

Dinham, S., & Scott, C. (2000). Moving into the third, outer domain of teacher satisfaction. *Journal of Educational Administration, 38,* 379–392.

Evans, L. (1997a). Understanding teacher morale and job satisfaction. *Teaching and Teacher Education, 13,* 831–845.

Evans, L. (1997b). Addressing problems of conceptualization and construct validity in researching teachers' job satisfaction. *Educational Research, 39,* 319–331.

French, J. R. P., Jr., & Raven, B. (1959). The bases for social power. In D. Cartwright (Ed.) *Studies in social power* (pp. 150–167). Ann Arbor, MI: Institute for Social Research.

Frymier, A. B., & Shulman, G. M. (1995). "What's in it for me?": Increasing content relevance to enhance students' motivation. *Communication Education, 44,* 40–50.

Gibson, S., & Dembo, M. H. (1984). Teacher efficacy: A construct validation. *Journal of Educational Psychology, 76,* 569–582.

Jacobs, L. C., & Chase, C. I. (1992). *Developing and using tests effectively: A guide for faculty.* San Francisco: Jossey-Bass.

Kearney, P., Plax, T. G., & Allen, T. H. (2002). Understanding student reactions to teachers who misbehave. In J. L. Chesebro & J. C. McCroskey (Eds.), *Communication for teachers* (pp. 127–140). Boston: Allyn & Bacon.

Kearney, P., Plax, T. G., Hays, E. R., & Ivey, M. J. (1991). College teacher misbehaviors: What students don't like about what teachers say or do. *Communication Quarterly, 39,* 309–324.

Kearney, P., Plax, T. G., Richmond, V. P., & McCroskey, J. C. (1985). Power in the classroom III: Teacher communication techniques and messages. *Communication Education, 34,* 19–28.

Keller, J. M. (1983). Motivational design of instruction. In C. M. Reigeluth (Ed.), *Instructional design theories: An overview of their current status* (pp. 383–434). Hillsdale, NJ: Lawrence Erlbaum.

Kennedy, D. (1999). *Academic Duty.* Boston: Harvard University Press.

Krathwohl, D. R., Bloom, B. S., & Masia B. B. (1964). *Taxonomy of educational objectives, Handbook II: Affective domain.* New York: McKay.

McCroskey, J. C. (1992). *An introduction to communication in the classroom.* Edina, MN: Burgess.

McCroskey, J. C. (1994). Assessment of affect toward communication and affect toward instruction in communication. In S. Morreale, M. Brooks, R. Berko, & C. Cooke (Eds.), *1994 SCA summer conference proceedings and prepared remarks* (pp. 55–71). Annandale, VA: Speech Communication Association.

McCroskey, J. C. (1998). *An introduction to communication in the classroom* (2nd ed.). Acton, MA: Tapestry.

McCroskey, J. C. (2001). *An introduction to rhetorical communication* (8th ed.). Boston: Allyn & Bacon.

McCroskey, J. C., & McCroskey, L. L. (1986). The affinity-seeking of classroom teachers. *Communication Research Reports, 3,* 158–167.

McCroskey, J. C., & Richmond, V. P. (1991). *Communication in educational organizations.* Edina, MN: Burgess.

McCroskey, J. C., & Teven, J. J. (1999). Goodwill: A reexamination of the construct and its measurement. *Communication Monographs, 66,* 90–103.

McCroskey, J. C., & Wheeless, L. R. (1976). *Introduction to human communication.* Boston: Allyn & Bacon.

McNeil, L. M. (2000). *Contradictions of social reform: Educational costs of standardized testing.* London: Routledge.

Morreale, S. P. (1994). Public speaking. In W. G. Christ (Ed.), *Assessing communication education* (pp. 219–236). Hillsdale, NJ: Lawrence Erlbaum.

Mottet, T. P., Beebe, S. A., Raffeld, P. C., & Medlock, A. L. (2004). The effects of student verbal and nonverbal responsiveness on teacher self-efficacy and job satisfaction. *Communication Education, 53,* 150–163.

Mottet, T. P., Beebe, S. A., Raffeld, P. C., & Paulsel, M. L. (2004). The effects of student verbal and nonverbal responsiveness on teachers' liking of students and willingness to comply with student requests. *Communication Quarterly, 52,* 27–38.

Mottet, T. P., Martin, M., & Myers, S. (2004). Relationships among perceived instructor verbal approach and avoidance relational strategies and students' motives for communicating with their instructors. *Communication Education, 53,* 116–122.

Parks, M. R. (1994). Communicative competence and interpersonal control. In M. L. Knapp & G. R. Miller (Eds.), *Handbook of interpersonal communication* (pp. 589–618). Thousand Oaks, CA: Sage.

Phillips, J. J. (1997). *Handbook of training evaluation and measurement methods* (3rd ed.). Houston, TX: Gulf.

Plax, T. G., Kearney, P., & Downs, T. M. (1986). Communicating control in the classroom and satisfaction with teaching and students. *Communication Education, 35,* 379–388.

Richmond, V. P., Gorham, J. S., & McCroskey, J. C. (1987). The relationship between selected immediacy behaviors and cognitive learning. In M. L. McLaughlin (Ed.), *Communication yearbook 10* (pp. 574–590). Newbury Park, CA: Sage.

Richmond, V. P., McCroskey, J. C., & Johnson, A. (2003). Development of the nonverbal immediacy scale (NIS): Measures of self- and other-perceived nonverbal immediacy. *Communication Quarterly, 51,* 504–517.

Ross, J. A. (1998). Antecedents and consequences of teacher efficacy, In J. Brophy (Ed.), *Advances in research on teaching* (Vol. 7, pp. 49–74). Greenwich, CT: JAI Press.

Rubin, R. B. (1999). Evaluating the product. In A. L. Vangelisti, J. A. Daly, & G. W. Friedrich (Eds.), *Teaching communication* (2nd ed.) (pp. 425–444). Mahwah, NJ: Lawrence Erlbaum.

Rubin, R. B., Palmgreen, P., & Sypher, H. E. (Eds.). (1994). *Communication research measures: A sourcebook.* New York: Guilford Press.

Sacks, P. (2001). *Standardized minds: The high prices of America's testing culture and what we can do to change it.* Reading, MA: Perseus.

Scannell, D. P., & Tracy, D. B. (1975). *Testing and measurement in the classroom.* Boston: Houghton Mifflin.

Sederberg, C. H., & Clark, S. M. (1990). Motivation and organizational incentives for high vitality teachers: A qualitative perspective. *Journal of Research and Development in Education, 24,* 7–13.

Shulman, L. S. (1986). Paradigms and research programs in the study of teaching: A contemporary perspective. In M. Wittrock (Ed.), *Handbook of research on teaching* (pp. 3–36). New York: Macmillan.

Spitzberg, B. H. (1995). The conversational skills rating scale: An instructional assessment of interpersonal competence. Annandale, VA: Speech Communication Association.

Teven, J. J., & McCroskey, J. C. (1997). The relationship of perceived teacher caring with student learning and teacher evaluation. *Communication Education, 46,* 1–9.

Vangelisti, A. L. (1999). Evaluating the process. In A. L. Vangelisti, J. A. Daly, & G. W. Friedrich (Eds.), *Teaching communication* (2nd ed.) (pp. 409–423). Mahwah, NJ: Lawrence Erlbaum.

Index